# The Life Cycle of Russian Things

# The Life Cycle of Russian Things

*From Fish Guts to Fabergé, 1600–Present*

Edited by
Matthew P. Romaniello, Alison K. Smith,
and Tricia Starks

BLOOMSBURY ACADEMIC
LONDON • NEW YORK • OXFORD • NEW DELHI • SYDNEY

BLOOMSBURY ACADEMIC
Bloomsbury Publishing Plc
50 Bedford Square, London, WC1B 3DP, UK
1385 Broadway, New York, NY 10018, USA
29 Earlsfort Terrace, Dublin 2, Ireland

BLOOMSBURY, BLOOMSBURY ACADEMIC and the Diana logo are trademarks
of Bloomsbury Publishing Plc

First published in Great Britain 2022
This paperback edition published 2023

Copyright © Matthew P. Romaniello, Alison K. Smith, and Tricia Starks, 2022

Matthew P. Romaniello, Alison K. Smith, and Tricia Starks have asserted their
right under the Copyright, Designs and Patents Act, 1988, to be identified as Editors of this work.

For legal purposes the Acknowledgments on p. xi constitute an
extension of this copyright page.

Cover image: © Print Collector/Getty Images.

All rights reserved. No part of this publication may be reproduced or transmitted in
any form or by any means, electronic or mechanical, including photocopying,
recording, or any information storage or retrieval system, without prior permission
in writing from the publishers.

Bloomsbury Publishing Plc does not have any control over, or responsibility for, any
third-party websites referred to or in this book. All internet addresses given in this
book were correct at the time of going to press. The editors and publisher regret any
inconvenience caused if addresses have changed or sites have ceased to exist, but
can accept no responsibility for any such changes.

Every effort has been made to trace copyright holders and to obtain their permissions
for the use of copyright material. The publisher apologizes for any errors or omissions and
would be grateful if notified of any corrections that should be incorporated in future
reprints or editions of this book.

A catalogue record for this book is available from the British Library.

Library of Congress Cataloging-in-Publication Data
Names: Smith, Alison Karen, editor, author. | Romaniello, Matthew P.,
editor, author. | Starks, Tricia, 1969– editor, author.
Title: The life cycle of Russian things : from fish guts to Fabergé,
1600–present / edited by Matthew P. Romaniello, Alison K. Smith, and Tricia Starks.
Description: First edition. | London ; New York : Bloomsbury Academic,
2021. | Includes bibliographical references and index. |
Identifiers: LCCN 2021012902 (print) | LCCN 2021012903 (ebook) |
ISBN 9781350186026 (hardback) | ISBN 9781350186033 (ebook) |
ISBN 9781350186040 (epub)
Subjects: LCSH: Russia–Social life and customs. | Soviet Union–Social
life and customs. | Russia (Federation)–Social life and customs. |
Material culture–Russia–History. | Material culture–Soviet
Union–History. | Material culture–Russia (Federation)–History. |
Consumption (Economics)–Social aspects–History.
Classification: LCC DK32 .L67 2021 (print) | LCC DK32 (ebook) | DDC 947–dc23
LC record available at https://lccn.loc.gov/2021012902
LC ebook record available at https://lccn.loc.gov/2021012903

ISBN: HB: 978-1-3501-8602-6
PB: 978-1-3501-8606-4
ePDF: 978-1-3501-8603-3
eBook: 978-1-3501-8604-0

Typeset by Newgen KnowledgeWorks Pvt. Ltd., Chennai, India

To find out more about our authors and books visit www.bloomsbury.com
and sign up for our newsletters.

# Contents

| | |
|---|---|
| List of Figures | vii |
| List of Maps | viii |
| List of Contributors | ix |
| Acknowledgments | xi |

The Life Cycle of Russian Things: An Introduction  1
*Matthew P. Romaniello, Alison K. Smith, and Tricia Starks*

## Part 1   Transforming Things

1   Immateriality and Intermateriality: The Vanishing Centrality of Apothecary Ware in Russian Medicine  17
    *Clare Griffin*

2   Lime and Limestone in Eighteenth-Century Russia  33
    *Alison K. Smith*

3   Underground Materials: The (Un)making of Samizdat Texts  51
    *Ann Komaromi*

## Part 2   Making Things

4   Making Fish Guts into Isinglass and Glue  71
    *Matthew P. Romaniello*

5   The Thickness of a Plaid: Textiles on the Chikhachev Estate in 1830s Vladimir Province  87
    *Katherine Pickering Antonova*

6   Sugar as a "Basic Necessity": State Efforts to Supply the Russian Empire's Population in the Early Twentieth Century  103
    *Charles Steinwedel*

## Part 3 Touching Things

7 Making Samovars Russian  119
*Audra Yoder*

8 "Constant Companions": Fabergé Tobacco Cases and Sensory Prompts to Addiction in Late Imperial Russia  135
*Tricia Starks*

9 Socialism in One Tank: The T-34 as a Microcosm  153
*Brandon Schechter*

## Part 4 Preserving Things

10 Binding Siberia: Semen Remezov's *Khorograficheskaia Kniga* in Time and through Time  171
*Erika Monahan*

11 "Rather Poor and Threadbare": Bogoras, Scratching-Woman, and the Intimacy of Material  191
*Marisa Karyl Franz*

12 "Kunstschutz" in the War of Annihilation or the Power of Images against Ideology  209
*Ulrike Schmiegelt-Rietig*

Select Bibliography  229
Index  243

# Figures

| | | |
|---|---|---|
| 0.1 | Photograph of a matryoshka | 2 |
| 1.1 | Laboratory and library of an apothecary-physician | 18 |
| 2.1 | Photograph of the ruin of the Forest Greenhouse, State Museum-Reserve "Gatchina" | 34 |
| 3.1 | *Nomer* 30 (1971), image 014, "Write Your Own": V. D'iachenko, "Sport-loto"; "Criticism" by Ry Nikonova | 55 |
| 3.2 | *Transponans*, no. 31 (1986), image 020, with a photo of Ry Nikonova and Sergei Sigei, performing their "Pneumatic Duet" | 57 |
| 4.1 | Table 1 from "An Account of the discovery of the manner of making isinglass in Russia" | 78 |
| 5.1 | Photograph of linen towel, spinning tools, and flax fibers | 88 |
| 7.1 | Photograph of a tea urn | 120 |
| 7.2 | *Kitchen* by V. G. Malyshev | 128 |
| 8.1 | Photograph of Fabergé case carved of Karelian birch embossed with the date 1915 | 136 |
| 8.2 | Photograph of case carved of Karelian birch and decorated with various charms | 143 |
| 8.3 | Photograph of gold-mounted silver presentation case of George C. de Dvorjitsky | 144 |
| 8.4 | Photograph of case with cloisonné decoration in the style of Viktor Vasnestov's *Battle of the Scythians* (1879) | 147 |
| 9.1 | Drawing of a T-34, from the cover of *Tank T-34 v boiu* | 154 |
| 11.1 | Illustration of Scratching-Woman's coat by Rudolf Weber originally published in Bogoras's *The Chukchee* | 192 |
| 12.1 | Icon of Saints Peter and Paul, around 1050 | 210 |
| 12.2 | View of the exhibition in the *Pogankiny Palaty*, 1942 | 221 |

# Maps

| | | |
|---|---|---|
| 5.1 | Map of Vladimir Province in the nineteenth century | 90 |
| 10.1 | Map of the source of the Tobol River in the Ural Mountains, by Semen Ul'ianovich Remezov | 179 |
| 11.1 | Map of the routes taken by Bogoras and Jochelson during the Jesup Expedition | 195 |

# Contributors

**Katherine Pickering Antonova** is Associate Professor of History at Queens College, City University of New York, United States. She is the author of *The Essential Guide to Writing History Essays* (2020) and *An Ordinary Marriage: The World of a Gentry Family in Provincial Russia* (2013). She is currently writing *Holy Men and Troublesome Women: Policing Faith in Russia after Napoleon* and researching a book about textile hand production in Russia and the Soviet Union.

**Marisa Karyl Franz** is a faculty fellow in museum studies at New York University, United States. She is the author of "A Visitor's Guide to Shamans and Shamanism: The Kunstkamera's Russian and Asian Ethnographic Collections in the Late Imperial Era." She is currently working on her manuscript *Near and Desired Things: Desiderata and the Collection of Shamanic Materials for Local Siberian Museums, 1880–1910*.

**Clare Griffin** is Assistant Professor of the History of Science and Technology at Nazarbayev University, Republic of Kazakhstan. She has published several articles on science and medicine in early modern Russia in journals such as the *Journal of Global History* (2020). She is also the coeditor of *Perpetual Motion? Transition and Transformation in Central and Eastern Europe & Russia* (2011) and the special edition "The Natural Turn in Early Modern Russian History," for *ВИВЛIОѲИКА: E-Journal of Eighteenth-Century Russian Studies* (2018). She is currently writing *Material Worlds: Materia Medica and the Global History of Early Modern Russian Medicine*.

**Ann L. Komaromi** is Associate Professor of Comparative Literature and Slavic Languages and Literatures at the University of Toronto, Canada. She is the author of *Uncensored: The Quest for Autonomy in Soviet Samizdat* (2015) and the electronic *Project for the Study of Dissidence and Samizdat* (2015). She is currently finishing a book on Soviet uncensored periodicals and publics, and she is working on studies of dissidence and the late Soviet avant-garde in comparative perspective.

**Erika Monahan** is Associate Professor of History at the University of New Mexico, United States. She is the author of *The Merchants of Siberia: Trade in Early Modern Eurasia* (2016) and "Locating Rhubarb: Early Modernity's Relevant Obscurity," in *Early Modern Things: Objects and Their Histories* (2013), and coeditor of *Seeing Muscovy Anew: Politics–Institutions–Culture* (2017) with M. Flier, V. Kivelson, and D. Rowland. She is now working on two books, one about the early mapping of Russia and an expanded second edition of Lindsey Hughes's *The Romanovs: 1613–1917*. She is the book review editor for *Canadian-American Slavic Studies*.

**Matthew P. Romaniello** is Associate Professor of History at Weber State University, United States. He is the author of *Enterprising Empires: Russia and Britain in*

*Eighteenth-Century Eurasia* (2019) and *The Elusive Empire: Kazan and the Creation of Russia, 1552–1671* (2012). He is also the editor of the *Journal of World History* and five edited volumes, including *Russia in Asia: Imaginations, Interactions, and Realties* (2020) with J. Hacking and J. Hardy. He is currently writing *Humoring Russia: Body Politics in the Eighteenth Century*.

**Brandon Schechter** has taught at NYU, Columbia, Brown, and UC Berkeley in the United States. He is the author of *The Stuff of Soldiers: A History of the Red Army in World War II through Objects* (2019) as well as articles in *Ab Imperio*, *Kritika*, and the *Journal of Power Institutions of Post-Soviet Societies*. He is currently working on *The Search for Salvation in the Second World War*, which compares the work of political officers in the Red Army with chaplains in the US Army.

**Ulrike Schmiegelt-Rietig** is Provenance Researcher at the Stiftung Preußische Schlösser und Gärten in Potsdam, Germany. She is author of *Eine Geschichte von Heiligen und Helden. Das Bildprogramm der Vladimirkathedrale in Kiev* (2018) and coauthor, together with Corinna Kuhr-Korolev and Elena Zubkova, of *Raub und Rettung. Russische Museen im Zweiten Weltkrieg* (2019). She is also teaching museum methodologies and exhibition narratives at the Department of Material Culture of the Carl von Ossietzky-University of Oldenburg, Germany.

**Alison K. Smith** is Chair and Professor of History at the University of Toronto, Canada. She is the author most recently of *Caviar and Cabbage: A History of Food in Russia* (2021). In principle, she is now working on two books about the palace of Gatchina and its surrounding area, but while she is Department Chair, in practice she is mostly tweeting about random archival finds and odd decrees @profaks.

**Tricia Starks** is Director of the Humanities Center and Professor of History at the University of Arkansas, United States. She is the author of *Smoking under the Tsars: A History of Tobacco in Imperial Russia* (2018) and *The Body Soviet: Propaganda, Hygiene and the Revolutionary State* (2008). She is also the coeditor, along with Matthew P. Romaniello, of *Tobacco in Russian History and Culture: From the Seventeenth Century to the Present* (2009). She is completing *Cigarettes and Soviets: Tobacco in the USSR*.

**Charles R. Steinwedel** is Chair and Professor of History at Northeastern Illinois University, Chicago, United States. He is the author of *Threads of Empire: Loyalty and Tsarist Authority in Bashkiria, 1552–1917* (2016).

**Audra Yoder** is an independent scholar and full-time mom in Oklahoma, United States. Most recently she was guest editor of a special issue of *ВИВЛIОѲИКА: E-Journal of Eighteenth-Century Russian Studies* on the "natural turn" in Russian historiography and coauthor, with Anna Graber, Clare Griffin, and Rachel Koroloff, of the introduction to the same. Other publications include such Instagram posts as "Thanking My Cat for That Lizard She Brought Me at 5:45 AM" and "Why Is There a Dump Truck in My Spice Drawer?" When she's not wiping small bums and noses, she fantasizes about having time to dust her shelf of Russian history books.

# Acknowledgments

*The Life Cycle of Russian Things* began as a workshop held at the University of Toronto in May 2019. The editors thank all of the participants for their intellectual collaboration in our project, not only those included in this volume but also Alexey Golubev, Kelly O'Neill, and Rebecca Woods. We benefited from the support of the History Department at Toronto and its staff to facilitate our discussions over two vibrant days.

Our editor at Bloomsbury, Rhodri Mogford, was an enthusiastic supporter of this project. We thank him for suggesting the title *From Fish Guts to Faberge* during our first conversation about the volume in San Francisco during the Association for Slavic, East European, and Eurasian Studies annual meeting in 2019. He and his team have provided exceptional guidance throughout the production process.

This volume has benefited from the numerous illustrations included, and we would like to thank all the institutions that have made this possible. The image captions throughout the text all provide proper citations, but this list includes the Wellcome Library, Forschungsstelle Osteuropa at the University of Bremen, the Royal Society, the Victoria and Albert Museum, the National Fine Arts Museum of the Republic of Sakha (Yakutia), the McFerrin Collection, Houghton Library at Harvard University, and the American Museum of Natural History.

Finally, Chapter 9 includes some material drawn from *The Stuff of Soldiers: A History of the Red Army in World War II through Objects*, by Brandon M. Schechter. Copyright (2019) by Cornell University; published by Cornell University Press.

# The Life Cycle of Russian Things: An Introduction

Matthew P. Romaniello, Alison K. Smith, and Tricia Starks

In November of 1992, one of us purchased the most Russian of souvenirs at the gates of a most Russian place, a matryoshka nesting doll from a souvenir kiosk at the entrance to the Aleksander Nevskii Monastery in St. Petersburg (Figure 0.1). Although now almost synonymous with Russian crafts, the matryoshka first appeared as a toy in the 1890s and came not from the depths of Russian history but from the center of the new school of Russian national art at the Abramtsevo artists' colony near Moscow. At Abramtsevo artists from all fields came to create and think and paint and conjure and, under the influence of their patrons, first the Slavophile Sergei Aksakov and then the industrialist Savva Ivanovich Mamontov, to develop arts and themes that spoke to a Russian national tradition—or at least, to a Russian national tradition that they were integral to inventing.[1] It was here, inspired to celebrate the Russian peasantry and traditional styles, that an artist transformed a Japanese nesting doll called a fukuruma with the application of Russian folk-art styles into the first matryoshka. The original matryoshka depicted a mother in peasant garb whose plump body encircled her seven children of diminishing size and age. In 1900, the colony's artists introduced the world to this new Russian folk-art object at the Paris Exhibition. Its popularity led to mass production of the dolls and the reforging of the monastery town of Sergiev Posad into a factory town.[2]

The student's nesting doll from 1992, however, dispensed with the traditional images of women and children and instead traced an interesting path of Russian-Soviet-and-then-Russian-again history. Boris Yeltsin, presented with grotesquely bulbous features, under a shock of silver hair, and above the resurrected double-eagle of the tsars, contained within him images of most of the Soviet premiers (sorry Andropov and Chernenko) and even several notable rulers from before 1917, including Nicholas II (the last tsar), Peter I (the Great), and Ivan IV (the Terrible). In an example of the resurrection of Russian nationalism that went with the collapse of the Soviet Union, the seller explained that the lone female inclusion was not the more famous Catherine the Great but instead Elizaveta Petrovna, because Elizaveta was actually Russian by birth, not simply by marriage. Examples of similarly "political" matryoshkas can be found at the Museum of Russian Matryoshkas in St. Petersburg, but this one, nestled in a suitcase filled with dirty laundry and books, made its way to North America. There it served first as a curiosity on a shelf and then journeyed with its owner to serve

**Figure 0.1** Photograph of a matryoshka. Photograph © Alison K. Smith.

as decoration in a new office and as demonstration tool in the classroom. Students twist and stack the figures, examine the accessories painted with each leader, and contemplate the historical memory that favors some rulers with an image and consigns others to the dustbin of history.

The story of this traveled matryoshka is the biography of a thing, as anthropologist Igor Kopytoff and others have defined it.[3] Its history begins as a concept passed across borders on the far east of Russia's territorial reach and then transported to her west European border. It is transformed into an object by the application of particular Russian themes and artistry backed by a specific political and cultural movement in the 1890s. It is packaged to the world as a symbol of Russia and mass produced for sale both internal and external over the course of the twentieth and now into the twenty-first century. In a specialized museum, and across collectors' sites on the internet, its earliest manifestations have been preserved, but it has also been brought home with travelers from across the world to serve as reminder of past excursions, token of affection for those left at home, toy for children, and pedagogical example for students. The matryoshka's smooth surface, the squeak of its sticking joints, the bright coloring of its decorations, and the sweet smell of lacquer evoke sensory reveries that intertwine with the material. On a shelf, it becomes a singular exhibition for the life of a person as represented in a thing. At some point, when Ivan IV finally goes missing or a crack appears in Brezhnev, perhaps it may itself go into the dustbin of history, surviving only as a memory of the thing that once was.

From idea to physical material, from material to product, from product to object, from object to exhibit, and from exhibit perhaps back to idea or memory, it is this "life cycle" of Russian things that occupies this book. From the transformation of raw materials into objects, the story of the production of these articles, the experience of interacting with these things, and the preservation (or disappearance) of these exhibits, this volume traces a distinctive path in understanding materiality and Russian life from the seventeenth century to the twentieth.

But Russian things are not just a crucible for blending theoretical approaches. Russia's position at the crossroads of multiple international networks, where different cultural adoptions reinforced regional variations among the diverse populations of the empire, highlights the ways in which material objects were central to the ever-evolving relationships between Russia and the wider world of global trade with Asia, Europe, and the Americas. The Russian Empire and its Soviet successor occupied a unique geographic and cultural space, hosting a complex mix of peoples varied in religion, language, culture, ethnicity, and race. Astride multiple trade routes across Eurasia, linking east and west as well as north and south, they benefited from their Asian and Middle Eastern connections to import luxuries as easily as their more famous neighbors in Europe. In the Soviet era, as the leader of the emergent Communist world, the area emerged as an exporter of essential products to its satellite states and navigated a new path in the global economy to retain its relationships with global capital. Throughout its history, materials consumed and created in Russia were undoubtedly "glocal," reflecting diverse geographic origins and habits at the local and global level.[4]

## The Life Cycle of Things

Analyzing the life cycle of things requires a multivalent approach. Yes, we use things as part of our daily lives, but where they came from or what value we see in them can be difficult to understand. Answering these questions in a different time and place makes the challenge that much greater. When material objects have disappeared through the vagaries of time or due to fragility or ephemeral use, we struggle to resurrect them through documents. Words, after all, develop new meanings over time, potentially changing something ordinary into something new or unfamiliar. Words even complicate the very way we write about things. The anthropologist Arjun Appadurai, for example, boldly stated that commodities are "the stuff of material culture," but "commodities are things with a particular type of social potential, that they are distinguishable from 'products,' 'objects,' 'goods,' 'artifacts,' and other sorts of things."[5] Appadurai gave scholars a plurality of terms to grapple with in order to understand the material world. One resolution to this dilemma was offered by Kopytoff who suggested that scholars could recover the life histories of an object, reflecting both its "economic, technical, or social meanings" as well as how it became "endowed with culturally specific meanings and classified and reclassified into culturally constituted categories."[6] This is not to suggest that Appadurai or Kopytoff wrote in opposition to one another, rather that attempting to understand the life cycle of things is a project decades in the making. When tracing its life story, an individual thing might be treated as a commodity at one point in its journey, as a product at another, and as an artifact at a third. Things carry a multiplicity of meanings in part as they move through time and space.

"Commodity" may be the easiest to define because its modern history begins with Karl Marx. Marx argued that any material produced by labor was a commodity, but certain objects were "fetishized" when a commodity gained value greater than the labor required to produce it.[7] Considering the history of European sumptuary laws, legal restrictions on consumption that preserved certain objects and materials for elites, it is not a surprise that fetishized commodities served Marx as a signpost of the accumulation of capital, affording middle-class consumers the ability to ape elite privileges.[8] The association of commodities and the growth of capital led to a long-lasting narrative of materials as capitalist "success" stories, as local products gained international prominence as part of the inescapable rise of the global economy. In *The Wheels of Commerce*, historian Fernand Braudel selected his examples based on their ability to cross borders, declaring "the most profitable commodity trades are those that operated over enormous distances. Distance is a constant indicator of wealth and success."[9] Be it sugar, salt, or the humble ear of corn, these commodities span distance and entice global consumption.[10]

Fetishizing commodities' narratives did not owe its popularity only to Marx, as the work of sociologist Immanuel Wallerstein gave it new attention in the 1970s. Wallerstein proposed a "world systems theory" as a mechanism for understanding the growth and transformation of the global economy. His theory posited a three-level hierarchy of global development—core, periphery, and semi-periphery. Europe was a "core" region of economic development, and European colonies around the world were its periphery, regions that it could exploit for its economic benefit. Russia, to Wallerstein, was part of the "semi-periphery," belonging neither to Europe's core nor to its periphery.[11] In his model of economic development, commodities played a role for their ability to track connections between world regions, even arguing that these goods acted as figurative "chains" linking the industrial core to periphery.[12] When the Soviet Union emerged as one of the world's primary exporters of oil and natural gas in the second half of the twentieth century, for example, the Soviets were linked to the capitalist West through their products, becoming a part of the West's periphery even if the Soviet Union defined itself as separate sphere of development.

While it is possible to "fit" Russia into Wallerstein's model as its history with oil demonstrates, his theory is not without its critics. Some scholars have suggested its focus on commodity chains restricted the view of goods to an aspect of dependence; things were links in exploitative economic relationships rather than subjects in their own right. In the 1990s, numerous critics of this early approach to world systems theory used the model to explain other issues in global development, particularly questioning its centering of Europe as the primary core. They noted that the West and the East were both "core" regions of the early modern world, leading to new questions about the "great divergence" that led to increased international stratification in the world economy.[13] Led by critics of world systems theory, studies of commodities moving from east to west, as well as the spaces in between, again demonstrated the value of understanding global processes through material culture.[14]

Another group of scholars suggested that the unidirectional examination of chains failed to consider the full complexity of materials, and instead advocated a "relational" approach that could account for multiple stages of production, as well as other influences on the product, such as marketing or resale.[15] This idea of a commodity network transformed the study of things/commodities/materials. Once again, consider Russia's oil production. Various machines and technical experts are required to identify oil fields and prepare to extract the resource. Labor is involved in the fields and in preparing and enabling transport to shipyards. Crude oil reaches Europe or the Americas, where it is transported to refineries, which crack the crude and produce multiple products, not only gasoline and oil but also various types of plastics. All of these products are sent to other factories to be transformed into finished goods, marketed to the public, and then used, worn, reused, or burned and destroyed.[16] There are labor and markets involved in all stages. There are multiple governments, multiple companies, and multiple consumers intervening in any or all of the stages.

Viewing commodities as the stuff of global development is far from the only approach to the study of things taken by previous scholars. At the end of the nineteenth century, the American economist Thorstein Veblen argued that the "conspicuous consumption" practices of the middle class were an essential component of establishing a public reputation.[17] The things we own, in other words, help define who we are perceived to be. In much the same way Marxist economic analysis was pushed in a new direction by the world systems approach of Wallerstein, consumption and its meanings gained new interest with the interdisciplinary work of Mary Douglas and Baron Isherwood, and a generation of anthropologists, economists, and historians in the 1970s and 1980s.[18] A focus on the consumption of things does not challenge the idea of world systems theory or global divergence but rather makes these global narratives feel more personal and individualized by thinking about how Chinese tea or Indian cotton left Asia and how Europeans received them.[19] Scholars following this approach can look into the past to think critically about how the same product was received by different people in disparate places to reveal cultural differences.

Much of the theoretical work on things found its origins among anthropologists. While Wallerstein and his critics debated the merits of economic chains or trade networks, anthropologists "drilled down" to the specific item to unpack its meaning within particular cultures. As things traveled and were incorporated in new contexts, anthropologists coined the term "localization" to capture the articulation of consumption habits as different ethnolinguistic groups refashioned products within their own communities.[20] Geographer Elaine Hartwick argued that commodity-chain analysis became more effective with a focus on its "materialist" outcomes; in other words, the culture of consumption was as important as the mechanism of production.[21] Without articulating the process in the same way, historians have often been interested in similar phenomenon. As early as 1966, Arcadius Kahan examined the possessions of the Russian gentry, including household goods but not neglecting serfs, as a mechanism for understanding the process of "Westernization" in the empire.[22] Atlantic historians have long considered the exchange of goods between Europe and the Americas a convenient method of evaluating cultural changes. For example, T. H. Breen investigated how material possessions implanted a sense of Britishness to colonial America.[23] This approach has continued to be productive, inspiring a large wave of consumption texts in the past two decades.[24]

Thinking about things has continued to evolve. Following the practice of "thick description" advocated by anthropologist Clifford Gertz, historian Ken Adler argued for capturing the history of "thick things," particularly as a way of "representing things in ways that at least partially and temporarily coordinate the diverse sets of human agents who design, make, and use them."[25] The focus on the local and specific has inspired attention to the materiality of commodities. In other words, this analysis of goods begins with an understanding of the relationship between the object and its user. Rather than focus on an object's significance to a community, this idea highlights the physical experience of using an object.[26]

Interdisciplinary techniques—moving across boundaries of literary, historical, anthropological, and cultural studies—infuse this approach. For instance, sensory studies change the questions asked of the past to focus on visceral interaction with the material. What did people see and hear when they walked down a street in Moscow at the end of the eighteenth century, and how did that differ from the smells and textures that a person could experience in the Second World War along the same street?[27] Alternatively, theories of subjectivity ask how emotions have changed, or not, throughout history and how that has altered human relationships to things.[28] If, for example, a matryoshka is purchased in Moscow as a souvenir of a year spent living in the city, is it the physical object or the memories attached to it that hold value? Both the history of the senses and the history of emotions focus on lived experiences. Each also highlights the importance of understanding rhetoric—how did people describe their emotions or the sensations they felt, and how do we understand what these words, ideas, and images signify? If one inherits a family quilt, is the material important, the craftsmanship, the generations who may have contributed, the emotions that are evoked by the way it feels, smells, or looks, or all of the above?

*The Life Cycle of Russian Things* opts not to limit the study of material culture to any one of these methodologies but hopes to highlight the interconnected nature of all of these approaches and how taking a multivalent and interdisciplinary approach can offer new avenues to understanding the past. This is not the first study of Russian things, nor has Russia been neglected by other scholars of commodities.[29] However, we argue that objects have a life history, not only defined by their production and use but also by their "afterlife" once they are preserved or even remade into new objects, not only by the physical material but also by the discussions and debates about their meaning and significance at various points in their lives. This is not intended to challenge those who study material culture with in-depth discussions of the composition and physical size of an object, nor those who view objects through the value placed on them for sale or inheritance, but rather to open the discussion to a broader audience, to consider new approaches, and to enliven the field with new connections and interpretations.

## Russian Things

The chapters that follow are grouped into four sections, each reflecting a way of interpreting physical objects. The first, "transforming things," examines both the ways that things could be agents of transformation and the ways that they were themselves transformed by human agency. The apothecary ware of the seventeenth century discussed by Clare Griffin was intended to transform ingredients into medicine; they were, as she puts it, "intermaterial" material objects. The lime and limestone discussed by Alison K. Smith were put to use in Peter I's efforts to transform his subjects and his state by creating a new-built environment, particularly around St. Petersburg. They were also, as materials themselves, part of a larger cycle of transformation that created one out of the other. The samizdat materials discussed by Ann Komaromi varied widely in their makeup; some samizdat producers delighted in transforming unexpected objects into pieces that blurred the line between text and art, but even more straightforward typed and reproduced manuscripts were often altered in the process of their creation and circulation. Furthermore, they were intended to transform those who read, interacted with, or even ingested them—the "wretched text" transformed into "a sign of the freedom of the spirit," and at the same time transforming readers into activists.

While these transformations are in some ways a series of processes of making and unmaking and making again, the chapters in the second section treat the question of making things in a more linear fashion. Here the processes by which raw materials—fish guts, flax, sugar beets—are made into valuable goods—isinglass, cloth, sugar—are centered. As becomes clear, however, this seemingly more linear process of making things is anything but simple. In Matthew Romaniello's telling, the process by which fish guts were turned into isinglass and fish glue was initially so obscure to both Russian and Western European observers that many of its consumers did not fully understand how to differentiate between the two products. In contrast, Katherine Pickering Antonova notes that the processes by which mostly women made flax fibers into thread and then into cloth were so well known and so common that they became almost invisible, leading many historians to underestimate their productive potential, thereby skewing much of their interpretation of Russian economic history. Finally, Charles Steinwedel focuses on a moment in the early twentieth century when state controls on sugar production—or at least state discussions of sugar production—shifted from seeking to protect sugar producers to seeking to protect sugar consumers, reflecting the now strange belief that sugar was a "basic necessity" of life and essential to health. Here, thinking about the process by which sugar beets were turned into sugar links into larger stories of industrial development and consumer societies.

How people interacted with things—how they literally handled, felt, touched them—is the focus of the third section. Audra Yoder traces the rise of the samovar as a signifier of something explicitly Russian by linking it to the specific domestic interior of a Russian home, and particularly to the Russian stove that spread a feeling of warmth and comfort in frigid northern spaces. Tricia Starks draws out the ways that cigarette cases—or more properly, papirosy cases—were handled as part of the larger sensory experience of smoking in tsarist Russia. As they were opened, shut, tapped, caressed, passed from hand to hand, they created not just physical dependency on nicotine but also a kind of emotional dependency on the entire act of smoking. Similarly, in Brandon Schechter's telling, the T-34 tank, mass produced during the Second World War, becomes not simply a machine of destruction but an entire ecosystem, where tank crews lived in close quarters, smelling, touching, feeling, hearing the same set of cues. The intimacy of the sensory crossed over into an intimacy of association, where tank crews felt an affinity to their tanks that blurred the lines between man and machine and machine and man. In all of these chapters, the sensory experience of interacting with objects becomes linked to the emotional experience of interacting with objects: drinking tea or smoking a papirosa as a moment of respite set off by a ritualized set of actions involving things; the experience of living in a tank creating an emotional bond with a killing machine on which a crew was dependent—and which was dependent upon them for its care and upkeep.

One of the things that becomes apparent in these first three sections is a particular issue that faces those of us who study the material culture of the past: destruction. As Clare Griffin points out in the volume's opening chapter, the apothecary ware that we know was used in Muscovy was an agent of transformation that has been transformed by time into immateriality—there are no extant pieces of apothecary ware to be examined, only hints at its production and use in written sources. Nor is this only a problem for historians of centuries far in the past; samizdat materials of the late twentieth century were fragile objects, subject to mishandling, to political control, and, at times, to their own transformative nature. Or there is the destruction of knowledge: changes in the global economy over the past century that have erased an easy familiarity with spinning and weaving, for example, not to mention the fires of war and revolution, that wreaked havoc and destruction of things as well as lives and systems.

Efforts to combat destruction, to preserve material objects, are the focus of the final section of this book. In large part these chapters explore the ways that individuals or institutions have collected materials, an act that removes them from their places of origin, where their purpose had an understood context, and places them in a radically different one. The act of collecting preserves things but also creates an entirely new layer of interpretation caused by their new context. The *Chorography*—an early atlas of Siberia—discussed by Erika Monahan is both an object that sought to preserve a record of the material world and also an object that itself has been preserved through an unusual twentieth-century peregrination. A coat that belonged to the shaman Scratching-Woman now sits in storage at the American Museum of Natural History, where its plain appearance keeps it off display but also belies, as Marisa Karyl Franz discloses, a rich history half a world and a century away. And Ulrike Schmiegelt-Reitig describes the world of art "protection" on the Eastern Front of the Second World War—"protection" that was influenced heavily by both overarching ideology and personal interests.

Beyond these four large groupings, however, yet other themes appear and reappear throughout the collection. One is the challenge of matching words to objects, to things, to commodities. In part this challenge reflects the chronological chasm between the times we write about and the times in which we are writing, and in part it reflects the transformation of translation. Whether the issue is differentiating between a *sklanka* and *sklannitsa* or recognizing "water-heaters" or "self-heaters" as early samovars, the historian must contend with the uncertain association between word and historical object. In some cases, furthermore, the problem of language was itself a historical question: understanding the difference between fish glue and isinglass is not only a problem for a historian trying to understand historical documents but also was a major challenge for bioprospectors of the seventeenth and eighteenth centuries as they sought to understand how best to reproduce a valuable product. Or, defining sugar as a "basic necessity" had important implications for the goals of sugar producers and for the diets of sugar consumers, and also brought up a bigger set of questions about the very definition of "necessity."

Many of the chapters also emphasize the interaction between people and objects, both the quotidian users of objects and the experts who were at times called to create or preserve them. Some of the experts have names. Semen Remezov's maps made the promise of early-modern Siberia tangible both to Muscovite audiences and to modern historians; the Italian-Swiss Placido Visconti's expertise at building with stone got him a lucrative contract to work near St. Petersburg; Mikhail Il'ich Koshkin went from Russian peasant to designer of the T-34 tank in an ideal early Soviet life; and Werner Körte played a role in preserving Russian art from the war raging around it. The chapters also hint at the scores of other experts who played roles in the material world of the past: many nameless stonemasons and plasterers; metalworkers who adapted the tea urn into the samovar; skilled weavers living in villages all across Vladimir Province; the fishermen who turned fish guts into isinglass; and the icon painters of nearly a millennium past. All these experts made things that yet more people interacted with every day as they made tea, got dressed, smoked a papirosa, prayed, walked, or drove around St. Petersburg. These interactions were pragmatic and practical but could also be layered with emotional, sensory, and physical responses—a tank crew feeling love for its tank, contemporary city dwellers upset when restoration changes the color of a stone building, an art historian shaken by a first interaction with an icon.

Finally, this focus on material culture also helps combat several long outdated but curiously persistent versions of Russian history. One is a vision of a Russia divided into two starkly separate worlds of wealth and poverty. At first glance, the subtitle of our volume suggests such a distinction: what could be more homely and base than fish guts, and what could be more symbolic of Russia's elite than the gorgeous works of the house of Fabergé? Even here, though, this apparent dichotomy is misleading. Fish guts were not base but instead a prized and expensive commodity; Fabergé smoking accessories were an elite version of a thing that linked Russia's royal family to millions of their subjects who shared their everyday habits—they were part of a spectrum of status and wealth, not an outlier. Many of the other chapters also demonstrate this broader array of Russian actors: not only emperors and serfs but also craftsmen and contractors; not only vast noble estates but also more modest noble households where the mistress spun and wove alongside her serfs; not only wealthy sugar producers but also an increasing number of sugar consumers, perhaps newly able to afford a daily treat for their tea.

Related to this vision is a second and perhaps more profound one: a vision of Russia's backwardness in comparison to an ideal West European world. Katherine Pickering Antonova notes that, at least in the world of economic history, this ideal opposite was the British textile industry—itself probably the true global outlier; by recovering long-ignored but once common processes of spinning and weaving, she argues that Russia's textile industry was not backward but instead eminently suitable to the specific locale and society in which it operated. Or, as Clare Griffin notes in her chapter, "Muscovite science does not look like West European science, did not function like West European science, but it was still science, and to appreciate it on its own terms we need to meet it on those terms, not on the terms of Western Europe." Similarly, Muscovite, Russian, and Soviet things did not always look like or function like Western European things, but that does not negate their importance. This framework was most egregiously destructive in the mindset of the Soviet Union's Nazi occupiers, who saw this backwardness as reason enough to wage a war of annihilation not only of people but also of things in Soviet space. Even here, though, actual confrontation with things, whether the mighty T-34 tank or haunting icons from Novgorod, shocked some Germans out of their comfortable feelings of superiority.

The chapters here reflect only a tiny fraction of the things that subjects of the Russian Empire made, used, consumed, preserved, of course, but they represent an attempt to recover the lives of a few things as they interacted with the lives of many people. Some played roles in countless lives in ways that resonate across the centuries: tea and sugar consumed by people sitting next to a Russian stove in the eighteenth century and in a tiny kitchen with an electric kettle today; hand-spun and hand-woven textiles that once clothed the masses but have now turned into a luxury item for an elite few; palaces and fine buildings that few entered but that many have passed by in the centuries since their construction; elaborate, beautiful cigarette cases that were held by elite hands in ways that echoed the many other hands that held a lit *papirosa*, later a cigarette, and now perhaps a vape pen. Some things had briefer lives, or lives cut short by sudden change: apothecary ware fallen out of fashion and eventually shattered or otherwise lost; the rare and mysterious isinglass, its value and use undercut by new technologies; a coat once embedded in the life of a Chukchi shaman, taken away to a museum on another continent where it lies in storage, rarely seen let alone worn; icons seized in the midst of a ferocious war from the sites where they had inspired the faithful for centuries. Other things in some ways outlived their times but still have a persistent place in memory: a bound book of hand-drawn maps, like the apothecary wares a victim of changing science, but this time preserved to be pored over today by anyone with an internet connection; tanks built in unimaginable numbers to win a war, now long surpassed as military technology but still finding a home in military monuments and song; samizdat creations that linked intellectuals and dissidents outside of official channels of communications in ways long outdated, but still resonant as a symbol of mental and artistic freedom for those who remember the constriction of the Soviet era.

Or there is the matryoshka. It persists as an object that has come to stand in for Russia (in 2020, the Unicode Consortium even approved a matryoshka emoji), perhaps above all to tourists who come home with one as the perfect souvenir. The particular matryoshka that opened this introduction, almost thirty years old, is just such a perfect souvenir. It has so far survived several moves and many eager undergraduate hands—although Ivan IV once went missing for a few hours, he was eventually found face-down in the corner of a classroom (quite an affront to a man very aware of his own dignity!). Every time it is opened, though, a few more flakes of paint and lacquer fall away, making the fragility of the physical object all too apparent. But also, every time it is opened it brings the same burst of pleasure, even of joy, as layer upon layer of history is uncovered, split apart, and reassembled, even knowing already that the last thrilling reveal will be a tiny, angry tsar. Perhaps it is too trite to link this pleasure of discovery to the pleasure of thinking historically about things, but there is something that connects the two. Things seem utterly obvious. What could be more real than a thing? But the act of uncovering the ways that people used things and tasted things and thought about things shows clearly that these most obvious pieces of materiality hide a multitude of meanings, a multitude of roles.

## Notes

1. Benedict Anderson, *Imagined Communities: Reflections on the Origin and Spread of Nationalism*, rev. ed. (London: Verso, 1991), is the now classic work on the intersection of capitalism and invented nations.
2. James H. Billington, *Russia in Search of Itself* (Washington, DC: Woodrow Wilson Center Press, 2004), 148, 208, fn. 24; Alexander and Barbara Pronin, *Russian Folk Arts* (South Brunswick, NJ: A. S. Barnes, 1975), 115–21.
3. Igor Kopytoff, "The Cultural Biography of Things: Commoditization as Process," in *The Social Life of Things: Commodities in Cultural Perspective*, ed. Arjun Appadurai (New York: Cambridge University Press, 1986), 64–91. Archaeologist Ann Brower Stahl also proposed the value of material biographies in her "Material Histories," in *The Oxford Handbook of Material Culture Studies*, ed. Dan Hicks and Mary C. Beaudry (Oxford: Oxford University Press, 2010), 151–73.
4. For a discussion of "glocal" analysis, see Noel Castree, "Commodity Fetishism, Geographical Imaginations and Imaginative Geographies," *Environment and Planning A* 33 (2001), 1519–25.
5. Arjun Appadurai, "Introduction: Commodities and the Politics of Value," in *The Social Life of Things: Commodities in Cultural Perspective*, ed. Arjun Appadurai (New York: Cambridge University Press, 1986), 3–63; quotes on 4 and 6.
6. Kopytoff, "Cultural Biography of Things," 68.
7. Karl Marx, *Capital*, vol. 1, chap. 1, "Commodities," section 4, "The Fetishism of Commodities and the Secret thereof," https://www.marxists.org/archive/marx/works/1867-c1/ch01.htm#S4, accessed July 9, 2020.
8. Ulinka Rublack and Giorgio Riello, eds., *The Right to Dress: Sumptuary Laws in a Global Perspective, c. 1200–1800* (Cambridge: Cambridge University Press, 2019).
9. Fernand Braudel, *Civilization and Capitalism, 15th–18th Century*, Volume 2, *The Wheels of Commerce*, trans. Siân Reynolds (New York: Harper & Row, 1979), 190.
10. For example, Sidney W. Mintz, *Sweetness and Power: The Place of Sugar in Modern History* (New York: Penguin, 1986); Mark Kurlansky, *Salt: A World History* (New York: Penguin, 2003); Arturo Warman, *Corn and Capitalism: How a Botanical*

*Bastard Grew to Global Dominance* (Chapel Hill: University of North Carolina Press, 2003).
11. Beginning with Immanuel Wallerstein, *The Modern World System: Capitalist Agriculture and the Origins of the European World-Economy in the Sixteenth Century* (New York: Academic Press, 1974). It should be mentioned that this theory was explored by historians as well, including Patrick O'Brien, "European Economic Development: The Contribution of the Periphery," *Economic History Review*, 2nd Series, 35:1 (1982), 1–18.
12. Terence K. Hopkins and Immanuel Wallerstein, "Commodity Chains in the World-Economy Prior to 1800," *Review* 10:1 (1986), 157–70.
13. Andre Gunder Frank, *ReORIENT: Global Economy in the Asian Age* (Berkeley: University of California Press, 1998); R. Bin Wong, *China Transformed: Historical Change and the Limits of European Experience* (Ithaca, NY: Cornell University Press, 1999); Kenneth Pomeranz, *The Great Divergence: China, Europe, and the Making of the Modern World Economy* (Princeton, NJ: Princeton University Press, 2000).
14. Maxine Berg, *Luxury and Pleasure in Eighteenth-Century Britain* (Oxford: Oxford University Press, 2005); Anne E. C. McCants, "Exotic Goods, Popular Consumption, and the Standard of Living: Thinking about Globalization in the Early Modern World," *Journal of World History* 18:4 (2007), 433–62; Eric Tagliacozzo and Wen-chin Chang, eds., *Chinese Circulations: Capital, Commodities, and Networks in Southeast Asia* (Durham, NC: Duke University Press, 2011); Maxine Berg, Felicia Gottman, Hanna Hodacs, and Chris Nerstrasz, eds., *Goods from the East, 1600–1800: Trading Eurasia* (London: Palgrave Macmillan, 2015); and Zoltán Biedermann, Anne Gerritsen, and Giorgio Riello, eds., *Global Gifts: The Material Culture of Diplomacy in Early Modern Eurasia* (Cambridge: Cambridge University Press, 2018).
15. Philip Dicken, Philip K. Kelly, Kris Olds, and Henry Wai-Chung Yeung, "Chains and Networks. Territories and Scales: Toward a Relational Framework for Analysing the Global Economy," *Global Networks* 1:2 (2001), 89–112.
16. Tom Fisher, "Fashioning Plastic," in *The Social Life of Materials: Studies in Material and Society*, ed. Adam Drazin and Susanne Küchler (London: Bloomsbury Academic, 2015), 119–36; and Gay Hawkins, "Plastic and Presentism: The Time of Disposability," *Journal of Contemporary Archaeology* 5:1 (2018), 91–102.
17. Thorstein Veblen, *The Theory of the Leisure Class* (Oxford: Oxford University Press, 2007). For a British application of conspicuous consumption, see Woodruff D. Smith, *Consumption and the Making of Respectability, 1600–1800* (New York: Routledge, 2002); or Bernd-Stefan Grewe and Karin Hofmeester, "Introduction: Luxury and Global History," in *Luxury in Global Perspective : Objects and Practices, 1600–2000*, ed. Karin Hofmeester (New York: Cambridge University Press, 2016), 1–26.
18. Mary Douglas and Baron Isherwood, eds., *The World of Goods: Towards an Anthropology of Consumption* (New York: Basic Books, 1979); Arjun Appadurai, ed., *The Social Life of Things: Commodities in Cultural Perspective* (New York: Cambridge University Press, 1986); John Brewer and Roy Porter, eds., *Consumption and the World of Goods* (New York: Routledge, 1993).
19. Giorgio Riello, *Cotton: The Fabric That Made the Modern World* (Cambridge: Cambridge University Press, 2013); Erika Rappaport, *A Thirst for Empire: How Tea Shaped the Modern World* (Princeton, NJ: Princeton University Press, 2019).

20. Marshall Sahlins, "Cosmologies of Capitalism: The Trans-Pacific Sector of the 'The World System,'" *Proceedings of the British Academy* 74 (1988), 1–51; David Howes, "Introduction: Commodities and Cultural Borders," in *Cross-Cultural Consumption: Global Markets, Local Realities*, ed. David Howes (London: Routledge, 1996), 5–7. This idea has been further explored by Peter Jackson, "Commodity Cultures: The Traffic in Things," *Transactions of the Institute of British Geographers*, New Series 24:1 (1999), 95–108.
21. Elaine Hartwick, "Geographies of Consumption: A Commodity-Chain Approach," *Environment and Planning D: Society and Space* 16 (1998), 423–37.
22. Arcadius Kahan, "The Costs of 'Westernization' in Russia: The Gentry and the Economy in Eighteenth-Century Russia," *Slavic Review* 25:1 (1966), 40–66.
23. T. H. Breen, "An Empire of Goods: The Anglicization of Colonial America, 1690–1776," *Journal of British Studies* 25:4 (1986), 467–99; Neil McKendrick, John Brewer, and J. H. Plumb, *The Birth of a Consumer Society: The Commercialization of Eighteenth-Century England* (Bloomington: Indiana University Press, 1982).
24. See the arguments for a "localized" analysis in Jonathan Curry-Machado, "Global Histories, Imperial Commodities, Local Interactions: An Introduction," in *Global Histories, Imperial Commodities, Local Interactions*, ed. Jonathan Curry-Machado (Houndmills: Palgrave Macmillan, 2013), 1–14.
25. Ken Adler, "Thick Things: Introduction," *Isis* 98:1 (2007), 80–3.
26. For example, see the essays in Daniel Miller, ed., *Materiality* (Durham, NC: Duke University Press, 2005).
27. Alexander M. Martin, "Sewage and the City: Filth, Smell, and Representations of Urban Life in Moscow, 1770–1880," *Russian Review* 67 (2008): 243–74; Steven G. Jug, "Sensing Danger: The Red Army during the Second World War," in *Russian History through the Senses: From 1700 to the Present*, ed. Matthew P. Romaniello and Tricia Starks (London: Bloomsbury Academic, 2016), 219–40. For a general introduction to history of the senses, see David Howes, *Sensual Relations: Engaging the Senses in Culture and Social Theory* (Ann Arbor: University of Michigan Press, 2003).
28. Stephanie Downes, Sally Holloway, and Sarah Randles, eds., *Feeling Things: Objects and Emotions through History* (Oxford: Oxford University Press, 2018).
29. Paulina Bren and Mary Neuberger, eds., *Communism Unwrapped: Consumption in Cold War Eastern Europe* (New York: Oxford University Press, 2012); Graham H. Roberts, ed., *Material Culture in Russia and the USSR: Things, Values, Identities* (London: Bloomsbury Academic, 2017); Paula Findlen, ed., *Early Modern Things: Objects and Their Histories, 1500–1800* (London: Routledge, 2013); Anne Gerritsen and Giorgio Riello, eds., *The Global Lives of Things: The Material Culture of Connections in the Early Modern World* (London: Routledge, 2016).

# Part 1

# Transforming Things

# 1

## Immateriality and Intermateriality: The Vanishing Centrality of Apothecary Ware in Russian Medicine

### Clare Griffin

In the summer of 1663, a specific person was sent to a specific place in search of a specific object for a specific purpose. The person was Master Ptitskoi, known in Moscow as a master of ceramics, especially those for apothecary purposes. The place was Gzhel, a village not far from Moscow famous then and now for its clay. The object was the Gzhel clay itself. And the purpose was to source and exclusively create apothecary ware from that clay for the Moscow court. Making a close reading of the order that sent Master Ptitskoi on his errand for Gzhel clay reveals how one short text can provide a broad insight into the complex material world of Muscovite pharmacy.

Material culture studies have become an essential part of the history of science, technology, and medicine, with investigations devoted to everything from water pumps to natural history collections to materials of chemical analysis. Each group of objects gives us a different perspective on the role of materials within historical, scientific, and medical practices and opens up new ways of thinking about the history of science. Here, I argue for the inclusion of one group of objects to which little attention has thus far been devoted, but which has unique features that merit attention: apothecary ware. Apothecary ware, in particular that subgroup of vessels used to transform ingredients into medical drugs, is a group of objects that functioned in an unusual way, existing only to interact with other objects. It was a group of items in heavy use at the seventeenth-century Russian court, where medical drugs were of notable interest.[1]

What were these objects? Apothecary ware is a category of objects that both contains different subgroups and is related to other categories of object. If one were to walk into an early-modern apothecary shop, the first thing to catch your eye would likely be ornate storage jars, typically ceramic, and often beautifully decorated as well as labeled as to their contents (see Figure 1.1). In the eighteenth century, Peter the Great had such storage jars, emblazoned with the Imperial insignia.[2] Many of those storage jars, sometimes also referred to as medical ceramic ware or pharmacy jars, would contain individual natural objects, being kept ready to be processed

**Figure 1.1** Laboratory and library of an apothecary-physician, showing books on shelves, drug jars, distilling, and so on, and the proprietor examining a flask. Credit: Wellcome Collection. Attribution 4.0 International (CC BY 4.0).

into ingredients. That production process takes us to a range of tools for creating medicines. The simplest kind were to cut or grind ingredients, such as a stone mortar and pestle. This transformed raw materials into ingredients suitable for being mixed together into medicines. Many early-modern medical drugs involved alcohols, so there was also equipment for brewing and fermenting alcohol from a range of natural objects, such as grains and fruits. This again involved tools for smashing up the raw materials, as well as heating them, and storing them during the long brewing or fermenting processes. Those tools were often metal or wooden. Those alcohols could then be distilled into stronger alcohol, involving another set of objects to heat the liquid, and glassware tubes and vessels to separate out the alcohol from diluting components. Once produced, those liquids would be stored in glass bottles. This already complicated processing of natural objects with the help of multiple kinds of technical object only takes us as far as creating ingredients.

The apothecary then needed to put these ingredients together into a medical drug according to a recipe, involving the paper material objects of a book or a physician's prescription on a scrap of paper. This could be a simple process, such as mixing a dried herb into an alcohol, which could be done with a glass or ceramic vessel and a wooden spoon. Or it could be a more complicated process, involving multiple steps, heating, and mixing. Such involved processes again required objects to create and to use fire safely, and vessels and stirring tools that could withstand heat, such as metals or ceramics. In either case, the apothecary would also use weighing and measuring devices such as metal scales. Once this process had been completed, the resulting medical drug would again go into a storage jar, either a large ceramic jar like those for natural objects and ingredients or a smaller vessel for a patient to take away. Apothecary ware is most properly the ceramic vessels for the production and storage of medical drugs, but it is important to remember that those items were part of a broader constellation of technical pharmacy instruments being brought into interaction.

We can study this apothecary ware using the perspective of material culture studies. Material culture studies places objects as the focus of historical inquiry, which leads to multiple further roads of analysis. Anne Gerritsen and Giorgio Riello have highlighted the historical existence of objects themselves, showing things can be different in different contexts, and thus how individual objects then effectively lived multiple lives when used and traded globally.[3] Looking at the material can also take us to considerations of culture. Scott Manning Stevens has shown how the tomahawk has been used as a key part of the racist stereotype of the Haudenosaunee (sometimes also called Iroquois) Native Americans as inherently violent in white American culture.[4] Objects can also tell us about knowledge and expertise. Pamela Smith has looked at what objects can add to histories of knowledge, asking, "We usually think about the production of knowledge as resulting in a body of texts, but what kinds of knowledge result from the production of things?"[5] We could rephrase that question here as: what kinds of expertise were inherent in the creation and use of apothecary ware to create medical drugs in Muscovy? And what does that then tell us about the possibilities and limitations of material culture studies? Directing our attention toward apothecary ware adds to our understanding of material culture as a perspective, and also reveals underappreciated facets of Muscovite science.

When I talk about apothecary ware, I am narrowly concerned with apothecary ware as objects that destroyed raw materials and, in the process, created medical drugs. These items functioned in a very specific way. They were objects that only existed to interact with, and indeed destroy and create, other objects. Their materiality—a term I use here to mean the sum total of their material properties—was fundamentally an intermateriality. In the Muscovite case, we do not have any identified examples of extant apothecary ware; the destructive objects were themselves destroyed. In this way—and others, as we will see later—these intermaterial objects are also immaterial. As such, lost Muscovite apothecary ware for creating drugs represents a subset of materials that behave in a unique fashion and so provide a rare opportunity for material culture analysis.

Apothecary ware can give us new perspectives on two vital trends within material culture-informed histories of science and technology: material specificities and object agency. Pamela Smith, in her consideration of early-modern West European artisanal scientific practices, has written, "Artisanal knowledge was inherently particularistic; it necessitated playing off and employing the particularities of materials (including, in some cases, the impurities in the material)."[6] This idea of materials and objects as each having some notable particularity, and the role of science as understanding and manipulating that particularity, has been key. We can see this in other studies, like Ursula Klein and Wolfgang Lefèvre's *Materials in Eighteenth-Century Science*, a study of chemistry as the science of understanding, manipulating, and experimental production of materials.[7] Apothecary ware had particular qualities, but those qualities were necessarily judged in terms of how they interacted with other things. Rather than looking at the particularities of the subjects of experimentation and artisanal creation, we can look at the particularities of the wares that facilitated creation. What was it about the specificity of apothecary ware as an object that allowed it to create another object?

Histories of technology informed by material culture have particularly been interested in the idea of object agency.[8] Technologies move, interface with other objects, and interact with people. One example of this approach is Marianne De Laet and Annemarie Mol's work on the Zimbabwe Bush Pump, showing how the pump only really fulfils its function of providing healthy drinking water when it is correctly installed in its location and used and maintained by the local community.[9] Objects like the Zimbabwe Bush Pump have their own kind of object agency. In the case of the Zimbabwe Bush Pump, De Laet and Mol talk about the pump as an actor, as when it functions it functions only in interaction with other materials and with people.

Apothecary ware presents a new perspective on this key issue of object agency. There are two basic ways in which a vessel designed for the production of drugs could work. In one variant, the specific properties of the vessel would actively take part in the transformation in some way, exerting object agency in the process. In the other variant, the vessel would be chosen to have the specific property of being chemically inert and would so have a meaningful and purposeful lack of object agency in the process. Apothecary ware thus complicates this already tricky question of agency, as it sits on a liminal point of having particular qualities but being unclear as to whether those qualities are there to create or to exclude object agency. As we look at our Muscovite apothecary ware, then, we must also ask—was the purpose of apothecary ware to act or to refuse to act?

Examining apothecary ware from this material-culture informed history of science and technology perspective also helps us understand Muscovy. Anglophone scholarship has inherited norms regarding the quantity and quality of evidence that count as sufficient for serious analysis from the long focus on Western Europe and its colonies. Yet documents are not neutral, and concepts of what constitutes a document are not either. We see this in how early-modern Russian documents are described by historians. For an example, we can turn to what has been referred to as the founding text for Muscovite studies in the modern West, Edward Keenan's "Muscovite Political Folkways." In this still-cited article, Keenan calls Old Church Slavonic a difficult language and complains that Muscovite genealogical books were not kept scrupulously.[10] Yet Muscovites themselves found both Old Church Slavonic and their genealogical books fit for use. Muscovite documents encode and express exactly the right amount of information and knowledge for Muscovy. When it seems that they do not, our issue is really with the chasm of time and culture between us and Muscovite document-creators, not with the document itself.

We can turn here to material culture studies as practiced in Native American and Indigenous Studies for guidance. Alyssa Mt. Pleasant, Caroline Wigginton, and Kelly Wisecup, talking of documentary practices in NAIS, have argued that we should challenge

> the field's conception of what materials count as evidence. Native peoples have their own documentary practices that pre-existed and continue alongside colonization. Historians can look to textual and non-textual archives and address the material circumstances of archive creation and arrangement in order to craft histories that escape the biases and assumptions of settler colonization and account for the contingency of the past.[11]

Mt. Pleasant, Wigginton, and Wisecup's reminder to challenge ideas of what material counts as evidence is a vital note that can be applied to many fields, including the history of Muscovite science in European context.

One example of how differences in materials cause a gulf between Muscovy and West Europe is printing. Western Europe joined East Asia in making use of print technologies to create large quantities of texts in the fifteenth century. Muscovy experimented with print in the sixteenth century, but as literacy was considered a practical skill only acquired by a limited professional group of scribes and clerks they did not require large print runs of books and so they found it insufficiently useful to bother investing in, and the project faltered.[12] In the eighteenth century, the Russian government took a different approach and realized that having a monopoly on printing presses within the empire meant that they could create official documents that were very hard to fake, which technological reframing eventually led to a return to printing books.[13] Muscovite science is then science in manuscript. This does not make it backward in comparison to West European science, in the same way that we do not talk of West European science as backward in comparison to East Asia, where they had been printing scientific texts centuries before Europe. It just makes it different. Muscovite science does not look like West European science, did not function like West European science, but it was still science, and to appreciate it on its own terms we need to meet it on those terms, not on the terms of Western Europe. Appreciating the documentary traces of materials like Muscovite apothecary ware for what they are helps us better understand Muscovy.

## The Valuable Specificity of Gzhel Clay

One document in particular highlights the issues and opportunities of focusing on Muscovite apothecary ware. On June 17, 1663, Tsar Aleksei Mikhailovich gave the following *Ukaz* relating to the affairs of the state medical department, the Apothecary Chancery:

> Search for clay in Gzhel *volost* [region] to make apothecary and alchemical ceramic vessels, and for that search send Master Pashko Ptitskoi [the master of] apothecary and alchemical ceramic vessels to Gzhel *volost*. And in such places Master Pashko Ptitskoi will search for clay, and the Tsar orders that 15 *vozy* [lit. loads, around 245–327 kg in total][14] of the clay [that Master Ptitskoi finds to be suitable] will be transported to Moscow by a peasant of Gzhel *volost*, and that clay will not be given out for other reasons but kept for apothecary purposes [only], and the Tsar has ordered that that clay from Gzhel *volost* should be kept and brought to Moscow by a peasant because it is appropriate/required/ suitable/necessary [for use by] the Apothecary Chancery.[15]

This short document about a trip to Gzhel, a village fifty kilometers southeast of Moscow that in the modern world has given its name to a style of Russian decorative ceramics, contains the major concerns of apothecary ware, in particular in the Muscovite case. Here we see not only apothecary vessels mentioned but also alchemical vessels. What was the terminology of Muscovite apothecary ware, and what do those terms denote? The document insists that clay suitable for creating apothecary ware will be identified. This takes us back to our issues of the particularity of objects, and their agency. What was it about certain kinds of clay from Gzhel that made it so suitable for apothecary ware, and how did those qualities express themselves in the drug-making process? We are also told that a specialist, a master, is going to determine which clay is suitable. Who is Master Ptitskoi, and what does his role here tell us about experts in Muscovy? One paragraph sets us up with the major issues of apothecary ware in early-modern Russia: words, qualities, and experts.

## Words

As speakers of modern English dealing with sources in early-modern Russian, first of all we must consider words. Words play more of a role in material culture studies than the name of the field might lead you to believe. To return to the work of De Laet and Mol, their article on the Zimbabwe Bush Pump heavily relies upon documents relating to that object, to the extent of including an appendix on how to install the pump.[16] Objects are the subject of material culture studies, but we often must approach those objects obliquely, using texts alongside objects, or even as proxies for lost objects. Such is the case with Muscovite apothecary ware, making the words for the things a fundamental starting point.

The vessels mentioned in the Gzhel *ukaz* are referred to by two words: apothecary and alchemical. The first is to be expected, the latter is perhaps less so. Alchemist can mean many things, from the once-common view of the seeker of gold, the philosopher of metals, to the more recent focus on the alchemist as practical expert in metals.[17] The usage at the early-modern Russian court hews closest to the latter, as "alchemist" was a rank within the Apothecary Chancery whose job was to create consumable medicines on the orders of the physicians.[18] The use of the word alchemist here then underlines the fact that the vessels being created are for the production of medicines.

Other contemporary documents give us different words, but similar issues of extracting meaning. In 1645, the Apothecary Chancery received one of their regular shipments of materials and equipment from Hamburg.[19] That list includes 360 *sklianitsy* and 90 *sklianky*.[20] What were these objects? The names themselves are tricky to interpret. A *sklianka* is familiar from modern Russian, meaning a small glass flask. What might a *sklianitsa* be? Perhaps a smaller kind of glass vessel? Except the 1645 import list specifies that the *sklianki* in question are in fact *ne bolshie*, not large. So we have here some small glass vessels and some even smaller glass vessels? Even establishing that point—if we can consider this sufficient to call it established—does not tell us the function of the objects. Were they for storage or for mixing medicines? It is not specified.

Perhaps we need to turn to a dictionary, but which one? The nearest contemporary dictionary is the late-sixteenth-century Russian-English dictionary attributed to the British physician Mark Ridley, but that text—although it is helpful on medicinal plants—does not list apothecary ware terms.[21] Indeed, most contemporary dictionaries are not helpful on medical terms in general. Scholars often point me toward the more numerous and voluminous nineteenth-century dictionaries, but this is a problematic approach. One famous example of why this is an issue is the word treacle. Treacle now means a sweet, sticky, cooking ingredient. In the early-modern period, it meant compound medicine also known as theriac and commonly including viper flesh.[22] Words change.

Closer to home, Russian medical terminology was also changing in this period. A herbal translated into Slavonic in 1534, the *Garden of Health*, does not use the modern term *lekarstvo* (medical drug), but rather *zel'ia*, a term designating a plant with important, and commonly—but not exclusively—medical, uses.[23] Interestingly for a dictionary compiled by a physician, Ridley's dictionary also does not include the term *lekarstvo*, but rather the terms *lechbe*—a cure—and *lechebnie*—medicinable.[24] Yet by the seventeenth century, prescriptions commonly used the term *lekarstvo* to refer to the finished, end product they describe.[25] By 1724, *lekarstvo* was a sufficiently normal part of Russian vocabulary to be listed—along with the terms *tselba*, *vrachestvo*, and *tselebtsvo*—in a Latin-Russian dictionary as equivalents to the Latin term *medicamentum*. *Zel'ia*, *lechbe*, and *lechebnie* are all absent from that list.[26] The familiar modern Russian word *lekarstvo*, then, seems to have only come into usage during the course of the seventeenth century. In the linguistic crucible of the Apothecary Chancery, it is easy to imagine that there would have been other evolutions. Even when later dictionaries list the terms we are interested in, there is no guarantee that the meaning would have stayed the same across the intervening time period.

The Apothecary Chancery owned and used *sklianki* and *sklianitsy*, and apothecary and alchemical ceramic vessels. This tells us less than we would like—there is that chasm again—but it does tell us something vital. Even the words themselves speak to a specificity, a particularity, a unique quality of object. We do not simply require a ceramic vessel but a ceramic vessel for alchemy or apothecary activities; we do not simply require a glass vessel but one of a certain dimension. Words tell us that these objects are specific, even when they do not reveal what the specifics are.

## Qualities

To find the specifics, the particularities, the qualities, and the agency of these objects, we can look at other points. The Gzhel *ukaz* does mention specific qualities of the clay, stating "that clay will not be given out for other reasons but kept for apothecary purposes [only], and the Tsar has ordered that that clay from Gzhel *volost* should be kept and brought to Moscow by a peasant because it is *nadobna* [for use by] the Apothecary Chancery." In the modern world, Gzhel clay is used for decorative ceramics, but it is not entirely clear whether Gzhel clay was used for decorative purposes in this period.[27] At the very least we can say that the specific batch of clay obtained by Master Ptitskoi was not intended for such a use. This specificity of purpose is expressed in the language of the *ukaz*. Central here is the word *nadobna*, a capacious word meaning—depending on context—suitable, appropriate, necessary, or required. In the Gzhel *ukaz*, this word indicates that the clay being gathered is specific to one purpose. This is not clay just for the tsar, or for the court, but clay with a notable property that makes it uniquely suited to the creation of apothecary vessels, and so it is reserved only for that purpose. Following one small word again reveals something much larger about the materials of Muscovite science.

That word *nadobna* appears in other Apothecary Chancery documents. In 1662 the department wrote to the military governor at Kaluga, a town 180 kilometers southwest of Moscow, to request that he send to Moscow various *sklianitsy* produced in Kaluga's Cossack towns (*cherkasskie gorody*). The document continues that those *sklianitsy* are *nadobny* (here most likely meaning required) for the Apothecary Chancery.[28] We should remember that the Apothecary Chancery also sourced *sklianitsy* from elsewhere, such as the Hamburg markets. This would then imply that there was something notable about Kaluga Cossack *sklianitsy*, a unique quality that was being sought out. When the Apothecary Chancery searched for its materials, it identified in particular ceramics made with clay from Gzhel and glassware from Kaluga Cossacks, in both cases implying a specificity of material that the department both understood and valued.

This apothecary ware, in particular the Gzhelware, was apothecary ware with a specific quality designed to be a liminal, generative object that existed only to create other objects, medical drugs. These objects have a translucent specificity: it exists, but we cannot clearly see what it was. This is the major reason these apothecary ware objects are immaterial. Not because they are lost but rather because a major aspect of their materiality, their intermateriality—the quality they had that made them uniquely suitable to create other objects—is not accessible to us. As Carla Nappi has argued in the case of ginseng, materials exist not only in space but also in time, and everything that ginseng in early-modern China was existed as a part of that flux. We cannot access early-modern ginseng outside of that flow of time, even if we had modern remnants of those early-modern objects.[29] Similarly, Muscovite apothecary ware was only itself when it was in the process of interacting with ingredients and drugs under the care of contemporary experts. Barring a reverse *Ivan Vasilievich Changes Profession* situation where modern historians could go back and directly view Muscovite apothecary ware in use, these objects are, for us, immaterial.[30]

Because of this immateriality of Muscovite Apothecary ware, their object agency is something of a Schrödinger's Cat: the materiality of apothecary ware was either to exert agency in the drug creation process or to refrain from agency in that process. If the clay had some special quality that would add to the quality or specific virtue of the end-product medical drug, it might have been chosen for that reason. If the clay would remain chemically inert during the process and allow the desired ingredients to interact without outside interference, it might have been chosen for this reason. We know it is one or the other, and that those two options are vitally important and mutually exclusive, yet we cannot open the box to check the exact state of the apothecary-ware-as-cat. This, then, is the immaterial intermateriality of Muscovite apothecary ware: objects with unique destructive generative qualities that we cannot precisely know.

## Experts

Devoting attention to apothecary ware as material culture shows us unique but unknowable immaterial intermaterial objects. Yet we do not need to leave it there. Focusing on objects, ironically, can take us back to people, more specifically to the experts who *did* know the specific nature of Muscovite apothecary ware's intermateriality. We can return here to what Pamela Smith has said of how artisanal knowledge was knowledge of the particularities of materials.[31] Having looked at the particularities, we can now also look at the owner of that artisanal knowledge of the particularities of materials, Master Ptitskoi.

Who was Master Ptitskoi? All I am currently able to tell you about him comes from this document. We are told that he is a master. He seems to have been based in Moscow. And he was a specialist in apothecary and alchemical ceramics, linking him to both those expert groups. Within the Apothecary Chancery, apothecaries and alchemists were apprenticed to existing masters to learn their practical skills, and once they had completed their training could then take on more responsibilities and exert their authority over other pupils.[32] From where did Master Ptitskoi derive his expertise, and how did he assert his authority? Those points are thus far unknown.

Master Ptitskoi was one of a number of different experts with practical knowledge in Muscovy. We have already met the Kaluga Cossack *sklianitsy* makers, whose reputation for creating glassware was valued as far away as Moscow. This is significant in part because Moscow had several of its own expert producers, alongside Master Ptitskoi. In 1630, the Apothecary Chancery purchased a copper vessel from Ivan Sverchkov, a merchant of the Moscow *Kotel' riad*, the copper or cauldron row; in 1684, a foreign artisan working in Moscow was paid by the Apothecary Chancery for making horn tubes for the department.[33] There were also *travniki*, herb collectors with knowledge of the local flora; unofficial healers peddling medical services; and writers composing Russian-language herbals.[34] Muscovy was full of experts.

The kind of expert that Master Ptitskoi represented is key. Over a decade ago, Pamela Smith noted that "the increased attention to everyday science and indigenous knowledge systems [in recent histories of science] has called into question the dichotomy between popular and elite."[35] Here the historiography of Anglophone West European science mirrors developments in Russophone historiography, notably those of *istoriia byta* (history of lived experience) and *istoriia posvednevnosti* (history of the everyday). Those trends have rebalanced histories of Muscovy from their focus on the elite. For example, P. V. Sedov has shown that the Moscow court can be better understood as an institution when looking at how it worked collectively on a day-to-day basis, rather than extracting one set of figures or events from the whole.[36] For both historians of Muscovy and historians of early-modern science, everyday practicalities have become central areas of study.

This is vital to understanding Muscovite science. We must here remember the "Silence of Muscovy" thesis, which long portrayed Muscovy as lacking literate expertise.[37] Although this thesis is rarely explicitly invoked today, it has cast a long shadow and influenced when, how, and even if we discuss Muscovite expertise. When experts are spoken of, they are often foreign servitors, like the West European physicians employed by the Apothecary Chancery.[38] Some Muscovites have been acknowledged as experts: the icon-painter Semen Ushakov and the cartographer Semen Remezov have both been framed in this way.[39] Yet Ushakov and Remezov were exceptional figures and are discussed as such. Moreover, both men broadly worked in the field of visual arts, and historians have long considered that Muscovites were both capable of and interested in art, as opposed to their supposed disinterest or incompetence in other fields of expertise. Ordinary Muscovites are not typically discussed as having expertise, especially not practical expertise.

When we do discuss expertise in Muscovy, we often discuss institutions. The remarkable production and survival of Apothecary Chancery documents has led us to overly privilege it, and its foreign employees in particular, in stories of early-modern Russian healing. The Apothecary Chancery was an exceptional bastion of literate expertise, whose interest in a range of subjects has left us vital resources on understanding Muscovite science. Yet the very documents of the department show us that other experts existed. The role of Kitai-gorod merchants and artisans, and Kaluga Cossack artisans here, as well as other local experts such the *travniki* (herb collectors) that K. S. Khudin and Rachel Koroloff have written about, the writers of the Russian-language herbals A. B. Ippolitova has examined, and the unofficial healers Eve Levin highlights, all show the Apothecary Chancery as a part of an Imperial Russian ecosystem of official, unofficial, and semi-official artisans, an ecosystem that functioned via the exchange of materials and expertise.[40]

So, to return to our earlier question, who was Master Ptitskoi? He was a locally known expert in creating ceramic vessels for use in preparing medical drugs, whose skills and knowledge were valued by the court. Compared to the visibility of elite expert creations like Ushakov's icons, this was a hidden kind of expertise, the creation of equipment to be used by invisible technicians to create medicines the availability of which was carefully policed, in a department most people would never be allowed to enter.[41] Yet expertise it was. We are told that the court sent Master Ptitskoi from Moscow to Gzhel specifically so that he could give his opinion on the local clay. We are told that he was given status there, to indicate which clay he found the most suitable, a decision he appeared to be taking by himself, without further oversight. Master Ptitskoi was not the only expert used by the Moscow court whose expertise is at best semi-visible: the *travniki*, alchemists, and apothecaries who also worked in the Apothecary Chancery were also behind-the-scenes figures. Master Ptitskoi was then one of a group of experts who were less visible than Ushakov or Remezov but whose knowledge was nevertheless highly valued and respected by the Moscow court.

## Conclusion

Compared to the more loquacious early-modern sources like those from Western Europe, Muscovite texts sometimes seem not to have a lot to say. But if we make a conscious effort to identify ideas regarding which materials are worth studying as culturally specific, and try to set aside those presumptions about documents and archives, one paragraph on the earth of Gzhel can be hugely revealing. A few short lines tell us much about the words, qualities, and experts that were central to Muscovite science. Threading that source together with other hints and notes on pharmacy equipment in seventeenth-century Russia, we can see what kind of object Muscovite apothecary ware was. We can see a common emphasis on local materials and production, and a clear sense that these objects had particular qualities that made them suitable for their vital role of destroying ingredients and creating medical drugs. Muscovite apothecary ware was a specific category of technical object created from materials with appropriate qualities to fulfil a particular practical function.

The presences and absences of Muscovite apothecary ware provoke new thoughts about material culture studies, and the key issues of particularities of materials and object agency. We know that Apothecary ware was a particular material, with specific qualities. Yet its potential agency is, in the most literal sense, ambivalent. There are two starkly opposed possibilities: apothecary ware was meant to express agency in the drug creation process; apothecary ware was supposed to be inert and express no agency in the drug creation process. This is our Schrödinger's Cat: it can only be one of these two mutually incompatible options, but we are unable to open the box to discover which one. We cannot give material culture studies the answer to this question, but the lack of an answer instead provides interesting theoretical points. Apothecary ware has a kind of immaterial, translucent specificity: we know the specificity existed but not what it was. Apothecary ware has an ambivalent, intermaterial agency: it either definitely expresses agency in mediating between other objects or definitely does not express agency as it does so. The very ambiguity of apothecary ware is its gift, as it reveals the nuanced possibilities of dealing with objects whose biographies are hard to read.

All this focus on objects takes us back to people. The ambiguous agency of Muscovite apothecary ware is only ambiguous to us, divided as we are from Muscovy by that gaping chasm of time, language, and worldview. The point of experts like Master Ptitskoi was that the agency of apothecary ware was entirely clear and comprehensible to him, yet—appropriate to a master protecting the arcane knowledge of his craft— he is not letting us in on the secret. Master Ptitskoi indeed does well not to tell us his secrets, for as we have seen, the early-modern Russian Empire was full of experts, many of whom peddled their expertise and their expertly created wares to the Russian court. Expertise was valuable; protecting one's tradecraft from the uninitiated was reasonable. This then, perhaps, can finally smash the so-called silence of Muscovy, with its presumptions of absences of expertise. The mindful hands of Muscovite artisans may not have spoken, but they were not silent.

## Notes

My thanks to the participants of the "Materials and Materiality in Russian History" workshop that took place at the University of Toronto in Summer 2019 for their comments on the first version of this chapter, to Emma Hagström Molin for her careful reading and excellent suggestions on the further development of this piece, and to Matthew Romaniello, Alison Smith, and Tricia Starks for organizing that workshop, putting together this volume, and for their productive comments and criticisms of earlier versions of this chapter. All remaining errors of fact and judgment are my responsibility alone.

1. Clare Griffin, "Russia and the Medical Drug Trade in the Seventeenth Century," *Social History of Medicine* 31:1 (2018), 2–23.
2. A 1710 account by Danish diplomat Just Juel, http://www.vostlit.info/Texts/rus11/Jul_3/text3.htm. See also A. V. Oreshnikov, "Danil Gurchin. Moskovskii aptekar' nachala XVIII veka," in *Sbornik statei v chest' grafini Praskov'i Sergeevny Uvarovoi* (Moscow: Tovarishchestvo Skoropechatni A. A. Levenson, 1916), 47–69, see 53.
3. Anne Gerritsen and Giorgio Riello, eds., *The Global Lives of Things: The Material Culture of Connections in the Early Modern World* (London: Routledge, 2015).
4. Scott Manning Stevens, "Tomahawk: Materiality and Depictions of the Haudenosaunee," *Early American Literature* 53:2 (2018), 475–511.
5. Pamela H. Smith, "Making and Knowing in a Sixteenth-Century Goldsmith's Workshop," in *The Mindful Hand: Inquiry and Invention between the Late Renaissance and Early Industrialization*, ed. Lissa Roberts, Simon Schaffer, and Peter Dear (Amsterdam: Koninklijke Nederlandse Akademie van Wetenschappen, 2007), 3–57, see 33.
6. Ibid., 43.
7. Ursula Klein and Wolfgang Lefèvre, *Materials in Eighteenth-Century Science: A Historical Ontology* (Boston, MA: MIT Press, 2007). See also Anita Guerrini, "The Material Turn in the History of Life Science," *Literature Compass* 13:7 (2016), 469–80.
8. On the agency of objects, see, for example, Janet Hoskins, "Agency, Biography and Objects," in *Handbook of Material Culture*, ed. Chris Tilley, Webb Keane, Susanne

Küchler, Mike Rowlands, and Patricia Spyer (London: Sage, 2006), 74–84; Bert De Munck, "Artisans, Products and Gifts: Rethinking the History of Material Culture in Early Modern Europe," *Past and Present* 224:1 (August 2014), 39–74.

9. Marianne De Laet and Annemarie Mol, "The Zimbabwe Bush Pump: Mechanics of a Fluid Technology," *Social Studies of Science* 30:2 (2000), 225–63.
10. Edward L. Keenan, "Muscovite Political Folkways," *The Russian Review* 45:2 (1986), 115–81, see 147, 153.
11. Alyssa Mt. Pleasant, Caroline Wigginton, and Kelly Wisecup, "Materials and Methods in Native American and Indigenous Studies," *Early American Literature* 53:2 (2018), 407–44, see 418.
12. Sergei Bogatyrev, "The Patronage of Early Printing in Moscow," *Canadian-American Slavic Studies* 51:2–3 (2017), 249–88.
13. Simon Franklin, "Printing and Social Control in Russia 1: Passports," *Russian History* 37:3 (2010), 208–37; Franklin, "Printing and Social Control in Russia 2: Decrees," *Russian History* 38:4 (2011), 467–92; Franklin, "Printing and Social Control in Russia 3: Blank Forms," *Russian History* 42:1 (2015), 114–35.
14. Richard Hellie lists a *voz* as 15–20 *pud*, and one *pud* as 16.38 kg. Richard Hellie, *The Economy and Material Culture of Russia, 1600–1725* (Chicago: University of Chicago Press, 1999), 648.
15. Original:

    Во Гжелской волости для аптекарскихъ и алхимическихъ глиняныхъ судовъ пріискать глины, которая глина годитца къ темъ оптекарскимъ судомъ, а для пріиску тое глины посланъ во Гжелскую волость аптекарскихъ и алхимическихъ глиняныхъ мастеръ Пашко Птицкой. А в которыхъ местехъ мастеръ Пашка Птицкой Во Гжелской волости глину пріищетъ, и тое глину указалъ Государь привезти къ Москве Гжелские волости крестьяномъ пятнатцать возовъ, а въ иные дела тое глины никуда не давать, а держать тое глину на оптекарские дела, и впередъ тое глины изо Гжелские волости указалъ Государь имать и возить тое ж волости крестьяномъ какъ та глина в Оптекарской приказе надобна будет.

    N. E. Mamonov, *Materialy dlia istorii meditsiny v Rossii* (St. Petersburg: M. M. Stasiulevich, 1881), ii, 267.
16. De Laet and Mol, "Zimbabwe Bush Pump," 254.
17. See, for example, Lawrence M. Principe and William R. Newman, "Some Problems with the Historiography of Alchemy," in *Secrets of Nature: Astrology and Alchemy in Early Modern Europe*, ed. William R. Newman and Anthony Grafton (Boston, MA: MIT Press, 2001), 385–431. For a discussion of this historiography and how it can be applied to a Slavic context, see Agnieszka Anna Rec, "Transmutation in a Golden Age: Reading Alchemy in Late Medieval and Early Modern Cracow" (PhD diss., Yale University, 2016), 4–10.
18. Maria Unkovskaya, *Brief Lives: A Handbook of Medical Practitioners in Muscovy, 1620–1701* (London: Wellcome Trust, 1999), 45–62.
19. Mamonov, *Materialy*, i, 79–86; Griffin, "Russia and the Medical Drug Trade."
20. Mamonov, *Materialy*, i, 82.
21. Gerald Stone, *A Dictionarie of the Vulgar Russe Tongue, Attributed to Mark Ridley, Edited from the Late-Sixteenth-Century Manuscripts and with an Introduction* (Cologne: Böhlau Verlag, 1996).

22. See, for example, Christopher Beckwith, "Tibetan Treacle: A Note on Theriac in Tibet," *Tibet Society Bulletin* 15 (1980), 49–51.
23. Central Academic Library of Kharkhiv National University V. N. Karazin (hereafter, TsNB), 121-r 159/c. Available online here: http://escriptorium.univer.kharkov.ua/handle/1237075002/1975 (accessed May 5, 2017).
24. Stone, *Dictionarie of the Vulgar Russe Tongue*, 201.
25. Prescriptions for the Tsar, 1663–4. Russian State Archive of Ancient Documents (RGADA), Moscow. Collection of the Apothecary Chancery, f. 143, op. 2, ed. khr. 706.
26. A 1724 Latin-Russian dictionary dedicated to Catherine I. Library of the Russian Academy of Sciences (BAN), St. Petersburg, Collection of Manuscripts from the Personal Library of Peter I, P.I.B 107, 434v–435.
27. The village was mentioned in documents as early as the mid-fourteenth century, and there were local workshops producing decorative ceramics there in the second half of the eighteenth century. Somehow or other the local clay had developed a reputation for being of good quality by the mid-seventeenth century, which strongly suggests that other ceramics were produced from that clay in the seventeenth century and/or earlier. However, I have not been able to identify any work or document confirming the production of decorative ceramics in the area before the mid-eighteenth century. On the earliest mentions of Gzhel in East Slavic documents, see E. L. Koniavskaia, "Dannye o russkikh kniaginiakh v kniazheskikh zaveshchaniiakh i dogovornykh gramotakh XIV-nachala XVI v.," *Drevniaia Rus'. Voprosy medievistiki* 3 (2020), 180–4. On the production of decorative ceramics in Gzhel in the eighteenth century, see Alison Hilton, *Russian Folk Art* (Bloomington: Indiana University Press, 1995).
28. Original: "те скляницы надобны в Аптекарский приказ"; Mamonov, *Materialy*, ii, 211–12.
29. Carla Nappi, "Surface Tension: Objectifying Ginseng in Chinese Early Modernity," in *Early Modern Things: Objects and Their Histories, 1500–1800*, ed. Paula Findlen (Abingdon: Routledge, 2013), 31–52.
30. *Ivan Vasilievich Changes Profession* (1973) is a comedy in which Tsar Ivan IV time-travelled to Soviet Moscow.
31. Smith, "Making and Knowing in a Sixteenth-Century Goldsmith's Workshop," 43.
32. Maria Unkovskaya, "Learning Foreign Mysteries: Russian Pupils of the Aptekarskii Prikaz, 1650–1700," *Oxford Slavonic Papers* 30 (1997), 1–20.
33. Mamonov, *Materialy*, i, 10–11; RGADA f. 143, op. 3, ed. khr. 136.
34. K. S. Khudin, "Stanovleniie mozhzhevelovoi povinnosti v Rossii v XVII v. (po materialam fonda Aptekarskogo prikaza RGADA)," *Vestnik RGGU* 21 (2012), 118–26; Rachel Koroloff, "Travniki, Travniki and Travniki: Herbals, Herbalists and Herbaria in Seventeenth-Century and Eighteenth-Century Russia," *ВИВЛIOθИКА: E-Journal of Eighteenth-Century Russian Studies* 6 (2018), 58–76; Eve Levin, "Healers and Witches in Early Modern Russia," in *Saluting Aron Gurevich: Essays in History, Literature and Other Related Subjects*, ed. Yelena Mazour-Matusevich and Alexandra Korros (Leiden: Brill, 2010), 105–33; A. B. Ippolitova, *Russkie rukopisnye travniki XVII–XVIII vekov: issledovanie fol'klora i etnobotaniki* (Moscow: Indrik, 2008).
35. Pamela H. Smith, "Science on the Move: Recent trends in the History of Early Modern Science," *Renaissance Quarterly* 62:2 (2009), 345–375, see p. 366. See also Pamela H. Smith, *The Body of the Artisan: Art and Experience in the Scientific Revolution* (Chicago: University of Chicago Press, 2004).
36. P. V. Sedov, *Zakat Moskovskogo tsarstva. Tsarskii dvor kontsa XVII veka* (St. Petersburg: Dmitrii Bulanin, 2008).

37. Robert O. Crummey, "The Silence of Muscovy," *The Russian Review* 46:2 (1987), 157–64.
38. Unkovskaya, *Brief Lives*; Sabine Dumschat, *Ausländischer Mediziner im Moskauer Russland* (Stuttgart: Franz Steiner Verlag, 2006).
39. Ann Kleimola, "Regulating Icon Painters in the Era of the Ulozhenie: Evidence from the Russian North," *Russian History* 34:1/4 (2007), 341–63; Valerie Kivelson, "Angels in Tobolsk: Celestial Topography and Visionary Administration in Late Muscovite Siberia," *Harvard Ukrainian Studies* 28:1/4 (2006), 543–56.
40. Khudin, "Stanovleniie mozhzhevelovoi povinnosti v Rossii v XVII v."; Koroloff, "Travniki, Travniki and Travniki"; Ippolitova, *Russkie rukopisnye travniki*; Levin, "Healers and Witches in Early Modern Russia."
41. Steven Shapin, "The Invisible Technician," *American Scientist* 77:6 (1989), 554–63.

2

# Lime and Limestone in Eighteenth-Century Russia

Alison K. Smith

In a corner of the huge park spreading out from the former Imperial palace in Gatchina, a small town outside St. Petersburg, lies the hollowed-out shell of the "Forest Greenhouse," one of a number of ruins scattered around the grounds. The building dates to the 1790s, built during the eventual Emperor Paul's most active period as the owner of the estate. Damaged during the Second World War, now its windows and roof are gone, and the internal components of its walls are laid bare to the eye (see Figure 2.1). The walls are mostly brick, but brick that was originally hidden on the inside by a thick layer of white plaster and on the outside by a cladding of stone. Remnants of the former remain, and the latter is still remarkably untouched, though stained by smoke. The informational plaque outside the ruin tells the park visitor more about one side of these walls. The cladding, it notes, is "Pudost' stone."[1] The note links this one ruined building in a corner of a park to a local material that helped to transform the built environment of the entire St. Petersburg region in the eighteenth century. As a geologist put it at the beginning of the nineteenth century, "the colonnade and porticos, if not the whole of the Cazan [sic] Church at Petersburg, the Palace at Gatchina, the colonnade in the garden opposite the north front of the palace at Peterhof, and many smaller ornamental buildings which decorate the environs of Petersburg, are constructed of this [Pudost'] stone."[2]

The plaque does not mention it, but the remnants of plaster on the inside of the building also link the building to the same local material, but the material transformed. Pudost', one of the villages belonging to the larger Gatchina estate, produced not only stone of a quality suitable for building colonnades or facing palaces and palace outbuildings but also the lime used to hold bricks together, to cover them with plaster, later to whitewash walls, or to create intricate decorations. Even after the quarries in Pudost' no longer produced stone suitable for building, they still produced limestone to burn into lime, thus continuing to add to the built environment of Gatchina and the St. Petersburg region.

Much of the scholarly consideration of material culture focuses on objects that are graspable, that can be picked up, held in a hand, moved about. This focus on the portable is perhaps linked to the concurrent interest in things that have "global lives," that literally or figuratively cross boundaries or borders and thereby carry meanings

**Figure 2.1** The ruin of the Forest Greenhouse (*lesnaia oranzhereia*) on the grounds of the Gatchina Palace Estate Museum, showing the layers of materials that went into its construction: a facing of "Pudost' stone," brick interior, and a layer of plaster coating the inside of the walls. Photo credit: © Alison K. Smith.

or otherwise construct networks linking disparate regions—like apothecary materials and wares, tea urns, isinglass, a shaman's coat held in a museum.[3] Buildings and the built environment hold people and objects rather than are held by them, but they are nonetheless part of the world of material culture. Buildings are objects; they are things that, as the architectural historian Carl R. Lounsbury put it, "serve basic functions but also embody culture and express the dynamics of its social, economic, and political fortunes," and which furthermore "achieve meanings in context."[4] Buildings are of course firmly situated in a particular place, but they are also part of the global world of materiality. The contexts that give buildings meaning are local, but they also may well reflect transnational trends—the buildings in Petersburg, Gatchina, and Peterhof listed above are all exemplars of that fact.[5] The colonnades and columns echo Rome, not Novgorod; the gardens at Peterhof echo Versailles, not Kolomenskoe. The particular location of these buildings is important too: around St. Petersburg, the new imperial capital that was simultaneously a colonial city, located as it was in a newly annexed imperial periphery. As a result, its built environment had to say many things to many people.[6]

One way to get at the materiality of buildings and to think about the layers of meaning they hold within them is to look at their literal building blocks, in this case limestone, and at the material that held them together and plastered over them, lime. At least in the eighteenth century, limestone and lime were excavated or produced locally and generally used within only a relatively small region.[7] At the same time, however, the knowledge of how to use these materials and the uses to which they were put had a much longer, transregional history—and eventually a transnational trajectory, as well. In other words, a focus on the materiality of building emphasizes the ways that transnational cultural projects, like the construction of St. Petersburg, were grounded in the extremely local. First stepping back to look at the "lime cycle" (the process by which limestone was turned into lime and then, in a way, back again) and the ways that its elements show up in eighteenth-century Russian laws, then looking closely at one particular site of production, the Gatchina imperial estate, and finally considering this process and this site in a longer chronological scope, lime and limestone become not merely component parts of buildings, invisible in their ubiquity, but also materials that are transformed by human and natural agency and that transform the world around them.

## Definitions and Transformations: The Lime Cycle

In an 1802 book on "town and country building, or a guide to knowing how to design and build any kind of building without having an architect," Prince Vladimir Lem, "architect and cavalier of the fourth degree," began by introducing the various materials that might be used for building in the Russian Empire. After briefly discussing different kinds of stone (including limestone) and brick, he spent a longer time describing lime and how it was produced. To make lime, chunks of limestone should be burned in "big and tall kilns so that they burn better." Once the limestone had been burned long and hot enough to turn into chunks of quicklime, the fire should be immediately doused with as little water as possible in order to avoid moisture getting back into the quicklime. According to Lem, damp quicklime or lime lost its strength, no matter how dry it seemed, so using it quickly or keeping it well covered was important (although it could be fired again to regain its strength).[8]

Lem was describing the first parts of the "lime cycle," a series of chemical reactions that transform limestone into quicklime into slaked lime and then back into limestone (albeit in a dramatically different form) again. Each of these materials has many uses in construction and industry. Although it can contain other materials, the basic chemical composition of limestone is calcium carbonate ($CaCO_3$). If limestone is burned at a very high temperature, roughly 1000°C, it produces lumps of calcium oxide (CaO) and releases the gas carbon dioxide ($CO_2$). Calcium oxide is known as quicklime, a material that is stable in air but which reacts with water. When quicklime is mixed with water ($H_2O$), the reaction produces heat and calcium hydroxide ($Ca(OH)_2$), known as slaked lime. Slaked lime can turn into a putty or is mixed in the right amount to form a powder. Over time, the carbon dioxide in air reacts with slaked lime to produce water and calcium carbonate—the basic component of limestone—again.[9]

According to Vladimir Dal' and then later etymologists, the Russian word for lime, *izvest'*, derives from the Greek word *asbestos*, meaning unquenchable or eternal, and the lime cycle helps to explain why that might have been so.¹⁰ When used in plaster or in mortar—two of the most important uses of lime in building—the last reaction of the lime cycle, through which slaked lime essentially becomes limestone again, means that the resulting surface or bind is potentially extremely strong—perhaps not literally eternal but certainly long-lasting. Lime was sometimes also called *izvestka*, although that could also be the term for a solution of lime used as whitewash. Limestone was *izvestniak*, or *izvestnyi* or *izvestkovyi kamen'*, though past sources sometimes refer to what is now known as limestone as simply *kamen'* or *plita*. Other terms are also now generally understood to refer to limestone—such as "white stone" (*belokamennyi*), an adjective used to describe the Mocow kremlin built by Grand Prince Dmitrii Donskoi in the 1300s that signified the beginnings of Moscow's rise to prominence. Although that kremlin was later replaced by one of red brick, the association of Moscow and "white stone" remained powerful.[11]

Each of these materials interacted with the people who produced them and the environment around them in a myriad of ways—and furthermore, despite the idea of eternity in its etymological source, each of the materials was transformed through these interactions. Limestone, of course, was physically taken from the ground, hewn into blocks or sheets or broken into smaller pieces, and used to build or to pave. Although it is just one of a number of different stones used in building, it is a particularly important one. For one thing, limestone is a family of sedimentary rocks ranging from the very soft (chalk) to the very hard. Because it always contains other material, it varies not only in hardness but also in color and general appearance. All of these differences mean that limestone is extraordinarily versatile in its use in terms of both structure and aesthetics.

Because of its versatility and utility, in the eighteenth century state decrees saw limestone as a significant natural resource to be discovered, quantified, mapped, exploited, and governed. Decrees that discuss governing the provinces, or incorporating new lands into the Russian Empire, note that those in charge were to keep an eye out for limestone pits on the state lands under their control. The 1712 decree integrating Ingermanland—the area around the newly founded St. Petersburg acquired during Peter I's Northern War—gave instructions for distributing farmland to nobles but noted that natural resources like clay pits and quarries should remain the property of the sovereign.[12] In part because of a new eighteenth-century desire to know the provinces better in order to exploit their resources, from limestone to fish guts, more fully, all sorts of provincial officials were tasked with sending in surveys of the resources around them—including quarries and new deposits of stone.[13] Although the Petrine law about Ingermanland noted that quarries ought to remain the property of the sovereign, later laws softened on this principle. In 1764, Catherine II's instructions for foreign settlers specifically noted that lime and limestone were resources that should be considered the communal property of a new settlement.[14] In the early nineteenth century, a guide to the geography of the Russian Empire went into detail about natural resources, including the limestone deposits found all across the empire.[15]

Lime, both the quicklime produced by burning limestone and the slaked lime produced by mixing quicklime with water, has a whole series of uses in the modern world. Lime solutions play into tanning, food preparation, agriculture, filtration and purification systems, and metallurgy, but in the eighteenth century its use was more limited.[16] For example, although eventually lime became an important part of agricultural techniques, helping to regulate the pH level of soil and thereby the effectiveness of other fertilizers, in the eighteenth century that use was not well developed. A mid-nineteenth-century Russian agricultural writer noted that although it was "one of the most ancient fertilizing materials after the waste of domestic livestock," lime had only come back into regular use as fertilizer during the nineteenth century.[17] In other words, although using lime as fertilizer has a long history, in tsarist Russia it was seen as an innovation. That idea is made even more clear in its one eighteenth-century appearance in connection with agriculture in the *Complete Collection of the Laws of the Russian Empire*: in Catherine II's 1765 decree encouraging the cultivation of potatoes.[18] Potatoes had been known before Catherine's reign, but active promotion of their cultivation was an innovation; this use of lime was not entirely unknown, but nonetheless an innovation, as well.

In the eighteenth century, however, lime was far more often considered to be a building material. It played three main roles in the world of construction: to make the mortar that held bricks or stone together, to make the plaster or stucco that covered the outsides or insides of buildings, and to make the whitewash that was regularly reapplied to the insides of buildings for reasons of appearance and hygiene. According to Vladimir Lem, preparing mortar was relatively simple. Lumps of lime were put through a screen to be ground fine, and then mixed in a hod with sand. The usual proportion was one part lime to one part sand, but if the lime was itself from a sandy rock, then less sand went into the mixture. Water was added and the mixture mixed until it thickened. Lem also gave instructions for how to test mortar: use it to stick together seven bricks one on top of the other. Once they dried a bit, raise the pile by the top brick. If only one or two bricks actually came off the ground, the mortar was weak and no good for "big and tall buildings" but acceptable to use for "low buildings for servants if you do not have better." If five or six came up together, then the mortar was good for more extensive projects.[19]

Lime shows up over and over again in decrees that link it to building projects. It shows up in a "resolution on a report of the Senate" touching on fortifications in Reval (modern Tallinn), specifically in a discussion about the supply of construction materials, which includes reference to royal decrees dating back to the fourteenth century.[20] After a fire in Vyborg, the empress's mercies to sufferers there included not only gifts of money but also materials to rebuild—three thousand barrels of lime among them.[21] A later fire in St. Petersburg also specified lime as a material necessary for rebuilding.[22] It is one of the materials listed in a decree from 1745 demanding that government buildings be properly kept up when they started to show signs of wear (specifically, 989 casks of lime were left over from a Moscow project to repair the town gates and now were being put to use to repair the walls of the old center, as well).[23] Later, when Catherine II ordered that towns around the empire be rebuilt according to new imperial plans, her decrees included provisions for producing sufficient lime. The decree about Kazan' specified that governors should find lands to build kilns for bricks and also to burn lime ("if bringing limestone to those places is found to be possible").[24]

Not only limestone and lime as materials but also the process of transforming one into the other appear in the *Complete Collection*. Burning lime required energy in the form of firewood and getting enough of that proved to be an occasional problem. By the 1760s, the brick and lime kilns on the Neva and Tosna rivers were having a hard time, particularly because the forests in the region had been allotted first to the Admiralty and then to another state office. That meant that only those institutions had the right to cut wood in the forests along the banks of the rivers—where, of course, the limestone and hence the kilns were. As the cost of firewood had just gone up, this was proving a huge problem for the production of bricks and lime. As a result, a decree of 1765 gave those (state) kilns the right to cut firewood near to them, contrary to previous decrees.[25] During Paul's reign, the discovery of new coal deposits led to decrees to govern its mining. They included notes that coal might well be particularly useful for firing lime (and brick) kilns.[26]

Burning lime also created smoke, and that led to its restriction in St. Petersburg in a July 1757 Senate decree. The decree was sparked by a day on which "here in St. Petersburg there is a great smog and it smells of burning," a fact that bothered some of the senators then in session. When members of the Senate inquired as to what was causing the smog and odor, they were told that it was caused by lime being burnt near the Trinity wharf. The Senate then sent a soldier named Ivan Metal'nikov to go investigate the situation. When he returned to say that there were indeed fires burning there, the Senate decided to decree that no more lime be burned within the city itself in order to protect it from unpleasant and potentially dangerous smoke and vapors.[27]

Of course, if lime was not to be produced in the city itself, that meant it had to be brought into the city, which created an additional set of potential problems. Starting well before the ban, decrees limited the transportation of lime, limestone, and other "heavy materials" on certain kinds of barges because they tended to wreck the barges and thereby disrupt traffic on the canals and other waterways. Rules for the Ladoga canal noted that such barges should not be more than one-third as wide as the canal itself in order to ensure that traffic move freely.[28] Some restrictions were later eased because of shortages in building materials in St. Petersburg, but the problem of ensuring safety on the all-important river and canal network remained.[29]

Another set of decrees reflected another danger posed by lime. The process of "slaking" quicklime—that is, mixing it with water to form the slaked or hydrated lime that was used in mortars and plasters—is a chemical reaction that generates heat. Quicklime therefore needed to be kept away from water except under controlled situations. But of course, that was particularly tricky in Russia, where river and barges were such a big part of the transportation infrastructure. As a result, another place that lime appears is in laws about safety. Lime appears in Peter's 1722 regulations on the Admiralty and navy. The regulations governing the "duties of the Captain over the port" stated (among many other things) that barges loaded with quicklime were only to dock "far from other boats, and do not get close to them or tie up to them." Docking in a place that was not safe could lead to a fine, confiscation of the boat and all its wares, and corporal punishment.[30] The same provision was repeated the next year in rules for "skippers and others" docking in Russian ports.[31]

Many eighteenth-century decrees also get at the idea that lime and limestone were not simply resources that sat there but resources that were extracted and transformed and worked and produced by people. Lime burning, for one, was an established job and listed in decrees as such. The 1721 decree that established magistracies in towns around the empire among other things listed the kinds of people who were likely to be found in towns. It ordered those people on a "form for the description of residents in the city and their crafts," which began with nonserving nobles (this was just before another Petrine innovation would force all nobles into service), then listed all sorts of different kinds of jobs. Town bureaucrats and religious servitors came at the top of the list and were followed by many different kinds of trades: gold- and silversmiths, "wine-sellers, who run drinking houses," skippers, shopkeepers, all sorts of other craftsmen, and gardeners. Toward the end of the list come "those who fire bricks" and "those who burn lime." There is certainly an implication here that these are low-ranking urban jobs: after them only come vodka distillers, carters, sailors, workers, the poor, and vagrants.[32]

Lime burning may not have had much prestige, but the use of limestone and lime in building constituted more skilled trades. Masons and plasterers did work that on the one hand literally held buildings together and on the other were central to their overall appearance. As such, they were important to regulate. Late in 1724, perhaps concerned over the quality of the stone construction taking place around him, Peter I released a decree stating that all stonemasons or contractors who had come to St. Petersburg to take on building work were to register with the Construction Chancellery. The goal was clearly one of quality control: henceforth anyone wishing to hire a contractor for stonework was to check first with the Chancellery to see if he had "built such buildings before, and whether his work was correct."[33] Attracting such skilled workers to places where construction was going on—like St. Petersburg—was a major goal. In 1732, for example, Empress Anna released a decree calling on workers skilled in building trades to come to St. Petersburg to help continue to build up the capital. It specifically listed stonemasons and plasterers among those in particular need.[34]

## Lime, Limestone, and Locality

Limestone and lime were simultaneously ubiquitous and local. This locality was in part a practical matter: they were used everywhere, but not necessarily traded much beyond their locality, in large part due to the challenges of transporting such heavy materials. More importantly, though, limestone was not generally known as limestone in the abstract. Instead, the stone quarried around St. Petersburg was usually called after its place of origin, generally along a river, rather than by the specific stone type. This means that the stone used to build St. Petersburg was often limestone but was referred to not as such but by the name of its village or river of origin: it was Putilov stone, Tosna stone, or Pudost' stone.[35] In other words, limestone was identified not so much as a generic good but as a specific, locally quarried one, with its own particular qualities: color, hardness, porosity.

According to the architect Vladimir Lem, the specific local origin of limestone was also important to the quality of the lime that it produced. He described the various limes and resulting mortars or plasters produced from limestone deposits around St. Petersburg:

> Svinaretskaia has a binding quality in thin walls, but in thick ones always remains loose; Siazskaia does not dry quickly, but when it dries out it holds fast; Bolkhovskaia is sandy and not good to use, because when it has been dried it always crumbles away; Tosnenskaia comes together strongly, but should be used quickly once in solution, for when it sits in the hod for five days or so it becomes weaker. All of these limes are of grey and yellowish color [and] are primarily used for any sort of masonry work; white Pudovskaia can be used for plastering and for whitewashing, and also for making walls, other than foundations, for it only sets firm on its exterior, and Borovitskaia can be used for plastering work and to make walls, other than foundations, because it does not set in the ground.[36]

Both limestone and lime, then, reflected extremely local conditions—not even a region but the bank of a particular bend in a river. The stone in different deposits was not only of varying color and density but also of different compositions; the result was lime of varying properties and uses.

One of these particular localities was the village of Pudost' and its adjacent lime pits and lime kilns. The limestone quarried near the village of Pudost' is a particular kind of limestone known as tufa. According to the nineteenth-century geologist Horner Fox Strangways, "Though coarse and porous, it is the best building stone in this part of Russia: its colour being a fine yellowish white, and its substance light and easily worked."[37] Although Strangways also noted that "it is hardly durable enough to withstand the vicissitudes of spring or the severity of winter," it was used widely in this region of severe winters and variable springs.[38] Its specific color was part of the attraction. Later, while arguing for the value of preserving elements of the tsarist past, the Soviet culture authority A. V. Lunacharskii noted that the Gatchina palace "would be severe and even gloomy" if not for the fact that it was built of Pudost' stone. The reason was "its color—light grey, almost the color of a cloudy sky." The result was a perfect fit between material and location: "Against the background of this northern sky the palace seems airy, almost a mirage, uncommonly light."[39] The lime Pudost' stone produced also had its own particular value—according to Lem it was very white, and it could be used for almost any purpose from the mortar that held walls together to plastering to whitewashing.

The village and its resources were part of the larger estate of Gatchina when it was given by Catherine II to her son Paul in 1783. This was an extravagant gift that consisted of an opulent palace (which had been built by Catherine's former favorite Grigory Orlov, the most recent owner of the estate), its park and grounds, and a couple of dozen villages scattered around it.[40] Pudost' was the most important source of limestone, but there were quarries at two other villages, Chernitsy and Paritsy, as well.[41] Although the central palace structure was already there, Paul added to the built environment of the region extensively. He expanded the palace structure, he commissioned a series of outbuildings for the larger palace grounds, he built a mill, a church, and fortifications on the road to St. Petersburg. All of this required material, much of it drawn from the estate itself. The quarries and the lime kilns all were put to work for the eventual emperor's building projects—they were allowed to supply other builders "only with the permission of the emperor."[42]

All of this building activity also required people who knew how to work with stone and lime. Utilizing the stone quarried in the region had long been one of the economic activities of the residents of Gatchina and its surrounding villages. According to a later history of the town of Gatchina, at the beginning of the eighteenth century "the village of Gatchina consisted of a few huts, settled by poor Finns, who occupied themselves other than farming with cutting wood, stone cutting, burning lime and charcoal, and also hauling, particularly sand, stone, and wood in the area of Petersburg."[43] Later, as the region became more fully incorporated into the Russian Empire and became part of the economic engine driven by St. Petersburg, more people came to the area to settle and to take advantage of its resources.[44]

During Paul's tenure as the master of Gatchina, the active exploitation of the region's resources only grew. Paul hired a Swiss-Italian stonework master named Placido Visconti to oversee construction on the palace and its grounds. Visconti signed contracts with contractors who promised to carry out the construction work or to deliver supplies and later reported on how well they had fulfilled their contracts.[45] The contractors then hired workers to fulfil their contracts. The workers themselves were usually not local peasants but instead peasants and serfs from other parts of the Russian Empire who came to the region sometimes on passports, sometimes illicitly, in search of employment. Because some of the men hired as workers either lacked passports or had let their passports expire, they might well end up arrested and questioned about their activities.

As a result, references to the stone and lime produced around Gatchina are rife in the archives of the Gatchina palace administration. There are of course the contracts and other documents associated with the various building projects around the town. In February 1793, for example, a man named Fedot Fedorov Okorchev signed a contract to build a hospital in the village of Gatchina. It was to have a lower floor of stone and an upper one of wood; the contracts included detailed building specs, and the file includes lists with costs for both material and labor.[46] The file also goes on to show some of the ways that even an autocrat in waiting could not get a contractor to finish his work on time and under budget. Already in August 1793 Okorchev sent in a petition lamenting that labor costs for stonemasons and carpenters had gone up. He continued to petition the Gatchina administration, then Paul himself, and eventually Paul's son Alexander, explaining why he had been unable to fulfil his obligations and asking for help. (In one of these petitions we learn among other things that he had also been contracted to deliver stone from Pudost' to Pavlovsk to help build a cascade there.)[47]

Another window into the role that Gatchina's quarries played in the local economy is the many statements made by workers who were brought in for questioning because they lacked passports. Many worked on the various building sites around the town or at the stone quarries in Pudost', Paritsy, and Chernitsy. In November and December 1797, for example, one of the local police officials, Andrei Delin, arrested groups of men at some of the quarries—four at the site in Paritsy and fifty-eight at the site in Chernitsy.[48] Some of the arrested men gave detailed statements about their work. For example, Grigorii Ivanov Parukhin was arrested in January 1799 and reported that he was fifty years old, illiterate, and a peasant from Arkhangel'sk province. In spring 1798 he had traveled to St. Petersburg on a passport, and after taking on several other jobs, "on last November 20 having been hired by the peasant Mokei Tropin I went to this district in the village of Paritsy to break stones, and was there until December 30 and then went to Gatchina where I was taken by a policeman under arrest." The Gatchina police then tried to find Tropin to follow up by going to the Paritsy quarry, where they were told by the stonecutters that Tropin had disappeared and "hidden himself from the artel" the previous October.[49] Nor was Tropin the only figure hiring people to work at the Paritsy quarry; a bit later in 1799, another man arrested for improper documents reported that a "contractor the St. Petersburg townsman Boris Zaitsov" had been the one to hire him to work at the Paritsy quarry.[50]

Records from the estate administration also show some of the ways that limestone and particularly lime were being used around the estate. The daily journals of the administration record all that went on in its office each day. They list (and copy out) instructions from the overarching administrator, Obol'ianinov, who was always close to Paul himself, or letters from other administrative bodies, generally with their own response. They also note everyone who came into the office each day, and what they were there for. One frequent reason the overseers of the various parts of the larger palace/town/village complex came in to the office was to ask for items from the palace stores to be used on properties belonging to the larger estate. Lime was a regular item requested.[51] It is also moderately clear that lime was being used above all for building/maintenance purposes. That was certainly true in one of the other places it came up. In July 1799, the administration received instructions from Obol'ianinov to move some of the palace cattle from the Silvia (part of the palace park) to the village of Rezino. He also ordered that the cowshed at Rezino should be fixed up, which specifically included "the insides should be whitewashed with lime."[52]

During Paul's reign, while he was investing heavily in the area, the work at cutting/breaking stone and burning lime was intended to be above all for the benefit of Gatchina itself. But after his death, when Gatchina's importance sank, the situation was very different. He left the palace to his widow, Maria Fedorovna, not to their son Alexander, the new emperor. By the time Maria Fedorovna died, and the estate passed on to the current emperor Nicholas I, lime burning for sale and profit had become a major part of the estate budget. In 1831, the estate overseers collected 12,410 rubles, 80 kopeks, in taxes and quitrent from the 252 *tiagla* (labor units) of peasants on the larger Gatchina estate. On top of that, the peasants owed certain dues in kind. They were to supply firewood to heat a number of the larger estate structures: orangeries, military barracks, and "for the firing of the lime kilns" (which demanded fifty units of firewood compared to the orangeries' sixty units). In addition, the Gatchina peasants had to supply a certain amount of labor duty to the production of lime. They also had to supply the labor to break stone, bring it to the kilns, and pack and fire the kilns: "Those kilns are fired two times a year, for which is demanded from each *tiaglo* five days."[53] From that work came significant income, as well. The estate had several additional sources of income other than quitrent: selling hay, rent from contracting out the mill, and collecting fees from people who used the estate's pastures to feed their cattle. But the single biggest item came from "the sale of lime from the Pudost' lime factory ... 17,959 ½ puds at 1 ruble 2 kopek each for 22,449 rubles 37 ½ kopeks."[54] That is about 324 tons of lime produced in Pudost' and at this point sold to consumers in the wider region.

## Transformations through Time

One of the reasons that the lime and limestone produced around Gatchina were so important, and one of the reasons that the materials appear so much in the *Complete Collection* in connection with construction, is that they were drafted into Peter I's effort to transform Russia. If the role of apothecary wares were intended to transform ingredients into medicines, the role of lime and limestones was to construct buildings that would transform the built environment of the country and thereby transform its people. Limestone and lime were not new materials, of course, nor were their basic functions in building much different. In his history of cementing substances, for example, Igor Znachko-Iavorskii describes lime plasters and mortars in use in ancient Novgorod.[55] Limestone construction was particularly prized in northern Rus' before the coming of the Qipchak Khanate in the thirteenth century, fell away during the worst years of the Mongol era that followed, and began to rise again as the Russian lands recovered.[56] Later, in seventeenth-century Muscovy, a stone chancery organized the supply not only of stone for building but also lime for mortar, for building up the city.[57]

By this time, too, Muscovy's ability to use lime, in particular, struck at least one traveler as remarkable. Paul of Aleppo, who traveled to Muscovy in the middle of the seventeenth century, reported on some of the buildings he saw there:

> The palaces in this city are mostly new, of stone or brick; and built on the European plan, lately taught the Muscovites by the Nemsas, or the Germans. We gaped with astonishment at their beauty and decoration, their solidity and skillful arrangement, their elegance, the multitude of their windows, and of the sculptured pillars on every side of them; the height of their stories, as though they were castles; their immense towers; and the manifold variety of the painting, in oil colours, both of their interior and exterior walls, which you might suppose were covered with slabs of real variegated marble, or with minute Mosaic; for the bricks made in this country are very fine and smooth, and like the best bricks of Antioch, in hardness, weight, and redness. They use as much sand as possible in their composition, and are possessed of great skill in their manufacture. They are vastly cheap: a thousand of them may be bought for a piaster: on this account, most of the buildings here are of brick. The lapidaries, with their iron tools, execute in it admirable engravings, not to be distinguished from stone. Their lime also is very fine and strong, and holds better than the lime of Aleppo: with this, when they have completed their brick building, they whiten it over; and it

adheres to it so firmly, that it will not fall off in a hundred years. By this means the fabric has all the appearance of stone.[58]

All their structures here are done with mortar, in the same manner as the ancients built the ancient edifices in our country. Having slacked their lime, they mix it with sifted sand: then they sprinkle their bricks with water, and dip them in lime; and having set them in a double layer along the wall, they cram the interstice with brickbats, and pour on mortar till it is filled up: in less than an hour's time the whole is firmly cemented, and becomes one solid mass.[59]

Stone might not be a major part of this building practice, but lime certainly was, and it gave the appearance of permanence that stone so often did.

Both limestone and lime gained new importance at the beginning of the eighteenth century in large part because of Peter I's desire to develop his new city, St. Petersburg, and to reconstruct his old city, Moscow, casting both in a new, modern, European mold. In early 1701 he released a decree stating that anyone building a new structure in Moscow to replace one that had burnt must build it of stone, or if that was too expensive, of stone and brick, and if that was too expensive, then of wattle and daub that would give the appearance of permanence.[60] Three years later, he followed with a stricter decree: all new buildings in the Kremlin and its adjacent Kitai-gorod area must be built of stone; if a property owner could not afford to build a new stone building, he was told to sell the property to someone who could.[61] A year after that, another decree hinted at a problem that hindered this goal of transforming the center of Moscow into a place of stone: a lack of materials. In May 1705, a decree noted that building of stone in areas other than Kitai-gorod should be stopped until building there was complete.[62] (It was eventually permitted in other areas, starting with Belyi gorod, in 1712.)[63] Later that year another decree aimed to get enough of a supply of stone to build bridges in the city by levying a special collection on certain villages. They were to supply stone and sand, the stone cut to certain sizes (or some in smaller pieces, but none "smaller than a goose egg"). The stone was to be cut in the fall, and the stone and sand delivered to Moscow over the winter, when the frozen world made transportation by sled more efficient.[64]

Peter's desire to create his new capital St. Petersburg out of virtually nothing, however, meant an even greater demand for stone. In 1714, he famously forbade all stone construction in his lands outside the new capital in order to preserve resources—both materials and mastery—for the new city.[65] From that point on, decrees expressed particular concern with making sure there was enough of both lime and limestone to build up St. Petersburg and that all new construction ought to be in stone.[66] According to Znachko-Iavorskii, the demand for lime in St. Petersburg in 1720 was more than 1 million *pudy* (16,380 tons).[67] A budget from 1710 allotted the lime from two hundred kilns, at a cost of 200 rubles per kiln, to the construction of the town—and a decree declared that all existing provinces of the empire would have to contribute extra money to ensure that supply.[68] Lime and cut limestone were among the goods deemed necessary for building and maintaining the new capital that were freed from internal taxation in a 1724 decree (the internal tariff had been applied in 1704).[69] In 1726 a decree stated that lime could be brought to Vyborg for construction without tariffs, as well.[70] In 1727, it was one of the materials listed in a decree on repairing the embankments of the Fontanka and other rivers and canals in St. Petersburg (already!), and in 1737 and again in 1745 for shoring up the banks of the Ladoga canal.[71] It was listed in instructions for rebuilding the Winter Palace in 1755.[72] A project to build a canal between the Sias' and Volkhov rivers (and possibly between the Mologa and Sias') listed some of the benefits to come; its specifications were governed in part by the idea that it was above all aimed at moving construction materials, including lime, to St. Petersburg.[73]

Perhaps more importantly, however, the mere fact that building should now be of stone was only part of the transformation Peter and his successors desired—he wanted new cityscapes that reflected his orientation toward Western Europe, and the later rulers of the eighteenth century continued to reform and rebuild Russian cities in models that followed transnational cultural trends. Famously, this involved new architectural styles that reached away from the Muscovite past first toward the baroque and then later toward neoclassicism.[74] It also involved a new arrangement of the built environment: Petrine decrees mandated that new stone buildings be laid out along streets in a line, not clustered around a central courtyard. This was, as other decrees regarding such building in Moscow put it, to make buildings in his city look like "buildings of other European States" and not *po staromu*—"as in olden times."[75] Another decree described one style of building—the clay- or stucco-covered brick structures that became ubiquitous in Russian towns—as "in the Prussian manner."[76] Other things about the new building style were opposed to how things had formerly been done—in 1723, for example, Peter I decreed that houses should now have plastered ceilings, not canopies "as in olden times."[77]

Limestone and particularly lime were central to this visual change. In some ways, buildings like the palace at Gatchina, clad in stone, were unusual examples of eighteenth-century architecture. In Moscow and Petersburg, on royal estates and in the new palaces built by the wealthiest of Russia's serf owners, plaster and stucco covered walls of brick or even wood.[78] The results were some of the Palladian structures that exemplified the newly established domestic world of the landed gentry and of the autocracy at the end of the eighteenth century.[79] Lime plasters and stuccos in all their possible uses could shift to reflect whichever architectural forms were currently in fashion.

## Conclusion

Bringing things full circle (or full cycle), in Gatchina itself limestone was and is central on its own, not simply transformed into lime. It links the borrowed form of the palace—built in the eighteenth century, it reached back to older Western European architectural forms and was thereby doubly borrowed—to the specific locale in which it was built, covering it with a local stone that appeared throughout the region. This is perhaps why there has been a minor tempest over recent restoration work on the palace exterior. When scaffolding on the building came down in early 2020, observers were surprised to see that the stone walls of the palace had changed color dramatically, losing their golden hue and turning a much plainer, starker grey. The officials in charge say it is a return to how the palace likely looked when it was originally built, but others doubt this story. In their eyes, the culprit was a water-repellant solution used as part of the restoration works that altered the color to something completely new.[80]

This most recent transformation of this particular structure composed of Pudost' stone highlights the instability of our certainty about the physical world of the past. Is the new, 2020 color a return to the eighteenth century, a return that will start over a slow transformation over the centuries, or is it a rupture? We cannot know precisely, in much the same way that we cannot know the exact size of a *sklanka* ordered to compound medicines, listed on a register but now long destroyed. The word *izvest* may etymologically suggest eternity, but in reality, even buildings of stone and mortar are not eternal, whether because of destruction due to war or renovation or because of the normal wear and tear of the elements. They transform the built environment and the everyday lives of the people who live in and among them, but that transformation is not a singular event but an ever-evolving series of interactions and transformations.

## Notes

1. See also V. Makarov and A. Petrov, *Gatchina* (Leningrad: Iskusstvo, 1974), 45.
2. Horner Fox Strangways, "Geological Sketch of the Environs of Petersburg," *Transactions of the Geological Society of London* 1:5 (1821), 392–458, here 438–9.
3. See Anne Gerritsen and Giorgio Riello, "The Global Lives of Things: Material Culture in the First Global Age," in *The Global Lives of Things: The Material Culture of Connections in the Early Modern World*, ed. Anne Gerritsen and Giorgio Riello (London: Routledge, 2016), 1–28.
4. Carl. R. Lounsbury, "Architecture and Cultural History," in *The Oxford Handbook of Material Culture Studies*, ed. Dan Hicks and Mary C. Beaudry (Oxford: Oxford University Press, 2010), 484.
5. On the ways we understand space as something created, see Henri Lefebvre, *The Production of Space*, trans. Donald Nicholson-Smith (Oxford: Blackwell, 1991).
6. On the ways that the built environment of imperial or colonial cities (for St. Petersburg was both) was and is particularly layered in meaning, see Brenda S. A. Yeoh, *Contesting Space: Power Relations and the Urban Built Environment in Colonial Singapore* (Kuala Lumpur: Oxford University Press, 1996); Saúl Martínez Bermejo, "Lisbon, New Rome and Emporium: Comparing an Early Modern Imperial Capital, 1550–1750," *Urban History* 44:4 (2017), 604–21; Rebecca Tinio McKenna, *American Imperial Pastoral: The Architecture of US Colonialism in the Philippines* (Chicago: University of Chicago Press, 2017).
7. Although the St. Petersburg's built environment included ornamental stone from well beyond its region, the bulk of the building in the area came from relatively local sources. On the variety, see A. G. Bulakh, "Ornamental Stone in the History of St Petersburg Architecture," *Global Heritage Stone: Towards International Recognition of Building and Ornamental Stones*, Geological Society, London, Special Publications 407:1 (2015), 243–52.

8. Vladimir Lem, *Opyt gorodovym i sel'skim stroeniiam, ili Rukovodstvo k znaniiu, kak raspolagat' i stroit' vsiakogo roda stroeniia po neimeniiu Arkhitektora* (St. Petersburg: Imperatorskaia tipografiia, 1802), 10–11.
9. Rory Young, "Lime-Based Plasters, Renders and Washes," in *Materials & Skills for Historic Building Conservation*, ed. Michael Forsyth (London: Blackwell, 2008), 58.
10. V. I. Dal', *Tolkovyi slovar' zhivogo velikoruskogo iazyka*, 2nd ed. (St. Petersburg: M. O. Vol'f,1881/reprint Moscow: Russkii iazyk, 1998), 2:13–14; M. P. Fasmer, *Etimologicheskii slovar' russkogo iazyka* (Moscow: Progress, 1964–73). One eighteenth-century source lists the alternative spelling *izviaz'*: *Slovar' kommercheskii, soderzhashchii poznanie o tovarakh vsekh stran, i nazvaniiakh veshchei glavnykh i noveishikh, otnosiashchikhsia do Kommertsii, takzhe do domostroitel'stva; poznanie khudozhestv, rukodelii, fabrik, rudnykh del, krasok, prianykh zelii, trav, dorogikh kamnei i proch* (Moscow: Tipografiia Kompanii Tipograficheskoi, 1789), 2:449.
11. *Moskva belokamennaia i ee dostoprimechatel'nosti* (St. Petersburg: Zhurn. "Mirskoi vestn.", 1864).
12. *Polnoe sobranie zakonov Rossiiskoi Imperii: Pervoe sobranie*, 45 vols. (St. Petersburg: Tipografiia II Otdeleniia Sobstvennoi Ego Imperatorskogo Velichestva Kantseliariia, 1830) (henceforth *PSZ*), vol. 4, no. 2540 (June 6, 1712).
13. *PSZ*, vol. 8, no. 6071 (May 26, 1732), which is about *konskie zavody* and instructs the people setting them up to keep an eye out for natural resources, including lime/limestone; vol. 9, no. 7086 (October 30, 1736), giving instructions for governors to keep an eye out for mining opportunities in their provinces.
14. *PSZ*, vol. 16, no. 12095 (March 19, 1764); similar language appeared in the decree released only days later, establishing regulations for settling New Russia: no. 12099 (March 22, 1764).
15. Evdokim Filippovich Ziablovskii, *Zemleopisanie Rossiiskoi imperii: dlia vsekh sostoianii* (St. Petersburg: Imperatorskaia Akademiia Nauk, 1810), 6:60, 93, 115, 126, 152, 156, and many more.
16. The *PSZ* includes decrees governing the use of lime in burials: *PSZ*, vol. 10, no. 7616 (July 7, 1738); vol. 12, no. 9269 (March 17, 1746); vol. 15, no. 11286 (July 6, 1761); vol. 16, no. 12032 (January 21, 1764); vol. 19, no. 13732 (1771). Although the *PSZ* does not often connect lime with tanning, in reality lime played an important role. Records from the Gatchina estate show that the St. Petersburg leather factory regularly requested significant quantities of lime from its production in the 1790s. See Rossiiskii gosudarstvenyi istoricheskii arkhiv (henceforth RGIA), f. 491, op. 5, d. 318, for one example.
17. I. Stebut, *Izvest', kak sresdstvo vosstanovleniia plodorodiia pochvy* (St. Petersburg: Tovarishchestva "Obshchestvennaia Pol'za," 1865), 1–2.
18. *PSZ*, vol. 17, no. 12406 (May 31, 1765).
19. Lem, *Opyt gorodovym i sel'skim stroeniiam*, 19.
20. *PSZ*, vol. 11, no. 8636 (October 15, 1742).
21. *PSZ*, vol. 10, no. 7635 (August 20, 1738).
22. *PSZ*, vol. 15, no. 11284 (July 4, 1761).
23. *PSZ*, vol. 12, no. 9180 (June 24, 1745).
24. *PSZ*, vol. 18, no. 12908 (June 4, 1767); also no. 13123 (May 26, 1768), rebuilding Astrakhan (after a fire, but the language is closer to the Kazan' decree than to the earlier fire-related decrees); vol. 19, no. 14136 (March 14, 1774), on reconstructing Moscow.

25. *PSZ*, vol. 17, no. 12308 (January 15, 1765).
26. *PSZ*, vol. 24, no. 18148 (September 22, 1797); vol. 25, no. 18638 (August 24, 1798).
27. *PSZ*, vol. 14, no. 10753 (July 31, 1757).
28. *PSZ*, vol. 8, no. 5327 (August 31, 1728).
29. *PSZ*, vol. 10, no. 7789 (April 4, 1739).
30. *PSZ*, vol. 6, no. 3937 (April 5, 1722).
31. *PSZ*, vol. 7, no. 4250 (July 19, 1723).
32. *PSZ*, vol. 6, no. 3708 (January 16, 1721).
33. *PSZ*, vol. 7, no. 4617 (December 16, 1724).
34. *PSZ*, vol. 8, no. 5995 (March 21, 1732).
35. S. V. Mamonov and L. S. Khar'iuzov, "'Putilovskii kamen'' kak ob'' ekt restavratsii," *Art Conservation Masterskaia*, https://web.archive.org/web/20180330093339/http://art-con.ru/node/1841, last retrieved November 18, 2018.
36. Lem, *Opyt gorodovym i sel'skim stroeniiam*, 11–12.
37. Strangways, "Geology of the Environs of Petersburg," 439.
38. Ibid.
39. Quoted in Makarov and Petrov, *Gatchina*, 6.
40. *PSZ*, vol. 21, no. 15808 (August 6, 1783).
41. Makarov and Petrov, *Gatchina*, 19.
42. S. Rozhdestvenskii, ed., *Stoletie gorod Gatchiny 1796 11/XI 1896 g.* (Gatchina: Gatchinskoe dvortsovoe upravlenie, 1896), 52.
43. *Materialy o gorodakh pridvornogo vedomstva. Gorod Gatchino* (St. Petersburg: Tipografiia Litografiia dvora ego imperatorskogo velichestva, 1882), 1–2.
44. Alison K. Smith, "New Town, New Townspeople: Transforming Gatchina in the 1790s," *Вивлиоѳика: E-Journal of Eighteenth-Century Russian Studies* 7 (2019), 86–101.
45. For example, in October 1797 Visconti reported on Gerasim Balin's work building a set of gates. RGIA f. 491, op. 1, d. 37, l. 6.
46. RGIA f. 491, op. 1, d. 11, ll. 1–7.
47. Ibid., ll. 8-8ob, 17-17ob, 32-33ob.
48. RGIA f. 491, op. 1, d. 98, ll. 30, 32. Other examples of men arrested while working stone are found in d. 238, ll. 1ob, 6, 18, 27–28.
49. RGIA f. 491, op. 1, d. 233, ll. 6–7.
50. Ibid., l. 36.
51. RGIA f. 491, op. 5, dd. 228–328.
52. RGIA f. 491, op. 5, d. 302, ll. 31ob-32.
53. RGIA f. 491, op. 1, d. 1825, ll. 1–2.
54. RGIA f. 491, op. 1, d. 1825, ll. 1–2. No, the math doesn't work out.
55. I. L. Znachko-Iavorskii, *Ocherki istorii viazhushchikh veshchestv ot drevneishikh vremen do serediny XIX veka* (Moscow-Leningrad: Akademiia Nauk SSSR, 1963), 286.
56. David Miller, "Monumental Building as an Indicator of Economic Trends in Northern Rus' in the Late Kievan and Mongol Periods, 1138–1462," *American Historical Review* 94:2 (1989), 360–90.
57. Znachko-Iavorskii, *Ocherki istorii viazhushchikh veschchestv*, 315.
58. Paul of Aleppo, *The Travels of Macarius, Patriarch of Antioch*, trans. F. C. Belfour (London: Printed for the Oriental Translation Fund of Great-Britain and Ireland, 1836), vol. 1, 397–8.
59. Ibid., 398.
60. *PSZ*, vol. 4, no. 1825 (January 17, 1701). Monasteries in Moscow were also told to build new buildings of stone (no. 1839 (March 11, 1701)); later decrees emphasizing

that buildings that burned down should be replaced with new stone structures include no. 2265 (April 20, 1710), on trading rows in Moscow.
61. *PSZ*, vol. 4, no. 1963 (January 28, 1704).
62. *PSZ*, vol. 4, no. 2051 (May 25, 1705); the decree was repeated in various forms, suggesting that not everyone listened, including in no. 2232 (May 12, 1709) and no. 2306 (October 17, 1710).
63. *PSZ*, vol. 4, no. 2531 (May 19, 1712), then in no. 2548 (June 25, 1712).
64. *PSZ*, vol. 4, no. 2072 (September 15, 1705).
65. *PSZ*, vol. 5, no. 2848 (October 9, 1714).
66. One or the other appears in connection with building St. Petersburg in *PSZ*, vol. 5, no. 2798 (April 16, 1714); no. 3424 (September 22, 1719); no. 3431 (October 12, 1719); vol. 6, no. 3766 (March 29, 1721); no. 3799 (June 24, 1721); no. 3822 (August 21, 1721); vol. 7, no. 4405 (January 5, 1724); no. 4505 (May 20, 1724).
67. Znachko-Iavorskii, *Ocherki istorii*, 321.
68. *PSZ*, vol. 4, no. 5592 (September 30, 1712).
69. *PSZ*, vol. 7, no. 4598 (November 13, 1724); vol. 4, no. 1972 (March 1, 1704).
70. *PSZ*, vol. 7, no. 4855 (March 14, 1726).
71. *PSZ*, vol. 7, no. 5014 (February 21, 1727); vol. 10, no. 7223 (April 12, 1737); vol. 12, no. 9215 (October 16, 1745).
72. *PSZ*, vol. 14, no. 10373 (March 9, 1755); extended in vol. 15, no. 10858 (July 9, 1758).
73. *PSZ*, vol. 17, no. 12452 (August 18, 1765).
74. Lindsey Hughes, "Russian Culture in the Eighteenth Century," in *The Cambridge History of Russia: Volume 2: Imperial Russia, 1689–1917*, ed. Dominic Lieven (Cambridge: Cambridge University Press, 2006), 65–91.
75. *PSZ*, vol. 4, no. 2548 (June 25, 1712); vol. 6, no. 3885 (January 19, 1722). Under Peter II, building in around courtyards was again allowed, reversing this visual signaling (vol. 8, no. 2262).
76. *PSZ*, vol. 5, no. 2850 (October 12, 1714). The decree stated that anyone wishing to build "*mazanki*, or in the Prussian manner, must build such a building on a stone foundation."
77. *PSZ*, vol. 7, no. 4321 (October 10, 1723).
78. William Craft Brumfield, *Landmarks of Russian Architecture: A Photographic Survey* (London: Routledge, 1997).
79. Priscilla Roosevelt, *Life on the Russian Country Estate: A Social and Cultural History* (New Haven, CT: Yale University Press, 1995).
80. "Serye steny Gatchinskogo dvortsa, kto vinovat i chto delat'?" *Gradozashchitii Peterburg*, https://protect812.com/2020/06/04/serye-steny-gatchinskogo-dvorca-kto-vinovat-i-chto-delat, retrieved July 2, 2020.

# 3

# Underground Materials: The (Un)making of Samizdat Texts

## Ann Komaromi

The word "samizdat" is a late Soviet neologism that gained currency in the late 1950s–80s in the Soviet Union. The word derives from the roots "sam-" (self) and "-izdat" (publish), resembling the older "samovar," discussed by Audra Yoder.[1] Samizdat can refer to a particular self-published work or set of texts as well as to the unofficial publishing system in which they circulate. Beginning in the late 1940s and 1950s, typed copies of hard-to-find poems by Osip Mandel'shtam, Boris Pasternak, and other authors whose prerevolutionary, émigré, or uncensored work was not available officially, circulated from hand to hand, establishing a basis for text-sharing networks.[2] Aleksandr Solzhenitsyn's *Gulag Archipelago*, first published abroad in 1973, circulated widely in the USSR in samizdat copies. There were also samizdat versions of Vladimir Nabokov's novel *The Gift* (*Dar*), written in emigration and banned in the USSR: copies were made in the early to mid-1970s out of photographs of a smuggled Western edition. The photographed pages were bound by hand in at least one case.[3] During the Cold War era, civic samizdat, including the internationally distributed and highly trusted *Chronicle of Current Events* (no. 1–65, 1968–82), a bulletin produced by Moscow rights activists, was perhaps the most broadly familiar samizdat publication.[4] However, as the samizdat copy of Nabokov's novel suggests, many writers, artists, and readers in the Soviet Union were interested in producing or reproducing creative texts and sometimes put special effort into the design and execution of samizdat editions.[5] Such creative samizdat texts, most of which were not obviously political, helped bridge the divides created by Soviet censorship between late Soviet culture, the repressed legacy of modernism and the avant-garde, and culture in the West. As samizdat writers and artists developed new forms of expression based on renewed cultural links, they also forged new types of relationships between Soviet authors and readers.

The production and distribution of late Soviet samizdat made it distinctive: samizdat differed from the underground press of the prerevolutionary era by being much less overtly political and by the technology of its production.[6] While photographic cameras were used in some cases, samizdat was typically made and copied on typewriters, low-tech machines widely available to Soviet citizens.[7] The life cycle of samizdat texts included being passed through trusted networks of friends and acquaintances. The texts were often reproduced along the way so that samizdat readers became publishers and distributors, and, on occasion, authors and editors. This blurring of roles complicates the life cycle of books as schematically illustrated by Robert Darnton with discrete nodes for author, publisher, and reader, and a unidirectional trajectory from one to the other.[8] Scholars working further on the history of books and publications noted the way external social forces impact this circuit of production and distribution.[9] These forces had obvious material impacts in the Soviet case: the political constraints and legal risks associated with samizdat resulted in the prevalence of thin and brittle onion-skin copies of texts that could be easily concealed.[10] Given the strict official control of xerox machines and other copy machines, samizdat typewritten texts were copied using carbon paper, for up to five or seven copies at a time, so that the copies at the back became almost unreadable.

Peter McDonald brought further nuance to Darnton's scheme by combining it with Pierre Bourdieu's concept of the field of literary production, thus adding another dimension to the two-axis (or flat) circuit in order to reflect the values and hierarchies created by writers and readers in the cultural field that exist in relative independence from the forces around them.[11] This approach lends itself to an analysis of how and why Soviet citizens valued the materially poor samizdat texts. The special aura of samizdat transformed the wretched text into a sign of the freedom of the spirit, of precious information and culture.[12] Therefore, many Soviet citizens willingly participated in the system, despite the risk. Indeed, a number of samizdat texts provoked enthusiastic, rhizomatic reproduction by readers that suggests not only a life cycle of the text but also its rebirth or afterlives. The samizdat text, because of its existence as an extra-Gutenberg object, illustrates in a vivid way the liberty of reading and writing that resists the authority imposed by and through printed books: such interaction with texts was, in the words of Roger Chartier, particularly "rebellious and vagabond."[13]

Full of energy as samizdat texts could be, they were also materially precarious. The survival of samizdat texts was never guaranteed—authorities might seize them; they might be locked away or destroyed; or they might be deemed of little value by readers and simply be ignored and eventually lost. Funded by the US government, Radio Liberty, based in Munich, established a Soviet Samizdat Unit in 1971 to collect and make available for Western researchers all samizdat texts deemed socially and politically significant.[14] The fate of literary or artistic samizdat was less certain. Soviet and former Soviet writers and unofficial historians did much to describe and preserve literary samizdat and the history of nonconformist art.[15] Recent digitization of literary and artistic samizdat journals that were too large and heterogeneous to be simply reprinted has expanded the materials available to researchers. A select number of these samizdat journals are the subject of this article.[16] Discussion here aims to show how these editions reflected the liberated potentials of samizdat texts while working in various ways through the "gaps" within Soviet culture. Speaking metaphorically, samizdat responded to "holes" in official Soviet culture, filling in information and work censored from official Soviet print. In a material sense, the samizdat text itself seemed poised to be destroyed, to disappear. Only the social activity around it could sustain its precarious existence.

## Transfurists and Neofuturist Texts

Scholarly interest has turned in recent years to the unofficial artists' groups that produced samizdat journals. These groups engaged the repressed avant-garde heritage and forbidden currents in Western culture as part of the Soviet artistic underground. Nonconforming artists' collectives grappled with the gaps and silences around them as they strove to revive a cultural heritage for the purposes of generating more creative potential than that afforded by restricted official culture.

The Transfurist group, like the Uktuss School which preceded it, grew up around the boundlessly creative couple Ry Nikonova (Anna Tarshis) and Sergei Sigei (Sergei Sigov). The couple lived in provincial cities but developed connections with unofficial culture in Leningrad and Moscow.[17] In addition to many handmade books, Nikonova and Sigei and their friends produced samizdat journals, the most important of which were *Nomer* (*Number*, 1965–74, Sverdlovsk and Rostov) and *Transponans* (*Transponans*, 1979–87, Yeysk and Leningrad).[18] These journals showed Sigei's familiarity with the Russian and early Soviet avant-garde legacy, which was far from widely known when he began researching it. Sigei and a few others—Vladimir Erl' and Tat'iana Nikol'skaia among them—contributed "lost" texts from Daniil Kharms and Aleksandr Vvedenskii. Their work appeared beside that of Aleksei Kruchenykh, Ol'ga Rozanova, and other important authors from the 1920s to 1930s in the pages of *Transponans*.[19] The journals also showcased Nikonova's remarkable capacity for generating new forms of creative practice according to her original and systematic adaptation of avant-garde principles.[20]

The samizdat books and journals created by the Nikonova-Sigei group recall the materials and techniques used to create Russian futurist books. In both cases, artists used poor materials, such as wallpaper or wrapping paper. They applied rudimentary binding with unevenly trimmed or unmatched pages serving to arrest the reader's attention and mark a significant difference from regular book production and artist's books or poetic editions.[21] The characteristic futurist technique of lithographing illustrations and text (often handwritten) together in books like *Starinnaia liubov'* (*Old-Fashioned Love*, 1912) or *Pomada* (*Pomade*, 1913) was cheaper than going through separate processes for producing illustrations and text. It also created new possibilities for blurring the boundary between visual and verbal elements.[22] These books brought futurist *zaum* (transrational language) to life with handwritten and specially printed letters, emphasizing the visual and phonic texture of letters and parts of words, which the poets took apart and recombined in nonstandard ways. Futurist poets Aleksei Kruchenykh and Velimir Khlebnikov described *zaum* as a verbal counterpart to the practice of cubo-futurist painters, who represented parts of bodies and sections of things in their compositions. Similarly, they said, "futurian speechcreators [*budetliane rechevortsy*] use chopped up words, half words and their clever combinations (*zaum* language)."[23] Aleksei Kruchenykh's poem "Dyr bul shchyl," which demonstrated what *zaum* looked like in the 1913 manifesto "The Word as Such," appeared in the book *Pomada* (*Pomade*, 1913), where the forms of the handwritten letters are echoed by the curves and angles of Mikhail Larionov's suggestive, mostly abstract Rayonist drawing on the same page.[24]

We find neofuturist principles articulated in issue 30 of *Nomer* (1971) from the Nikonova-Sigei group. The text "Budetliane i budushchely Predposlan'e recheritelia" (*Futurians and Future-Dwellers: The Preface of a Speechsmith*) recalled futurist neologisms.[25] In it, Sigei stated, "*Zaum* is the mother of art." The numerous subsections of point five of Sigei's preface on the lessons of painting for writing appeared on the facing page, with handwritten statements set at different angles within triangles printed on wrapping paper that bears the logo of the Sverdlovsk department store (*TsUM, Sverdlovskii univermag*). The overwritten paper with its geometrical facets thus evokes cubo-futurist aesthetics in the context of the issue.[26]

Although Sigei explicitly referenced the avant-garde lineage, the differences are important, too: the printed department store paper functions as a ready-made or "found" element that shows the influence of postwar Pop Art in its provenance as a mass-produced, labeled item from everyday Soviet culture. Found images and texts play a large role in both *Nomer* and *Transponans*: already in 1968, the artists defined a cardinal working principle they called *transponirovanie* as the "transfer of any printed product into a different semantic tonality."[27] One striking example of the transformation of found texts appears on the cover of *Nomer*, issue 18. It features a visual work called "The New Dress," consisting of a schematic drawing of the American excavator "Lima" (from a plant in Lima, Ohio), adapted with India ink (*tush'*), and surrounded by a paper image of a heavy gilt painting frame cut out of the Soviet journal *Poland* (*Pol'sha*).[28] The issue also contains a stunning work called "The Holy Spirit" (*Dukh sviatyi*): what looks like a drilling apparatus (also from the "Lima" drill machine schematics) is altered with India ink and watercolor paints in pink, red, and blue hues that make the estranged object appear to be flying through the heavens. Transparent overleaf pages, somewhat stiffer than the onion-skin paper used for producing carbon copies of pages in other samizdat editions, protect the drawings and paintings as they would in a fine printed edition. The group made the journal *Nomer* at home in Sverdlovsk in one copy, departing from the norms of printing (including from the processes of small print runs of Russian futurist books), *and* from the practices of regular samizdat, while referring to those norms and practices.[29] As art projects, these journal issues refracted and exaggerated the characteristics of extra-Gutenberg culture in samizdat, such as additions by hand, transparent paper, and eccentric content.

In addition, the journal *Nomer*, which Sigei described as a programmatically "open" journal, turned the collective and processual aspects of samizdat production into a systematic artistic practice. The journal *Nomer* featured sections such as "Write Your Own" (*Vpishi svoe*), for reader-contributors to add works, and "Criticism" (*Kritika*) for later response to works. Valerii D'iachenko's "Sport-Lotto" in the "Write Your Own" section of *Nomer* 30 consisted of a blue Sport Lotto ticket cut into pieces and pasted onto a page made of what looks again like rough wrapping paper (Figure 3.1). The facing page shows altered printed text: by blocking out certain letters, the page title "Questions of Radio and Television Technology" becomes something like "Questions of those, for the sake of veins, and it is visible" (*Voprosy tekh radi ven i viden*). The blocked-out letters significantly alter the sense of the original, opening it up to the ambiguity of *zaum*. In fact, this entire issue was created by writing over and pasting sections and pages into a copy of an official Soviet journal called *Radio and Television*: the title on

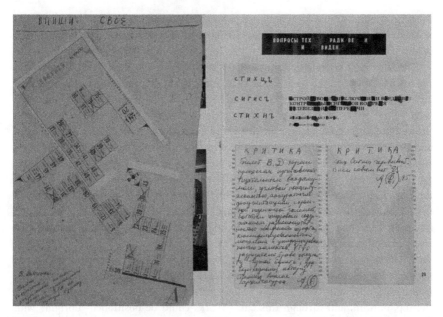

**Figure 3.1** *Nomer* 30 (1971), image 014, "Write Your Own": V. D'iachenko, "Sport-Loto" with "Criticism" by Ry Nikonova in *Nomer* 30 (1971). Credit: Research Centre for East European Studies at the University of Bremen, F. 01-097 (Sigei and Tarshis).

the colorfully altered cover has been transformed by the same technique from *Radio i televidenie* to *Dno idei*, that is, *The Dregs of an Idea*.[30]

Projects like the journals *Nomer* and its successor *Transponans* illustrated the way samizdat and unofficial artistic activity were neither totally separate from nor combatively opposed to Soviet print culture and institutions: they emerged from within that culture opening it up via material transformations. The Nikonova-Sigei group creatively altered ready-made printed texts and introduced into them their own techniques and materials. Early futurist *zaum* as avant-garde innovation involved breaking up conventional words into discrete phonemes and letters and reassembling them to generate new semantic potentials out of their visual and phonic texture. This late Soviet neofuturist intervention involved breaking apart and opening up the materials of language and culture at multiple levels, from the word to printed books, journals, and other mass-produced (consumer and bureaucratic) papers. In another striking example, the cover of *Nomer 23* was made out of a typical heavyweight file folder featuring standard lines for labeling, enumerating, dating, and specifying the expected duration of conservation of the contents: in that last line, "Preserve ___ years," they wrote "many" (*mnogo*) by hand. The upper left portion of the cover features a standard printed portrait of Karl Marx with a futurist eye drawn over part of his face and a *zaum* word bubble: *Khr*.[31] By showing that such bureaucratic paper and propaganda texts (and the conventionalized practices and ideas they represent) may be altered, written over, filled, and used for purposes other than those originally intended, the artists demonstrated the ubiquitous possibility of art and creative practice. This was not fighting the Soviet regime—it was living creatively within it, using the materials at hand.

The journal *Transponans*, begun in 1979 by Nikonova and Sigei, who had moved to the town of Yeysk on the Azov sea in 1974, came to encompass a much wider circle of authors, reaching readers in Leningrad and Moscow, thanks to ties the couple developed with fellow artists and writers in those cities. All thirty-six issues of *Transponans* showed the same complex intermedial character as *Nomer*; most were much longer, and all were handmade. The group produced a "run" of five copies. Leningraders Boris Konstriktor and Vladimir Erl' became contributors to *Transponans*, providing links for the Yeysk-based artists to Leningrad circles.[32] In his survey of Leningrad samizdat journals, Konstriktor described how difficult it was to cut, paste, stencil, and "produce" (*srezhissirovat'*) five copies of the intermedial *Transponans* by hand.[33] The first ten issues of *Transponans* were formatted vertically on A5-sized paper. After that, the issues exhibited a square (210 × 210 mm) format, and beginning with issue 28 (1985), they exhibited the complex Ry-structure (*Ry-struktura*) shape, the name of which was a play on Ry Nikonova's name: the square shape featured a triangular cut on the right (unbound) side, and a triangular wedge inserted so that the corners protrude from the top, bottom, and through this cut.[34] Works could be positioned "upright" with the binding on the left, or "sideways," so that the binding was at the top. In the latter position it is easy to see why the group referred to the Ry-structure also as "pants" (*shtany*) (Figure 3.2).[35]

As with *Nomer*, the "transposition" of avant-garde techniques to the late Soviet context implied creative adaptation of those techniques. The Nikonova-Sigei group developed their own principles and lines of investigation through a combination of theoretical statements and practical demonstrations pursued over years. Moreover, in addition to relatively well-known avant-garde forebears such as Aleksei Kruchenykh and Kazimir Malevich, the couple aimed to engage more obscure figures and aspects of the legacy into a living heritage and practice. Sigei showed special interest in those artists who had been forced into the "lower stratum" (*nizovoi sloi*) of Soviet culture beginning in the 1920s: he and Nikonova drew particularly on the little-known avant-garde work of Vasilisk Gnedov and Aleksei Nikolaevich Chicherin.[36] In his major theoretical tract of 1926, "Kan-Fun" (a title derived from the conjunction of Constructivism and Functionalism), Chicherin rejected the conventional discursive word because, as he said,

> WHEN OUR DESCENDANTS ESTABLISH AN INTERPLANETARY
> CONNECTION,
> THEY WILL BE FORCED TO SPEAK
> IN THAT LANGUAGE OF THE COSMOS
> FOR WHICH
> WE
> ARE FIGHTING[37]

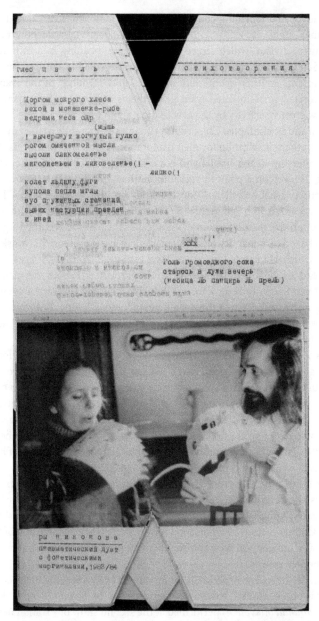

**Figure 3.2** This issue of *Transponans*, no. 31 (1986), features the Ry-structure shape. The photo shows Ry Nikonova and Sergei Sigei, performing their "Pneumatic Duet." Credit: Research Centre for East European Studies at the University of Bremen University, FSO-01-037 (Erl').

Chicherin advocated replacing conventional words with other verbal and nonverbal material (lines, signs, etc.) in poems and using that material according to the basic laws of Constructivism, which aimed to concentrate meaning in a minimal unit of material.[38] Sigei's "lower stratum," where Chicherin resided in cultural history of his period, represents another manifestation of the "underground" of the avant-garde—the unconsecrated, unassimilated avant-garde that is still capable of furnishing a fertile basis for new creative activity by those who dig it up to use.

Nikonova and Sigei adapted Chicherin's principles exuberantly in their own practice. They found in them inspiration for their exploration of unusual "platforms" for poetry (a concept referring to the spatial and material support for the artistic work)[39] and for attempts to overcome poetry's verbal limitations. In "Kan-Fun," Chicherin wrote about a poem, or what he called a "construction," entitled "Aveki vekov" ("For ages of ages," 1924), realized in a "gingerbread (*prianichnoe*) edition, tasty, with a generous amount of mint; the theme formed of chocolate, the board carved in Sergiev Posad; printed and baked in a quantity of fifteen pieces in Mossel'prom at Miasnitskie gates."[40] Reportedly, Chicherin printed his poem "Aveki vekov" ("For ages of ages") on a piece of gingerbread and sent it to friends. M. L. Gasparov heard about the incident many years later from Sergei Bobrov, a former futurist, who had received a copy of "Aveki vekov" on gingerbread. It was a time when people were starving, Bobrov recalled. The printing was unreadable, but a note glued to the outside said, "For internal use!—With greetings, Chicherin." So, Bobrov and his wife ate it.[41]

Nikonova quoted Chicherin's description of the "gingerbread edition" in her theoretical article "Culinart" (*Kulinart*), a form of art based on "one of the most common human … functions: swallowing." Nikonova contrasted her idea of Culinart action to a performance by the Austrian Actionist artist Hermann Nitsch, which featured the dismembering of sheep in a kind of ritual sacrifice. If Nitsch's performance brought people closer to the level of predatory animals, Nikonova said her concept was predicated on the "humanization of the animal sphere in us." In one of her group's actions, letters written on a plate in jam were licked so that the poetry is ingested (rather like a Eucharist, she says). This does not bring people harm and grief, but "the opposite," as she described it: "The human body becomes at least for a short time a vessel for poetry. And that is nice. All hail sweet, salty and marinated art inside of us!"[42] Poetry in a Culinart action becomes food for the body. The consumption of the poetic text—normally understood as a spiritual activity—is transformed (like a Eucharist) into an embodied process.

The samizdat journal provided a site for theorizing and preserving such performance. In the essay on "Culinart" Nikonova also referred to Sigei's "Bottled Lettvodka" (*Konservirovannaia bukvodka*) performed at the second show of "Trans-Poets" on July 3, 1983, in Leningrad. Sigei cut white, brown, and black letters out of paper, first a "Kh," then U," followed by an "O." While the letters simply spelled "EAR" (*UKhO*), the first two inevitably suggested the obscene word "Prick" (*Khui*) to the audience. Sigei put the letters in an empty bottle, filled it with vodka, and used a bottling machine to seal it, affixing a label: "Serg. Sigei. Bottled Lettvodka." In his description of the event, Sigei shared the off-stage continuation of the event: Boris Kudriakov insisted they open and drink the vodka. However, it proved to be undrinkable, because the paper and ink of the letters ruined the taste.[43] This coda to the event, the attempt to drink "Lettvodka," was, said Nikonova, the most relevant part for "Culinart."[44]

Samizdat texts were often read aloud in performances that could engage the whole body. They were linked to social practices for which a model of modern silent reading of print cannot account.[45] Among the Nikonova-Sigei group, poetry was often realized in performance. Important for Nikonova was the way eating art objects also modeled the process of creating a vacuum. Her extensive exploration of the possibilities of "vacuum poetry" had additional roots in the work of Egofuturist poet Vasilisk Gnedov. Gnedov performed his "Poem of the End" (*Poema kontsa*, 1913), in which the poem was reduced to a blank page, on multiple occasions using sometimes provocative gestures.[46] As she did with her humanizing twist on the bestial art action of eating, so in the case of vacuum poetry, Nikonova took elements with potentially negative signification (nothingness, the void) and transformed them to reveal their positive potential. The "Complete Vacuum" is a storehouse (*sklad*) of existence, Nikonova wrote, because out of nothing something new may appear.[47]

The "holes" in Soviet culture, resulting from the suppression of avant-garde artists and much of their legacy, provided an opportunity for engagement and creative work, according to Nikonova and Sigei. Moreover, their commitment to the avant-garde "underground" (lower strata, *nizovoi sloi*) suggests that the creative renewal they effected could be replicated by appealing to minor or forgotten parts of the cultural legacy. The systematic elimination of material—by blacking out letters or covering over portions of a printed page, of eating a poetry sandwich, or licking poetry jam—became in their practice a transformative process revealing the possibility for creative intervention everywhere and by everyone, given the ordinary, everyday materials they used and their location in the provinces. Unofficial culture had its blind spots, too: nearly everything happening outside of the capital cities of Moscow and Leningrad failed to register as cultural activity. Nikonova and Sigei made art in their own provincial "hole," like the exiled or repressed artists to whom they referred.[48] They transposed Chicherin's attempt to use unconventional material and forms for poetry in order to convey a language of the cosmos (typical of the utopian aspirations of that period) into their own neo-avant-garde practice, emphasizing the creative transformation of everyday life in any location through poetic and artistic activity. The attention to *Transponans* then and subsequently along with the participation in the journal by Moscow and Leningrad artists showed that their efforts were not isolated or lost—they emerged out of a void, bringing other "lost" avant-garde works and artists with them, to impart a highly distinctive flavor to the unofficial cultural process in the late Soviet Union, like mint in gingerbread.[49]

## The Moscow Conceptual Circle and the Afterlife of Art

The Moscow Conceptualist artists—including Il′ia Kabakov, Andrei Monastyrskii, Dmitrii Prigov, Lev Rubinshtein, Vladimir Sorokin, and others[50]—derived inspiration from Western art trends, especially Pop Art and Conceptualism. According to Marek Bartelik, Soviet Sots Art[51] and Soviet Conceptualism took from Western Pop Art a tendency to portray the Platonic forms of ideas along with the decomposition of material culture.[52] Soviet Conceptualist artists differed from the Nikonova and Sigei group by being more sharply polemical in their relationship to the historical avant-garde, whose utopian aspirations they parodied or rejected.[53] There was dialogue between the groups, however. In a 1982 letter to Ry Nikonova, Dmitrii Prigov argued that far from being already outmoded as Nikonova thought, Conceptualism had the potential for addressing "our [Soviet] problems":

> Because our present culture, with its absence of an idea of the object [*predmet*] and its qualities, is a culture of ideology where the object is replaced by the language of its description, while the language of description of the object (the language characteristic of an object culture) is replaced by the language describing the object which represents the object. Therefore, what we call conceptualism is, of course, not classical Conceptualism in the western sense.[54]

Prigov believed Soviet artists could reveal new potentials in Conceptualism by adapting it to the situation of Soviet ideology, in which language had become progressively detached from material objects in the world. Il'ia Kabakov also talked about the difference between the Western person's orientation to an object (from whence the interest of "dematerializing" the art object derived) versus the Soviet person's orientation to the context for things and people.[55] Conceptualist artists and theorists in the USSR worked within a Soviet culture in which material reality was displaced by concepts and ideal representations in official Soviet ideology and Socialist Realist art.

Unexpected uses of verbal and visual materials characterized both Soviet Conceptualist art and the neofuturist work of the group of Nikonova and Sigei. However, if the latter group hearkened back to the early avant-garde emphasis on the materiality of the "word as such," Conceptualists drew attention to the ramification of functions of writing, which could appear as theoretical or philosophical discourse; as information; as documentary record of instructions, events, and participant reactions; as literary work; and/or as a formal element of the composition.[56] In this way, the Soviet Conceptualists parodied the official cultural displacement of material objects with discourse, infusing the practice with ambivalence and aesthetic function. The samizdat folio series *MANI* (*Moskovskii arkhiv novogo iskusstvo* = *Moscow Archive of New Art*, nos. 1–4, 1981–2) illustrates the adaptation of Conceptualist art for critical engagement with Soviet attitudes and reality. The series was produced in four copies, with envelopes and texts grouped into folios designed by a succession of editors. Yelena Kalinsky described the project as a way of facilitating dialogue among artists who shared similar concerns: the *MANI* folios "contributed to the consolidation of the group known today as the Moscow Conceptualist circle."[57]

The standardized envelopes of the *MANI* folios contain highly disparate contents: in addition to essays, and textual and photographic records of visual works and staged events, one finds things like the sixteen proposals from "the Author" to "get together" (*sobrat'sia*): each proposal was carefully handwritten and folded into its own envelope.

Occasionally the contents surprise the reader with their materiality: one envelope containing pencil lead shavings is followed by another filled with colorful confetti (posing challenges for containment). In another instance, a paper banner reading "All Men Are Scum," unexpectedly packed into a standard-size envelope, unfolds into a more than four-foot long piece shaped like a penis.[58] Thus, the tendency to circumscribe art objects is opposed from within the folios by moments of material expansion.

In an overt allusion to Western Conceptualism, Viktor Skersis riffed on Joseph Kosuth's classic "One and Three Chairs" (1965). Photographs documenting Skersis's attempts to demonstrate the proposition, "In order to humanize things, the means for contraception and an apparatus for execution are necessary," appeared in *MANI* 2 (1981). In one photo, a chair is tipped over with its legs up and a sheet draped over it in imitation of a woman's body positioned for a gynecological procedure. In another, an axe is fixed on the wall over a chair so that it might be released to fall on the chair, in an arrangement resembling that of a guillotine.[59] Skersis's work underscores the absurdity of applying an inappropriate philosophical discourse to things. Rather than the real object disappearing behind the idea, the chair's static form appears humorously to resist the title's attempt to "humanize" it with reproductive or mortal capacities. As Skersis repeats Kosuth's gesture, he highlights the parodic function that gesture takes on in the Soviet context.

Kabakov offered a more ambivalent reflection on the relationship between materiality and cognition, in his "Discourse on the Perception of the Three Layers, Three Levels, into Which an Ordinary, Anonymous Written Product—Notices, Slips, Menus, Bills, Tickets, etc.—May Be Broken Down," which appeared in folio one of *MANI*.[60] In the essay, Kabakov posits three levels of perception of regular, everyday paper products, which may be focused on the material carrier, the paper "good quality, bad quality, smooth, rough, and so on"; or on the "white" of the surface; or on the printed message. Kabakov goes on to parse out the possible meanings of the white surface, which may evoke utilitarian emptiness or an "energistic" flow. The white might further serve to symbolize death, or it might signify metaphysical fullness. Those who know Kabakov's other works and writing might connect these possible meanings to his other reflections on the ambivalent potential of white painted canvases, which indicated utopian fullness for Malevich: Kabakov reconceived those white surfaces also in terms of a vampiric emptiness.[61]

As with Skersis's chair, the interest of this work derives from its unlikely combination of highly philosophical discourse (suggesting at the limit the sacred) with banal information and everyday items. That paper is headed for the trash, as Kabakov acknowledges:

> The cardstock, the paper itself, is presented as a thing, that is, in its lowest, natural form. As we know from experience, it quickly changes from new to old, from clean to dirty, from whole to torn, crumpled, and wrinkled. I would especially like to note the inevitable future it is heading toward—it will become garbage, filth, refuse that can be easily crammed into the wastepaper basket. This "paper future" can be seen very clearly in the present of every paper, especially if it carries the stamp of short- term use: packing paper, newspaper, tissue paper, and such.[62]

Ultimately, Kabakov writes, the reader/viewer may adopt utilitarian perception of the flat emptiness of the white, paying attention only to the information—a bill for international phone calls, a warning notice for failure to pay the telephone bill, a movie ticket, and so on. When the ephemeral use of that information has been exhausted, the paper degenerates to the level of useless material and goes to the trash can. By contrast, if the reader/viewer relates to the whiteness as self-sufficient fullness, the mundane text becomes a visual grid through which she perceives the light and energy pouring out, transforming the ordinary, nondescript, bureaucratic document.[63] Such an outcome seems unlikely, and Kabakov's parodic intent is clear.

Kabakov enhances the manipulation of objects and concepts with his use of the Russian literary technique of *skaz* (imitation of a character's oral speech) so that the voice of the text never quite lines up with our perception of the author's intention.[64] The essay is likely to confuse the unaccustomed reader with its lurching from banal items and trash to metaphysical realms: it is not clear what should be taken seriously. In addition to parodying the Soviet ideological tendency to pile inflated concepts onto a Soviet life of relative material poverty, the disconcerting ambivalence of this text conveys the anxiety the Soviet nonconformist artist or writer had that his or her work might soon be junked. The nonconformist artist, like the unofficial author, had no guarantee that this work would endure. It might be seized, or it might be sent to the trash when judged by audiences at home or abroad to be of no value. The samizdat text and/or artwork was potentially as ephemeral as an everyday paper item of Soviet life: perhaps there was nothing more substantial to it outside of the context in which nonconformist art was read (annoyingly for those artists themselves) as a sign of rebellion against the oppressive state. Kabakov's later success internationally suggests that his distinctive blend of Western, Soviet, and Russian legacies did transcend that nonconformist moment—his works have endured.

## Conclusion

As shown in this article, the nonconformist artists producing samizdat editions reflected on the making and potential unmaking of uncensored and marginal works. Both the neofuturist artists, around Nionova and Sigei, and the Soviet conceptualist artists, including Viktor Skersis, Il'ia Kabakov, and their associates, engaged everyday materials from the late Soviet context as they transposed ideas and practices from the historical avant-garde and the West to their own situation. This meant working through the "holes" and "gaps" in a repressive and limited official Soviet culture. The artists showed how much energy could come from such empty spaces. Suspended over those voids, their precarious works drew attention to the social context needed to activate and sustain their material lives. Coming out of artists' collectives of remarkable energy, such works, with their unconstrained use of the material to hand, aimed to project creative and intellectual possibilities for their audiences.

We have seen that certain artists in both groups took their presumed disadvantages—of lacking official support, of living in the provinces, of only having poor and banal materials to hand, of producing for a small circle of friends—as grounds for critical reflection and innovative realization of artistic tasks. By doing so, these artists expressed the hopeful futurity of samizdat as a cultural practice designed to enable people to think and act outside of institutions. Artistic samizdat editions represented the possibility of creative activity for everyone anywhere with any materials: they were rhizomes of artistic freedom designed to transform Soviet people and their society.

## Notes

I would like to acknowledge the useful feedback provided by the volume editors and the expert advice of Ilja Kukuj and helpful comments of Rebecca Smith.

1. See Chapter 7 of this volume. Peter Steiner discussed the genealogy of samizdat and scholarship on it in "On Samizdat, Tamizdat, Magnitizdat and Other Words That Are Difficult to Pronounce," *Poetics Today* 29:4 (2008), 613–28.
2. Aleksandr Daniel', "Istoki i smysl sovetskogo samizdata," in *Antologiia samizdata: Nepodtsenzurnaia literatura v SSSR, 1950-e–1980-e*, 3 vols., ed. V. V. Igrunov and M. S. Barbakadze (Moscow: Mezhdunarodnyi institut gumanitarno-politicheskikh issledovanii, 2005), 18.
3. Photos of this edition appeared in Ann Komaromi, "Samizdat and Tamizdat," in *Vladimir Nabokov in Context*, ed. David Bethea and Siggy Frank (Cambridge: Cambridge University Press, 2018), 169.
4. An introduction to the bulletin in English appeared in Peter Reddaway, trans. and ed., *Uncensored Russia: The Human Rights Movement in the Soviet Union: The Annotated Text of the Unofficial Moscow Journal "A Chronicle of Current Events" (Nos. 1–11)* (London: Jonathan Cape, 1972). Amnesty International published English editions of the bulletin beginning with *A Chronicle of Current Events: Number 17* (London: Amnesty International, 1971).
5. For a broad sampling of texts produced originally as samizdat, see A. Strelianyi et al., eds., *Samizdat veka* (Moscow: Polifakt, 1999), and the *Antologiia samizdata*.
6. While Soviet rights activists seemed political to other samizdat users, they did not advocate for then-unthinkable regime change. By contrast, the revolutionary underground in tsarist Russia publicized its political goals through uncensored printed editions. Information about prerevolutionary press and organizations from "Land and Freedom" (*Zemlia i volia*) to Lenin's *Pravda* appeared in Leonard Schapiro, *The Communist Party of the Soviet Union* (London: Eyre & Spottiswoode, 1962), 6–130.
7. The typewriter acquired something of a cult status as a machine in the later decades of the Soviet Union. Lev Rubinshtein wrote, "O, the typewriter. O, the longed-for dream of my poor youth," in "Mashinka vremeni," in *200 udarov v minutu: pishushchaia mashinka i soznanie XX veka*, ed. Anna Narinskaia (Moscow: Politekhnicheskii muzei, 2016), 65. This catalog features photographs of common brands of typewriters and copy paper (*kopirka*) used for samizdat.
8. Robert Darnton, *The Kiss of Lamourette: Reflections in Cultural History* (New York: W. W. Norton, 1990), 112.
9. Thomas R. Adams and Nicolas Barker modified Darnton's scheme, outlining five events in the life of a book, including publishing, manufacturing, distribution, reception, and survival. These events were linked in a circle and set in a context made up of spheres of intellectual influences; political, legal, and religious influences;

commercial pressures; and social behavior and taste. See Thomas R. Adams and Nicolas Barker, "A New Model for the Study of the Book," in *A Potencie of Life: Books in Society: The Clark Lectures, 1986–1987*, ed. Nicolas Barker (London: British Library and Oak Knoll Press, 1993), 14–15.

10. See, for example, the photograph of a dog-eared samizdat copy of Mikhail Bulgakov's *Heart of a Dog* (*Sobach'e serdtse*), in Ann Komaromi, "The Material Existence of Soviet Samizdat," *Slavic Review* 63:3 (2004), 604.

11. Peter D. McDonald, "Implicit Structures and Explicit Interactions: Pierre Bourdieu and the History of the Book," *The Library* ser. 6, 19:2 (1997), 107. This type of Bourdieusian analysis was taken up in the Soviet case by Mikhail Berg, *Literaturokratiia* (Moscow: Novoe literaturnoe obozrenie, 2000); and Ann Komaromi, *Uncensored: The Quest for Autonomy in Soviet Samizdat* (Evanston, IL: Northwestern University Press, 2015).

12. Komaromi, "The Material Existence," 615.

13. Roger Chartier, *The Order of Books: Readers, Authors, and Libraries in Europe between the Fourteenth and Eighteenth Centuries*, trans. Lydia G. Cochrane (Stanford, CA: Stanford University Press, 1994), viii. On the creation of epistemological uncertainty and openness in the "extra-Gutenberg" system of samizdat, see Ann Komaromi, "Samizdat as Extra-Gutenberg Phenomenon," *Poetics Today* 29:4 (2008), 629–67.

14. While enormous, the corpus of samizdat, published in *Sobranie dokumentov samizdata* (*Collection of Samizdat Documents*, 1972–8) and *Materialy samizdata* (*Materials of Samizdat*, 1972–91), was not comprehensive because it included only texts considered strategically significant according to Radio Liberty's mission.

15. See, for example, the massive and idiosyncratic series compiled by Konstantin Kuz'minskii and Grigorii Kovalev, *Antologiia noveishei poezii u Goluboi Laguny*, 5 vols. (Newtonville, MA: Oriental Research Partners, 1980–6); and the more systematic and descriptive *Samizdat Leningrada. 1950-e–1980-e: Literaturnaia entsiklopediia*, ed. D. Ia. Severiukhin et al. (Moscow: Novoe Literaturnoe Obozrenie, 2003).

16. Digitized issues of editions treated here, *Nomer, Transponans*, and the *MANI* folios, are found as electronic editions under "Journals and Folios," in the *Project for the Study of Dissidence and Samizdat*, ed. Ann Komaromi (Toronto: University of Toronto Libraries, 2015), https://samizdatcollections.library.utoronto.ca/, hereafter PSDS. Originals of these samizdat editions are held in the Archive of the Research Centre for East European Studies at the University of Bremen.

17. Sigei explained that he was an "anar-fut" (anarchic futurist) from 1962 to 1965. The "Uktuss School" formed in 1965 in Sverdlovsk, and that group produced the journal *Nomer*, as detailed in Sigei's letter "A. Niku," in *Antalogiia noveishei poezzii* (vol. 5B, 546). The group called Transfurists (or Transpoets) dates its beginning to 1979, the year Nikonova and Sigei started the journal *Transponans*. On the latter group, see the catalog *Transfurizm*, comp. Sergei Koval'skii, Il'ia Kukui, Boris Konstriktor, and ed. Il'ia Kukui (St. Petersburg: Muzei nonkonformistskogo iskusstva, 2017), 16. Other sources include Gerald J. Janecek, "A Report on Transfurism," *Wiener Slawistischer Almanach* 19 (1987), 123–42.

18. The group working on *Nomer* included Nikonova, Sigei, E. Arbenev, V. D'iachenko, A. Galamaga, M. Tarshis, and a few others. After Nikonova and Sigei alone produced the first issues of *Transponans*, the production group expanded, and the circle of contributors eventually became quite wide ("Vmesto manifesta," *Transfurizm*, 18–22).

19. Nikolai Khardzhiev, who survived from the former avant-garde generation, was an important source for works by these historical avant-garde authors, some of which were published for the first time in *Transponans*. Khardzhiev appeared in a photo with Kazimir Malevich in *Transponans* 29 (1985), image 056, PSDS. Among the contemporary authors and artists who contributed were Leningrad poet Kari Unksova and Moscow poets Genrikh Sapgir and Vladislav Len, and Moscow Conceptualists Andrei Monastyrskii, Dmitrii Prigov, and Lev Rubinshtein. For the long list of authors represented in the journal, see Il'ia Kukui, "Laboratoriia avangarda: zhurnal *Transponans*," *Russian Literature* 59:2–4 (2006), 233–4.
20. Janecek acknowledged he could only address a select set of the five hundred handmade books Nikonova alone produced; Gerald Janecek, "Tysiacha Form Ry Nikonovoi," *Novoe literaturnoe obozrenie* 35 (1999), 284.
21. Against such deluxe editions, Russian avant-garde book artists asserted their rough aesthetic in editions of three hundred to four hundred copies. Deborah Wye, "Art Issues/Book Issues: An Overview," in *The Russian Avant-Garde Book: 1910–1934*, ed. Margit Rowell and Deborah Wye (New York: Museum of Modern Art, 2002), 17.
22. Janecek detailed the production processes for futurist books and drew attention to the interpenetration of text and illustration; Gerald Janecek, *The Look of Russian Literature: Avant-Garde Visual Experiments, 1900–1930* (Princeton, NJ: Princeton University Press, 1984), 70–3. Marjorie Perloff echoed many of the same points in "The Word Set Free"; Marjorie Perloff, *The Futurist Moment: Avant-Garde, Avant Guerre, and the Language of Rupture* (Chicago: University of Chicago Press, 1986), 116–61.
23. A. Kruchenykh and V. Khlebnikov, "Slovo kak takovoe" (The Word as Such, 1913), in *Literaturnye manifesty: Ot simvolizma k Oktiabriu*, vol. 1 (Munich: Wilhelm Fink Verlag, 1969), 82.
24. Nancy Perloff explored the phonetic texture of the "gruff syllables" of Kruchenykh's zaum poem in *Explodity: Sound, Image, and Word in Russian Futurist Book Art* (Los Angeles: Getty Research Institute, 2006), 71–5. See the page online at https://www.getty.edu/research/publications/explodity/index.html.
25. The neologisms "budetliane" and "budushchely" were used by Velimir Khlebnikov and Aleksei Kruchenykh. See, for example, the manifesto "The Word as Such" for their use of "budetliane" and "rechetvortsy" (meaning "poets"); Kruchenykh and Khlebnikov, "Slovo kak takovoe." Sigei wrote "O budushchelakh" to clarify the difference between "Budetliane" and "Budushchely," in *Transponans* 2 (1979), images 011–12, PSDS.
26. *Nomer* 30 (1971), image 018, PSDS.
27. Kukui, "Laboratoriia avangarda," 228.
28. *Nomer* 18 (1970), image 001, PSDS.
29. Kukui remarked on the way *Nomer*, as a household project by and for the intimate circle of friends, appeared to violate principles for distinguishing samizdat (which would be publicly circulated) from private projects; Kukui, "Laboratoriia avangarda," 229. The later and more widely known journal *Transponans* and subsequent scholarly recognition of the sustained and meaningful character of Nikonova and Sigei's practice show the editions they produced to be more than ephemeral private projects.
30. *Nomer* 30 (1971), image 003, PSDS.
31. *Nomer* 23 (1970), image 001, PSDS. On the early Russian avant-garde practice of painting faces, see Ilya Zdanevich and Mikhail Larionov, "Why We Paint Ourselves: A

Futurist Manifesto, 1913," in *Russian Art of the Avant-Garde: Theory and Criticism*, ed. John E. Bowlt (London: Thames & Hudson, 2017), 79–83.
32. Leningrader Konstriktor (born Boris Aksel'rod) married Nikonova's sister Nadezhda Tarshis after becoming acquainted with the artists in 1978. *Transfurizm*, 275–7.
33. From the discussion of *Transponans* in Boris Konstriktor, "Dyshala noch' vostorgom samizdata," *Labirint/Ekstsentr* 1 (1991), 42–5.
34. *Transponans*, no. 28 (1985). Kukui, who detailed the changing shape and dimensions of the *Transponans* issues, observed that the Ry-structure realized a "square within a square" with all the avant-garde connotations such a configuration evoked—most obviously Kazimir Malevich's suprematist squares. Kukui, "Laboratoriia avangarda," 231–2.
35. *Transponans*, no. 31 (1986), image 20, PSDS.
36. Sigei wrote, "The tradition of Russian poetry ... had been destroyed by the fact that its main continuers (the 'stock holders') exited into the lower stratum of literature ... The main task is the transposition (*transponans*) of the achievements of those who exited into the lower stratum, existing only there." From Sigei, "O 'zadachakh' transpoezii," in *Transponans* 1 (1979), images 4–5; reprinted in the catalog *Transfurizm*, 16.
37. A. N. Chicherin, "Kan-Fun," in *Zabyti avangard. Rossiia, pervaia tret' XX stoletiia*, ed. Konstantin Kuz'minskii, Dzheral'd Janecek, and Aleksandr Ocheretianskii (Vienna: Gesellschaft zur Forderung slawischer studien, 1988), 193.
38. Gerald Janecek, "A. N. Chicherin, Constructivist Poet," *Wiener Slawistischer Almanach* 25 (1989), 504, 510.
39. Kukui, "Laboratoriia avangarda," 232.
40. Chicherin, "Kan-Fun," 192. *Prianiki* (gingerbread, spice, or honey cookies) are often decorated by being cooked in a carved wooden mold, and mint is sometimes used for flavoring them.
41. Janecek, "A. N. Chicherin," 509.
42. Nikonova, "Kulinart," *Transponans* 18 (1983), images 25–7, PSDS. Nikonova also referred to Chicherin's statement in her "Attestation," featuring a label for "prianiki" from the Kuibyshev regional food store, followed by B. M. Konstriktor's outline of a hand over which the words "I ate the cookies!" (*Prianiki s"el*!) was written, followed by Chicherin's name. *Transponans* 19 (1983), images 029–030, PSDS.
43. Kuz'minskii and Kovalev, *Antologiia noveishei poezii*, vol. 5B, 541–2.
44. On a different type of informal text sharing consisting of manuscript cookbooks, see Anastasia Lakhtikova, "Professional Women Cooking: Manuscript Cookbooks, Social Networks and Identity Building in the Late Soviet Period," in *Seasoned Socialism: Gender and Food in Late Soviet Everyday Life*, ed. Anastasia Lakhtikova, Angela Brintlinger, and Irina Glushchenko (Bloomington: Indiana University Press, 2019), 80–109.
45. Poetry seminars and unofficial apartment readings or performances were central to unofficial cultural life in this period. Gerald Janecek described this in *Everything Has Already Been Written: Moscow Conceptualist Poetry and Performance* (Evanston, IL: Northwestern University Press, 2018). Grigorii Kovalev, who was blind and worked with Kuz'minskii to collect samizdat poetry for the *Antologiia noveishei poezii*, reportedly had a special talent for recalling a poet's words and her or his manner of reading, as reported by Viktor Krivulin, "Zolotoi vek samizdata," in *Samizdat veka*, 344. Roger Chartier wrote about the need for historians to account for the networks of practices associated with reading, including reading aloud as embodied and social performance. Reading aloud may give access to texts the listeners cannot themselves

read (for lack of skills or lack of access to copies of the text) and it may "cemen[t] the interlocking forms of sociability" organized around the text (Chartier, *Order of Books*, 8).

46. Janecek discussed Nikonova's vacuum poetry in "Tysiacha form," 304–6. Gnedov's "Poem of the End," from the book *Death to Art* (*Smert' iskusstvu*), 1913, consisted of a title and a blank page as printed in the book. In performance, Gnedov reportedly tried out a variety of gestures, including arm movements back and forth that suggested cancellation, and a fist raised to the audience: see Crispin Brooks, "On One Ancestor: Vasilisk Gnedov in the Work of Sergej Sigej and Ry Nikonova," *Russian Literature* 59:2–4 (2006), 184–6.
47. Ry Nikonova, "What is a Vacuum?" *Transponans* 13 (1982), images 32–3, PSDS.
48. Former convicts or those in disfavor were often banned from living in the major cities. Nikonova and Sigei took up "provincialism" and "dilettantism," derided by most Russian intellectuals, as positive principles. Kukui, "Laboratoriia avangarda," 227.
49. Nikonova and Sigei also participated in international mail art networks beginning in the late 1980s. Charlotte Greve, "Zaumland. Serge Segay and Rea Nikonova in the International Mail Art Network," *Russian Literature* 59:2–4 (2006), 445–67.
50. Moscow Conceptualism was described by Boris Groys and Il'ia Kabakov. See *NOMA, ili Moskovskii kontseptual'nyi krug*, ed. Il'ia Kabakov (Zurich: Cantz, 1993).
51. Soviet Sots Art, often discussed together with Soviet Conceptualism, was a Soviet version of Pop Art that reflected artistically on the typical images and forms of Soviet culture. Famous Sots-Art works include the parodies of propaganda banners by Vitaly Komar and Aleksandr Melamid or the "branding" of Lenin's profile, juxtaposed to the Coca-Cola logo by Aleksandr Kosolapov (Konstantin Akinsha, "Between Lent and Carnival: Moscow Conceptualism and Sots Art (Differences, Similarities, Interconnections)," in *Moscow Conceptualism in Context*, ed. Alla Rosenfeld (New Brunswick, NJ: Jane Voorhees Zimmerli Art Museum, 2011), 24–47).
52. Marek Bartelik, "The Banner without a Slogan: Definitions and Sources of Moscow Conceptualism" (*Moscow Conceptualism in Context*, 8). Boris Grois first applied "Conceptualism" to parts of Soviet nonconformist artistic practice. His article, originally titled "Moscow Romantic Conceptualism," was reprinted as Boris Grois, "Nulevoe reshenie," in *NOMA, ili Moskovskii kontseptual'nyi krug*, ed. Il'ia Kabakov et al. (Zurich: Cantz, 1993), 42–59.
53. An example of such parody would be the mock advertisement by Vitalii Komar and Aleksandr Melamid of ideal Suprematist geometric shapes for use in everyday situations to address human dissatisfaction: "Circle, Square and Triangle," *Metki* 1 (1975), image 015, PSDS.
54. The correspondence between Prigov and Nikonova, originally published in *Transponans* 12 (1982), was quoted by Janecek, *Everything Has Already Been Written*, 137.
55. Kabakov contrasted the attitude among Western audiences, for whom objects matter more than spaces, to Russian or Soviet audiences, for whom the objects are typically wretched and insignificant, and for whom the spatial context determines the attitude and behavior of audiences. Ilya Kabakov, *Uber die "Totale" Installation/O "Total'noi" installiatsii/On the "Total" Installation* (Ostfildern: Cantz, 1995), 244.
56. Mary A. Nicholas cited Charles Harrison's taxonomy of writing as "documentary accompaniment to artistic practice," as well as "literature," and "art" in Western Conceptualism. She quoted Soviet Conceptualist artist Iurii Al'bert's assertion that "neither the word as such (*slovo kak takovoe*), nor the image as such" interested him. Mary A. Nicholas, "Rereading Moscow Conceptualism," *Slavic Review* 75:1 (2016), 25.

57. Yelena Kalinsky, "The MANI Archive," *Zimmerli Journal* 5 (Fall 2008), 120. Editors of the *MANI* folios included Andrei Monastyrskii (no. 1); Vadim Zakharov and Viktor Skersis (no. 2); Elena Elagina and Igor' Makarevich (no. 3); Natal'ia Abalakova and Anatolii Zhigalov (no. 4), with the participation of Georgii Kizeval'ter as photographer. A fifth issue was begun, but finished during Perestroika and not circulated. See Aleksandra Danilova and Elena Kuprina-Liakhovich, "MANI: An Experiment in Modelling Cultural Space," trans. Mikhail Grachev, in *Anti-Shows: APTART 1982-84*, 232-44, ed. Margarita Tupitsyn, Victor Tupitsyn and David Morris (London: Afterall Books, 2017), 241.
58. Lev Rubinshtein, "The Author Proposes Getting Together," in "Two Works (*Dve raboty*)," *MANI* 2 (1981), envelope 34, PSDS; the "Untitled work" by V. Skersis and V. Zakharov is composed of the envelopes with surprising contents, *MANI* 4 (1982), envelopes 22 and 23, PSDS. The work by E. Shnitser and E. Volodina, "All Men Are Scum (*Vse muzhchiny—podonki*)" appeared in *MANI* 4, envelope 27, PSDS. Shnitser and Volodina are fictional artists created by Skersis and Zakharov (Danilova and Kuprina-Liakhovich, "MANI," 237).
59. See *MANI* 2 (1981), envelope 38, images 0391 and 0397, PSDS. Photos of Skersis's version of "One and Three Chairs" appeared in the preceding envelope.
60. See Kabakov, "Rassuzhdenie o vospriiatii trekh sloev …" *MANI* 1 (1981), images 0122–0126, PSDS. The text subsequently appeared with English translation in *A-Ya* 6 (1984), 30–6, and as "Discourse on the Perception …," in Il'ia Iosifovich Kabakov et al., *On Art* (Chicago: University of Chicago Press, 2018), 50–3.
61. Il'ia Kabakov, *60–70e …: Zapiski o neofitsial'noi zhizni v Moskve* (Moscow: Novoe literaturnoe obozrenie, 2008), 45. See also Amei Wallach, *Ilya Kabakov: The Man Who Never Threw Anything Away* (New York: Harry N. Abrams, 1996), 44.
62. Il'ia Kabakov, "Discourse on the Perception," in Kabakov et al., *On Art*, 50.
63. The perception of metaphysical fullness (Kabakov et al., *On Art*, 52-3) seems humorously tacked onto the banality of everyday paper.
64. Boris Eikhenbaum used the term *skaz* to describe the voice of the narrator of Nikolai Gogol's story "The Overcoat." Boris Eichenbaum, "How Gogol's 'Overcoat' Is Made," in *Gogol from the Twentieth Century*, ed. Robert A. Maguire (Princeton, NJ: Princeton University Press, 1974), 269–91. Kabakov's allusions to Gogol and his *skaz*-like use of "characters" and their voices have been widely noted.

# Part 2

# Making Things

# 4

# Making Fish Guts into Isinglass and Glue

Matthew P. Romaniello

Russia's bountiful fish produced multiple valuable resources including not only caviar but also isinglass and glue. Europeans consumed all three in significant quantities.[1] Caviar was generally known to be fish roe, but the origins of isinglass and glue remained obscure. Isinglass was dried swim bladders extracted from sturgeon. Russia was home to several varieties, including beluga, ossetra, sevruga, and sterlet. Isinglass was in high demand throughout Europe, particularly needed by brewers and vintners to strain particulates from beer and wine (a process known as "fining"). Fish glue was simply glue rendered from any of the remaining parts of the fish, typically bones and cartilage, and then prepared for sale as dried cakes. Isinglass and glue served distinct purposes and were created from different parts of the fish, but the finished materials had a similar texture, color, and an absence of a recognizable odor, and were both soluble in water, each becoming a "rich thick Jelly," even if glue failed to "fine" beer or wine as effectively.[2] Furthermore, early-modern Russians used one word for both isinglass and glue (*klei*), which makes identifying the correct product particularly difficult for historians. It was not until the end of the eighteenth century that export records began to distinguish between the two, revealing the significant cost difference between the two products. In 1793, for example, St. Petersburg's export records note that isinglass sold for ten times the cost of glue by weight.[3] Maintaining the confusion in terminology and the similarity in appearance of *klei* created an opportunity for Russian merchants to sell common glue as the far more valuable isinglass; Western consumers quite literally paid for their ignorance. Once the products were understood as two separate items, Russia lost its advantage.

Scholars of early-modern Europe often investigate a practice called "bioprospecting," which was the process of exploiting the natural world for potential commodities and improvements to production of materials. Merchants seeking new goods and naturalists exploring new lands sought out unfamiliar plants and animals in hopes of locating a marketable commodity for Europe, which historian Londa Schiebinger called the hunt for "green gold."[4] For example, cochineal was an insect discovered in the Americas from which a valuable red dye could be produced. As the Spanish controlled the export market, the British attempted to smuggle the insects from Central America to India in hopes of developing their own industry in the eighteenth century.[5] Isinglass and glue were not new products in the early-modern world, but learning to distinguish between the two or uncovering Russia's unknown production methods offered the potential for increased profits. Teasing out a production method that turned a common material like fish into higher-value materials was bioprospecting as much as smuggling insects was.

It is unsurprising that Russia's foreign consumers attempted to uncover the fabrication methods for their animal materials to free themselves from their dependency on Russia. In a mercantilist world, replacing imports with domestic goods was a desirable goal for improving the balance of payments.[6] Russians exported the best-quality isinglass, but Europeans had no knowledge of how the Russians manufactured it, much less whether it was glue or something else entirely. Reverse engineering the production process would not be the work of a single individual, nor was it easily achieved. First the difference between isinglass and glue had to be clearly understood, which surprisingly took both Russians and their consumers more than a century to distinguish.

Once this distinction was understood by consumers of isinglass and fish glue, the method to process each had to be uncovered, which required moving beyond the scant knowledge of production that reached European markets through merchant exchanges. When the British developed an industrial process to transform the swim bladder from any type of fish into isinglass at the end of the eighteenth century, this technological breakthrough permanently altered the isinglass trade. For Europeans, bioprospecting the method of transforming fish guts into isinglass was a success; but, for Russians, bioprospecting destroyed one of their most valuable early-modern exports.

## Identifying Isinglass and Glue

Long before Muscovite Russia's conquest of the Volga Region, local communities produced isinglass and glue for sale across Eurasia. In 985, the Islamic geographer al-Muqqadasi mentioned both products as exports from the Bulghar Khanate and its trade center of Kazan'.[7] After Russia's conquest of Kazan' in 1552, the state regulated the fishing industry with as much attention as it gave to the cultivation of grain or hunting for fur.[8] Fishing remained an occupation for non-Russian communities throughout the region, including Chuvashes, Maris, Mordvins, and Tatars. Not only were Russians unfamiliar with how to make fish into isinglass and glue but also the language and cultural differences between Russians and their non-Russian subjects made exchanging this knowledge difficult. The Russians lacked firsthand knowledge about where to fish, what types of fish to gather, or how to prepare the fish for transportation to Moscow or beyond. All of these tasks remained in the hands of Russia's new subjects.[9]

Even after decades of experience managing the local population, Russian authorities' knowledge of the fishing industry had scarcely advanced. For example, when the central government dispatched a set of directions to the governor of Kazan' in 1613, it reminded him of his responsibility to monitor and tax both the grain and fish supplies produced throughout the region, but that was the only requirement. The governor of Kazan' had to regulate the "fish market" (*rybii dvor*) in the same manner as the grain market. The state expected yearly reports on prices and the volume of the supply but did not request any information about the methods for gathering fish or preparing finished goods for the market.[10]

The state profited from the fishing industry operating on the Caspian Sea, but its command of the intricacies of the Astrakhan market was no more sophisticated. In a 1634 instruction to its governor, the state regulated sales of sturgeon (specifically beluga, ossetra, and sevruga, but not sterlets), noting the higher cost of fish that contained caviar, *viziga* (the spinal cord used in cooking), and *klei*.[11] The instruction specifies that these three items, as materials extracted from the fish, could be sold separately; this *klei* is likely the swim bladder (in other words, isinglass), not glue that could be rendered from any of the remaining parts of the animal. While the sturgeon swim bladder itself was the source of isinglass, it required artisanal experience to properly extract the complete organ and skill to dry, fold, and roll the material for shipping. There is no indication that the state or its local administrators possessed any knowledge of how fish became isinglass or glue. The state's focus was on the revenue generated by the fishing industry, not on the material side of production.

As time passed the state expressed little interest in the industry's efficiency at making or exporting those products. New regulations promulgated for Kazan' in 1649 limited the number and size of the beluga, ossetra, and sevruga that could be sold, warning against the sale of "fish of a smaller size," presumably to protect the fisheries. It also provided guidelines for the proper way to salt and pack caviar for transportation to Moscow, which indicated that the state possessed technical information on the techniques to prepare and preserve this luxury food. Furthermore, the state instructed the governor of Kazan' to report on similar activities throughout the region, including sales in the fish markets in Samara and Saratov further down the Volga.[12] Subsequent regulations mentioned no fish products other than caviar.[13]

This disinterest in the production methods for isinglass and glue is only more surprising considering the earliest accounts of Russia's economy always mentioned *klei* as being among Russia's most valuable exports. Simply noting the value of *klei*, however, revealed neither if it was isinglass or glue, or both, nor how Russia's fishermen should prepare either good for the market. For example, Johann Kilburger's analysis of Russia's foreign trade in the year 1673 mentions that "*rybii klei*, or '*karluk*' as the Russians knew it," was gathered near Astrakhan along the Volga. Kilburger mentions two terms for two products (*rybii klei* and *karluk*), making it tempting to conclude that the former meant glue and the latter isinglass, but he used the two terms as synonyms, not separate products. Kilburger estimated the *klei* exports from Russia to be 300 *pudy* yearly (approximately 11,000 lbs.).[14] A *pud* is only a measure of weight, not value or quality, so whether this *klei* was glue, isinglass, or both is unknown.[15]

Nor was the confusion about the products only a problem for merchants like Kilburger. Samuel Collins, the English physician in Tsar Aleksei Mikhailovich's court, only mentions isinglass as an afterthought to his discussion of caviar in his well-known *Present State of Russia* (1671). Collins wrote, "Near Astracan they kill many hundreds of *Bellugas* for the spawn [roe], and thro away the rest; but 'tis pitty, seeing the Fish is one of the greatest Dainties that comes out of the watry Element, especially his belly, which surpasses the marrow of Oxen. The glew which they call *Isinglass* is made of the *Beluga*'s sounds."[16] The "sounds" is the swim bladder, which is the part of the fish that was used for isinglass. Collins's account is one of the first to identify isinglass as the swim bladder, which makes it noteworthy, but he offered no further information, including no reference to another type of fish glue.

The reason merchants and physicians mentioned this unique Russian export during the seventeenth century was a result of the increasing demand for it throughout Europe; consumers wanted not only to purchase these materials but also to understand their origins. Surprisingly, a French apothecary, Pierre Pomet, wrote the lengthiest account of making isinglass, despite never having traveled to Russia. He included it in his description of medicaments: "That which we call Fish-Glue, or Isinglass, ... is the mucilanginous Part of a Fish, whose Back is full of little white Scales that are prickly and ranged in Order, commonly found in the Muscovy Seas."[17] The French word for isinglass is literally "fish glue" (*ichtyocolle*), so like the Russian in this context, glue and isinglass were synonyms. He then provided a lengthy description of a production method that he never observed:

> The sinewy Parts of the Fish are boiled in Water, till all of them be dissolved that will dissolve; then the gluey Liquor is strained, and set to cool. Being cold, the Fat is carefully taken off, and the Liquor itself is boiled to a just Consistency, then cut into Pieces, and made into a Twist, bent in the Form of a Crescent, as commonly sold, then hung upon a String, and carefully dried. That which is clearest and whitest is best; and which being boiled in Water and Milk, will almost all dissolve. It is chiefly made in Muscovy; and that which is called the Patriarch Sort, which is four square, very thin and white, almost transparent, is the choicest; the next is the Czar's Sort, which is the large Horse-shoe, or twisted Kind, that is in thin Rags, and clear; a meaner Sort is that which is yellow and brown within; and that in square Books or Cakes, is the worst of all.[18]

Pomet's description of the manufacturing process was for glue: "the sinewy Parts of the Fish are boiled," not isinglass that was dried (not boiled) swim bladders. However, the products he described were types of isinglass, which were graded based on color and shape. It would be more than a century until a European realized that the grades of isinglass reflected the skill of the craftsman, not a boiling process to render fish guts into glue. Pomet's text circulated across Europe; it was first published in Paris in 1694 and translated into English and German by 1712. He frequently would be cited as an expert on isinglass in the eighteenth century. His error became institutionalized as fact.[19]

As an apothecary, Pomet's primary interest was in the medical uses of isinglass, but he mentioned that its primary use was that it served "the Wine-Merchants and Vintners, who use it to fine their Wines."[20] With the popularity of Russia's isinglass among French winemakers and British brewers, demand for the export continued to increase. It was sufficiently important for Russia's economy that Tsar Peter the Great turned *klei* into a state monopoly in 1701, alongside other high-volume exports like pitch, potash, tar, and caviar. The *klei* monopoly could be isinglass, glue, or both. According to historian R. I. Kozintseva, the average sale of *klei* in the twenty-two years of the monopoly for which we have data was 780.1 *pudy* per year (28,083 lbs.). The markets for Russia's exported *klei* were Amsterdam, London, and Hamburg, in order of decreasing value.[21]

The success of the Petrine monopoly may have inspired the turn toward Russia's first investigations of its fish products. As remarkable as it seems, before the eighteenth century there was no mention of such an effort. Distinguishing between isinglass and common glue could segment the market and allow better products to command premium prices. One of the early texts in the process was Philip Johan von Strahlenberg's *Das Nord- und Ostliche Theil von Europa und Asia*, published in Stockholm in 1730 and translated into English, French, and Spanish in the next decade. Strahlenberg was a Swedish officer captured at the Battle of Poltava in 1709 who lived as a prisoner of war in Tobol'sk from 1711 until 1721. Following his ten years in Siberia, Strahlenberg produced his extensive summary of the peoples, materials, and current political and economic developments in the region. Daniel Gottlieb Messerschmidt's (1685–1735) "official" scientific expedition to Siberia for the Russian government in the 1720s relied on Strahlenberg's expert knowledge as well. Through Messerschmidt, Strahlenberg's expertise was enshrined within the Russian Academy of Sciences. In Strahlenberg's study of Siberia's economy, he described,

> Ising-Glass, or *Carluck*, in the Russian Tongue, *Kley-Ribey* is brought from Russia, as well as Hungary; It is made of the Bladder of the Fish Beluga; The best Sort is that which is roll'd up in long Rolls; The other Sort is press'd into Cakes. Some make it also of the Sturgeon or *Sevringa* [sevruga]; But this is not near so good, and may easily be known from the other, that being smooth and white, this, on the contrary, yellowish, and full of Cracks.[22]

While Strahlenberg still used *karluk* and *rybii klei* as synonyms, he described isinglass, not glue.

Other contemporary members of the Russian Academy of Sciences observed glue production, suggesting that the academy at large was aware of the distinction between the materials, even if some of the members had errors in their field notes. For example, glue appeared in the records of the Academy's Second Kamchatka Expedition (1733–43). This expedition gathered accounts of the peoples of the empire, along with mineral, animal, and plant samples, in an attempt to document the natural resources of Siberia, Kamchatka, and the North Pacific. The Russian naturalist on the expedition, Stepan Krasheninnikov, observed indigenous communities of Kamchatka producing glue from whale parts (*kitovyi*), which only added to the complexity of possible techniques employed throughout Russia to render aquatic waste products into useful goods. Krasheninnikov complimented the ingenuity of the local fisherman, who had found another valuable product in whales beyond blubber and oil.[23]

Naturalists like Strahlenberg and Krasheninnikov pioneered Russia's first steps toward a general understanding of the long-unknown process of converting fish into isinglass and glue. Foreign merchants' ongoing interest in these products only added to the importance of this investigation. Britain's long-serving envoy during Peter the Great's reign, Charles Whitworth, knew that isinglass (not glue) was one of the principle exports for the British Russia Company, alongside "hemp, flax, train-oil, linen, pot-ash, [and] rhubarb."[24] George Forbes, the British envoy extraordinary in 1734, complimented Russia's fishing industry, mentioning that

> the Waters are no less abundant than the Land, many of them are covered with all sorts of Water fowle, and swarm with various kinds of Excellent Fish. ... the Caviare is made of the Roes of the Beluga and Sturgeon of which they take such quantitys that they throw all the other parts of the Fish away except the gristle, of which they make that Glew called Isinglass.[25]

As Forbes never left St. Petersburg, his description of Russia's fish could only reflect secondhand knowledge, like that possessed by Collins or Pomet in the seventeenth century. The Russian Empire had long since produced multiple products from its fish, including valuable exports like caviar and isinglass and domestic ones like *viziga* (the spinal cord) and glue. Since Forbes mentions fish "gristle" as isinglass, it is uncertain if he meant the swim bladder (isinglass) or the glue-making staples of bones and cartilage. If the men negotiating to export Russia's valuable isinglass had no knowledge of what the product was, it is no wonder more detailed information about the material was a necessity not only for European merchants and physicians but also for the Russian Academy of Sciences.

## Making Isinglass and Glue

Russia possessed an advantage in any commercial negotiations over *klei* as long as the difference between isinglass and glue remained unknown in the West. By the middle of the eighteenth century, however, export records began to distinguish between the two. There was no single law or regulation that required this major change, but records in St. Petersburg, the Danish Sound Toll (the gateway to and from the Baltic Sea), and in London all marked this change.[26] When Britain prepared to renegotiate its commercial treaty at the beginning of the 1760s, the British Board of Trade and Plantations' comments on the first draft of the new treaty focused attention on Britain's key exports: isinglass, hemp, flax, iron, timber, wax, tallow, and rhubarb.[27] In 1758, 31,384 rubles of isinglass were exported from St. Petersburg, but this value increased to 79,000 rubles by 1768. The end of the Seven Years' War at the beginning of the 1760s led to a steady increase in St. Petersburg's exports, so an increase of more than 150 percent during a decade of relative peace appears reasonable.[28] Furthermore, in 1768 isinglass was Russia's fifth-most valuable export, following iron, hemp, flax, and wax, a position it still held in 1780.[29] Over the next decade, other products surpassed isinglass's revenue, but it remained the tenth-most valuable export as late as 1788.[30] Isinglass held a prominent position in Russia's export trade for the remainder of the century, increasing to a significant 451,539 rubles in 1793, even as it diminished in overall importance as an export. It was only the thirteenth-most valuable export from St. Petersburg that year, even if the monetary value of the export reflected an increase of 570 percent since 1768.[31] At the same time, glue was only one-tenth as expensive as isinglass and only sold one-third as much by weight.[32] By both value and volume of sales, it was isinglass and not glue that drove sales of *klei* exports.

In light of the continuing expense of importing isinglass, the British aspired to secure the trade on a better footing by observing the production process and then finding a domestic substitute. This effort was led by a Scottish chemist, Humphrey Jackson, who received a patent in 1760 for using a chemical process to produce an alternative to the Russian import utilizing American sturgeon gathered in the Delaware River.[33] In 1765, Jackson published *An Essay on British Isinglass*, which blamed the "Merchants at Petersburgh in this respect, that those who principally deal in Isinglass know nothing of its Preparation, except its being made from a particular Kind of Fish, the very Name of which they are unacquainted with." His lengthy study redressed this lack of information, serving as "a free Enquiry into the Merits of each Species of Isinglass, with the most advantageous Methods of converting them into Fining, and its real Mode of Action in clarifying Malt Liquors, hitherto misapprehended."[34] He criticized Britain's brewing industry for its reliance upon imported Russian isinglass, when other versions of the product were available, including the "domestic" types imported from the American colonies.

While Jackson's study failed to disclose any new information about Russia's production process, during the same period the Russian Academy of Sciences pursued its own research. Gerhard Friedrich Müller, a historian by training, published a study on the production method for rendering fish into glue in 1768, drawing upon his extensive ethnographic fieldwork throughout the empire.[35] In an unusual choice for a member of the Russian Academy, Müller published his report at the French Académie des sciences, which the Russians typically avoided, as its foreign specialists were overwhelming hired in Britain and Germany.[36] Müller reviewed the varieties of fish useful for making glue, with a focus on the Volga Region and the Ural Mountains, but concluded that ossetra and sterlet (not beluga or sevruga) produced the best quality. The decision to publish on glue in France may have been an intentional choice to develop a new market for a low-volume Russian export. Britain already consumed a significant volume of isinglass; perhaps France could be persuaded to do likewise for glue?[37]

Shortly after Müller's publication, Humphrey Jackson traveled to Russia to investigate their methods of producing isinglass. He reported the results of his expedition to the Royal Society, publishing his study in 1773.[38] He observed that Russians made isinglass from the swim bladders, but "any other part of cartilage could be used to make fish glue." Notably, Jackson's report on Russia's production method was the first publication to identify two separate processes—one for isinglass and another for glue, made from different parts of the fish. Müller may have discussed multiple parts of the fish but did not make a single mention of air bladders or producing isinglass.

Jackson's mission to Russia was to uncover the secrets of producing the various grades of isinglass available in the marketplace. Russian craftsmen began by removing the sounds:

> From the fish while sweet and fresh, slit open, washed from their slimy *sordes*, divested of every thin membrane which invelopes the sound, and then exposed to

stiffen in a little air. In this state, they are formed into rolls about the thickness of a finger, and in length according to the intended size of the staple: a thin membrane is generally selected for the center of the roll, round which the rest are folded alternately, and about half an inch of each extremity of the roll is turned inwards. The due dimensions being thus obtained, the two ends of what is called short staple are pinned together with a small wooden peg; the middle of roll is then pressed a little downwards, which gives it the resemblance of a heart shape, and thus it is laid on boards, or hung up in the air to dry. ... In this state, it is permitted to dry long enough to retain its form, when the pegs and sticks taken out, and the drying completed; lastly, the pieces of isinglass are colligated in rows, by running packthread through the peg-holes, for convenience of package and exportation.[39] (See Figure 4.1.)

Jackson's research allowed him to reject Pomet's claim that boiling the internal organs was necessary for isinglass; Pomet's process was for preparing glue. Jackson further delineated the methods for producing short and long staple isinglass described above, as well as "book" isinglass that was folded long staple isinglass and "cake" isinglass that was "formed of the bits and fragments of the staple sorts." He dismissed earlier theories related to the quality being linked to the species of fish, arguing that Atlantic cod would make an acceptable substitute if the same process of preparing isinglass were followed.[40] In other words, his claims in his first publication on isinglass were correct, despite some resistance from British brewers for his American alternative.

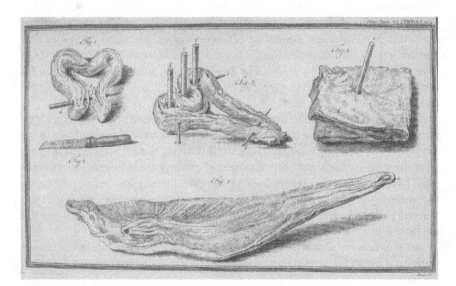

**Figure 4.1** Table 1 from "An Account of the discovery of the manner of making isinglass in Russia ... In a letter from Humphrey Jackson, Esq.; F.R.S. to William Watson, M.D. F.R.S.," *Philosophical Transactions of the Royal Society* 63 (1773). Credit: © The Royal Society.

Jackson's efforts were an eighteenth-century episode of industrial espionage, although the Russian state made no attempt to protect this "secret." Nevertheless, his observations threatened Russia's monopoly on isinglass by confirming Russia's *klei* was not one product, but two, and, more importantly, that Russian sturgeon was inessential for the product to work. Meanwhile, the Russian Academy of Sciences began its own fact-finding mission. Samuel Gottlieb Gmelin, a professor of botany at the Academy, led a new expedition to southern Russia and Iran in 1770. The notes from his expedition would be published in the four-volume *Reise durch Russland zur Undersuchung der drey Natur-Reiche*, followed closely by the three-volume Russian translation. Volume two contained an extensive description of the fishing industry in Astrakhan, published in 1774 (in German) and 1777 (in Russian), arriving after Jackson's report to the British Academy. Gmelin's account was the most comprehensive study of fishing produced by the Russian government since its conquest of Kazan' and Astrakhan in the sixteenth century, including the current methods of preparing caviar for transport and producing isinglass from a swim bladder, with no mention of glue. However, Gmelin's notes on producing isinglass were far less detailed than Jackson's, because Gmelin's primary interest was in the types of fish caught, the types of boats used, and the best methods for catching large volumes of fish in the Caspian Sea and the Volga River delta.[41] Jackson's intention, of course, was to glean enough information to end Britain's dependence on the Russian export.

Since Jackson's 1773 account preceded Gmelin's publication, the Russian Academy of Sciences lagged behind Britain's Royal Society in recognizing isinglass and glue as separate products. Perhaps in an attempt to reclaim a leading role in the study of fish materials, Peter Simon Pallas, a member of the Academy, wrote to the Royal Society in 1778 that Jackson had made some errors in his assessment, and suggested the society review Müller's report to the French Académie published in 1768, without mentioning Gmelin's 1774 corroboration of Jackson's work.[42] Pallas was a botanist by training, so he was an odd choice to respond to Jackson's report. He either hoped to focus Britain's attention on glue, which the British rarely imported, wished to defend the Russian Academy's reputation, or was simply unaware of the difference, as seemingly the Russian government had been for two centuries. Subsequently in 1780, the Academy of Sciences produced a Russian translation of Müller, twelve years after its publication in France.[43]

There is no doubt that the Russian government became more interested in glue production following the scientific work of the 1770s. In Russia's commercial treaty with the Kingdom of Sardinia in 1783, for example, it promised to export "strong glue" (*colle forte*) to the Mediterranean alongside hemp, linen, iron, leather, fur, wax, and caviar, with no mention of isinglass.[44] In 1785, Ivan Ivanovich Lepekhin recorded the volume of glue and locations of its production for the Russian Academy. While Müller had focused on the older production areas along the Volga River and south of the Ural Mountains, Lepekhin detailed the new glue production in the Russian north, particularly in the region around Arkhangel'sk. It was not a small enterprise, with at least thirteen different workshops involved.[45] Johann Friedrich Gmelin, Samuel Gottlieb Gmelin's cousin and another member of the Academy, published the results of his own chemical experiments on the process. In an article on "Cooking Glue," Gmelin detailed six different types of glue capable of being produced from fish parts, with the most valuable "carpenter's glue" (*stoliarnoi klei*) requiring a chemical additive. The other varieties were produced by different parts of the fish; for example, cartilage produced appropriately named "cartilage glue" that held higher value than typical "fish glue" (*rybii klei*), which properly should be made from the bones and fatty membranes of the fish.[46] This *rybii klei* was unquestionably glue, and not isinglass.

Pallas returned to the isinglass/glue issue after his last expedition for the Academy to New Russia in 1793 and 1794. Traveling down the Volga River to Astrakhan, Pallas would have observed the robust fishing industry in the region and could have settled the ongoing debates about the best method to dry bladders (as Jackson discussed) or offered local formulas for producing alternate fish glues. However, his only comments on fish related to the ongoing economic importance of isinglass exports.

> [Isinglass] is principally exported from St. Petersburg to England, where it is used in large quantities, in the beer and porter breweries. The English supply the Spaniards, Portuguese, Dutch, and French, with this commodity for clarifying their wines. According to the list of exportation printed by the English Factory at St. Petersburg, there have been exported in British vessels, from 1753 to 1758, between one and two thousand pood of isinglass: from 1769 to 1786, from two to three thousand; in late years usually upwards of four thousand; and in 1788, even six thousand eight hundred and fifty pood of that article.[47]

In arguing for the continuing importance of Russia's isinglass exports, Pallas ignored all the scientific work published with the express intent of replacing Russia's product, and thus misleading his readers on the current situation. His own intent, as with his response to the Royal Society after Jackson published, was to defend Russia's commercial interests.

In 1795, a Scottish inventor, William Murdoch, developed an affordable substitute for isinglass using Atlantic cod. The decades of effort to study isinglass turned out to be less important than using chemistry to transform a different bladder into a substitute for the Russian product. Using Russian isinglass for British beer fining was a centuries' old practice, but the rapidly escalating cost of the material due to the disruption of trade during the Napoleonic era made a domestic alternative more appealing. By 1800, the Committee of London Brewers had paid Murdoch £2,000 for his process. It was not necessarily a popular substitution in Britain, as the Customs and Excise Office prosecuted the brewers for adulterating both fish and stale beer in 1809, but Customs and Excise lost their case.[48] Murdoch's chemically produced "isinglass" became an industry standard in the nineteenth century.

Following the initial decline of the isinglass trade during the Napoleonic era, Russian authorities began to focus on the quality of their product as its most valuable feature, as a cheaper product was readily available in Western markets. Arguing for quality over cost was a strategic decision, as the British public seemed resistant to the taste of the alternative. British merchants living in Russia, the men who were involved in the export trade, emphasized that Russian isinglass and glue were only produced from sturgeon, making these products more valuable than anything manufactured from the common Atlantic cod.[49]

Meanwhile, the Russian Academy of Sciences began to investigate other countries' glue production methods, raising the possibility of replacing Russian techniques with new manufacturing processes. The Academy translated a German study of industrial processes in 1801, which featured a variety of methods for rendering glue, including manufacturing methods from Britain and the United States.[50] A St. Petersburg publication from 1809 advocated for the production of "strong glue" (*krepkii klei*) as a better product for the British and French markets. The anonymous author suggested that neither the type of fish nor the region in which it lived was as significant as the processing of the material.[51]

When European trade recovered from the Napoleonic-inspired disruptions by the 1820s, isinglass regained its position as a high-volume Russian export, but it was only a temporary recovery. The trade steadily declined, starting in the 1840s, and it would never regain its eighteenth-century highs.[52] When the recovery first began, the Russian government attempted to capitalize on the market, leading Russia's College of Manufacturing in 1828 to promulgate formal guidelines to standardize the processing of fish across the empire. The instruction was extensive, detailing a lengthy method to produce the highest-quality isinglass and included warnings to make sure that any caviar from the sturgeon was properly prepared for export.[53] However, industrial techniques had by this time outstripped any attempt to shore up the market of expensive, hand-produced isinglass. As Russia focused on producing consistent, high-quality goods, the chemical process for preparing isinglass made the swim bladders from a variety of fish suitable substitutes. Not only were Murdoch's cod used but also the plentiful tropical fish from Africa's lakes and rivers found their way into the industry by the middle of the nineteenth century.[54] Any European country with a fishing industry, at home or in the colonies, was now free from any dependence on Russia.

## Conclusion

Isinglass and glue had been exported from the Volga Region and Caspian Sea long before Russia was a state. When Muscovite Russia expanded into this territory in the sixteenth century, its officials guaranteed the production of these materials as much as they did with grain, fur, and honey. Local non-Russians possessed the knowledge to catch, process, and sell these fish-derived materials; it was not necessary to understand how the trade was managed as long as the state controlled its outcome when the goods reached the market. If the Russian state did not recognize isinglass and glue as separate products, much less understand the production method for either, how could foreigners discover this information?

Russia's animal materials were important export products for the empire, as successful as better-known plant materials such as hemp or flax.[55] In a mercantilist world, Russia's ability to manufacture materials from domestic goods and export these products to foreign markets was a marker of a successful economy. Britain was Russia's largest foreign trade partner in the eighteenth century, importing large volumes of hemp and flax but also isinglass. While Britain's hope to produce hemp and flax in its North American colonies to free itself from its Russian dependency was never realized, British naturalists succeeded with at least one of Russia's most famous animal materials.[56] Chemists like Jackson traveled to Russia to investigate the production of isinglass and fish glue, while his contemporary Murdoch developed a successful chemical alternative to relying on Russian sturgeon. Murdoch's new isinglass product was sufficiently concerning to Russian authorities that multiple members of the Academy of Sciences investigated its domestic version to verify its quality at the beginning of the nineteenth century. Russia's attempt to salvage the export industry failed; cheaper industrial alternatives trumped the natural and valuable product.

For isinglass and glue, naturalists from multiple countries, employed by Britain and Russia, were deeply enmeshed in the production of industrial knowledge. This was not an abstract process of discovering new information to further science but deliberate investigations of products that held commercial value. This type of bioprospecting, uncovering production methods rather than discovery of new materials, did not end in the early-modern era. Industrial alternatives to animal materials may have come into existence but regularizing the production of commodities from the natural world was the priority.[57] Its resources were to be supplemented or replaced at an industrial scale. Locating valuable body parts, authenticating the value under the auspices of scientific experimentation, and ultimately domesticating the industry to replace expensive imports with factory- or laboratory-enhanced products was an intrinsic part of European engagement with the natural world.

## Notes

1. On the fish trade in general, see Richard Hellie, *The Economy and Material Culture of Russia, 1600–1725* (Chicago: University of Chicago Press, 1999), 71–84. For caviar, see Maria Salomon Arel, *English Trade and Adventure to Russia in the Early Modern Era: The Muscovy Company, 1603–1649* (Lanham, MD: Lexington Books, 2019), 121–31.
2. Humphrey Jackson, *An Essay on British Isinglass* (London: J. Newbery, 1765), 24–5.
3. Russia exported 6,221 *pudy* for 451,530 rubles (or 72.58 rubles per *pud*), compared to 2,041 *pudy* of glue for only 15,184 rubles (or 7.43 rubles per *pud*). William Tooke, *View of the Russian Empire during the Reign of Catharine the Second and to the Close of the Eighteenth Century* (London: T. H. Longman and O. Rees, 1799), vol. 3, 627, 628.
4. Among the many works on this subject are: Londa Schiebinger, *Plants and Empire: Colonial Bioprospecting in the Atlantic World* (Cambridge, MA: Harvard University Press, 2004); Paula de Vos, "The Science of Spices: Empiricism and Economic Botany in the Early Spanish Empire," *Journal of World History* 17:4 (2006), 329-427; Inez G. Zupanov and Angela Barreto Xavier, "Quest for Permanence in the Tropics: Portuguese Bioprospecting in Asia (16th–18th Centuries)," *Journal of the Economic and Social History of the Orient* 57:4 (2014), 511–48; Stefanie Gänger, "World Trade in Medicinal Plants from Spanish America, 1717–1815," *Medical History* 59:1 (2015), 44–82; Clare Griffin, "Disentangling Commodity

Histories: *Pauame* and Sassafras in the Early Modern Global World," *Journal of Global History* 15:1 (2020), 1–18.
5. James W. Frey, "Prickly Pears and Pagodas: The East India Company's Failure to Establish a Cochineal Industry in Early Colonial India," *The Historian* 74:2 (2012), 241–66; Edward D. Melillo, "Global Entomologies: Insects, Empires, and the 'Synthetic Age' in World History," *Past and Present* 233 (2014), 233–70.
6. Seeking replacements for expensive imported luxuries was a common process. See, for example, Maxine Berg, "In Pursuit of Luxury: Global History and British Consumer Goods in the Eighteenth Century," *Past and Present* 182 (2004), 85–142; Wouter Ryckbosch, "From Spice to Tea: On Consumer Choice and the Justification of Value in the Early Modern Low Countries," *Past and Present* 242 (2019), 37–78.
7. David Christian, "Silk Roads or Steppe Roads? The Silk Roads in World History," *Journal of World History* 11:1 (2006), 7–8.
8. Matthew P. Romaniello, *The Elusive Empire: Kazan and the Creation of Russia, 1552–1671* (Madison: University of Wisconsin Press, 2012), 37–45, 72–82.
9. For example, Russian State Archive of Ancient Documents, Moscow (RGADA), f. 281, op. 1, d. 232, March 4, 1564, for Arzamas; I. P. Ermolaev, and D. A. Mustafina, eds., *Dokumenty po istorii Kazanskogo kraia: Iz arkhivokhranilits Tatarskogo ASSR (vtoraia polovina XVI—seredina XVII)* (Kazan′: Izdatel′stvo Kazanskogo universiteta, 1990), #24, 60–2, July 13, 1606, for Sviiazhsk; and RGADA, f. 281, op. 4, d. 6448, March 4, 1616, for Kazan′.
10. RGADA, f. 16, op. 1, d. 709, l. 3ob., April 16, 1613, copy from 1720.
11. *Akty istoricheskie, sobrannye i izdannye* (St. Petersburg: Izdatel′stvo arkheograficheskoi kommissii, 1842), vol. 3, #124, 192–5, September 20, 1623. Richard Hellie translates this *klei* as glue and not isinglass; Hellie, *Economy and Material Culture*, 81.
12. RGADA, f. 16, op. 1, d. 709, ll. 16ob.-21, May 16, 1649, copy from 1720.
13. For example, RGADA, f. 281, op. 8, d. 11532, August 27, 1653, for Simbirsk; f. 159, op. 2, d. 1161, September 1, 1670, for Saratov and Tsaritsyn; and f. 1455, op. 1, ed. khr. 2510, October 5, 1690, for Saransk.
14. B. G. Kurts, *Sochinenie Kil′burgera o rosskoi torgovle v tsarstvovanie Alekseia Mikhailovicha* (Kiev: Tipografiia I. I. Chokolova, 1915), 104. Richard Hellie records forty-eight sales of glue (*klei*) between 1607 and 1710, at a median price of .1325 rubles per funt (14.4 oz. US). See Hellie, *Economy and Material Culture*, 141.
15. The language and translation issue for these terms was not unique to fish products, as Clare Griffin discusses similar challenges in her essay in this volume.
16. Samuel Collins, *The Present State of Russia* (London: John Winter, 1671), 134. Collins passage was included in another physician's account of Russia: Jodocus Crull, *An Account of the Antient and Present State of Muscovy* (London: A. Roper and A. Bosville, 1698), vol. 1, 164.
17. Translations taken from Pierre Pomet, *A Complete History of Drugs*, 4th ed. (London: J. and J. Bonwicke, 1748), vol. 2, 58.
18. Pomet, *Complete History*, vol. 2, 59.
19. See, for example, Humphrey Jackson's discussion of Pomet's text Humphrey Jackson, "An Account of the Discovery of the Manner of Making Isinglass in Russia," *Philosophical Transactions* LXIII (January 1773), 3–4.
20. Pomet, *Complete History*, vol. 2, 59.
21. R. I. Kozintseva, "Uchastie kazny vo vneshnei torgovle Rossii v pervoi chetverti XVIII v.," *Istoricheskie zapiski* 91 (1973), 267–337; the *klei* data is on 317. On the monopolies, also see the discussion in Arcadius Kahan, *The Plow, the Hammer, and the Knout: An*

*Economic History of Eighteenth-Century Russia* (Chicago: University of Chicago Press, 1985), 187–90.
22. Philip Johan von Strahlenberg, *An Historico-Geographical Description of the North and Eastern Parts of Europe and Asia* (London: W. Innys and R. Manby, 1738), 388.
23. Stepan Krasheninnikov, *Opisanie zemli Kamchatki* (St. Petersburg: Imp. Akademiia nauk, 1755), 42.
24. Charles Whitworth, *An Account of Russia as It Was in the Year 1710* (Twickenham: Strawberry Hill, 1758), 82–3.
25. Michael Bitter, "George Forbes's 'Account of Russia,' 1733–1734," *Slavonic and East European Review* 82:4 (2004), 909.
26. The London and St. Petersburg records are discussed below. The modern word for isinglass (Danish: *husblas*) first appeared in the Sound Toll Registers in the 1710s on rare occasion, but consistently was noted by the 1760s alongside *lim* (glue). *Sound Toll Registers Online*, www.soundtoll.nl, *husblas* and *lim*, accessed on April 14, 2019.
27. The National Archive, Kew, Richmond, Surrey (TNA), CO 389/31, ff. 25–98, "Letter to the Earl of Bute, Inclosing Representation to His Majesty, upon the Project of a Treaty of Commerce with Russia," May 18, 1762, here 30.
28. "Isinglass" is used in the British translation of the Russian export records. The 1758 data is from the British Library, Hardwick Papers, Add. MS 35495, "A Computation of the Value of the Goods Exported Anno 1758, from Petersburg in 161 Vessels," f. 83; 1768 from Tooke, *View of the Russian Empire*, vol. 3, 632. For Russia's overall trade in this era, see Matthew P. Romaniello, *Enterprising Empires: Russia and Britain in Eighteenth-Century Eurasia* (Cambridge: Cambridge University Press, 2019), 164–83.
29. 1768 data is from Tooke; 1780 data is from TNA, FO 65/1, f. 145, "Goods Exported from St. Petersburg by the Foreign Ships, Anno 1780."
30. See the export records for 1788 in John Dalrymple, *Queries Concerning the Conduct Which England Should Follow in Foreign Politics in the Present State of Europe* (London: J. Derrett, 1788), 5–6.
31. 1793 data from Tooke, *View of the Russian Empire*, vol. 3, 626–8.
32. According to the data from 1793, as reported in Tooke, *View of the Russian Empire*, vol. 3, 627, 628.
33. John H. Appleby, "Humphrey Jackson, F.R.S., 1717–1801: A Pioneering Chemist," *Notes and Records of the Royal Society of London* 40:2 (1986), 147–68; patent discussed on 157.
34. Jackson, *Essay on British Isinglass*, 22, vi–vii.
35. Gerhard Friedrich Müller, "O rybem klei," *Akademicheskiia izvestiia na 1780 god*, ch. VI (1780), 403–8.
36. For example, see Nicholas Hans, "Russian Students at Leyden in the 18th Century," *Slavonic and East European Review* 35 (1957), 551–62; Thomas H. Broman, *The Transformation of German Academic Medicine, 1750–1820* (Cambridge: Cambridge University Press, 1996), 40–5.
37. In the late 1750s, French authorities offered to import tobacco and beef from Russia, in an attempt to secure a permanent trade between the two countries that did not impinge on products already exchanged between Russia and Britain. Glue would fit this pattern. See Romaniello, *Enterprising Empires*, 164–74.
38. Jackson, "Account of the Discovery."
39. Ibid., 9–10.
40. Ibid., 10–11.

41. Gmelin's work was not translated into English until the twenty-first century, but this does include volume two with its observations on the fishing industry. Samuel Gottlieb Gmelin, *Astrakhan Anno 1770: Its History, Geography, Population, Trade, Flora, Fauna, and Fisheries*, trans. Willem Floor (Washington, DC: Mage, 2013), 157-91. There were further comments on Astrakhan's fishing industry included in Gmelin's final volume concerning his return trip from Iran; see *Puteshestvie po Rossii dlia izsledovaniia trekh tsarstvestestva* (St. Petersburg: Imp. Akademiia nauk, 1785), ch. 3, 350-1.
42. Appleby, "Humphrey Jackson," 162-3.
43. Müller, "O rybem klei."
44. National Library of Scotland, Special Collections, Sir Robert Liston Papers, MS 5524, ff. 67-88, "Projet d'un Traité de Commerce entre S. M. le Roy de Sardaigne, et S. M. l'Imperatrice de toutes les Russies, divise en les quatre chapitre suivants," [1783], f. 74r.
45. I. I. Lepekhin, *Puteshestv Akademika Ivana Lepekhina*, ch. IV (St. Petersburg: Imp. Akademiia nauk, 1805), 285-8.
46. Johann Friedrich Gmelin, "Varenie Kleia," *Khimicheskiia osnovaniia remesl i zavodov*, ch. I (St. Petersburg: Imp. Akademiia nauk, 1803), 144-6.
47. P. S. Pallas, *Travels in the Southern Provinces of the Russian Empire in the Years 1793 and 1794* (London: A. Strahan, 1812), vol. 1, 220.
48. John Griffiths, *The Third Man: The Life and Times of William Murdoch, 1754-1839* (London: André Deutsch, 1992), 222-4.
49. This varying quality was the primary issue of William Tooke's critique of the product. Tooke was British but also a member of the Russian Academy of Sciences. See his *View of the Russian Empire*, vol. 3, 465-7.
50. Johann Samuel Halle, *Otkrytiia tainy drevnikh magikov i charodeev*, trans. V. A. Levshin (Moscow: Universitetskaia tipografiia, 1801), ch. 2, 299-300, 305, 321.
51. *Sekretnyi ekonom, khudozhnik, remeslennik i zavodchik ili polnoe sobranie redkikh, poleznykh, novishikh otkrytii* (St. Petersburg: Tipografii Gubernskago Pravleniia, 1809), 42-3.
52. Sound Toll Registers Online, www.soundtoll.nl, *husblas* and *lim* accessed on April 14, 2019.
53. *Svod zakonov Rossiiskoi Imperii* (St. Petersburg: Tip. Vtorago Otd. Sobstvennoi E. I. V. Kantseliarii, 1833), v. 11, pt. 1-3, 787-854.
54. J. F. Royle, *On the Production of Isinglass Along the Coasts of India* (London: W. H. Allen, 1842).
55. These works include Alfred W. Crosby Jr., *America, Russia, Hemp, and Napoleon: American Trade with Russia and the Baltic, 1783-1812* (Columbus: Ohio State University Press, 1965); Kahan, *The Plow*; Herbert H. Kaplan, *Russian Overseas Commerce with Great Britain during the Reign of Catherine II* (Philadelphia, PA: American Philosophical Society, 1995).
56. On Britain's attempts to grow hemp and flax, see Romaniello, *Enterprising Empires*, 44-6, 88-91, 118-20.
57. Industrial replacements for natural materials position this narrative alongside new examinations of the environmental consequences of Russia's export trade. See Paul Warde, "Trees, Trade and Textiles: Potash Imports and Ecological Dependency in British Industry, c. 1550-1770," *Past and Present* 240:1 (2018), 47-82.

5

# The Thickness of a Plaid: Textiles on the Chikhachev Estate in 1830s Vladimir Province

Katherine Pickering Antonova

If you were browsing the market stalls in Suzdal, Russia, in the 1830s, you might find yourself tempted by an attractive bolt of plaid linen fabric in dark blue, white, and yellow (see the reproduction in Figure 5.1). The Chikhachev plaid was produced and marketed by the local gentry family of that name. It was well known in a small region outlined by four towns staking out an almost perfect square north of their provincial capital, Vladimir, with Teikovo marking the northwest corner, Shuia the northeast, Kovrov the southeast, and Suzdal the southwest corner (Map 5.1). The Chikhachev family lived in the tiny village of Dorozhaevo on the eastern line between Shuia and Kovrov, and they also owned small parcels of land just outside Teikovo, where Natalia Chikhacheva grew up, and in a larger village, Ivanovo, just north of the Teikovo-Shuia line. This northeast quarter of Vladimir province would, a few decades later, become the center of Russia's textile industrialization, and the village of Ivanovo was to grow into a substantial city that is today known mainly for (textile) labor unrest, especially its role in instigating the 1905 Revolution.

In the 1830s, all this was not yet imaginable, but the region was already a center of textile hand production and trade, through a specialized network of peddler traders, the *ofenia*, who efficiently moved goods from producers to buyers across the region and on to other market zones, doing annual business to the tune of 7.5 million rubles in 1852.[1] The Chikhachev plaid was one of many similar products made on other estates, sold alongside other local goods such as vodka from Shuia or sheepskins from Dunilovo, not to mention a large handknitting operation that occupied over five thousand souls in nearby Gorokhov district in 1852 and was spilling over into the village of Yakushevo in Shuia district because business was so good.[2]

The Chikhachev plaid was specialized—the pattern, colors, and quality were known and its reputation made it marketable—but it was also ordinary, in the sense that it was interchangeable with similar fabrics produced in similar ways on other estates of the region, it was affordable to most townspeople and gentry, and it was used to make common household items like tablecloths, pillow cases, or pantaloons. Linen is long-wearing and grows softer over time, and the flax fiber used to make it was a local crop, lowering the cost of its production. The tricky dyeing process that gave the fabric its distinct color pattern was done by serfs in villages owned by the

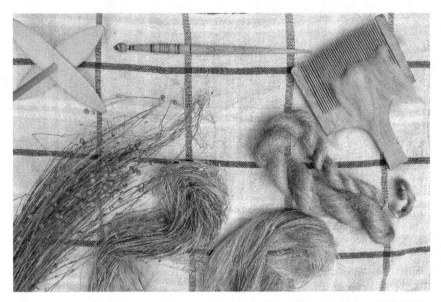

**Figure 5.1** The linen towel in the background was made by Alisa Beer using dyed threads in a cotton/linen blend but handwoven according to patterns found in the Russian textiles in the Metropolitan Museum collection and using the colors named by N. I. Chikhacheva in her diary. Lying on the towel across the top, right to left, are a basic Russian wool comb (twentieth century) with cleaned wool across it, ready to spin; a mid-twentieth-century Russian spindle typically used for flax; and a "Turkish"-style spindle with two arms crossing its shaft, a modern reproduction of what was likely a typical spindle for wool spinning in most of Russia. Across the bottom, from left to right, are dried flax, the same fiber after it is "broken" and then "scutched" (roughly combed through a set of nails), and then a "strick" of combed fiber, ready to spin. Flax samples were provided by the Hermitage, a Harmonist community in Pitman, Pennsylvania, that processes flax fibers into linen entirely by hand. Credit: Photograph by the author.

Chikhachevs but without their direct supervision: one group of their serfs paid their quitrent in dyed thread. The weaving required moderate skill. A plainweave structure was made more pleasing by alternating the colors of threads in both the warp and weft, the most efficient means of producing a visually complex result. The weavers were serfs in the Chikhachevs' home village of Dorozhaevo, who worked directly under the supervision of their mistress, Natalia Ivanovna Chikhacheva.

Borrowing the term "thick thing" to mean "a thing that attracts multiple meanings," textiles are one of the thickest things around the world at any time in human history, yet postindustrial developments have made that thickness invisible to most people living today.[3] Paradoxically, the very thickness of textiles before industrialization contributes to their historical invisibility: they were so well understood by almost every living person that describing the technical details of their production or function was like describing breathing.[4] Today we "weave" metaphorical connections, "knit" ideas or people together, conceptualize time as "threads," refer to maternal lineages as "the distaff side," and use old spinning wheels to decorate nostalgia-themed restaurants, yet most people have no firsthand sense of the materiality or technical processes behind textiles.

Textiles "attract meaning"—or become "thick"—in several intersecting ways. Technically, they are limited in form, quality, appearance, and function by the constraints of making them, which change depending on the maker, the time and materials available, and the availability of tools or machines. Aesthetically, textiles are worn, displayed, and admired to the extent they please the human eye and sense of touch. Economically, textiles are an essential good that all humans have had to devote considerable resources to producing or purchasing. They are a global trade good that dominates the economies of vast regions around the world, encompassing everything from essential needs to the most desired luxury items. The labor involved in making and trading textiles is one of the largest, most long-standing, and exploitative labor markets across time.[5] Yet even while textile labor is almost synonymous with the worst forms of exploitation, it can also be a hobby or even a status symbol depending on who does it, what they make, and for what purpose. Finally, but perhaps most palpably, textiles attract meaning as intimate material objects. The word "material" itself is synonymous with textiles. Textiles provide necessary protection, cater to our modesty, or highlight our lack thereof. They offer comfort and reflect our identities. Textiles are associated with caring when given to others, with status when used to display, with productivity, pride, and even piousness when made by hand. They are also associated with strength and sustenance in the form of ropes, sails, and fishing nets. Individual forms of textile—from fishing nets to fishnet stockings—are themselves thick things, rich with literal and metaphorical associations.

Looking at the intersection of meanings attached to the Chikhachevs' plaid and the other textile products of their estate, we find a stark duality between sets of deeply weighted meanings. On one side of the duality, the Chikhachev textiles were handmade by peasants, overseen by a woman, in rural private spaces, traded only regionally. Such materials are traditionally categorized as "craft," not "industry," and the associations of all these characteristics imply lower quality, skill, and value—except their long-after-the-fact value as tokens of nostalgia for a world that no longer exists. The other side of the duality, in symbolic opposition to everything the Chikhachev textiles represent, is urban, factory mechanized industry, peopled primarily by "skilled" men and far more profitable.[6]

Virtually none of the weighty associations on either side of that opposition is true. We are able to attach those associations only because we have so completely forgotten the materiality of material. The technical details of choosing and preparing fibers, spinning them into threads, manipulating threads into cloth in any number of ways using any number of tools, sewing cloth into objects of infinite variety, and marketing those objects to nineteenth-century users determined the thick associations of textiles for the people making and using them in the past and are therefore essential to our historical understanding of that past as it was lived.

## The Chikhachevs' Things

Behind the dual, opposed associations we carry about textiles in the past there was an everyday reality that happened to be recorded by Natalia Chikhacheva as part of her efforts to keep track of the work, purchases, and production she oversaw.[7] Thus we know that weaving at Dorozhaevo took place in outbuildings arranged near the main house, with two young men, "Efimushka" and "Aleshka," dedicated to weaving for at least most of the year, and one additional female weaver, Vasilisa, a household serf who worked there only at times of high activity. Natalia Chikhacheva oversaw the weavers while she also spun, knitted, made bobbin lace, and sewed herself, and while her women household serfs spun and sewed (but never cut out fabric, as only the mistress of the house could take on the risk of wasting such labor-intensive material).[8] Most of the weaving was carried out during the first half of the year and resulted in their annual plaids, produced at a rate of three yards a day, resulting in about forty-five yards in two months.[9]

Woolen fabric was also woven at Dorozhaevo, probably in the later months of the year that were not recorded directly in the surviving diaries, and plainweave linen fabrics were woven by peasants in their own huts at other villages, often sewn by Natalia or her house serf women into shirts or used as towels or work cloths.[10] The yarn and threads spun by Chikhacheva and dozens of her serfs in Dorozhaevo and elsewhere seem to have been used only for their own needs, and the stockings Natalia knitted were for family use. She sewed largely for her own family but her lace was marketed,

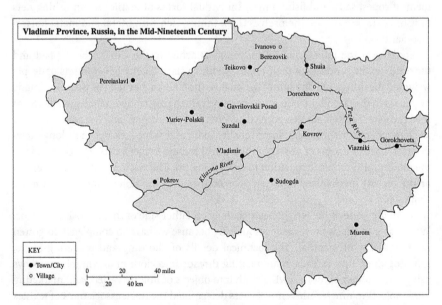

**Map 5.1** The Chikhachev Estate in the nineteenth century, map adapted from Katherine Pickering Antonova, *An Ordinary Marriage: The World of a Gentry Family in Provincial Russia* (New York: Oxford University Press, 2012).

which she took pride in.[11] None of this multilayered, multipurpose production was understood as a workshop or manufactory, although small dedicated workshops did exist in this region at this time for spinning, dyeing, weaving, knitting, and likely also for felting wool cloth and other aspects of hand textile production.[12] The Chikhachevs' cloth production was simply part of the production of any estate in a region where flax and sheep grew better than cereal grains.

Nonestate-centered manufactories similarly made a variety of qualities, from canvas to decorative cloth, though many of the earliest manufactories were associated especially with fabrics that could not be made in peasant huts, such as silks, a limited niche centered around Moscow. Printed cottons were popular for clothing and required imported raw material and the additional skills of hand printing and, later, large machinery. These were the purview mainly of Sheremetev-owned Ivanovo and a main driver of that village's growth into an industrial city after the emancipation of serfs, as they specialized in mechanized printing, eventually buying finished cloth and thread from elsewhere.[13]

In other words, a wide range of manufacturing methods produced a range of goods for a range of needs across a differentiated market. There was no threshold between "better," "more skilled," or "more marketable" fabrics that was out of reach of peasant labor. Some, like silk and printed cotton, could only be made in factory settings (but sometimes by serfs) while other textiles that were made on smaller looms in the same ways for a century or more were actually the result of higher skill, like linen damask (a complex weave pattern). Even a plain weave of fine wool or linen could not be mechanized before the late nineteenth century. The rollers of early spinning machines that drafted out loose fibers while adding twist would break delicate wool fibers, while long-stapled, combed flax could only turn into rope if spun on the machines of the time.[14]

Skill level was also unrelated to whether peasants worked in their own home or a specialized building. When Natalia listed the linen fabrics she received from the peasants of Budyltsy village in 1835, her comments mirror those recorded of inspectors in "real" manufactories: of sixteen total lengths of fabric received from different households, six were "bad," eight were acceptable, and two were "very good."[15] The two best were also the shortest lengths, because greater care, and therefore time, must be taken by even the most skilled weaver to produce a superior fabric.

The only constraint imposed by weaving in peasant huts was the width of finished fabric: wide fabrics require wide looms. Home looms were narrow to save space, so fabrics made on them would need more seams if sewn into large items like clothing or tablecloths. The issue of fabric width was a matter of marketability rather than skill or quality, however. One of the most well-known Russian textile objects was the table runner, narrow but highly decorated. It was made with a single continuous length of fabric woven on a narrow home loom but required enormous skill for the fine, high-quality cloth and embroidery added after the cloth was complete.[16] While the eighteenth-century tsars made attempts to encourage manufactories and therefore wider, more exportable cloths to match those European markets where manufactories had already become commonplace, this did not imply, as most historians have assumed, that wider cloth required greater skill from the weaver or was higher quality.[17] In fact, highly decorated narrow cloths that required more seaming—but could be decorated along the seams to emphasis how much more work went into them to preindustrial eyes that recognized such facts at a glance—could be more desirable, albeit only to a narrower market. Saving a few seams is always welcome, but for locally marketed goods in the Ivanovo-Teikovo region of the early nineteenth century, that factor could not outweigh the greater availability and lower price of otherwise perfectly competitive fabrics made on narrow home looms.

Similarly, historians have looked for other markers of "advancement" in preindustrial textile production that fell back on assumptions about hierarchies of quality or marketability that derive from twentieth-century prejudices rather than preindustrial realities. One of the most notable examples of this historiographical error is the search for spinning wheels. The spinning wheel is a more complicated machine than the spindle, though both are used to spin fiber into thread or yarn. The assumption of economic historians has long been that the "development" of textile production would follow a straight line from tools to simple machines to steam-powered machines. However, depending on the fiber, the intended use of the resulting thread or yarn, and other working conditions, the spindle can actually produce more, can produce a better-quality product, or both. A spinning wheel is faster only within its very significant constraints: wheel spinners must remain at the wheel, and the significant investment in a wheel limits what kinds of fibers can be produced to what parameters: some wheel setups that produce linen thread easily in great quantity are not as effective for spinning a woolen knitting yarn.

A spinning wheel could be made locally by hand but was still much more expensive than a spindle (see Figure 5.1). A spindle is in fact so cheap and simple that it defies the imagination of modern observers that it could ever be preferable to the wheel. Moreover, spindles have been used almost exclusively by women, whereas wheels, as a larger investment, have often been used in workshop settings, overseen by male managers or owners, thus associating wheels with the proto-industrial model of a "stage" of development between (lesser) handwork and (better) machine production.

A spindle is a simple mechanical aid for adding twist at the same time that the spinner draws fibers out to the desired density. The knack of managing both twist and drawing out ("drafting") simultaneously can be taught in a few minutes and mastered with a few weeks of practice, as children as young as five did all over the world before the industrial revolution, using only an easily replaceable weighted stick. Spinning, regardless of tool, becomes a true skill—allowing a spinner not only to produce consistent thread but also to control the drafting and twist to get exactly the thread characteristics she wants—with years of practice and experiment. Spindles are preferable to wheels when the majority of spinning is done alongside and between other tasks, because spindles are eminently portable. A spindle can easily be slipped into a belt and worked for a minute here or there, while walking from place to place or while cooking or taking care of children. Thus spindle-spinning can be "slower by the hour but faster by the week," in the words of anthropologist Edward Franquemont.[18] Even the poorest household can afford as many spindles as they could want, so everyone could spin at once on long winter afternoons. The weight, or whorl, attached or built into the spindle shaft makes it spin longer, while other easily altered characteristics of weight and form eased the making of different end products and offered more minute quality control.

One of the many frustrations of the textile historian is that even in the rare instances where a diarist such as Chikhacheva did write about spinning, she did not bother to mention whether she worked a wheel or a spindle. However, since there is no mention in her extensive papers of any building dedicated to spinning yet she does record days when she and her "women" (household serfs) were all spinning, it is implied that they used spindles, or at least the serfs did.[19] Either way, they produced enough thread and yarn to sustain estates peopled by up to a thousand peasants with sufficient surplus for marketing the plaids and occasionally other fabrics; their methods were as "developed" for their goals as was possible at the time.

The seasonal nature of pre-emancipation industrial labor, with peasants working in manufactories in the agricultural off-season and then returning to their villages, undermines the supposed distinction between "skilled labor" and rough peasant "craft." A weaver does not gain or lose his skill as he moves from village to town or hut to "large stone building." One reference in Natalia's diary suggests that at least one of their serfs was working for pay in a workshop (he had probably been apprenticed there as a boy), and she made an agreement with his employer for especially expensive fabric she planned to use for a tablecloth and dessert napkins.[20] In this case a specially trained workshop weaver was providing textiles for his owner, which is often supposed to be one of the factors distinguishing estate-based serfs from their town counterparts, yet clearly was a distinction without a real difference.

As a linen producer, Chikhacheva also sometimes bought linen from others, paying in one instance thirty-two kopecks per yard for "fine linen" and getting ninety-three yards in one purchase for "everyday use." It seems likely that her own estates' production did not meet her needs that year, rather than that her best serf weavers could not meet the quality of purchased fabric for linens in "everyday use" at a reasonable price, less than half the cost of "ordinary chintz."[21] Rather, this and frequent additional references to Natalia's purchases from peddlers, of fabric and other items, demonstrate a general availability in this unique region of manufactured goods, despite the infamous obstacles of transportation and Russia's small trading class. It turns out that the same people who made such goods occasionally bought comparable goods, depending on the vagaries of supply and timing.

In fact, the Chikhachev papers describe a community in the Ivanovo-Teikovo region that was generally more porous than historians expect based on imperial Russia's rigid social estate structure and relatively underdeveloped towns. Here, freed serfs became magnates, peddlers were highly organized and prosperous, serfs were apprenticed in towns while rural serfs were masters of specialized crafts, and most serfs moved casually and often between an outbuilding on their resident landlord's property to market day in Suzdal or Shuia to a factory in Ivanovo. Social distinctions certainly mattered, but they were far from simple and cannot be described as feudal, capitalist, or proto-industrial.[22] Most of this social complexity was continuous at least from the early eighteenth century to the middle of the nineteenth, and the technological and economic changes that altered it were gradual. The most sudden and undoubtedly tectonic change was not the invention of a machine or the opening of a new market, but the end of serfdom in 1861.[23]

Emancipation not only theoretically released more peasants to work in towns and cities (though this was a gradual, not overwhelming, transition), it largely broke up the smaller, village-based textile production that had been organized through middling landowners like the Chikhachevs, disrupting the continuity from male field serfs growing and processing flax to household women and the mistress handspinning it into thread, to skilled weavers turning thread into linen cloth, the "cutting up" of fabric by the mistress, and the "sewing up" by her and her household ladies.[24] This tremendous disruption left many such rural hand manufacturing operations to shrink or fade while more mechanized and urban operations like Ivanovo expanded rapidly. The fluid continuum of production across a mostly rural Ivanovo-Teikovo region where serfs engaged in the full range of textile production using a full range of techniques shifted to an urbanizing and proletarianizing Ivanovo-Voznesensk specializing in cotton, while the middling nobility abandoned domestic industry for professions (or poverty) and many of the fabrics that had been viable or even preferable alternatives to machine-made cotton, like plain linen, became scarce until they, too, were eventually mechanized.

## What Have We Learned

One of the most important factors in the history of textile production that historians have so far failed to understand is that the complexity of textile tools does not impact and may even reduce the complexity or quality of the product. The most complex and highest-quality textiles must, to this day, be made by hand using simple tools. It is a deep irony that the history of textile industrialization as a story of graduated stages of development leading to a higher plane, fully realized only through mechanization, was first written in a period dominated by the poorest-quality textiles in the history of the world: the first primitive synthetics, produced in the 1970s but subsequently refined or supplanted.[25]

In measuring value or level of economic development according to the numbers of items sold, the distance of markets reached, and profits earned, historians have undervalued the significance of regional markets and overvalued the relatively short-term and uneven nature of the advantages offered by quantity over quality. Time has shown that industrial-scale output and global trade leads to cycles of market saturation and increasingly false "innovation," where new products are constantly introduced only to lose their marketability as they lose their novelty, or products are manufactured to be disposable, prompting consumers to buy more to replace what does not last in order to maintain profits. The preindustrial or semi-industrial regional industry has been understudied by historians because it was seen as failing to meet this standard of growth. It is less profitable, lacks global reach, and does not "lead to" anything else, yet regional industry can offer greater quality to regional consumers, who are more likely to be knowledgeable judges and may even know the producer. It represents a different understanding of value: quality, longevity, and stability over high but unstable quantity and profits.

Britain dominated the globe for two centuries through, initially, the textile industry. They provided the model that also dominated the history of industrialization, setting the standard of profitability and marketability against which the rest of the world was measured and inevitably found wanting. Over the past few decades, revisionist historians have shown two major problems with this interpretation. First, it holds the entire world to a false standard, as if any development that did not "follow" the British model was "behind," rather than accurately seeing the British model as an outlier.[26] Second, the British model became used to define a series of "stages" of economic development from pre-mechanized to "proto-industrial" (defined by early mechanization, specialization, and expanding markets), to fully industrialized, in a straight line from lesser to greater. This theory developed in the 1970s and was shaped by the ideological standoff of the Cold War: both capitalist and Communist historians saw economic development in "stages" following Marx, though they differed in their judgment of which stages were ultimately the preferable outcome. Research since has shown that actual development (even in Britain) varies enormously across time and space and there is no trajectory that leads inevitably from one "stage" to another. In fact, the stages as initially defined cannot be pinned down with any clarity in real cases, and they can occur in any order.[27]

In 1950, the Soviet historian I. V. Meshalin described a pre-emancipation economy of Russian peasants who were taught specialized skills in factories and then returned home to make the same products there, and who by the 1850s had become an "army" of trained hereditary weavers who could always "be moved to a factory" if necessary.[28] He assumed that "moving to a factory" was preferable and that the historical significance of his research was how long this took in Russia. He described a porous boundary between peasants making, he assumed, rough homespun in their huts for quitrent payments and factory "skilled laborers" in a large merchant-owned workshop making finer cloth for the market. He knew that sometimes the weavers in one or the other "type" of manufacturing must have been literally the same people, but he assumed the factory setting meant more advanced or more skilled work was done. In reality the weavers were likely to have made far finer linen runners at home and rougher but faster plain cottons in the factory.

Meshalin also made the same omission common to all the major works on mid-nineteenth-century Russian textile development: historians did not consider ordinary, middling-income landowners taking in textile products from serfs as quitrent payments as a part of textile "industry," because in their minds such "craft" had to be a "backward" holdover from an earlier, "feudal" economic stage.[29] Thus, in his overview of preindustrial Russian textile production synthesizing both Western and Soviet works, Wallace Daniel argues that a conflict between merchants and peasants that was supposed to have delayed or impeded Russian industrialization in the mid-nineteenth century "emerged because the social values of the middle rank were patrimonial; having struggled to build an enterprise, members of the middle rank did not want to share it with small producers and peasant traders."[30] By "middle ranks" Daniel refers to registered "entrepreneurs," including in his sample four foreigners, eight noblemen, thirty townspeople or other "middle ranks," and one former serf (who we must assume had opinions about patrimony but likely not the same ones as the others in this group). The noblemen included in his study were all owners or investors of manufactories, not producers like Natalia Chikhacheva, who collected wool, thread, and dyes from serfs on outlying estates, had her household ladies spin and sew, and male serfs resident on her demesne lands specialize in high-quality weaving.

Rural producers were certainly also patrimonial and certainly also came into conflict with their peasant laborers. However, the relevant question was not what "delayed" Russian industrialization but what advantages sustained rural, mostly unmechanized operations. The answer is: abundant cheap labor, high skill levels, and cheap local raw materials. Moscow had advantages, too: much more capital available for investment, state support, greater access to markets through its urban, central location, and guild organization that could organize a complicated labor force of free and serf laborers, some of them seasonal, as well as regulating other aspects of the industry. But instead of competing directly with each other, Moscow specialized in what Vladimir province could not produce—silk and other products based on imported raw materials or technology—while Vladimir province specialized in what Moscow could not produce—the incredibly labor-intensive and slow linen-making process.[31]

Much confusion has resulted not only from historians ignoring serf-based rural production as part of textile industry but also from equating Moscow's silk-dominated operations with the Sheremetev-owned operations centered in Ivanovo that became more urban in the second half of the nineteenth century and came to most closely resemble the model they sought. Yet Ivanovo properly marks a third case: at the time Daniel describes, the influence of the noble capitalist Sheremetev was already becoming supplanted by some of his most successful former serfs, who in turn were becoming mired in conflict with labor that was already taking on the forms of "modern" class conflict for the printed cotton industry, even while the linen and handknitting industries continued to operate nearby as they had for centuries.[32] Specialty goods produced in Moscow filled a different market niche from the mass-produced and highly mechanized printed cotton of Ivanovo, and from still another niche of linens and local woolens produced across the Ivanovo-Teikovo region. Silk factories, spinners, and looms cannot produce linen shirts and bedsheets or cheap calico dresses, and vice versa, because these are completely different technologies, both operating at their most efficient level possible. There is no meaningful ranking in the relative development of an industry if they produce different products by different means for different markets.

## Conclusion: The Importance of Place and Thing

To understand the development of textile labor and economics before industrialization, we must add to the technicalities of tools and processes an understanding of the regional circumstances that were equally determinative. The term "terroir" as applied to consumable foods refers to "the specific locale of production" that is "important to the quality and essence" of the product.[33] There is no equivalent for textiles, but a modern neologism attempts to capture something similar as part of activist efforts to support sustainable and transparent postindustrial textile production: "fibershed." As defined by Rebecca Burgess and analogous to a watershed, a fibershed is "place-based textile sovereignty, which aims to include ... all the people, plants, animals, and cultural practices that compose and define a specific geography." The term is also useful to describe how textiles were produced before mass industrialization, as it places the focus on "the source of the raw material ... and the connectivity among all parts, from soil to skin and back to soil."[34]

It was no accident that the Ivanovo-Teikovo region emerged as the main textile-producing center in Russia already by the early eighteenth century, long before the introduction of machine-made printed cotton. This area was uniquely suited for the production and marketing of, primarily, linen and, secondarily, domestic wool. While there are parts of Vladimir province with good soil for grains,[35] the area around Ivanovo-Teikovo was less hospitable. The Chikhachevs did meet their own needs via cultivation of cereal grains and vegetables, but it was not a profitable endeavor. Flax, on the other hand, grew robustly and provided a low-cost raw material for linen cloth production.[36] The region was not especially conducive to raising sheep for fiber, but sheep were frequently raised for both meat and a medium-to-coarse wool that was adequate for everyday stockings and other basic uses.[37]

The availability of cheap raw materials and cheap labor (through the relatively high concentration of noble-owned estates) joined the relatively high concentration of market towns as well as the organized peddlers, the *ofenia*, to concentrate textile production in this region from at least the early eighteenth century, and likely much longer.[38] The skills were passed on and a reputation was built, providing additional factors that maintained the viability of this form of production over time.

The regional factors that made it worthwhile to hand-produce textiles for market in Dorozhaevo but not in, say, Poltava also directly affected the nature of what was produced and the methods of production. When your raw materials are limited to linen and medium-to-coarse wool, the only luxury fabrics that can be made are linens with complicated weave structures or fine plain-weave linens with complicated embroidery, both of which were major commodities of the region, as opposed to silks, which were made in more urbanized manufactories in Moscow where foreign investment companies and imperial sponsorship made it possible to import silk from the far East, stocking knitting machines as early as the seventeenth century, and, by the late eighteenth century, Jacquard silk looms.[39] Alongside luxury goods, the majority of flax and wool would necessarily be used for more ordinary textiles to take advantage of the relatively long-wearing qualities of linen and long-staple wools.

Unlike linen, the wools of the region could theoretically be adapted to mechanized spinning and weaving as those technologies were developed in Britain in the mid-nineteenth century. The British banned export of their machines for decades, however, so the Ivanovo-Teikovo region was unable to compete on the global wool market (along with every other wool industry of the time).[40] It could, however, offer local and regional buyers a similar, much less expensive product, since the abundant cheap labor provided by serfs working in off times and seasons could produce sufficient quantities even without mechanization, until the lifting of export restrictions on the machines and the saturation of railroads changed that calculation in the last few decades of the century. None of this made the textile hand production of the region before 1861 more or less "developed" than any other. It made it take the specific form it did and marked the point at which that form changed.

In 1831 when Natalia Chikhacheva was in Moscow, her husband Andrei was left alone on their estates to handle what was normally Natalia's business. He recorded how he was confused by questions from a serf woman about "whether the calico should be woven two threads thick—saying that the lady [Natalia] wants it thicker—and into this reed [of the loom] one thread does not quite do it." Not understanding any of the complexities of this question, Andrei helplessly "resolved her difficulty by ordering [her] to weave two threads thick in [those] cases [where] Nat. Iv. wanted it thicker: because the samples are all different."[41] The relative thickness of a fabric, familiar to readers today as "thread count," was a factor in fabric quality that depended not on what kind of loom was used or where but on the weaver's use of time and materials: that is, the thickness of the threads themselves (how they were spun and how much fiber was used in spinning the threads), how many were set in the warp (how much finished thread was used up), and how long it would take to weave (how much of the weaver's valuable time). These questions were normally negotiated between an attentive and knowledgeable owner and the serf weaver. In the same way, the "thickness" of the thing, as in the multiple meanings attached to a material object, depends on details of process, skill, and tools that are not directly preserved in archives but can still be recreated with sufficient attention to detail.

## Notes

The author thanks the participants of the conference on materiality at the University of Toronto, May 2019, for their input on an early draft of this chapter, and Abby Franquemont for her generous time in reading the manuscript for technical errors. The author promises reparations for any remaining errors.

1. *Voenno-statisticheskoe opisanie Rossiiskoi imperii*, vol. 6, pt 2. Vladimirskaia guberniia (St. Petersburg, 1852), 220.
2. *Voenno-statisticheskoe opisanie*, 6:2, 210, 212, 218.
3. Ken Alder, "Making Things the Same: Representation, Tolerance and the End of the Ancien Regime in France," *Social Studies of Science* 28:4 (1998), 400–545; Ken Alder, Introduction," *ISIS* 98:1 (2007), 80–3.
4. The plant and animal fibers textiles are made of leave little direct evidence, and the simplicity of most preindustrial textile tools makes them easily confused with other objects.
5. An entry point to the recent explosion of interest in cotton, capitalism, and labor is Sven Beckert, *Empire of Cotton: A Global History* (New York: Knopf, 2014); Giorgio Riello, *Cotton: The Fabric That Made the Modern World* (Cambridge: Cambridge University Press, 2013); Giorgio Riello and Prasannan Parthasarathi, eds., *The Spinning World: A Global History of Cotton Textiles, 1200–1850* (Oxford: Oxford University Press, 2009); and on the cotton industry in Russia see Dave Pretty, "The Cotton Textile Industry in Russia and the Soviet Union," in *The Ashgate Companion to the History of Textile Workers, 1650–2000* (Farnham: Ashgate, 2010), 421–48.

6. On the false dichotomy of craft versus science, see Pamela Smith, Amy R. W. Meyers, and Harold J. Cook, eds., *Ways of Making and Knowing: The Material Culture of Empirical Knowledge* (Ann Arbor: University of Michigan Press, 2014), introduction.
7. See Katherine Pickering Antonova, *An Ordinary Marriage: The World of a Gentry Family in Imperial* Russia (Oxford: Oxford University Press, 2013), on Natalia Chikhacheva's role as estate manager and the broader context of the Chikhachev family.
8. *Gosudarstvennyi istorichskii arkhiv Ivanovskoi oblasti* (GAIO), *Fond* 107, *opis'* 1, *delo* 67, *list* 53. Hereafter "CH" refers to this Chikhachev *fond*, followed only by *delo* and *list* numbers.
9. Yarn and cloth were both "given out for dyeing." CH 63, l.3. Many of the Chikhachev serfs living on their nonresidential properties seemingly divided their time between working for merchant workshops and working for the Chikhachevs, producing fleeces, flax, yarn, or cloth, or performing labor like building or dyeing, as quitrent payments. On dyeing see Alica Weisberg-Roberts, "Between Trade and Science: Dyeing and Knowing the Long Eighteenth Century," in Smith et al., *Ways of Making and Knowing*.
10. For more detail on the estate's needlecraft, see Katherine Pickering Antonova, "'Prayed to God, Knitted a Stocking': Needlework on a Nineteenth-Century Russian Estate," *Experiment: A Journal of Russian Culture* 22 (2016), 1–12. The making of rough linen and sewing and distribution of peasant shirts on the Chikhachev estates is comparable to the large-scale manufacture and trade in rough so-called "negro cloth" in the American colonies for slave use, even while some individual slaves or particular estates made their own. Peggy Hart, *Wool: Unraveling an American Story of Artisans and Innovation* (Atglen, PA: Schiffer, 2017), 39–40.
11. Antonova, *An Ordinary Marriage*, 80.
12. Irena Turnau documented several such workshop communities through extraordinary research in the 1980s; see "Aspects of the Russian Artisan: The Knitter of the Seventeenth to the Eighteenth Century," *Textile History* 4:1 (1973), 10–11, and her many other contributions to that journal, as well as passing mentions in reference works of the period such as *Voenno-statisticheskoe opisanie*.
13. The copperplate printing of cotton and linen began in the seventeenth century. Later mechanization used larger rollers. On copperplate printing see Elena Phipps, *Looking at Textiles: A Guide to Technical Terms* (Los Angeles, CA: J. Paul Getty Museum, 2011), 23.
14. Hart, *Wool*, 58.
15. CH d. 63, l.118. Compare to Wallace Daniel, "Entrepreneurship and the Russian Textile Industry: From Peter the Great to Catherine the Great," *Russian Review* 54 (1995), 18.
16. Robert Smith, "Runners and Rituals in Early Russia," *Costume: Journal of the Costume Society* 38 (2004), 41–9.
17. I. V. Meshalin, *Tekstil'naia promyshlennost' krestian Moskovskoi gubernii v XVIII i pervoi polovine XIX veka* (Moscow: USSR Academy of Sciences, 1950), 42–55.
18. The fullest explanation of the differences between spindle and wheel spinning can be found in Abby Franquemont, *Respect the Spindle* (Loveland, CO: Interweave Press), 2009, 6–47, which derives not only from her expert practice but also the anthropological research on Andean spinning conducted by her parents: Edward and Christine Franquemont, "Learning to Weave in Chinchero," *Textile Museum Journal* (1987), 55–79. Edward Franquemont noted that "despite the availability of several spinning wheels in the town, people continue to prefer the handspindle methods."

"Andean Spinning," in *Handspindle Treasury: Spinning around the World*, compiled by Amy Clarke Moore and Liz Good (Loveland, CO: Interweave Press, 2000, 2011), 14. Contrast this to influential historian Lynn White's assumption that "we may be sure that the people making and selling textiles recognized at once—although none seems to have recorded his views—that the new instrument [wheel], by speeding yarn production, considerably reduced the labor component of the final cost of plain cloth." Lynn White Jr., "Technology Assessment from the Stance of a Medieval Historian," *American Historical Review* 79:1 (February 1974), 12. The differences he was seeing were actually due to the organization of spinning labor into male-run guilds, not a technological advantage.

19. Chikhacheva did mention knitting while she walked the fields to oversee the men's labor. Antonova, *Ordinary Marriage*, 80.
20. CH d. 63, l.110. She may have turned to Mishka for his access to a wider loom, but since her own Dorozhaevo weavers worked in an outbuilding, it's likely their looms were already wider than ordinary. Instead, Mishka was probably skilled in a decorative weave pattern, like damask. The false assumption that *izba* looms must only have been able to produce "rough" fabrics is so persistent that many local Russian museums today place what looks like a pile of fabric scraps on their display loom. It is obvious which museums enjoy the intervention of a skilled weaver, as they display the appropriately breathtakingly complex and beautiful fabrics that actually were made on such looms for centuries.
21. CH d. 63, l. 116ob and d. 67, ll. 7, 15ob.
22. On the Chikhachevs' social landscape, see Antonova, *An Ordinary Marriage*, chapters 2, 5, and 8 (note especially p. 169, where the Chikhachev family visited a cotton mill "run by steam engine"), and on the peculiar social composition of Ivanovo, see Alison K. Smith, "A Microhistory of the Global Empire of Cotton: Ivanovo, the 'Russian Manchester,'" *Past & Present* 244:1 (2019), 163–93, and on Russia's estate structure being less rigid than believed, see her *For the Common Good and Their Own Well Being: Social Estates in Imperial Russia* (New York: Oxford University Press, 2018).
23. Smith, "Microhistory of the Global Empire of Cotton."
24. Antonova, *Ordinary Marriage*, ch. 4, esp. p. 80. Tracy Dennison emphasizes the "inherently antagonistic" relationship within a system of production built around serfdom, in which lords and managers could manipulate circumstances that not only harmed individual serfs but also the productivity of the enterprise. Tracy Dennison and Sheilagh Ogilvie, "Does the European Marriage Pattern Explain Economic Growth?" *Journal of Economic History* 74:3 (2014), 651–93. This is certainly the case and would have been true to some degree even on smaller estates owned by middling-income nobles like the Chikhachevs, but the difference in intimacy of relations and negotiations—for better or worse depending on the character of individual owners—would have been significant, also.
25. Proto-industrialization was first defined by Franklin F. Mendels, in "Proto-Industrialization: The First Phase of the Industrialization Process," *Journal of Economic History* 31 (1972), 269–71, based on his 1969 dissertation.
26. The most relevant source is the tip of the iceberg of recent studies on alternative modernities: Prasannan Parthasarathi, *Why Europe Grew Rich while Asia Did Not: Global Economic Divergence, 1600–1850* (Cambridge: Cambridge University Press, 2011).

27. An entry point in this immense literature is Sheilagh Ogilvie and Markus Cerman, *European Proto-Industrialization: An Introductory Handbook* (Cambridge: Cambridge University Press, 1996). A starting point on the literature about gendered textile labor is Hunter and Macnaughton, "Gender and the Global Textile Industry" in *The Ashgate Companion to the History of Textile Workers, 1650–2000*, ed. Lex Heerma van Voss et al. (Farnham: Ashgate, 2010).
28. Meshalin, *Tekstil'naia promyshlennost' krestian Moskovskoi*, 55, 118.
29. See especially William L. Blackwell, *The Beginnings of Russian Industrialization, 1800–1860* (Princeton, NJ: Princeton University Press, 1968); Klaus Gestwa, *Proto-Industrialisierung in Russland: Wirtschaft, Herrschaft und Kultur in Ivanovo und Pavlovo, 1741–1932* (Göttingen: Vandenhoeck & Ruprecht, 1999).
30. Daniel, "Entrepreneurship and the Russian Textile Industry," 4.
31. The availability of cheap serf labor was especially important to linen production because flax requires several time-consuming steps to even prepare it for spinning (see Figure 5.1).
32. Daniel, "Entrepreneurship and the Russian Textile Industry," 21. Alison Smith in "A Microhistory of the Global Empire of Cotton" points out that Ivanovo's cotton industry, "with its demands for mechanized factories on the one hand and wide trade networks on the other, made apparent the limits of the kinds of economic development possible under serfdom." Her microhistorical study of Ivanovo's early cotton industry highlights distinctions between the cotton industry and the linen and wool industries that were still operating through specialized handwork in the surrounding area and that tended to be very compatible with serfdom, and the chronological break that Emancipation brought by disrupting those handwork alternatives, leaving much of that work to either be absorbed into factories (linen) or reduced to a much more peripheral domestic activity (wool spinning and weaving) for those unable or unwilling to buy the relatively cheap imported woven cloth that flooded global markets with full textile mechanization by the close of the nineteenth century. Knitting, lacemaking, and embroidery continued to be produced and traded via "domestic industry" well into the twentieth century. See Turnau, "Aspects of the Russian Artisan"; Sof'ia Davydova, "Russian Lace and Laceworkers: A Historical, Technical, and Statistical Investigation," *Experiment: A Journal of Russian Culture* 22 (2016), 161–72; Vladimir Stasov, "Russian Folk Ornamentation: Embroidery, Weaving and Lace," *Experiment: A Journal of Russian Culture* 22 (2016), 178–98.
33. On the uses of "terroir" see, for example, Richard Bundel and Angela Tregear, "From Artisans to 'Factories': The Interpenetration of Craft and Industry in English Cheese-Making, 1650–1950," *Enterprise & Society* 7:4 (December 5, 2006), 705–39; Michael DeSoucey, "Gastronationalism: Food Traditions and Authenticity Politics in the European Union," *American Sociological Review* 75:3 (2010), 432–55; Tamara L. Whited, "Terroir Transformed: Cheese and Pastoralism in the Western French Pyrenees," *Environmental History* 23:4 (October 1, 2018), 824–46.
34. Rebecca Burgess and Courtney White, *Fibershed: Growing a Movement of Farmers, Fashion Activists, and Makers for a New Textile Economy* (White River Junction, VT: Chelsea Green, 2019), introduction. It is merely a happy coincidence that the word "shed" is also the word for the space made in a loom for the weft to pass through the threads of the warp, creating fabric.
35. The *opol'e* region in the western part of the province, described in Susan Smith-Peter, *Imagining Russian Regions: Subnational Identity and Civil Society in Nineteenth-Century Russia* (Leiden: Brill, 2018), 27. Smith-Peter offers deep context on the

regions of Vladimir province as part of her larger discussion of "subnational identity" across the Russian Empire.

36. Flax was equally useful for its oil. On the long-standing reliance on flax as a local source of fiber for textiles in Eastern Europe as well as the technology and methods of flax processing, see Pippa Cruickshank, "Flax in Croatia: Traditional Production Methods, the Use and Care of Linen in Folk Costumes and Implications for Museum Conservation," *Textile History* 42:2 (2011), 239–60. On the wider uses of flax and the cloth made from it, linen, see Joshua MacFadyen, *Flax Americana: A History of the Fibre and Oil That Covered a Continent* (Montreal: McGill-Queen's University Press, 2018); Christian and Johannes Zinzendorf, *The Big Book of Flax* (Atglen, PA: Schiffer, 2011); Linda Heinrich, *Linen: From Flax Seed to Woven Cloth* (Atglen, PA: Schiffer, 2010). Hemp grows more easily than flax and produces a similar fiber. It was more widely grown in nineteenth-century Russia, but mainly for personal use; linen fabric was more marketable. Hemp requires more work with a smaller yield, so it was usually processed with a mix of premium long and lower-quality shorter fibers together that result in fabric considered adequate only for peasant use. For technical detail comparing every step of the process, see Stephanie Gaustad, *The Practical Spinner's Guide: Cotton, Flax, Hemp* (Loveland, CO: Interweave Press, 2014).

37. In the nineteenth century the softest merino wool had to be imported from Spain. British wools offered a range of useful textile fibers but dominated in the global marketplace primarily because of their development of means for finishing high-quality wool cloths, such as broadcloth. Hart, *Wool*. Russian sheep raising seemingly did not consider breeding for wool characteristics to be a priority. However, the Orenburg region was home to cashmere goats whose down was used in luxurious shawls for export from the eighteenth century to the present. Galina Khmeleva and Carol R. Noble, *Gossamer Webs: The History and Techniques of Orenburg Lace Shawls* (Loveland, CO: Interweave Press, 1998), 11–12.

38. See Turnau, "Aspects of the Russian Artisan."

39. Turnau, "Aspects of the Russian Artisan"; Meshalin, *Tekstil'naia promyshlennost' krestian*.

40. Which machines worked successfully with which fibers, for what uses, and when such machines went into use in a given country in a complicated subject. See Hart, *Wool*, 58–60; Gillian Cookson, *The Age of Machinery: Engineering the Industrial Revolution, 1170–1850* (Woodbridge: Boydell Press, 2018), introduction; Gail Fowler Mohanty, *Labor and Laborers of the Loom: Mechanization and Handloom Weavers, 1780–1840* (New York: Routledge, 2006), Ch. 9.

41. CH d. 54, l. 23ob.

# 6

# Sugar as a "Basic Necessity": State Efforts to Supply the Russian Empire's Population in the Early Twentieth Century

Charles Steinwedel

Sugar and sweets are everywhere in contemporary Russia, just as they are in the United States and other European countries. Whether it takes the form of chocolate for a pick-me-up, sugar to spoon into tea, or cake and sweet champagne to celebrate, sugar is a staple. Even during the difficult economic times of the 1990s, Russians boasted of their high-quality chocolate and ice cream. At that time, a visitor from the United States with a sweet tooth (such as the author) faced an embarrassment of riches. One could enjoy a new favorite, such as homemade pastry rolls (*pliushki*). Stores offered both local cakes and spice cookies, such as *prianiki*. If one sought a taste of home, kiosks offering Snickers bars were on nearly every corner. As Russia has recovered from the economic crisis of the 1990s, sugar consumption has increased.[1]

A typical consumer might not realize that this bountiful presence of sugar in Russia was—like the now-ubiquitous matryoshka—only a century old. Russia's sugar consumption accelerated in the decade before 1917 due, in large part, to a shift in government policies toward the promotion of sugar consumption that emerged from debates in the State Duma and among Russian officials. These debates established that the Russian elites considered providing greater access to sugar as a government priority. How to achieve this remained unclear.

Russia had produced sugar from beets since 1799, shortly after Prussian Franz Carl Achard perfected a process for using beets to produce sugar that was chemically identical to sugar from sugarcane.[2] Only in the late nineteenth century, however, did the Russian Empire's sugar production surge. Between 1892 and 1911, it grew 421 percent—the fastest in Europe.[3] By 1914, Russia became one of the world's largest sugar producers, reaching fourth or fifth place depending on how one counts US colonial possessions. Russia's increase in sugar production was part of a continental European phenomenon. Led by Germany and Austria-Hungary, European beet sugar production overtook that of tropical cane sugar that has received much more attention.[4]

Yet sugar consumption in the Russian Empire did not keep up with production. Consumption a little more than doubled between 1892 and 1911, from 8.3 pounds per person to 17.6 pounds per person.[5] This represented a substantial increase, to be sure, but per-capita consumption remained low by European standards.[6] In 1909, the tsar's subjects consumed only about 14.5 pounds per capita, far below English consumption of 84.3 pounds, Germany's 39.7 pounds, France's 36.1 pounds, and Austria-Hungary's 26 pounds per capita.[7] Consumers abroad largely enjoyed the increased production from Russia's sugar factories.

This essay addresses how sugar consumption became a subject of political discussion in the Russian Empire during the same decades that writers such as Thorstein Veblen drew attention to consumption in Europe and the United States. In the early twentieth century the disconnect between Russia's increasing sugar production and relatively low sugar consumption became controversial. In 1908, deputies to the State Duma began to attack existing sugar regulations, called *normirovka*, or "norming," and began to discuss sugar as an "item of first necessity" (*predmetom pervoi neobkhodimosti*), what I have rendered as "a basic necessity." How to encourage sugar consumption by keeping consumer prices low while cultivating a prosperous sugar industry and still providing the state treasury with sugar excise and tariff revenue became a vital question. State officials initially resisted defining sugar as a basic necessity, likely because collaborating to raise the price of a "basic necessity" was a crime under imperial law. But they agreed on the need to lower sugar prices and increase consumption.[8] The perception that a productive, economically developed, and healthy society required sugar to provide fuel for the empire's workers and peasants became widespread. Sugar producers' economic interests and state officials' desire for revenue prevented any dramatic reform of sugar regulations. Nonetheless, in the period 1908–10, Minister of Finance Vladimir N. Kokovtsov and ministry officials oversaw a shift in policy emphasis from the satisfaction of the energetically expressed needs of producers and the treasury toward satisfying consumers' desires for greater access to sugar at lower prices.

## The Development of "*Normirovka*"—State "Norming" of the Sugar Market

The shift in imperial officials' efforts to increase sugar consumption after 1905 was the culmination of a longer history of state regulation of sugar. In Russia and elsewhere, sugar prices were notoriously unstable.[9] Weather and large capital requirements lay at the root of sugar market volatility. Harvest size and sugar content in beets varied with the weather from year to year. Poor harvests resulted in high prices for beets, which, in turn, made sugar quite expensive for ordinary people. At the same time, high prices meant high profits that drew entrepreneurs and investment into growing and processing beets. If weather patterns shifted in subsequent years, bumper crops could drive prices down dramatically. In such cases, prices no longer sustained investments in equipment to harvest, transport, and refine sugar. Then producers complained of the imminent demise of the industry. Imports made this situation even more fraught: imported sugar could flood the market and put local producers out of business.

For these reasons, states have intervened heavily in sugar production and marketing. With the notable exception of Great Britain, import duties were widespread in

Europe. Many countries that had import duties did not levy an excise tax on domestic production. The Russian Empire featured both. Russia enacted a tariff in gold on sugar in 1877, then added another 10 percent to that in 1881. These virtually eliminated foreign imports of sugar. When in 1881 Russia applied an excise tax by weight along with import duties, the difference between the import duties and domestic excise was so great economist Isaak Levin wrote in 1908 that protectionism "nowhere, it seems, reached such a level as ours in Russia."[10] Tariffs and excise taxes did not prevent instability in the sugar market, however. In the early 1880s, poor harvests drove up prices of sugar several rubles to 7 r 50 k per *pud* (set at 16.38 kg or 36.11 lbs. in 1899). Between 1881 and 1884, high prices led Russian producers to nearly double production. Prices then collapsed, reaching as low as 3 r per *pud* in 1884. Panicked producers pleaded for help from state officials, who temporarily instituted a premium for sugar exports to Asia, essentially paying producers to export.[11] Sugar producers again raised the idea of stabilizing prices through the institution of norms for each factory's production. In 1886, Minister of Finance Nikolai Bunge wrote to the Kiev Market Committee, the most important Russian sugar market, that such limits on production would have to be implemented privately. Since the new harvest promised to be another excellent one, in 1887 sugar producers gathered in Kiev and established limits on sugar production for each factory. This was the first private, voluntary sugar cartel in Europe.[12] Production over a set limit would have to be exported or be subject to a 2 r 50 k fine. By 1893–4, 206 of 226 factories participated. This provided an incentive to export sugar from the empire. Although the private cartel kept prices from going too low through overproduction, it failed to stabilize the market since no mechanism controlled prices when poor harvests caused prices to climb.

In 1892 a poor harvest, exhausted reserves, and speculation pushed sugar prices from their normal range of from 3 r 90 k to 5 r to as high as 5 r 70 k. In response, state officials imported sugar and sold it for 5 r 10 k along railway stations in the southwest. Sugar producers continued to pressure state officials to undertake official, state-administered production norming, which they argued would be more effective at controlling prices. All producers would have to take part.

When in 1895 the London sugar price fell, Russian sugar producers faced a decline in export prices and downward pressure on domestic prices as well. A special commission recognized a state-enforced *normirovka* as desirable and introduced such a policy by the end of 1895. According to this policy, the Ministry of Finance set a production target for sugar on the domestic market each year, established a quota of 60,000 *pudy* that each factory could produce and market, and created a reserve supply of sugar. If a factory produced more than the factory's quota, it could either keep the sugar in reserve or pay an additional tax on it of 1 r 75 k.[13] If the price of sugar rose, the state could order sales from reserves to combat inflation. If a producer sold sugar abroad, neither the excise tax nor the additional tax was applied to the sugar.

The state *normirovka* succeeded in stabilizing prices at a relatively high level and spurred the growth of the industry. The sugar industry in the empire's southwest—now in Ukraine—became a model for how a mix of entrepreneurial energy, technological expertise, and state sponsorship could catalyze economic growth. In essence, producers were guaranteed a high price on the domestic market: the price limit was typically set at 4 r 50 k to 5 r at a time when the price of sugar in London was about half that. Producers could not speculate as easily on higher prices but could sell from their reserves while paying the normal excise but no additional tax. They could still dump sugar on the world market without paying any excise tax at all. Beyond high prices and protection from imports, sugar producers benefited from state-sponsored railroad construction, low freight prices, and funding through the State Bank's branch in Kiev.[14] Four ministers of finance associated with Russian industrialization in the late nineteenth century—Alexander A. Abaza, Nikolai Kh. Bunge, Ivan A. Vyshnegradskii, and Sergei Iu. Witte—had connections to the sugar industry and the southwest.[15] The state benefited from the sugar trade as well. By the early twentieth century, the excise tax on sugar was the second most lucrative in the empire after that on vodka.[16] By 1914, sugar accounted for 21 percent of all excise tax revenue generated in the empire.[17]

These policies had a very different effect on the Russian Empire's sugar consumers. *Normirovka*'s high domestic prices put sugar out of the reach of most of Russia's rural population and of working people in the cities as well. The relatively high prices for domestic sugar compared to the prices at which Russian producers could sell on the London market, along with the wealth generated by the sugar trade, did not escape the notice of the empire's press. Journalists and editorials routinely criticized state policy for producing high prices and wealthy sugar industrialists. Observers abroad—who had their own interests to be sure—also interpreted Russian policy as a means to support the sugar industry. The 1902 Brussels Sugar Convention found that Russia's sugar regulations represented unfair support for sugar production and kept Russia out of the London sugar market from September 1903 to September 1908.[18] This reduced Russian sugar producers' profits and increased their stocks of sugar.

## The Sugar Question in the Third Duma

Deputies in the Third State Duma (1907–12) initiated a broad discussion of sugar policy that, over the next two years, elevated consumer interests in greater access to sugar because it was considered essential to ordinary Russians' health. The discussion began in May 1908 as part of the Duma Budget Commission's annual review of the budget for the government department that supervised the collection of sugar and alcohol taxes.[19] Rather than sticking to budget numbers and tax estimates, deputies on the Budget Commission sought to completely review the regulation of sugar in the empire. Two commission members who were also doctors were particularly outspoken on the subject. Andrei I. Shingarev stated that sugar was "undoubtedly a basic product of consumption (*osnovnym produktom potrebleniia*)." Mikhail Ia. Kapustin argued that ninety-three million rubles collected in taxes on sugar were essential to the state budget, but sugar prices should be reduced in some manner.[20] Budget Commission chairman Mikhail M. Alekseyenko and Minister of Finance Kokovtsov rejected these assertions. Alekseyenko argued that sugar was "of course, not a basic necessity," and that the sugar excise and exports generated essential revenue for the treasury. Kokovtsov argued that a fundamental review of the sugar *normirovka* exceeded the responsibility of the commission and ought to be addressed with the "greatest caution."[21]

The Budget Commisson's final report, issued on May 2, 1908, reflected Shingarev's and Kapustin's belief that sugar was a necessity and that regulations needed to change in order to lower sugar prices. Budget Commission members accepted the projection for sugar revenues of 93.2 million rubles but maintained that "since sugar constitutes a nourishing product for the population, then all measures must be taken toward making it less expensive."[22] The existing *normirovka* was directed "toward the protection of the interests of large factory owners, and not of consumers." For this reason, the government's policy direction in this branch of industry required a "fundamental review." Budget Commission members concluded that sugar prices could be reduced by reducing the excise tax on sugar, eliminating *normirovka*'s regulation of Russia's domestic market and reducing tariffs that protected domestic producers from foreign competition.[23] The Duma Budget Commission, in essence, endorsed a much freer market in sugar to reduce prices and to improve supplies for the empire's population.

In May 1908, discussion of sugar regulations moved from the Duma Budget Commission to the Duma itself. Evgenii M. Sheideman, vice chair of the Agricultural Committee, focused more on the health of the industry. Overproduction and the loss of markets due to the Brussels Sugar Convention of 1902 had put the sugar industry in crisis.[24] He proposed a solution similar to that of Budget Commission deputies. Sheideman proposed reducing the excise tax on sugar from 1 r 75 k to 75 k. Such a move would reduce excise tax revenue, but he predicted that much lost revenue would be regained through increased consumption and would be good for the industry. Moreover, reduced taxes would "create the opportunity for the poor population to consume this necessary product, that is to say, a product without which our poor peasant and working population cannot live."[25] Another deputy spoke against indirect taxes more generally, stating, "Matches, kerosene, tea, and sugar—these are necessary materials of popular consumption, without which a person cannot live."[26] A resolution requiring "the development of measures directed toward lowering the price of sugar" passed easily.[27]

The Ministry of Finance responded relatively quickly to this resolution. Vice Minister of Finance Senator Iosif I. Novitskii chaired a "Conference on the Development of Measures Directed toward Lowering the Price of Sugar," only five months later, in October 1908. The Ministry of Finance brought together officials, sugar producers and traders, and scholars to examine how the industry operated. The conference was a substantial affair, meeting over three days. The stenogram listed twenty-seven participants. Representatives of St. Petersburg officialdom from the Ministry of Finance predominated. Three professors at St. Petersburg technological schools were present, nearly equaling representation from the Board of the All-Russian Society of Sugar Industrialists, including its chairman Andrei A. Bobrinskii and three of its members. Five men from the St. Petersburg Fruit, Tea, and Wine Exchange attended.[28] Notably, neither State Duma deputies who had raised the issue nor consumers were represented. Novitskii framed the conference as an internal administrative and fact-finding exercise. Novitskii had invited two Duma deputies as observers who could neither address the conference nor vote, which prompted them to decline to participate.[29] Only participants from the St. Petersburg Fruit, Tea, and Wine Exchange would represent consumers' interests. They sold sugar to producers of chocolate, candy, and preserves that consumers ate.

Chair Novitskii actively directed the Special Conference's discussions. His introductory remarks on sugar's place in the Russian Empire stressed the industry's close ties to agriculture and how it had become a factor of "no small importance in the national economy." Over twenty years the amount of land under beet cultivation had doubled, the number of factories increased by about 25 percent, and sugar production had tripled. Russia contended with Austria-Hungary to be the second largest European sugar producer after Germany. If the Russian Empire's sugar industry occupied such a "brilliant position" with respect to production, it occupied only twelfth place in consumption per person. In Novitskii's words, Russian consumption was "not at the level that would be desirable, taking into account the physiological significance of sugar." The fact that "economists recognize that per capita consumption of sugar is, to a certain degree, an indicator of the culture of a country and of its economic prosperity" increased his sense of disappointment. It was extremely important to illuminate what was limiting sugar consumption and what could be done to expand it.[30]

In Russia itself, Novitskii stated, a "rich and passionate literature" existed for and against the empire's sugar regulations. Those in favor of *normirovka* argued that it strengthened the sugar industry, reduced price volatility, and delivered inexpensive sugar to the consumer. Those opposed to *normirovka* argued that it allowed the industry to maintain a high domestic price for sugar that weighed on the consumer and reduced consumption. Indeed, Novitskii stated it was fair for consumers to question why, even without excise taxes, sugar had a wholesale price of 2 r 25 k within Russia, while consumers of Russian sugar in England paid only 1 r 80 k Russian consumers felt they were paying the price for cheap sugar sold abroad, and that *normirovka* was responsible for this state of affairs. The primary purpose of the conference, then, was to examine the relationship between sugar regulations and sugar prices. Novitskii seemed most interested in identifying the production price of a *pud* of sugar so that the state could specify a price that would allow producers to make a profit but sell sugar to consumers for less than the then-current price of about 4 rubles.[31]

When Novitskii directed discussion toward the cost of sugar production, Andrei A. Bobrinskii, chairman of the Board of the All-Russian Sugar Industrialists, provided an estimate of 1 r 70 k to 2 r per *pud*. Novitskii pointed out that this information reflected the cost of production at only twenty-one factories and for only 1906/7. Novitskii seemed skeptical of the desire of sugar producers "to take on the characteristics of major capitalistic enterprises." He seemed very interested in the size of and costs associated with joint-stock companies, which spent, he thought, large sums on administration, paid more for their sugar beets, and incurred expenses raising capital. Novitskii concluded that bigger factories were supposed to produce sugar more cheaply, but, in fact, increased costs of production. Novitskii questioned the power of banks over large enterprises. Nikolai V. Monakhov from the Board of the All-Russian Sugar Industrialists replied that sugar industrialists paid high interest rates, 10 percent, but typically for commercial paper (*veksel'noi*) operations rather than bank loans. Novitskii asserted that it was easier for joint-stock companies than individual proprietors or partnerships to get bank credit. Moreover, he thought that finance also explained why the sugar industry developed in the empire's southwest. It had to do with the "Jewish question." Joint-stock companies were good for resolving the "difficulties in property rights" that Jews faced.[32] In sum, Novitskii seemed to view the participation of joint-stock companies in sugar production somewhat skeptically. He favored smaller factories run by landowners who grew beets nearby.

When the conference turned to discussion of *normirovka*, Novitskii found himself refereeing a clash between representatives of the St. Petersburg Fruit, Tea, and Wine Exchange and sugar industrialists present. A representative of the former, Mikhail N. Miller, argued that any effort to lower prices that left in place *normirovka* was only a palliative that would not address the fundamental cause of high prices.[33] Sugar industrialists stressed the need for state regulation to counteract sugar production's dependence on weather conditions. Moreover, Russian sugar factories differed from their European counterparts. They were not individual buildings but entire settlements. The factory owner had to build storage for sugar, a workshop, housing for the factory director and employees, a school, a barracks for workers, and a hospital. These drove up production costs. Without the stability provided by *normirovka*, the industry would not have grown as it had.[34] Vasilii V. Prilezhaev from the Department of Trade offered an alternative cultural and developmental explanation for low sugar consumption. It resulted "not from high prices" but from "the insufficient culturedness and solvency of our purchasers, and likewise from the insufficient organization of our trade."[35] Such a noneconomic perspective made sugar prices essentially irrelevant to consumption.

Novitskii's summary of three days of discussion reflected these differences of opinion. Those in favor of *normirovka* argued that the policy made possible the growth of the empire's sugar production over the past two decades. He thought it fostered growth and protected the industry, including smaller factories that preserved the agricultural basis of the industry. Proponents of *normirovka* argued that the policy accompanied a long-term decline in prices from 5 r 35 k to 3 r 90 k on the Kiev market. Russian beet cultivation had improved to the point that the amount of sugar produced from a given quantity of beets equaled levels in Europe. True, it took more land to grow beets in Russia, but proponents of *normirovka* pointed to climatic factors, the quality of the soil, and the "general level of culture of the country" to explain this.[36] Sugar exports benefited Russia's trade balance and provided jobs for the empire's agricultural workers. *Normirovka* ensured a steady supply of sugar within Russia, as excess production was held in reserve against the following year's possible shortfall. Consistent prices reduced the vulnerability of the sugar market to speculation and prevented boom and bust cycles that left producers in difficult straits.[37]

Novitskii then took up the arguments of *normirovka* opponents. They countered that, since the policy maintained high prices, it ran counter to technical innovation. They argued that *normirovka* maintained higher prices than foreign consumers paid and believed, most of all, that the policy defended the interests of producers, not consumers. The policy reduced incentives to innovate, preserving weak factories with the guarantee of high prices. Eliminating *normirovka* would subject factories to competition. *Normirovka* made possible syndicates of producers that maintained high prices. Sugar exports were a good thing but need not require sacrifices from consumers.[38]

Novitskii seemed to find arguments in favor of *normirovka* more convincing than those of its opponents but was not ready to dismiss either side of the issue. So, he turned attention to the production price of sugar. He and other officials seemed to fixate on the idea that a precise understanding of production costs could enable the government to regulate the price of sugar so as to make possible lower prices without fundamental change in sugar regulations. When discussion turned to a deeper consideration of prices, however, representatives from the sugar industry asserted that they had not had time to gather the data required to examine prices thoroughly. In-depth discussion was put off until Novitskii could convene another special conference to investigate sugar prices more thoroughly.

Novitskii convened just such an expanded special conference two months later in December 1908. Eighty-one experts initially joined Chair Novitskii to discuss the sugar industry and its regulation. Those institutions represented in October returned with more representatives, but now were joined by two State Duma deputies and representatives from essentially every industry and state institution that had a conceivable interest in sugar production. Notably, consumer organizations as such still were not present. The exchange committees again were expected to represent consumers' interests.[39] The size of the meeting demonstrated the seriousness with which state officials regarded the need to supply sugar.

All present accepted that sugar needed to be made available to as much of the population as possible through the reduction in prices. Mikhail V. Krasovskii, a member of the State Council and of the All-Russian Society of Sugar Producers, argued, "The question of the accessibility of sugar for the broad mass of the Russian population is one of the most important questions of our contemporary condition and must concern the government and society alike." A lack of nutrition threatened "the Russian people with gradual degeneration." Since the development of grain production would take many years, "the introduction of sugar to the people's daily diet, although in modest quantities, is recognized as one of the best means to support [the people's nutrition]. Sugar is a particularly essential means for the support of the health and development of children to the age of five."[40] Indeed, the military had included sugar in soldiers' rations the previous year.[41]

Conference participants, however, differed as to how lower prices and greater accessibility could be brought about and the consequences of doing so. The largest contingent at the December Conference—the sugar producers—argued that consumers benefited from *normirovka*. They made the same arguments they had in October, but now in greater numbers, with more data at hand, and with greater passion. Sugar producers were so quick to argue that change in *normirovka* would destroy the sugar industry that at the end of the first day, Novitskii took time to remind everyone that no one wanted the sugar industry's destruction. Rather, the question before the Special Conference was how to ensure the industry's healthy development "without forgetting the interests of the consumer of sugar."[42] Sugar industrialists argued that, absent state-organized limits on production, private agreements would take their place and likely be less advantageous to consumers. Representatives closer to agricultural interests stressed the important role small sugar factories played in local agricultural economies, too. A reduction in prices would result in factory closures and job losses. In sum, sugar industrialists argued that *normirovka* kept prices low, while the professors and representatives from the Fruit, Tea, and Wine Exchange thought *normirovka* kept market prices high.[43]

Two professors, Mikhail D. Zuev from Khar′kov and Kazimir I. Smolenskii from St. Petersburg, prepared written estimates of the cost of production of a *pud* of granulated sugar in the empire, and Graf Andrei Bobrinskii offered one as he had promised in October.[44] The three estimates differed substantially: Zuev's was lowest at 1 r 61 k, Smolenskii's was 1 r 85.74 k, and Bobrinskii's was highest at 1 r 93.55 k—20.2 percent higher than Zuev's. Much of the Special Conference was spent interrogating Zuev's low estimate. Sugar industrialists and their representatives attacked Zuev's every assumption, while representatives of the Fruit, Tea, and Wine Exchange again provided the most vigorous defense of Zuev's work and the strongest critique of *normirovka*. Vice chair of the Exchange Miller stated that Zuev's analysis was a "true ray of light in the sugar kingdom." The purpose of the conference, he asserted, was not to destroy the sugar industry but to regard sugar consumers' and traders' interests equally with those of sugar factory owners. Hitherto, sugar industrialists had become used to "identifying their interests with the interests of the population of the Russian Empire" and "everything had taken place between closed doors." Now they must abide by the "same rules that other branches of industry did, and not have any special privileges."[45] Some representatives of exchange committees from outside sugar-producing areas also criticized the industry. The chair of the Rostov-on-Don exchange, Efim S. Gol′din, argued that consumers had little ability to pay high prices for sugar. The price of sugar had to be lowered, and better today than tomorrow, for the good of all concerned.[46]

Miller and Gol′din were likely disappointed with the limited nature of the conversation, which only occasionally addressed large issues. Much of the discussion so addressed fairly specific elements of sugar production costs that the stenogram often reads as if the Ministry of Finance had convoked all institutions of government relevant to the industry in order to analyze its accounting standards. Sugar producers attacked their critics' assumptions at such great length that it seemed impossible to define a particular cost price for the entire empire. As Novitskii observed toward the end of the third day, differences of opinion between scholars and industry were such that little progress had been made. Some argued that many sugar factories were on the verge of collapse, while others that the industry was in a relatively prosperous position.[47] On day four, Miller expressed his frustration that so much time had been spent arguing over sugar industry costs and that a "mass of questions" lay before the Special Conference. He suggested that the conference accept cost estimates offered by the sugar producers so it could move on.[48] Chair Novitskii accepted the sugar producers' cost of production and reasonable profit as 2 r 18 k.[49] Indeed, one can question the decision to fixate on sugar production costs. As Bobrinskii's estimate indicated, the excise tax of 1 r 75 k was more than five times greater than the 32.55 k difference between the highest and lowest production cost estimates. Even a modest reduction in excise tax could have reduced the price of sugar as much as price adjustments based on the production cost. Over the nine days the conference met, interest dwindled. By day nine, only forty or so people were present and voting out of the more than eighty listed initially as participants.[50]

The consistent and vocal presence of sugar industrialists meant the conference would not endorse immediate and fundamental changes in laws regulating sugar.

Although sugar industrialists succeeded in forestalling fundamental reform in *normirovka* at the special conferences in 1908, thereafter the Ministry of Finance and the State Duma sought again to increase sugar supplies on the domestic market. Whereas previous ministers of finance had fostered the sugar industry as an engine of economic development and state revenue, in 1909, Minister of Finance Kokovtsov gradually shifted the thrust of state policy from protecting nearly exclusively the interests of sugar producers toward providing more sugar to consumers at lower cost. On March 9, 1910, Kokovtsov wrote to ministry officials regarding events that had driven sugar prices upward. A good wheat harvest had enabled more peasants to buy sugar. At the same time, a poor beet harvest and the elimination of the Vladivostok *porto franco* in the Far East increased prices for Russian sugar. Then, speculators withheld sugar from the market in anticipation of still-higher prices.[51] Novitskii cited "the special urgency of the matter at hand" when he asked that the State Council address the measure on March 23, 1910. A few weeks later, Kokovstov asked that the Duma take up sugar prices.[52] The ministry and the State Duma proposed legislation that would reduce the excise on sugar by 75 k, from 1 r 75 k to 1 r. Ministry of Finance officials could also prevent price spikes, if necessary, by (1) ceasing to return excise taxes to producers exporting sugar; (2) lowering the import duty on sugar; and (3) lowering import duties when prices exceeded established limits in major cities such as Odessa, Kiev, Warsaw, or Kharkov, rather than only in Moscow and St. Petersburg. The Duma and the ministry also recommended doubling the production quota for new and existing sugar factories to 280,000 *pudy*.[53] The legislation passed on March 31.

The State Council's discussion of the legislation in April 1910 seemed as though it might go the way it had in the special conferences. The State Council included several sugar industrialists, most notably Andrei A. Bobrinskii, all of whom vigorously attacked the Duma's proposals as having harsh consequences for the sugar industry. Sergei Witte, who presided over the creation and introduction of *normirovka*, also was present, so it seemed that the project faced formidable opposition. Minister of Finance Kokovtsov calmly defended the Duma project, saying he hardly recognized the current condition of the industry or the contours of the Duma's legislative proposal in the attacks of the legislation's opponents.[54] The basic goals of the government with respect to sugar—to prevent supply instability and price spikes—remained the same. The government needed to protect sugar consumption by setting and enforcing upper limits on prices for what Kokovtsov described as "a product recognized by many as a basic necessity."[55] If the government saw that the "Russian consumer" could not receive the sugar he or she needed, the government needed more weapons with which to limit sugar prices. The sugar industry had always been a "favorite child" of the government. The government needed to avoid being one-sided in defense of the industry. Regulations had not been created for the industry alone, but for the industry and for the Russian consumer. Kokovtsov asked, "Is it necessary to give the Russian consumer the opportunity to obtain that quantity of sugar that he cannot obtain right now, and for a price which is guaranteed by the government, or is it necessary to calmly look on while the law on *normirovka*, having served its purpose, in practice leads us to a dead end?"[56] Witte replied with a general defense of *normirovka*, arguing that protection of the sugar industry was common throughout Europe, and the Russian case was nothing extraordinary. He stated, "Probably sugar is a basic necessity" that should be protected from price increases.[57] The law was created with both the industry and consumer in mind, he claimed, and excusing his "openness," he said he had been thinking much more about the "pocket of the treasury than the pocket of the sugar industrialist" in developing *normirovka*. He saw defects in the legislation but thought it better that a law be passed than not.

In the end, the State Council approved the law, with some adjustments. Members of the State Council met with Duma deputies in a special commission to reconcile their legislation. Members of the State Council considered a 75 k decrease in excise tax too abrupt a blow to the treasury. Instead, excise on sugar would be reduced by 10 k each year for the next four. The norm for a single factory's production was reduced from 280,000 *pudy* to 240,000. The legislation became law on April 15, 1910. The sugar producers did not take long to react. In December 1910, officials in Kiev learned that sugar producers had taken steps to form a private syndicate with the goal of raising sugar prices.[58]

## Conclusion

Since only three sugar harvests were recorded after the 1910 legislation took effect and before the First World War broke out, the legislation's effectiveness is difficult to assess. Nonetheless, by the harvest of 1913, the amount of sugar on the domestic market increased by 12.1 percent and per-capita consumption was up by 8.4 percent.[59] Other evidence suggests that by the First World War, sugar had become a "basic necessity" and a product people considered an essential part of their diet.[60] In historian Iurii Kir'ianov's study of food riots during 1916–17, he identified sugar's absence or expense as playing an important role in nineteen of the thirty-seven events for which he could identify a cause of unrest.[61]

The extensive discussion of sugar policy in the period 1908–10 made clear that the empire's elite considered the sugar supply essential. The need to produce sugar was something on which all officials, industrialists, traders, and consumers could agree. The question was how to deliver more of this essential material to more of the empire's population. Much of the conversation on sugar supply was very dry and technical then and reads very much so now. In basic structure, the 1895 *normirovka* remained largely unchanged. The fact that it changed at all is significant, however. The sugar industry had been a fundamental part of the Russian Empire's economic dynamism of the last thirty years of the Romanov dynasty. Ministers of finance before Kokovtsov, and many others in the imperial elite as well, profited greatly from the sugar trade, and so did the empire as a whole. Sugar became a source of wealth and power. The relatively greater stress given to consumers' desire for sugar demonstrated its new importance as a material to which all should have access. In treating sugar as a basic necessity, Russian imperial officials were looking toward Europe. Access to sugar was an important feature of modern economies. By the 1920s and 1930s, awareness of the cost of such a feature in obesity, diabetes, and tooth decay would be more widespread. These concerns about sugar, so familiar to us, were present in Germany already by 1900, but completely absent from Russian discussions at the time.[62] For officials, sugar producers, and academic economists in 1910, sugar provided energy necessary for industrialization. The desire to increase consumption was one policy that connected Duma deputies, government officials, sugar producers, and consumers.

## Notes

1. Martin Todd et al., *Russian Federation Sugar Sector Review* (Rome: Food and Agriculture Organization of the United Nations, 2013), 8; *Food Outlook: Biannual Report of Global Food Markets* (Rome: FAO UN, 2019), 43.
2. Susan Smith-Peter, "Sweet Development: The Sugar Beet Industry, Agricultural Societies and Agrarian Transformations in the Russian Empire, 1818-1913," *Cahiers du monde Russe* 57:1 (2016), 105–6; I. Levin, *Nasha sakharnaia promyshlennost'* (St. Petersburg: Gramotnost', 1908), 5.
3. Truman G. Palmer, *Cost of Producing Sugar in the United States, Germany, Austria-Hungary, Russia, and Cuba* (Washington, DC: United States Beet Sugar Industry, 1913), 32.
4. Sydney Mintz's *Sweetness and Power: The Place of Sugar in Modern History* (New York: Penguin, 1985) was the seminal work on Caribbean sugarcane as a commodity.
5. Palmer, *Cost of Producing*, 32. The first consumption figure, 8.3 pounds/person, is for 1891/2 and comes from "Sakhar," in Brokgauz and Efron, *Entsiklopedicheskii slovar'*; the second figure, 17.6 pounds/person, is for 1911/12. See Upravlenie delami osobogo soveshchaniia po prodovol'stviiu, *Potreblenie sakhara v Rossii* (Petrograd: Ekaterininskaia Tipografiia, 1916), 6.
6. Sidney Mintz describes sugar as a product of mass consumption in Britain by 1850. Mintz, *Sweetness and Power*, 148–9. Martin Bruegel argues that although French sugar consumption grew in the late nineteenth century, members of the working classes and especially those outside of Paris remained skeptical about sugar as a food. Nonetheless, French consumption increased from 11 kg per capita in 1900 to around 17 kg by 1914. Martin Bruegel, "A Bourgeois Good? Sugar, Norms of Consumption and the Labouring Classes in Nineteenth-Century France," in *Food, Drink and Identity: Cooking, Eating and Drinking in Europe since the Middle Ages*, ed. Peter Scholliers (Oxford: Berg, 2001), 111.
7. *Zhurnal soveshchaniia o vyrabotke mer, napravlennykh k ponizheniiu tseny sakhara. Stenograficheskie otchety zasedanii 3, 4, i 7 oktiabria 1908 goda* (St. Petersburg, 1908) (hereafter *Zhurnal soveshchaniia Oktiabria 1908*), 2–3.
8. Article no. 1,684 of the imperial law code declared collaboration to raise the price of basic necessities to be a criminal act. *Svod zakonov Rossiiskoi Imperii*, vol. 15 (1857), 433.
9. Horacio Crespo, "Trade Regimes and the International Sugar Market, 1850–1980: Protectionism, Subsidies, and Regulation," in *From Silver to Cocaine: Latin American Commodity Chains and the Building of the World Economy, 1500-2000*, ed. Steven Topik, Carlos Marichal, and Zephyr Frank (Durham, NC: Duke University Press, 2006), 147–73.

10. Levin, *Nasha sakharnaia promyshlennost'*, 5.
11. "Sakhar," in Brokgauz and Efron, *Entsiklopedicheskii slovar'*, 26.
12. Roger Munting, "The Russian Beet Sugar Industry in the XIXth Century," *Journal of European Economic History* 13:2 (1984), 304.
13. *Nasha sakharnaia promyshlennost'*, 19–20. In 1903, the factory quota was raised to 80,000 *pudy*.
14. Alfred J. Rieber, *Merchants and Entrepreneurs in Imperial Russia* (Chapel Hill: University of North Carolina Press, 1982), 107.
15. Rieber, *Merchants and Entrepreneurs in Imperial Russia*, 107.
16. *Kratkii ocherk 50-letiia aktsiznoi sistemy vzimaniia naloga s krepkikh napitkov i 50-letiia deiatel'nosti uchrezhdenii, zevedivaiushchikh neokladnymi sborami* (St. Petersburg, 1913), appendix 12, cited in Yanni Kotsonis, *States of Obligation: Taxes and Citizenship in the Russian Empire and Early Soviet Republic* (Toronto: University of Toronto Press, 2014), 220.
17. Munting, "Russian Beet Sugar Industry in the XIXth Century," 303.
18. *Briussel'skaia mezhdunarodnaia sakharnaia konventsiia* (St. Petersburg: Tipografiia V. F. Kirshbauma, 1911), 17–18, 20.
19. The department was called the Main Administration of Non-Assessed Levies and the State Sale of Beverages. Like temperance activists elsewhere in Europe, those in Russia considered sugar as an alternative to alcohol.
20. Stenogram April 3, 1908, *Doklady biudzhetnoi komissii* (1912), 2104–5.
21. *Doklady biudzhetnoi komissii po razsmotreniiu proekta Gosudarstvennoi rospisi dokhodov i raskhodov na 1908-1916 gg., s prilozheniiami* (St. Petersburg: Gosudarstvennaia tipografiia, 1912), 2049.
22. The total sugar excise received for that year was 93.6 million rubles. *Doklady biudzhetnoi komissii*, 1989. By contrast, revenue from direct taxes amounted to 194.2 million r and from tariffs, 279.3 million r. The alcohol monopoly and excise taxes generated 509.3 million r. Kantseliariia Gosudarstvennoi dumy, comp., "Prilozhenie pervoe, Raboty gosudarstvennoi dumy po rassmotreniiu proektov gosudarstvennykh rospisei dokhodov, 1908–1912," in *Obzor deiatel'nosti Gosudarstvennoi dumy tret'iego sozyva* (St. Petersburg: Gosudarstvennaia tipografiia, 1912), 8–9.
23. *Doklady biudzhetnoi komissii* (1912), 1987–9. *Sakharnaia promyshlennost'. Otnoshenie G. Dumy k voprosu ob udeshevlenii sakhara* (n.p., n.d.).
24. *Tretii sozyv gosudarstvennoi dumy: biografii, portrety, avtografii* (St. Petersburg: N. N. Ol'shanskii, 1910), 52.
25. *Gosudarstvennaia duma, Tretii sozyv, sessiia I, zasedanie* 63, 10 V 1906, 271.
26. *Gosudarstvennaia duma, Tretii sozyv, sessiia I, zasedanie* 63, 10 V 1906, 297–8. On Chelyshev, see *Tretii sozyv gosudarstvennoi dumy: biografii, portrety, avtografii*, 80.
27. *Gosudarstvennaia duma, Tretii sozyv, sessiia I, zasedanie* 63, 10 V 1906, 303.
28. The October Conference generated a stenogram of ninety-six legal-sized pages. *Zhurnal soveshchaniia Oktiabria 1908*, 1–2.
29. Ibid., 5–6.
30. Ibid., 2–3.
31. Ibid., 4.
32. Ibid., 22, 25, 27.
33. Ibid., 28.
34. Ibid., 45–6.
35. Ibid., 54.

36. Ibid., 67–9.
37. Ibid., 67–72.
38. Ibid., 72–5.
39. *Zhurnal soveshchaniia o vyrabotke mer, napravlennykh k ponizheniiu tseny sakhara. Stenograficheskie otchety zasedanii 8, 9, 10, 11, 12, 13, 15, 16 i 17 Dekabria 1908 goda* (St. Petersburg, 1909), 1–3, 393. Hereafter *Zhurnal soveshchaniia Dekabria 1908*. The stenographer's report ran to 520 legal-sized pages.
40. *Zhurnal soveshchaniia Dekabria 1908*, 349.
41. The French army introduced sugar into a soldier's daily ration already in 1876. Frank Trentmann, *Empire of Things: How We Became a World of Consumers, from the Fifteenth Century to the Twenty First* (New York: Harper Perennial, 2016), 166–7.
42. *Zhurnal soveshchaniia Dekabria 1908*, 50.
43. Ibid., 418.
44. Ibid., 508–11.
45. Ibid., 92–3.
46. Ibid., 102–3.
47. Ibid., 138.
48. Ibid., 194.
49. Ibid., 197.
50. Ibid., 414, 420.
51. Rossiiskii Gosudarstvennyi Istoricheskii Arkhiv (RGIA), f. 575, d. 655, l. 41ob-42.
52. RGIA, f. 575, d. 655, l. 52; Ibid., 53-63ob.
53. Kantselariia Gosudarstvennoi dumy, comp. *Obzor deiatel'nosti Gosudarstvennoi Dumy tret'ego sozyva*, 352. *Sakharnaia promyshlennost'. Otnoshenie G. Dumy*, 16.
54. *Gosudarstvennyi sovet: Stenograficheskie otchety, 1909–1910 gody. Sessiia piataia* (St. Petersburg: Gosudarstvennaia tipografiia, 1910), 2284.
55. Ibid., 2295.
56. Ibid., 2298.
57. Kokovtsov and Witte both qualified their statements that sugar was a "basic necessity" perhaps due to the fact that, as Witte stated, anyone "who entered into an agreement with regard to the establishment of a high price for a basic necessity" was "subject to criminal responsibility." They may have hesitated to declare sugar a basic necessity because they found the prospect of opening sugar industrialists to criminal prosecution undesirable. *Gosudarstvennyi sovet: 1909–1910 gody*, 2303.
58. RGIA, f. 575, d. 657, November 19, 1910, handwritten memorandum to Novitskii, l. 3. The document started with the article from the law code identifying agreements to establish a high price for a basic necessity as a crime.
59. *Potreblenie sakhara v Rossii*, 6.
60. Barbara Alpern Engel, "Not by Bread Alone: Subsistence Riots in Russia during World War I," *Journal of Modern History* 69:4 (1997), 721.
61. Iurii Kir'ianov, "Massovye vystupleniia na pochve dorogovizny v Rossii, (1914-fevral' 1917 g.)," *Otechestvennaia istoriia* 3 (May–June 1993), 12–13; Engel, "Not by Bread Alone," 718–19.
62. John Perkins, "Sugar Production, Consumption and Propaganda in Germany, 1850–1914," *German History* 15:1 (1997), 29–30.

# Part 3

# Touching Things

# 7

# Making Samovars Russian

## Audra Yoder

In the opening scene of Denis Fonvizin's comedy *The Brigadier* (1769), the eponymous brigadier's son, a self-absorbed dandy called Ivanushka, sits drinking tea with affected gestures. Flirting with him from across the tea table, the frivolous (and married) Avdotia Potapova theatrically pours out tea for herself. Her daughter, the virtuous Sofiia, sits demurely embroidering in a corner. Throughout the play Sofiia, the personification of maidenly honor, speaks only Russian, abstains from tea, and engages in occupations traditionally considered appropriate for Russian women. The contrast with the proceedings at the tea table could not be greater, where the superficially Frenchified Avdotia Potapova drinks in the sexual overtures made in absurdly bad French by the shallow Ivanushka. Later in the play, when Sofiia's suitor, the chaste Dobroliubov, desires to speak to her father about his honorable intentions, the latter interrupts him rudely, saying, "Better let's go and have a little cup of tea" (*Poidem-ka luchshe da vyp'em po chashke chaiu*).[1] The depraved characters in *The Brigadier* drink tea, while the upright do not. Throughout, Fonvizin portrays tea drinking as an idle pastime indulged in by people with short-sighted pretensions to refinement, whose Western possessions and habits corrupt them morally and drain them financially.

For Fonvizin and other social satirists of eighteenth-century Russia, tea and its expensive accessories represented everything excessive and decadent about Westernized elite culture. Less than a century later, the samovar had morphed into a beacon of wholesome Russian domesticity, immortalized in the canon of nineteenth-century literature as a cultural touchstone setting Russian hospitality apart from other nations. Whence this change? To be sure, the samovar's transformation from a foreign-inflected luxury into a symbol of authentic Russianness was a multifaceted process shaped by economic, social, political, and cultural forces. Yet the principal reason the samovar was around at all in nineteenth-century Russia, having fallen into relative disuse elsewhere in Europe, was its eminent practicality. Before the samovar could become a national symbol, it had to become a common household appliance. This is the story of how that came about.

First, a definition. A samovar is a metal urn-shaped vessel featuring a heat source (typically a charcoal brazier) in its base and, above this, a central interior chimney or tube through which hot air travels and heats the water chamber. The hot water is dispensed through a tap rather than a spout (Figure 7.1). The terms "tea urn"

**Figure 7.1** Photograph of a tea urn, made in London by an unknown silversmith, 1777–8. © Victoria and Albert Museum, London.

and "samovar" are interchangeable, and I use the latter when referring to tea urns manufactured in Russia. "Samovar" derives from the Russian words *samyi*, meaning "self" or "same," and *varit'*, "to boil." There is no doubt of the word's Russian origin, and the term is not normally used to designate a vessel for coffee, *sbiten'* (an ancient Russian drink made from water, honey, herbs, and spices), or any other beverage aside from tea.[2]

The tea urn has been called "an icon of the eighteenth century" and reached the height of its popularity in Western Europe in the 1760s and 1770s. In those years it rode a wave of convergent economic and cultural trends: the continuing growth of tea drinking, technological advances in metals production, an explosion of consumer goods for the home, and the neoclassical obsession with urns and vases.[3] About one hundred years before the height of the samovar's popularity in nineteenth-century Russia, it throve in the context of the Europe-wide consumer culture that flowered in the eighteenth century, into which wealthy Russians were thoroughly integrated. Throughout eighteenth-century Europe and especially in Russia, tea remained an expensive—and decidedly foreign—luxury. Although leaf tea itself came from China, Western doctors had first introduced tea to the Russian court as a medicine in the seventeenth century, and when tea evolved into a social pastime in the early eighteenth century, it retained the cultural baggage of a Western, rather than an Eastern, habit. Curiously enough, even though Russia shared a long land border with China, Chinese cultural influence on tea consumption in European Russia was minimal; instead, the chinoiserie style popular in European courts since the late seventeenth century predominated.[4] Russian tea drinkers of the period used that beverage to create new spaces where their assimilation of Western culture could be displayed and performed.[5] Since tea must be prepared and drunk using specialized equipment, such display was not possible without ownership of tea accessories; physical objects have always been inextricably bound up with the world's tea cultures.

In the late 1990s, the renowned Cambridge archaeologist Christopher Tilley reasoned that to be human is to speak and to make and use things; neither language nor material culture has ontological primacy in the study of culture. Both are essential. This represented a shift away from the linguistic model of material culture studies, dominant in the 1960s, that had inspired both archaeologists and anthropologists to "read" material culture using Ferdinand de Saussure's system of signs. Saussure's model of semiotics taught that all signs are arbitrary, and in a trend known as the "linguistic turn" of the 1960s, some scholars used his ideas to argue that language constructs reality. Accordingly, items of material culture became stand-ins for abstract concepts and were valued for the symbolic role they played in social relations. When thinkers like Jacques Derrida were added to the mix, the arbitrary nature of signifiers meant that there was nothing outside the text. This way of thinking consigned material objects to be read as texts rather than "actively *doing* something in the world" (to borrow a phrase from Tilley). Remembering Tilley's charge not to forget the "materiality" of material culture by treating objects as mere texts, I follow the example of another archaeologist, Nicole Boivin, in assigning historical agency to material objects and to the constraints and opportunities furnished by the material world.[6] Specifically, I contend that the samovar's becoming "Russian" in the nineteenth century resulted from the material conditions of the eighteenth. The samovar was and remains a multivalent object and symbol, incorporating moral, economic, technological, gendered, and political dimensions; the focus here is on the material.

The samovar—that most Russian of objects—is in fact an integral part of Russia's shared European cultural heritage.[7] A comparison between the historical development of British and Russian tea cultures makes this abundantly clear. British tea culture exerted a formative influence on Russian tea culture in the eighteenth century; the rise of the samovar during the reign of Catherine II (r. 1762–96) resulted partly from the Russian "Anglomania" of that period. More importantly for my purposes here, in both Britain and Russia, the material conditions of the domestic interior shaped the development of their distinctive tea cultures. The first section of this essay sketches how the samovar made its way into Russia and uses unpublished household inventories of noble families to track their ownership and use of tea ware. I then compare the conditions under which tea was prepared in British and Russian households in order to demonstrate how the physical configuration of the Russian domestic interior caused the samovar to become a permanent fixture in Russian culture, long after its fashion had faded in the West.

## The Origins of Metal Tea Ware in Russia

Though tea appears in Russian sources from the second decade of the seventeenth century, no teapots, kettles, or other tea equipage are documented in Russia until the early eighteenth century.[8] While the exact origin of the tea urn remains murky, a general timeline can be established using documents and museum collections. Dutch and English silversmiths produced both lamp-heated tea kettles with spouts and tea urns with taps by 1700. Larger hot water urns with interior box irons had emerged in those countries by 1729. Modern charcoal-burning tea urns, the equivalent of the samovar, appeared no later than 1740, and the fad for neoclassicism in the decorative arts fueled their popularity in the 1750s and 1760s.[9] Archival documents attest that the earliest known samovars manufactured in Russia date to the 1740s, though no specimens or images survive.[10] The earliest extant Russian samovars were made in the 1760s and resemble Western European tea urns in almost every detail.[11]

After about 1650, sources attest to the increased presence of both European- and Russian-made tableware of silver and other prestige metals in Russia. The wealthiest Russian nobles owned self-contained vessels for heating food during this period, though little is known of their design. The inventory of Vasilii Vasil'evich Golitsyn's possessions made upon his fall from power in 1690 includes a number of braziers (*zharovni*) for cooking and warming food, at least one of which was probably made of silver.[12] European silver wine fountains, which closely resemble modern samovars, are also known to have existed in the homes of elite Russians from the first decades of the eighteenth century. Prince Vasilii Lukich Dolgorukii, Peter's ambassador to Denmark, owned one.[13] In the first half of the eighteenth century, many early works of the London-based silversmith Paul de Lamerie, considered one of the greatest silversmiths of the century, came to Russia. Notable among these is a fountain he produced in 1720–1.[14] Around that same time, in 1721, Prince Aleksandr Menshikov commissioned over 1,700 rubles' worth of silver objects from London, including a teapot, a tea kettle with burner, two tea caddies, and other accessories for tea and coffee.[15]

Solid evidence of habitual tea consumption and the ownership of silver tea ware among the Russian nobility dates to the 1720s. Archival documents reveal that the Mikhailovich branch of the Golitsyns, one of the oldest, wealthiest, and most influential noble families in Russia, were early adopters of tea drinking, and inventories of their possessions made between 1729 and the 1790s attest to the range of tea wares available to wealthy eighteenth-century Russians. A list of silver dishes dated 1729 includes one plain silver teapot of English make, along with other tea and coffee vessels of Dutch and German provenance.[16] The inventory specifies that the Golitsyns' British silver teapot had a wooden handle, as did the earliest British silver teapots.[17] The 1729 inventory also includes one stamped silver teapot of Russian (*Moskovskii*) make weighing over two pounds, as well as a slightly smaller plain coffee pot, also of Russian origin. The vessels described above are the earliest documented tea and coffee vessels manufactured in Russia, and the Golitsyns almost certainly had them custom-made. Secondary literature dates the first silver teapots produced in Russia to the 1730s, but the Golitsyns' 1729 inventory allows us to date the genesis of this industry slightly earlier.[18] By 1742 the Golitsyns also owned a variety of silver coffee pots, silver tea cups, tea spoons, and sugar bowls.[19] The modern tea service, which eventually evolved to include creamers, sugar bowls, specialized spoons, strainers, and other accessories, did not coalesce until around the middle of the eighteenth century.[20] Therefore the variety of tea accessories owned by the Golitsyns at the early date of 1742 testifies not only to their extraordinary wealth but also to their lifestyle on the cutting edge of fashion and technology.

Among the earliest recorded tea kettles in Russia—forerunners of the modern samovar—is one included in Prince Menshikov's order of table silver from London in 1721. The invoice includes one "tea kettle with burner" (*chainyi kotel i s kanforom*) weighing 122.7 ounces.[21] Other early records of tea kettles in Russia appear in a Golitsyn inventory dated April 1740, which lists one small and one large tea kettle. Described as "teapots with burners" (*chainik s konforkoi*), these vessels probably closely resembled British and Dutch kettles equipped with stands and spirit lamps, which had emerged at the turn of the eighteenth century.[22] The Golitsyns' kettles probably originated in Russia, since their household inventories tend to specify the country of origin for vessels purchased abroad. Alongside these "teapots with burners," the Golitsyn inventory for 1742 lists a "white silver English heating teapot" (*chainik zzharovnaia aglitskoi* [sic] *raboty beloi serebrenoi*).[23] How or whether the "English heating teapot" differed in function or structure from the Russian "teapots with burners" is impossible to determine, since early in the history of both British and Russian metal tea ware, multiple terms existed for the same vessels.[24] The handwriting on the 1740 Golitsyn inventory differs significantly from that on the 1742 inventory, suggesting that the lists were drawn up by two different individuals, which could also help explain the discrepancy in the description of the tea kettles. In any event, the multiplicity of terms for similar vessels testifies to their novelty. From the second half of the eighteenth century, tea kettles on stands with burners would come to be known in Russia as *bul'otki*.[25]

While the earliest Golitsyn inventories indicate that Russian silversmiths—and also European silversmiths resident in Russia's capital cities—were producing silver teapots and kettles for a tiny elite market in the 1720s, the manufacture of Russian copper samovars began somewhat later in the Urals. The imperial government required Russian copper works operating in the first half of the eighteenth century to produce coinage. The German-born engineer Georg Wilhelm de Gennin (1676–1750), who had been recruited into the Russian army by Peter I's associate Franz Lefort in 1697, managed the state copper manufactories in the Urals for twelve years in the 1720s and 1730s. In the factories he oversaw, Gennin introduced the practice of offsetting the cost of minting coin by manufacturing turned and cast copper dishware for the domestic market, as well as the large pots and tubes required by distilleries—technologies prerequisite to the development of Russian samovar production. Gennin's innovation soon spread to other Urals copper works.[26] Beginning in the 1740s, the Russian government imposed tariffs on "tea and coffee pots, candlesticks, trays, holders and similar small items," indicating that commerce in metal tea ware, imported and otherwise, was significant enough to make taxation worthwhile.[27]

The word "samovar" first appears in a Russian document from 1740. That year, at the customs house in Ekaterinburg, a soldier named Zakhar Gilev detained Timofei Pushniakov, who ran a metals factory in the region, and several of his compatriots for transporting, among other things, a "tin-plated copper samovar" (*samovar mednyi, luzhenyi*). This is the earliest document attesting to samovar manufacture inside the borders of the Russian Empire.[28] Grigorii Akinfevich Demidov, grandson of the great industrialist Nikita Demidov, left his family's iron and munitions factories to establish Russia's first known samovar manufactory, which was producing copper samovars in a village called Suksun in the Perm' region by 1745.[29] In 1746, a monastery near Nizhnii Tagil owned "two brass (lit. 'green copper') samovars with tubes" (*dva samovara s trubami zelenoi medi*).[30] The copper works at Suksun, along with those in Nizhnii Tagil, were among the first copper production sites in Russia. The design of these early "samovars" of the 1740s remains mysterious. They may have resembled cauldrons with interior tubes more closely than proper tea urns.[31] Or they may have been simply tea kettles with spirit lamps, like those listed in the Golitsyn inventories for 1740–2.[32] While documentation is lacking and specimens nonexistent, it seems likely that the first Russian samovars were based on European designs. The scarcity of surviving samovars is doubtless due to the value of the material they were made from, which could be sold, exchanged, or melted down.[33]

Part of the difficulty in parsing these samovar-like devices (*samovariashchie sosudy*) stems from the fact that the word "samovar" did not become the standard Russian term for a tea urn until the 1770s. "Water-heating vessel" (*vodogreinyi sosud*) was an early Russian phrase used to denote any device that could be used to heat water. Before "samovar" became the norm, they were known variously as *vodogrei* (water heater) in Tula, *samogar* (from an old word for "cinder") in Iaroslavl', and *samogrei* (self-heater) in Viatka.[34] A 1769 inventory of table silver belonging to the Kochubei family lists one *chainyi vodavar'* (tea water boiler).[35] The wide range of terminology for domestic implements, as has been demonstrated with apothecary ware, building materials, and fish guts, typifies the early modern period across Europe and makes precise tracking of these technologies difficult.[36]

Archival evidence of samovar ownership among the eighteenth-century Russian nobility is fragmentary and attests to a range of designs and terminology; again, precisely what the word "samovar" meant in the eighteenth century is not always clear. The Demidovs owned a green copper samovar in 1789.[37] In 1795, the Iusupov family had several copper contraptions for tea and hot water, including one samovar, a "teapot for water," and two copper "cubes for distilling water" (*kubikov dlia gnaniia vody*). These last were probably reservoirs for hot water designed to rest inside a stove, which the English called "coppers." The Iusupovs also owned a yellow British ceramic tea service.[38] In 1792, the Shcherbatov family boasted porcelain tea services from Britain and Saxony, together with two copper samovars and a third equipped with a cast iron hot plate.[39] Curiously, no vessels described as samovars appear in the Golitsyn family inventories, but a list of silver objects compiled sometime after 1758 includes several teapots, candlesticks, and a number of turned, plain, and patterned urns (*urny*).[40] Prince Aleksandr Mikhailovich Golitsyn had served as Russia's ambassador to Britain from 1755 until he returned to Russia to assist with the coup that brought Catherine II to power in 1762. Aleksandr Mikhailovich, whose personal expense records indicate his enthusiasm for English table silver, was doubtless familiar with the English term "tea urn," and thus it is possible that one or more of the urns appearing on this inventory were tea urns.[41] Aside from this possible exception, I did not find the phrase *chainaia urna* (tea urn) in eighteenth-century Russian sources.

We can associate the rise of the term "samovar" in the 1770s with the establishment of the celebrated Lisitsyn samovar workshops in Tula (Ivan Lisitsyn, 1778) and Moscow (Grigorii Lisitsyn, late 1770s).[42] Arms manufacture in the town of Tula, two hundred miles south of Moscow, began in the seventeenth century with the establishment of a Dutch iron foundry. Late in the seventeenth century, the Dutch were exporting almost a thousand cannons back to the Netherlands annually and selling the inferior pieces to the Russian military.[43] Peter the Great established a state arms manufactory in Tula in 1712 and gave manufacturers the right to purchase iron ore independently and to produce goods for the domestic market. As in the Urals, metals production for the state did not yield a high profit margin, but luxury consumer goods did. Catherine's interest in Matthew Boulton's products resulted in a marked British influence on the luxury goods produced at Tula during her reign.[44] The arms and decorative arts industries helped transform Tula from a small settlement into an important provincial city, and by 1808, eight distinct samovar manufactories operated there.[45] Later in the nineteenth century, Tula became known as the samovar capital of imperial Russia.

In sum, the history of the true Russian copper samovar is on firm documentary footing only from the 1770s, about a decade after the neoclassical tea urn had enjoyed the height of its popularity in Britain. The weight of evidence strongly suggests that the Russian samovar, extant in some form as early as 1740, evolved from British and Dutch silver tea urns, which had existed since 1700 and had assumed their larger, modern form no later than 1729.

## Tea Urns into Samovars

Whatever the origin and design of the earliest samovars, when the word "samovar" and its synonyms first came into Russian usage in the middle of the eighteenth century, they all conveyed the same, novel idea: a device that could heat water indoors by itself, *samo*, that is, without the use of a Russian stove.[46] Occupying a massive space both in the folk imagination and in the domestic interior, the Russian stove (*pech'*) played a central role in both heating and cooking, and curiously enough, exerted a formative influence on the development of a distinctively Russian tea culture beginning in the second half of the eighteenth century.[47] Between roughly 1770 and 1840, the ubiquity of the Russian stove helped ensure the continued popularity of samovars in Russia, while the particularities of British domestic interiors, specifically the continued prevalence of fireplaces and the emergence of cooktop stoves, contributed to the downfall of the tea urn in Britain. After 1800, the tea urn gradually became dissociated from its roots in Western Europe and inextricably embedded in Russian culture.

In exploring the causes of the British tea urn's decline at the end of the eighteenth century, it must be noted that wall fireplaces had become standard in British country houses by the medieval period and would remain so until the end of the eighteenth century. Like many other Europeans, the British used brick-lined ovens for baking and open fires for all other cooking. In the words of one historian, "it was the chimney hearth that made the kitchen a 'kitchen.'"[48] The eighteenth century saw the enclosure of the cooking hearth, which permitted the emergence of horizontal cooking surfaces. As early as the 1740s in London, real estate advertisers sought to attract buyers with kitchen ranges.[49] Even then, open fireplaces remained a fixture in many houses across the socioeconomic spectrum, and not only in kitchens but also in sitting rooms and bedrooms as well.[50] The proliferation of fireplace accessories such as fenders, irons, small brooms, trivets, and scuttles signaled the rise of the fireplace as a site of social interaction and display—just like the tea table, which experienced its own explosion of accessories in the eighteenth century.[51]

Thus, when the fashion for drinking coffee, and later tea, first developed in the seventeenth century, the English heated water for these beverages in large, round-bottomed cooking pots over open fires. Since both cooking pots and spacious indoor fireplaces were ubiquitous, this process was straightforward. For this reason, when the self-contained charcoal-burning tea urn appeared in the middle of the eighteenth century, fashion and the allure of new technology, rather than efficiency, sustained its popularity. The vogue for classical vases, combined with a sharp rise in the amount of tea consumed, created a heyday for the British tea urn in the 1750s and 1760s. When neoclassicism declined after about 1770, the tea urn's popularity declined with it. Simultaneously, as kitchen conditions changed with the enclosure of the hearth, older cooking staples such as cooking pots on legs began to disappear, and flat-bottomed saucepans, pots, and notably kettles emerged to complement the new heating arrangements.[52]

Since both tea and fireplaces had become symbols of British national identity by the second half of the eighteenth century, it was perhaps only natural that the two should become more closely connected in the popular imagination as time went on. Because of the technological and cultural factors sketched above, the kettle, rather than the tea urn, embodied this connection. In his celebrated 1839 book *Tea: Its Effects, Medicinal and Moral*, a physician by the name of George Gabriel Sigmond articulated a sentiment that had apparently been growing in early nineteenth-century British tea-drinking circles:

> Alas! For the domestic happiness of many of our family circles, this meal [tea] has lost its character, and many of those innovations which despotic fashion has introduced, have changed one of the most agreeable of our daily enjoyments. It is indeed a question amongst the devotees to the tea-table, whether the bubbling urn has been practically an improvement. Upon our habits, it has driven from us the old national kettle, once the pride of the fireside.[53]

Sigmond's work helped to cement the tea kettle as a national symbol in the British imagination. He acknowledged that fashion, rather than practical considerations, had been responsible for the tea urn's rise and called for a return to the more efficient kettle.

And that is exactly what happened. Once the novelty and fashion of the tea urn had worn off, British tea drinkers reverted to the older and, for them, more convenient kettle. Of course, tea urns remained in use in Britain and across Europe throughout the nineteenth century, but there was no question of the kettle's practical superiority, and tea urns would never again rival them in popularity or symbolic import. After the turn of the nineteenth century, the inhabitants of virtually all British homes, from grand manors to working-class row houses, had access to one or more of three options for heating water indoors: hanging a kettle or cauldron in an open fireplace, heating a kettle on a cooktop surface, or drawing hot water from a copper inside the stove. The latter two, cooktop surfaces and coppers, were common even in middle- and working-class Victorian homes.[54] Compared to these, lighting a charcoal-burning tea urn was tedious, dirty, and time-consuming.

Heating and cooking technologies in Russia were very different. More architectural feature than appliance, Russian stoves were built from clay, stone, or brick, and enclosed a fire that could be tended through a semicircular stoke hole. The stove was a multipurpose domestic technology, often with a flat top for sleeping, one or more ovens, and the ability to supply radiant heat to warm a room or an entire cottage (Figure 7.2). Little is known about the history of stoves and cooking methods in medieval and early modern Russia. Until about 1600, domed clay stoves seem to have predominated. Flat-topped, tiled stoves often described in the sources as "Dutch" appeared in wealthy households in the late sixteenth century, shortly after glazed tiles of Italian origin appeared in Ukraine. These were generally constructed from clay, and more rarely, brick or stone. One 1682 document refers to the refurbishing of a bread-making establishment that contained sixteen cooking stoves but only two open hearths.[55] In the late seventeenth and eighteenth centuries, open hearths were not unknown, but stoves predominated, and modern cooktop ranges remained unusual until the second half of the nineteenth century. The evolution of these basic heating and cooking technologies is very difficult to track in Russian documentary sources, as stoves and ovens were not considered movable property and hence do not appear in inventories.

Western travel accounts of eighteenth-century Russia help fill this lacuna because almost without exception, foreign travelers commented on the ubiquity and sheer size of Russian stoves. John Bell, a Scottish physician who first came to Russia in 1714 and later journeyed on to Beijing, divided Eurasia into stove-using and nonstove-using peoples. His first impression of Tatars was, "They use no stoves, as the Russians do."[56] The notorious Venetian Giacomo Casanova, who visited Russia in 1765, wrote that Russia was a land of stoves, and that only Russians know how to build stoves properly.[57] Jacques Jubé, a French priest who spent three years serving as a tutor in Russia during the reigns of Anna and Peter II, described stoves at length in his book on the habits and customs of Russians.[58] Elizabeth Justice, who spent three years as a governess in a wealthy English family in St. Petersburg during Anna's reign, noted that the Russian "Peach" (*pech'*) was "a compleat Way of warming a Room."[59] Jane Rondeau, wife of the British envoy to Russia during Anna's reign, described stove-warmed halls filled with blooming myrtle and orange trees in the dead of winter.[60] Visiting foreigners immediately noticed and became interested in the stove's centrality

**Figure 7.2** *Kitchen* by V. G. Malyshev. Credit: National Fine Arts Museum of the Republic of Sakha (Yakutia).

to Russian interiors. Almost universally in Western European eighteenth-century foreign travel accounts of Russia, the stove figured prominently in descriptions of the differences between Russian and Western lifestyles.

The British, in particular, often compared the relative merits of the Russian stove and the British fireplace in their diaries and letters, and many British expatriates considered the lack of fireplaces to be one of the defining characteristics of life in Russia. As early as the reign of Peter the Great, the English engineer John Perry, who published his description of Russia in 1716, described Russian stoves with an engineer's eye for detail and, in the same passage, recounted his attempt to make "a Fire after the English Fashion."[61] Many British families living in St. Petersburg longed for fireplaces so acutely that they went to the expense of having them installed in their homes. The account of James Brogden, a young Englishman with a variety of commercial interests who visited Russia as part of a European tour in 1787-8, reveals that his familiarity with the reputation of the Russian stove predated his arrival there. Brogden complained that in some places, Russian stoves were not as effective at heating interiors as he had been taught to expect, and that in others, it was all he could do to withstand excessively heated rooms. Knowing very little Russian, Brodgen frequented the houses of British merchants and other expatriates in St. Petersburg and remarked that hardly any of them lacked British-style grates and fireplaces.[62] Lady Elizabeth Craven (née Berkeley, 1750–1828), a prolific author of plays and travel journals, published an account of her journey through Russia in 1789. "*Dans le ligne Anglais*," Craven wrote of what is now called the English Embankment, "... I find English grates, English coal, English hospitality, to make me welcome, and the fire-side cheerful."[63] British people living or traveling in eighteenth-century Russia drank tea and built themselves fireplaces in order to enjoy domestic comfort and to assert their Britishness in a foreign environment.

Russian high society's fascination with all things British peaked under Catherine, who freely confessed to her own "Anglomania," and the British living in St. Petersburg willingly supplied wealthy Russians with the goods necessary to indulge their interest.[64] Russian Anglophilia in the eighteenth century may be partially attributed to the Anglo-Russian commercial treaties of 1734 and 1766, which led to a steady increase in both British goods and British people in Russia. A British shop called Hubbard's on Vasilievskii Island advertised the sale of many imported items, including "tea and coffee machines." Elsewhere in St. Petersburg, in the 1790s, one could buy British-made nickel-plated tea urns (*nakladnye samovary*).[65] Vessels for brewing tea and coffee had appeared on Russian tariff schedules beginning in the 1740s. In 1782, the category that included these items was expanded to include Old Sheffield plate, a popular material for tea urns.[66] The British also supplied small amounts of leaf tea to Russia throughout the eighteenth century.[67]

But long after Russian Anglophilia had faded, one object once popular in Britain would become a permanent fixture in Russian culture: the tea urn, already known in Catherinian Russia as the samovar. Unlike other aspects of British tea culture, the samovar remained widespread in Russia primarily because, unlike in Britain, it was the easiest and most convenient method of boiling water indoors. Heating water using a Russian stove required more time and effort than lighting a samovar. The Russian stove was designed to cook food slowly at declining temperatures, without direct contact with the heat source, as the fire inside it slowly died. To heat water using a Russian stove, a cauldron full of water would be placed on top of a skillet inside the stove.[68] This was a slow and cumbersome way to heat water. Cooktop surfaces and Western-style wood- and coal-burning stoves appeared in Russia at the turn of the nineteenth century, soon after they appeared in Britain and America. But since these new technologies were costly and made the preparation of traditional Russian staples such as black bread difficult, they were widely adopted only toward the end of the nineteenth century, and then primarily in urban areas.[69]

Throughout the eighteenth century, then, when variations on the Russian stove were the norm even in elite households, the samovar represented a great improvement in domestic technology. The Russians embraced the tea urn for the same reasons that the British ultimately rejected it: efficiency and convenience. British fireplaces and cooktop stoves ultimately made the tea urn obsolete, whereas in Russia, the relative absence of cooktop surfaces and open indoor fireplaces made the samovar the easiest and most practical option for boiling water, since heating water using an enclosed Russian stove was time-consuming. The material conditions of domestic interiors shaped the distinctive tea cultures of Britain and Russia, leading to the kettle becoming a national symbol in Britain, and the samovar in Russia. As a distinctively Russian tea culture developed during the reign of Catherine, the samovar quickly became its focal point. The growth of tea drinking in eighteenth-century Russia owed a great deal to widespread British influence on Russian fashion, noble behavior, and luxury technologies, but once established, Russian tea drinking quickly took on a life of its own. The samovar, on its way out in the West, seemed to have been designed for the specific needs of stove-bound Russian homes, and as a result, its popularity increased dramatically. Long after the tea urn's popularity faded in Western Europe, and the fashion for all things British declined in Russia, the samovar continued to serve the water-heating needs of tea-drinking Russians because it was the most efficient and practical technology available.

## Conclusion

While tea had been present in Russia for more than a century previous to her accession, the reign of Catherine the Great saw the consolidation of a distinctively Russian tea culture—that is, ways of preparing, serving, and understanding tea that set Russia apart from other tea-consuming cultures. A number of factors came together during this period to shape its distinctive evolution. From about 1700, Russian fashion and the decorative arts synchronized with contemporary developments in Europe, although they retained some distinctive characteristics. Crucially, the technologies necessary for the production and processing of luxury materials such as silver and porcelain also arrived in Russia during this period and were heavily influenced by Dutch, British, and German innovations in these fields. The rise of neoclassicism in Britain, and the Anglophilia Catherine shared with other Russian tastemakers, drove the ascendancy of the tea urn in both empires. The tea urn appealed to Russian elites under Catherine on a number of levels. It satisfied the craze for classical vases, chinoiserie, tea itself, and everything British in one elegant package. And because most Russian homes were not well equipped to boil water quickly, it ultimately proved to be the most efficient option.

Scholars tend to shy away from giving objects historical agency, because doing so can eclipse human agency and often fails to account for cultural factors. The physical characteristics of British and Russian interiors were, of course, only one factor among many that shaped their distinctive tea cultures. Yet it was most certainly not cultural conservatism that caused Russians to hang on to the samovar long after their fellow Europeans had abandoned the tea urn. Had a reluctance to experiment with foreign customs exerted a strong influence on noble behavior, they would not have drunk tea at all, but stuck with that more traditional, widely available, and cheaper hot beverage, *sbiten'*. Instead, both the Russians and the British clung to their beloved adopted beverage, tea, and embraced the vessels for its preparation that were the most economical in terms of time and energy.

## Notes

1. Denis Fonvizin, *The Brigadier*, in Harold B. Segel, *The Literature of Eighteenth-Century Russia* (New York: Dutton, 1967), 2:322, 353.
2. Robert E. F. Smith and David Christian, *Bread and Salt: A Social and Economic History of Food and Drink in Russia* (Cambridge: Cambridge University Press, 1984), 237. Samovars fitted with coffee filters existed, but sources specify them as such (e.g., *samovar dlia kofe* or *kofeinyi samovar*). An array of similar devices (*samovariashchie sosudy*) for preparing and warming food were also available in eighteenth-century Russia. These were sometimes referred to as "samovar-kitchens."
3. Maxine Berg, *Luxury and Pleasure in Eighteenth-Century Britain* (Oxford: Oxford University Press, 2005), 164. Excavations at Pompeii and Herculaneum began in the 1730s and 1740s, and the classical vase in particular captured European imaginations in the 1760s and 1770s; the resemblance of tea urns to Greek and Roman vases is not coincidental, and they were sometimes called "tea vases." Jenny Uglow, "Vase Mania," in *Luxury in the Eighteenth Century: Debates, Desires, and Delectable Goods*, ed. Maxine Berg and Elizabeth Eger (New York: Palgrave, 2003), 153–6.
4. Audra Yoder, "Tea Time in Romanov Russia: A Cultural History, 1616–1917" (PhD diss., University of North Carolina at Chapel Hill, 2016), ch. 1–2.
5. See Woodruff Smith, "From Coffeehouse to Parlour: The Consumption of Coffee, Tea and Sugar in North-Western Europe in the Seventeenth and Eighteenth Centuries," in *Consuming Habits: Deconstructing Drugs in History and Anthropology*, ed. Paul E. Lovejoy, Andrew Sherratt, and Jordan Goodman (London: Routledge, 1995); and Smith, *Consumption and the Making of Respectability, 1600–1800* (New York: Routledge, 2002).
6. Christopher Tilley, *Metaphor and Material Culture* (Oxford: Blackwell, 1999), 265; Nicole Boivin, *Material Cultures, Material Minds: The Impact of Things on Human Thought, Society, and Evolution* (Cambridge: Cambridge University Press, 2008) .
7. Yoder, "Tea Time in Romanov Russia," ch. 2.
8. Ibid., chapter 1.
9. Erika Schrijver, "Europe's Earliest Silver Tea-Kettle," *The Connoisseur* (October 1969), 83; Jane Pettigrew, *Design for Tea: Tea Wares from the Dragon Court to Afternoon Tea* (Stroud: Sutton, 2003), 32, 43–5; Elizabeth de Castres, *A Collector's Guide to Tea Silver, 1670–1900* (London: Muller, 1977), 13, 28, 32, 48; Victoria and Albert Museum, http://collections.vam.ac.uk/item/O89145/urn-unknown/, accessed July 22, 2020; http://collections.vam.ac.uk/item/O93393/urn-albrink-otto/, accessed May 15, 2016 and July 22, 2020; http://collections.vam.ac.uk/item/O90600/urn-unknown/, accessed July 22, 2020; Herbert Brunner, *Old Table Silver: A Handbook for Collectors and Amateurs* (New York: Taplinger, 1967), 175.
10. Liudmila Britenkova, *Samovary Rossii: populiarnaia entsiklopediia* (Moscow: Khobbi Press, 2010), 113.
11. See Yoder, "Tea Time," for a thorough discussion of Russian tea culture being more closely aligned with Western than Eastern tea cultures.

12. Richard Hellie, *The Economy and Material Culture of Russia, 1600–1725* (Chicago: University of Chicago Press, 1999), 591.
13. Britenkova, *Samovary Rossii*, 8; E. A. Ivanova, *Russkie samovary* (Leningrad: Khudozhnik RSFSR, 1971), 13; Robert E. F. Smith, "Whence the Samovar?" *Petits Propos Culinaires* 4 (1980), 65.
14. Antique vases probably supplied the basic designs for European silver fountains, the earliest example of which is a table fountain given to Charles II by the City of Plymouth in 1660. The garden vases of Louis XIV also probably provided inspiration for silver table fountains. Marina Lopato, *State Hermitage Museum Catalog: British Silver*, trans. Catherine Phillips (New Haven, CT: Yale University Press, 2015), 18–19.
15. Russian State Archive of Ancient Documents (hereinafter RGADA), f. 198, op. 1, ed. khr. 495, f. 2, published in Lopato, *British Silver*, 320.
16. RGADA, f. 1263, op. 1, d. 6104.
17. Bennett Alan Weinberg and Bonnie K. Bealer, *The World of Caffeine: The Science and Culture of the World's Most Popular Drug* (New York: Routledge, 2002), 79, 82.
18. Britenkova, *Samovari Rossii*, 27; T. Gol′dberg, F. Mishukov, N. Platonova, and M. Postnikova-Loseva, *Russkoe zolotoe i serebrianoe delo XV-XX vekov* (Moscow: Nauka, 1967), 94.
19. RGADA, f. 1263, op. 1, d. 6104, ll. 1–4, 11.
20. Berg, *Luxury and Pleasure*, 241; de Castres, *A Collector's Guide*, 34.
21. RGADA, f. 198, op. 1, ed. khr. 495, f. 2, in Lopato, *British Silver*, 321. The Russian word *chainik* normally denotes both kettles and teapots, the distinction usually being clear from context; my research did not uncover any other instances of the word *kotel*, a transliteration of the English "kettle." It appears here probably because the document is a Russian translation of an English-language invoice.
22. RGADA, f. 1263, op. 1, d. 6104, ll. 1, 4.
23. RGADA, f. 1263, op. 1, d. 6104, l. 18.
24. The first English tea kettles of the late seventeenth century were sometimes referred to in household inventories as "furnaces." Pettigrew, *Design for Tea*, 43.
25. Ivanova, *Russkie Samovary*, 13.
26. Britenkova, *Samovary Rossii*, 105.
27. Smith, "Whence the Samovar?" 66, citing Mikhail Dmirievich Chulkov, *Istoricheskoe opisanie Rossiiskoi kommertsii* (St. Petersburg: Imperatorskii akademii nauk, 1781-8), vol. 6, i, 375.
28. Britenkova, *Samovary Rossii*, 105–6.
29. Ibid., 113; A. A. Gilodo, *Russkii samovar* (Moscow: Sovetskaia Rossiia, 1991), 8, citing documents housed at the Nizhnii Tagil branch of the Sverdlovsk regional archive (GASO).
30. Britenkova, *Samovary Rossii*, 113.
31. Ibid.; Gilodo, *Russkii samovar*, 8.
32. Britenkova acknowledges that the earliest Russian "samovars" may have actually been tea kettles, not tea urns. Britenkova, *Samovary Rossii*, 28.
33. Sara Pennell, *The Birth of the English Kitchen, 1600–1850* (New York: Bloomsbury Academic, 2016), 74.
34. Britenkova, *Samovary Rossii*, 9, 28, 103.
35. RGADA, f. 1445, op. 1, d. 143, l. 1.
36. Pennell, *Birth of the English Kitchen*, 64.
37. RGADA, f. 1267, op. 7, d. 39, l. 2.
38. RGADA, f. 1290, op. 3, d. 20, ll. 4, 10, 11.

39. RGADA, f. 1289, op. 4, d. 189, ll. 1–2.
40. RGADA, f. 1263, op. 2, d. 24, l. 8.
41. Anthony Cross, *"By the Banks of the Thames": Russians in Eighteenth Century Britain* (Newtonville, MA: Oriental Research Partners, 1980), 13; RGADA, f. 1263, op. 1, d. 6105, ll. 2, 57; d. 6163, ll. 13, 62; see also dd. 3457, 3458, 6106.
42. Smith, "Whence the Samovar?" 63.
43. W. Bruce Lincoln, *The Great Reforms: Autocracy, Bureaucracy, and the Politics of Change in Imperial Russia* (DeKalb: Northern Illinois University Press, 1990), 4.
44. Tamara Rappe, "Catherine II and European Decorative Arts," in *Catherine the Great: Art for Empire*, ed. Nathalie Bondil (Montreal: Montreal Museum of Fine Arts, 2005), 242.
45. Britenkova, *Samovary Rossii*, 119–20.
46. Ivanova, *Russkie samovary*, 16; Britenkova, *Samovary Rossii*, 103.
47. See Snejana Tempest, "Stovelore in Russian Folklife," in *Food in Russian History and Culture*, ed. Musya Glants and Joyce Toomre (Bloomington: Indiana University Press, 1997).
48. Pennell, *Birth of the English Kitchen*, 43.
49. Ibid., 64, 73.
50. Mark Girouard, *Life in the English Country House: A Social and Architectural History* (New Haven, CT: Yale University Press, 1978), 246–63.
51. Lawrence E. Klein, "Politeness and the Interpretation of the British Eighteenth Century," *The Historical Journal* 45:4 (2002), 885.
52. Pennell, *Birth of the English Kitchen*, 73.
53. George Gabriel Sigmond, *Tea, Its Effects, Moral and Medicinal* (London: A. Spottiswoode, 1893), 88–9.
54. Ruth Goodman, *How to Be a Victorian: A Dawn-to-Dusk Guide to Victorian Life* (New York: Liveright, 2013), 263; Pennell, *Birth of the English Kitchen*, 67.
55. Smith and Christian, *Bread and Salt*, 18–23.
56. John Bell, *A Journey from St. Petersburg to Pekin, 1719–22*, ed. J. L. Stevenson (New York: Barnes and Noble, 1966), 11.
57. Giacomo Casanova, *The Memoirs of Jacques Casanova de Seingalt*, trans. Arthur Machen (New York: G.P. Putnam's, 1894), vol. 5, 502.
58. Jacques Jubé, *La Religion, Les Moeurs et Le Usages Des Moscovites* (Oxford: Voltaire Foundation and the Taylor Institution, 1992), 160–5.
59. Elizabeth Justice, *A Voyage to Russia* (York: Thomas Gent, 1739), 21.
60. Jane Vigor, *Letters from a Lady, Who Resided Some Years in Russia, to Her Friend in England* (London: J. Dodsley, 1777), 93–5.
61. John Perry, *The State of Russia under the Present Czar* (London: Cass, 1967), 109–12.
62. James Cracraft, "James Brogden in Russia, 1787–1788," *Slavonic and East European Review* 47:108 (January 1969), 232.
63. Elizabeth Craven, *A Journey through the Crimea to Constantinople* (London: G. G. J and J. Robinson, 1789), 125.
64. Adreas Schönle, *The Ruler in the Garden: Politics and Landscape Design in Imperial Russia* (Oxford: Peter Lang, 2007), 48.
65. Anthony Cross, *By the Banks of the Neva: Chapters from the Lives and Careers of the British in Eighteenth-Century Russia* (Cambridge: Cambridge University Press, 1997), 16–17.
66. Smith, "Whence the Samovar?," 67, citing Chulkov, *Istoricheskoe opisanie*, vol. 6. Sheffield plate, invented in 1743 by the English cutler Thomas Boulsover, was made

by plating silver onto copper. The first known English tea urn in Old Sheffield plate was made in 1762.
67. Smith and Christian, *Bread and Salt*, 233; Chulkov, *Istoricheskoe opisanie*, vol. 6, ii, p. 242.
68. Cauldrons were not placed directly in the ashes, but on top of skillets or some other flat metal surface. Smith and Christian, *Bread and Salt*, 22.
69. V. I. Pokhlebkin, *Natsional'nye kukhni nashikh narodov* (Moscow: Pishchevaia promyshlennost', 1978), 13–14; Joyce Toomre, "Introduction," in *Classic Russian Cooking: Elena Molokhovets' A Gift to Young Housewives* (Bloomington: Indiana University Press, 1998), 37–8.

# 8

# "Constant Companions": Fabergé Tobacco Cases and Sensory Prompts to Addiction in Late Imperial Russia

Tricia Starks

Tsar Nicholas II (r. 1894–1917), like many of his subjects, smoked the unique, Russian, hollow-filtered cigarette called a papirosa (-a singular; -y plural), but from the moment he pulled his smoke out of a delicate, jeweler-crafted case until he stubbed it out in an expensive, custom ashtray, elegance flavored his habit.[1] The tsar's smokes were not the ready-made brands manufactured in one of the many factories of the capital. He enjoyed custom-blended and rolled papirosy filled with aromatic, Oriental-leaf tobacco (*nicotiana tabacum*) rather than the cheaper, foul-smelling, nicotine-intense Russian makhorka (*nicotiana rusticum*) smoked by the majority of the population. Nicholas inherited a taste for oriental leaf from the Black Sea region from his father Alexander III, who also smoked.[2] Not just his papirosy were distinct. At times, the tsar used a holder designed to keep the burning embers away from his face, a health consideration at the time. To light up, he pulled his match from a hard-stone stand or employed one of the new compact-fuel lighters, because lighting from a candle or using a still from the fire was beneath him. A photo dated to 1895 shows Nicholas II at Peterhof smoking at a desk with a brick match holder. This unassuming "brick" was pricey—twenty-seven to seventy-five rubles apiece from one maker.[3] Poor peasant household incomes of the time averaged about 221 rubles per year.[4]

Even the butts of the tsar's smokes received special treatment. Rather than crushed underfoot or thrown into a gutter, in his wing of the Alexander palace over seventy ashtrays awaited his ashy residues, or perhaps those of his wife, Empress Aleksandra Fedorovna, who also smoked.[5] Once Nicholas stubbed one papirosa out, he had the leisure and means to continue smoking, pulling another smoke out of one of the many cases he possessed, lighting up again and again, and repeating the experience throughout his day—twenty-five to thirty times on average. Even during imprisonment, the tsar continued to be provided with tobacco. In just nine months of 1917 he smoked some eight thousand papirosy—about a pack and a half a day.[6]

Tobacco even supposedly accompanied the tsar's final moments—in the form of an exquisite case made by the St. Petersburg goldsmith and jeweler Peter Carl Fabergé (1846–1920) (Figure 8.1). Fashioned of Karelian birch sourced from the area between

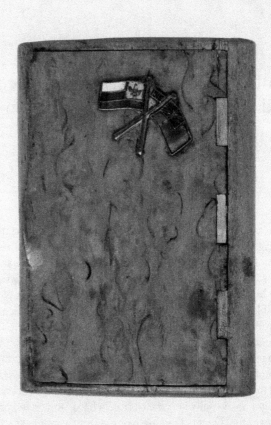

**Figure 8.1** Photograph of Fabergé case of carved Karelian birch embossed with date 1915 and believed to belong to Tsar Nicholas II. St. Petersburg. Photo courtesy of the McFerrin Collection.

Finland and Russia, the case featured two flags: the personal flag of Nicholas II from 1914 to 1917 and the British red ensign that had been the mark of the Royal Navy to 1801 and in the First World War served as the flag of the British merchant navy. Fabergé experts theorize that the piece commemorated the provision of Russia with supplies by the British merchant marine, a mark of the connections of tobacco accessories and military matters.[7] The lightweight wood was a favorite of the royals for personal gifts, the humble material allowing for the workmanship to take center stage rather than ostentatious jewels and precious metals.[8]

The many artisans under the auspices of the House of Fabergé produced exquisitely designed and worked cases of metal, stone, and wood decorated with jewels, enamels, and metalworks for the tsar, his court, and other elite smokers. These represented the epitome of the craft and many have been preserved in excellent form. Not only are these beautiful objects but they serve as a unique source. Smoking, a habit of daily life for many as mundane as breathing, often escaped record keeping much like many of the quotidian samovars and spindles featured in this volume. Like other items—the shaman's coat or the maps of Remezov, for example—these cases have taken on a remarkable second life. Found, auctioned, collected, repatriated, and displayed, they have come to represent a fallen regime rather than punctuate the rituals of smokers' daily lives. Even as they are resurrected in this new guise, Fabergé objects, well-preserved, stamped with names of craftsmen, and documented with provenances of ownership and often dates and price of purchase, provide a rare view into a habit many enjoyed but few considered worthy of notice.

Cases served a utilitarian purpose—to protect the fragile papirosy from moisture, crushing, and tobacco loss—but they held meaning alongside the smokes. Exchanged as gifts, they served as reminders of important events and people. Alexander III received them from his children.[9] Engraving, a service regularized by Fabergé, solidified this association. Empress Alexandra Feodorovna gave Nicholas II a Karl Hahn case for New Years in 1895 inscribing it, in English, "for darling Nicky."[10] The court awarded cases as recognition for service, which smokers then displayed as signs of status. Other users bought cases for themselves and the themes of design, color of enamel, and choice of materials, all could convey messages of social standing, fashionable pretensions, political affiliation, or cultural aspiration that users displayed in a social argot understandable to other aficionados.[11]

For the user, the case held implications personal, social, and physical. The effects reached well beyond the relationship of owner to object. Fabergé's colleague and biographer Henry Charles Bainbridge noted that cases "serve a useful purpose" but also became for the smoker "constant companions."[12] As this essay argues, these "constant companions" held meanings for social status and identity. Even more, they affected the smoker physically, intimately, and immediately. Since cases never fully left the sensibility of the smoker, cases served as reminders to users of their habit and triggered continued use. Lighters, ashtrays, holders, and, most especially, cases became accessories to addiction and embedded the smoker in a web of prompts to continued use outside of the biological cues of withdrawal. The tsar experienced a style of smoking that dripped with luxury, but tobacco was democratic in its availability and cheaper accessories were available to simulate the experience for those unable to afford a Fabergé case.[13] Although Fabergé cases were luxury items, they triggered use in their visibility and imbued tobacco use with glamour spreading their effects well beyond the elite. In this way cases influenced bystanders too.

The role of the case in encouraging tobacco use—as an extravagant consumable, a social signifier, or a trigger to withdrawal—may have been important to the early development of tobacco dependency in Russia and might have been party to the higher amount of female smoking seen there. Whereas in narratives of tobacco in the United States, Britain, and China, historians argue mass use developed because of mass production of cheap smokes by machine, expansion of markets through seductive advertising, transitions to more addictive leaf, or manipulation of product qualities to increase use, such arguments do not hold true within the Russian context.[14] Russia developed into a society of smokers before large-scale mechanization, mass advertising, or product manipulations.[15] Other explanations must be sought for Russian mass use such as more nicotine-laden tobacco, more addictive styles of use, early associations with the military and masculinity, or substitution of tobacco in areas and eras of food scarcity. But the pull of smoking accessories is an aspect of habit formation not often discussed. Perhaps the early cases of Fabergé and the sensory allure they gave smoking provide one additional factor in the unique story of early, Russian, tobacco dependency.

## Cases, the Sensory, and Prompts to Use

The tsar enjoyed a distinctive experience of a habit that had become nearly universal. On the eve of the First World War, contemporaries estimated a large mass of the urban, male population in European Russia smoked about a pack a day. Women smoked in sufficient numbers to merit custom marketing, specialized brands, and gendered accessories.[16] Manufacturing statistics indicated the size and growth of smoking. From 1861 to 1900 the production of Russian tobacco increased from 1.3 billion to 8.6 billion items with the largest growth being in papirosy.[17] While no usage statistics are available for the empire, and much rural use escaped count, the more than one thousand Russian papirosy brands recorded by 1913 implied a market of diversity and size. By 1914, papirosy accounted for almost half of all processed tobacco in Russia; by 1922 they were 80 percent of processed tobacco.[18] Russians entered the First World War with perhaps the world's most intense tobacco habit. This switch to smoking, a possibly more addictive form of tobacco because of the speed and intensity of nicotine delivery, may explain the early spread of tobacco use in Russia. Most global markets continued with snuff, chaw, or pipes.[19]

Goldsmiths and jewelers catered to elite smokers with luxurious accessories but none so prolifically, inventively, and notably as the many artisans of the House of Fabergé, who provided unique, beautifully constructed accessories to smokers of the imperial family and accoutrements for rising numbers of Russians growing wealthy during the industrial boom of the 1890s.[20] For specialists in the art of Fabergé it is these cases, perhaps the most widely produced items from the artisans, that inspired the greatest interest. As Fabergé's business colleague Henry Charles Bainbridge observed in 1949,

> I say of all the productions of Fabergé, it is, in my opinion, his cigarette cases which should finally bring about this happy consummation [of his reputation]. Not only should the extraordinary [sic] large number of them contribute towards this but the main reason is that in them is the whole, not a portion, of the art of Fabergé. In the range of them every material made use of by Fabergé is employed; platinum, gold, silver, enamel, stone, wood (those in Karelian birch and other woods attract many people on account of their light weight and the simplicity of ornamentation in gold), precious stones, and they give an opportunity not only to the goldsmith but the lapidary and stone setter to display their separate crafts.

It was not just in their exquisite workmanship and fine materials, however, that these items held value. Bainbridge waxed on that the cases "are pleasing to look at and pleasant to feel, and above all have in them that quality I have called 'substance' which creates the sense of well-being which I believe to be the main reason for the attraction of all Fabergé objects."[21] To Bainbridge, the case was important because it was both simple and opulent. It infused the daily life of the user with luxury, quality, and "substance." The "pleasing" sensory experience—in feel, in look, in weight—attracted users as much as their utility. As Queen Mary said, upon picking up a case belonging to King George V of Britain, "there is one thing about all Fabergé pieces, they are so satisfying."[22] As a scholar noted, Fabergé's objects "have the quality of being artistic toys, pleasing to touch and turn in the hands."[23] As Cynthia Coleman Sparke, Russian art consultant for Bonhams auction house in London, argues, "It is in the *touché* or feel of a piece that its attribution [as a Fabergé piece] is secured."[24]

More than a pleasing experience, the feel of the case reminded the smoker of their habit. Through their physical intrusion on the senses, felt on the person or even perceptible in the possession of others, cases became more than inanimate objects—they became actors in smokers' lives triggering withdrawal and inducing use. The chemical nicotine is often depicted as the primary reason for smokers' continued use of tobacco, but sensory stimuli—the sight of a pack, the feel of a case in a pocket, the smell of smoke—can cue cravings and trigger the symptoms of withdrawal.[25] For the elite smoker, the case became a seductive, sensory stimulus. Nestled in the pocket or purse, cases repeatedly reminded the smoker of the ease and proximity of another papirosa. Even unseen, the case was sensible—the weight of a case in a pocket changed the fit of a jacket, arms crossed over the chest pushed it into the ribs, or an embrace communicated the feel of the case to both parties. The sensory prompts from tobacco accessories and other smokers stimulated the need for more for user and bystander. Even the lack of sensation had its place in the pull to continued use. Fabergé objects were famed for their "insensibility." Many styles of closure, most hidden, characterized Fabergé cases. Observers commented of the hinges and clasps—neither seen nor heard.[26] A satisfying swoosh of air, then silence, punctuated their shutting. So ingenious was his design that it was widely copied.[27]

Smokers did not just use cases; cases changed smoker behavior. Anthropologist Daniel Miller theorizes that while objects can serve as signifiers to other, conveying meanings important to identity, items can also influence user behaviors.[28] A case changed the ritual of the smoker—opening the case, extending it as an offer to a companion, perhaps tapping a papirosa upon its lid, removing a match from a hidden compartment, closing it with one or two hands (perhaps with a whoosh), and the return of the case to pocket—all became part of the smoking experience. Smoking rituals of the case had social as well as personal implications. They could encourage the smoker to ostentatiously display a case or inspire a companion to pull out their own in a competing spectacle of ritual and object. Passing around a lit tinder cord, a feature of some cases, created yet another social ritual.[29]

By exciting the senses of the smoker, Fabergé presaged developments in industrial design central to smoking's later seductions in the West. Sensory reminders to smoke intruded upon the tsar as with any smoker—be it the feel of a case in his pocket, the sight of accessories around him, or the smell of tobacco (fresh or stale) from his family members who also smoked. The *touché*, luxury, and beauty of his accessories created a further inducement to use, an aspect of habit formation that was not fully exploited by tobacco manufacturers until years later. Industrial designers in the West eventually considered every sense in construction of consumer appeals and researched the interaction of multiple senses so as to unlock "subconscious" consumer desires.[30] In terms of tobacco, the sensory appeal of the pack or case is made more intense by the fact that the "subconscious" of the consumer is already in play because of the biological functions of the product. The primary component of tobacco dependency—nicotine— creates physical responses within the body and habituates users to desire these effects even before the sensory appeals of the package are added.[31] Sensory historian David Howes argues that the senses are intimately bound to capitalist consumption with its luring of buyers to purchase luxury items made more affordable and available by mass production. He points out that the view of the product sparked desire but also the sensual experience of its packaging—opening, smelling, handling, and hearing— triggered consumption.[32] The sight of a papirosa or a case could elicit a visceral as well as aesthetic response, triggering the biological pull for addicts or the revulsions of committed nonsmokers.[33]

In their beauty and style, Fabergé cases were meant to be displayed, presented, and shown. They prompted others to touch, caress, and explore their shape and function, and they therefore became ideal cues for tobacco use for all around the smoker. The case was not just an individual prompt but a social invitation to addictive behavior. Other makers also produced cases, and while perhaps not of the same quality as those of Fabergé, they still held meaning for their users and influenced behavior. On the front lines, soldiers occasionally fashioned their own cases from spent shell casings infusing experience and memory into a habit they carried into peacetime.[34] Cases, be they luxurious or humble, prompted, poked, and prodded the body, reminding the smoker of their habit and inducing a desire for nicotine. In their "substance" and in their constant sensibility cases carried the seeds for further tobacco dependency.

## Smoking, Distinction, and the Case as Social Signifier

In the late imperial Russian city, smokers could buy papirosy easily and most everywhere—in pubs or restaurants, through retail and factory stores, and on the streets from sellers with cases of different brands or even from itinerant hustlers selling a few singles. Brand-specific artwork on packaging helped to differentiate papirosy at even a casual glance. The many vendors who offered their wares along the streets opened up display trays with dozens of boxes, packs, and portcigars. These miniature museums full of pieces of portable, affordable, collectible, and usable art tempted passersby. Prices ranged from .25 kopek to a full kopek per papirosa for factory-rolled smokes. Low-price brands like *Sladkie* (Sweetness) and *Zolotye* (Golden) nestled aside more expensive brands like *Modnye* (Fashionable) and *Diushess* (Duchess). Once purchased, the pack became a signal of a smoker's economic status or pretensions but also indicated political leanings (worker's *Trezvon*), an unsophisticated palate (cloying

*Dessert*), or even aesthetic tastes (heavy *Cigarnae*). Advertising posters carried the message further. *Vazhnye* (Great) celebrated its filtered smoke and sturdy portcigar case in its posters for distribution through the city.[35]

Cigarette packs were many things at once—marketing, art, symbol, protection, and collectible. In the Western context, tobacco was on the front lines of advertising as manufacturers pioneered many of the most inventive marketing strategies such as the first use of color, promotions with coupons and premiums, flamboyant skywriting, and product placements in cartoons and movies.[36] Seductive appeals, smooth messaging, and enticing packages lured new smokers to the habit and kept older smokers hooked.[37] Russian manufacturers similarly employed innovative means of attracting attention. New research on the effects of advertising and brand recognition has led to implementation in the West of plain packaging and pushes for graphic warning labels.[38] Printed advertising on packs presented an opportunity to not just lure the consumer to purchase in public. The case followed the smoker home even as they enticed new users on the street.

If alluring packs are considered an inducement to smoke today, it does not seem a major leap to consider that an expensive Fabergé case may have encouraged use in the past. Although not employed by the tobacco industry, Fabergé made more durable, and expensive, cases and tobacco accessories to tempt the growing market of smokers to another level of consumption. These stunning cases, holders, lighters, and ashtrays became some of the most popular items sold by the jeweler.[39] Smokers of means need not display the artwork of the manufacturer but instead could purchase a case that imbued the habit with custom connotations of affluence, status, and taste.

In their conception, Fabergé cases underscored the jeweler's focus upon what experts term "taste" over "noisy demonstrations of wealth" as the craftsmanship was emphasized over the price and size of the jewel decorations.[40] This did not mean items were cheap. For members of the elite, these were indulgences. For the lower classes they were completely out of reach. Although in their daily use the cases mirrored Fabergé's attempts to bring design elegance to mundane objects like desk sets and light switches and while Fabergé stood at the forefront of a new movement of "industrial arts" attempting to democratize beauty, he did not do the same for luxury.[41] According to records from the Bolshevik seizure of the shop in 1919, one of the most expensive pieces was an ashtray worth some 6,500 rubles, the equivalent of a year's salary for a lieutenant colonel.[42]

Although seemingly anyone could get hold of a passable papirosa, smokers could distinguish their consumption as more cultured than others with attention to type of tobacco, manufactured or self-rolled papirosa, quality of manufacture, and accessories to use. Papirosy smokers came from across the empire and up and down the social ladder. A smoker of means indulged in luxurious accessories for their habit such as special smoking rooms in houses, smoking jackets and hats, papirosy holders, ashtrays, lighters, and, most essentially and portably, cases. Using expensive accessories, the upper-class smokers of the late imperial period supplied their tobacco habit, shared with a growing number of lower-class smokers, with specialized trimmings to show how their consumption was more refined, more specialized, and more considered and therefore less brutish and base. The emphasis upon the value of the case as not evident in its materials but in an educated appreciation of its "substance," and the many ways in which tobacco products could be judged, required a new set of skills from the smoker—connoisseurship. Connoisseurship emerged through educated consumption, modeled from others' reactions, and displayed through orchestrated presentation of the self, not just from an outlay of cash. Even within the royal household good taste could not be bought. A snide commentary from one of the craftsmen in the House of Fabergé told of the lack of artistic appreciation and "middle-class" stinginess of the Empress Aleksandra and mocked orders from the court as displaying "absolutely no knowledge of art."[43]

Material displays of class distinction took on particular significance in the tumultuous scene of the late nineteenth and early twentieth centuries as large numbers of migrants moved to cities and large numbers of middle-class people moved into roles of affluence.[44] In the city they found the space to create new personae and encountered a developing consumer culture with the latest goods and fresh entertainments to consume in novel venues.[45] Swiftly rising social groups—recently emancipated peasants, newly urbanizing workers, an emerging class of business owners, and professionalizing doctors, lawyers, and bureaucrats—came together in the quickly developing urban areas, unmoored from past considerations of estates, localities, and tradition.[46] Nearly everyone smoked, but a case served as a signifier of class status and social distinction, and the materials, themes, and costs associated with cases contributed to efforts to establish the self and solidify status during disorienting social change. The case became a sign of discerning consumption, a means of its communication, and a language for its replication that also served as a solid symbol of a hard-won, yet perhaps tenuous, new identity.

The case brought the social and individual into tension. Carried on the body, the case was a personal item bound up in the definition of the self. The case itself—showing discernment and understanding—placed the smoker within a group. At the same time the cases of Fabergé allowed personalization that identified the user as an individual and distinct, such as a case carved of Karelian birch, which featured a picture and various charms to remind the user of events of his life (Figure 8.2). Dated with an inscription of July 29, 1915, the case showed a charm of a lady's fan and name along with a man's photograph, a fly, and snippets of inside jokes or messages. The decorations, a style of display often used by soldiers, perhaps sparked social interactions and conversation.[47] Even as the case indicated belonging in the community of tobacco connoisseurs, the many charms prompted personal reveries for the smoker that reinforced addiction by not just the "substance" of the case but with sweet reveries of times gone by.[48]

More formal presentation cases could be an even greater symbol of differentiation for a universal habit. In 1885, Tsar Alexander III named Fabergé as the Purveyor to the Imperial Court, and in 1890 Goldsmith by Special Appointment to the Imperial Crown. Under these auspices, the workshops began creating items that could be given for special recognition from the royal family.[49] A presentation gift from the tsar could come as medals or badges, or at times, snuffboxes and cases.[50] The item could be immediately turned back in for its cash equivalent or kept for use, but the value of an object was not just in the workmanship and materials. Case decoration accorded to a

**Figure 8.2** Photograph of case carved of Karelian birch and decorated with various charms, workmaster Julius Rappaport of St. Petersburg. Photo courtesy of the McFerrin Collection.

complex hierarchy of significance.[51] For ordinary occasions and gifts, the simple state emblem was chosen. For those of more significance, a cypher of the initials of a royal personage, the tsar or empress, could show this higher connection. At the ultimate stage of influence, power, and significance, a portrait of the tsar or his family indicated the highest esteem.[52]

A striking gold case with the double-headed eagle was presented around 1890 to George C. de Dvorjitsky (1889–1971) who served as a senior lieutenant of the imperial Russian navy (Figure 8.3). Shining beams of wavering heights radiated out from the symbol of the imperial family and would have confronted any user with the proximity of the smoker to the highest of powers. Such cases carried all the "substance" and beauty of other Fabergé pieces but layered upon them an added dose of social capital.

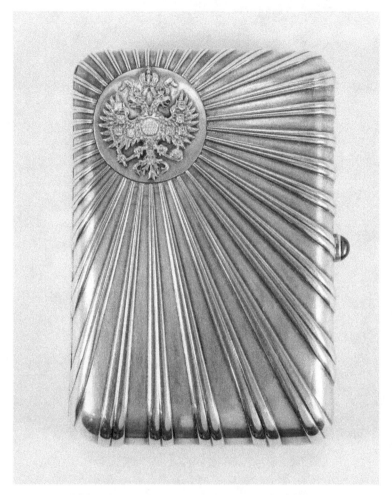

**Figure 8.3** Photograph of gold-mounted silver presentation case of George C. de Dvorjitsky with double-headed eagle, workmaster Mikhail Perkhin, St. Petersburg, *c.* 1890. Photo courtesy of the McFerrin Collection.

Historian Ulla Tillander-Godenhielm muses that presentation cases could serve as a material "curriculum vitae" for the user.[53] Pulled from a jacket pocket to afford a smoke the case became a sign of the user's status in the court as well as their wealth as an individual. On a personal level, the case opened conversation of one's merit or could even be a reminder to the user of their own self-worth, as mirrored back from the shining surface. In a system where precedence and proximity to power were of such import, in a society where economic status was in flux, the ability to show one's worth easily and quickly must have been of great use. The added incentive, and comfort, this gave to the actions of pulling out the case, showing off the emblem, and lighting up, is incalculable.

Other elite figures similarly used objects from Fabergé to reward those around them. The items became a language unto themselves that created bonds, smoothed associations, and recognized contributions. It was a language that eased social relationships when it was unclear how to proceed. As one Fabergé enthusiast remembered, "When any member of the community has something very personal or private to say to someone else ... [and] he has come to the conclusion that the saying may be done more delicately by a third party, then he goes to the goldsmith and jeweler who says it for him."[54] Among the lower classes, the silver case of less lofty manufacture could serve as a similar recognition of service to a foreman or boss—an impersonally personal object.[55]

## Cases, Gender, and Empire

A notable number of women smoked around the tsar. His mother, like his father, smoked heavily.[56] His wife supposedly took up the habit after the "nervous shock" of the Revolution of 1905.[57] Tsar Nicholas II's daughters smoked, too.[58] For women of means the Fabergé case was a delightful crossover from his opulent jewelry to their chemically addictive habit. The range of enamels and colors available in cases from Fabergé, from brilliant sapphire blue to delicate mauve, far exceeded the palette of other makers and allowed women to create ensembles of case, match case, and holder to glorify entire outfits. A delicate mauve ensemble of case and holder, currently in the McFerrin collection, showed the ways in which the combination of items could create a thematic whole.[59] The attraction of cases may have helped build the number of Russian female smokers, a group unique in their early visibility and seemingly accepted status.

Tobacco, manliness, and the military had strong associations in popular literature, paintings, branding, and advertising of the period. Cases accompanied men in combat, served as rewards, and commemorated battles. They were an expected accompaniment to military uniform, and soldiers used the cases not just to protect their papirosy but as records of their service, as may be the point of the charmed Karelian birch case (Figure 8.2).[60] A simple metal case from 1915, adorned with double-headed eagle and the number 1914–15, brought together the reminder of service with the use of tobacco.[61] A case in the State Historical Museum honors the battleship Azov, famous for its service against the Ottomans and Egyptians in the Battle of Navarino (1827).[62] Empress Mariia Feodorovna gave Emperor Alexander III a leather case inscribed with the dates 1877–8 to memorialize the end of the Russo-Turkish War.[63]

The military associations of cases echoed the connections of tobacco, smoking, and papirosy with imperial conquest. The Russian papirosa was an imperial affair—from leaf to manufacture. Most essentially, the leaf drew together the frontiers of imperial power. Oriental-leaf tobaccos were grown in Crimea and the regions of the Black Sea. Makhorka came from Ukraine, and tobacco seed accompanied invading forces into Central Asia.[64] Conflict threatened regular provision of leaf in the areas bordering the Ottoman Empire, yet also could bring opportunity. Nicholas II joked that war had helped him with his Turkish habit, chortling, "I am very happy that the Sultan brought a new supply of tobacco to the Crimea right before the outbreak of the war. Now I find myself in quite favorable conditions in this regard."[65] The tsar's quips regarding captured tobacco were but one entry in a cultural campaign connecting tobacco with the edges of empire, which entered into tobacco advertising and branding and influenced case design. One famous case showed a map of Crimea with jewels to depict Black Sea resorts along a coastline of sparkling blue sapphires. Produced by special order, the client hoped the item might convince a recalcitrant landowner to allow passage of the Crimean Railway across their lands to expand access to the resort area.[66]

The English critic Sir Sacheverell Reresby Sitwell went into rhapsodies over Fabergé's cases, and their materials, as symbols of Russia, sighing,

> Why, and how is it, that so simple an object as a cigarette case can speak to us with a Russian accent, and be as strong of flavour as a phrase out of a Russian song? The cigarette case can be in "red," or "green," or "yellow" gold; it does not matter. The finished object, as you handle it, is as "Russian" as any character in Russian history.[67]

This association with Russia was not, however, accidental. Fabergé evoked the strength of the Russian Empire not just in his themes but also in basic materials—the wood, hard stone, and gemstones of the land. The royal family preferred wood objects for personal gifts such as the Karelian wood of the case purportedly belonging to the tsar, which in its border origins secured imperial agendas. Using precious stones from the Urals and Siberia, worked in lapidaries established in the eighteenth century and fostered by Catherine the Great, Fabergé created cases of carved agate, quartz, rhodonite, and nephrite set with diamonds, rubies, tourmalines, topazes, and aquamarines gathered throughout the empire.[68] These carved cases, ashtrays, and match holders became displays of the riches of Russia.[69] Nephrite, a jade-like stone of Siberia, was used for a significant number of cases and other accessories such as a fuel lighter whimsically carved into the shape of a hippopotamus with diamond set eyes.[70]

These stones represented not just an expedience of using locally sourced materials but also evoked national pride. The expedition of the German naturalist Alexander von Humboldt (1769–1859), as well as that of mineralogist Christian Gottfried Ehrenberg (1795–1876), had revealed the rich geological resources of Siberia and the Urals to global notice, and the attention of Fabergé to techniques for working stone and training of artisans allowed full utilization of this wealth.[71] The use of Russian hard stone also coincided with state priorities. In 1912, Nicholas II promoted the "production of artistic objects made from Russian minerals."[72]

The materials and artistic themes of Fabergé celebrated Russian resources and the decorative styles utilized Russian folklore, native designs, and imperial imagery. The creation of museums to celebrate early East Slavic art, the display of Scythian artifacts, and the Abramstevo workshops of Savva Ivanovich Mamontov, all contributed to the style.[73] Fabergé resurrected older methods of applied art for his cases, part of a trend for imperial kitsch encouraged by the state.[74] A case in the old Russian style might display seventeenth-century techniques of cloisonné enameling (metal wires encasing enameled patches of color) and filigree ornamentation.[75] The fanciful bogatyr, a mythic warrior of the East Slavic past who thundered across the steppe and defended the frontiers of old Rus', became a staple of decorative arts and tobacco imagery. The bogatyr image called to mind military valor, imperial ideals, and masculine strength. He appeared on many cases and featured in Russian tobacco advertising and branding.[76] A case image attributed to the painter Alexander Borozdin (1880–1918) combined the figure of the bogatyr with enamel work and cloisonné.[77] The case of Colonel Oleg Ivanovich Paniukhov (1882–1973) used imagery of bogatyrs in the style of the painter Nicholas Roerich (1874–1947).[78]

One exquisite case combining Old Russia styling and the bogatyr came from the Moscow workshop and has been dated from the period 1908–17 (Figure 8.4). Men in battle—here Slavs and Scythians—struggle on horseback in a field of grain. The small

**Figure 8.4** Photograph of case with cloisonné decoration in style of Viktor Vasnetsov's *Battle of the Scythians* (1879) belonging to Colonel Oleg Ivanovich Pantiukhov, workmaster Feodor Ruckert, Moscow, 1908–17. Photo courtesy of the McFerrin Collection.

painting echoed the works of the painter Viktor Vasnetsov (1848–1926), famed for pictures like "Knight at the Crossroads" and "Bogatyrs." In the case, from the Moscow workshop, Vasnetsov's 1879 painting "Battle of the Slavs and Scythians" brought history, masculinity, militarism, and bravado to the act of smoking.[79] The elaborately enameled cloisonné patterning created a case that would have had a distinctive feel on the exterior as well as a beautiful clash of colors, patterns, and images. The case belonged to Colonel Oleg Ivanovich Pantiukhov, founder of one of Russia's first scout troops and a hero of the First World War, and may have been given him alongside his Order of St. George in 1915. Together imagery and owner showed the tradition of cases as awards and the connection of military men with tobacco.

## Conclusion

As utilitarian object, prompt to nicotine craving, mark of character, and social signifier, the cigarette case furthered the visibility and spread of smoking behavior in late imperial Russia. The cases of Fabergé provided incentives to smoking for those of the upper classes. They were invested with meaning for nation and empire that connected tobacco to larger issues of character and identity. For women, they imbued their habit with elegance and femininity through dainty, softly enameled accessories. For men, their figures of heroic derring-do underscored connections to archetypical masculine characteristics foundational to Russian imperial and military strength. The value of the case was amplified by the social meaning it gained either in the imperial awards system or because of familial connections. Finally, in addition to the beauty of their execution, their sensory allures encouraged continued tobacco use. Analysis of the tobacco accessories and cases of Fabergé show one more way in which smoking became part of Russian culture and associated with luxury, enjoyment, and status.

Beautiful cases may have encouraged uptake and prompted continued tobacco use in the imperial era, but after 1917 tobacco accessory use declined. The artistry and luxury of Fabergé did not long survive the period of war, upheaval, and revolution. In the First World War many of the Fabergé artisans were called or volunteered to service, and those who remained saw the workshops turned over to produce artillery shells and syringes instead of cases and jewelry.[80] With the revolution, the stocks of the workshop were seized and the artisans moved into other pursuits.[81] Carl Fabergé left the country soon after 1917, and his son Agathon was pressed into service evaluating the riches of the bourgeoisie and weighing their value.[82] Fabergé cases dispersed onto the world market with refugees and Bolshevik sales even as Soviet citizens smoked in greater and greater numbers. The cases disappeared, but the habit remained.

## Notes

I am indebted to Dorothy McFerrin and Jennifer McFerrin-Bohner for access to the McFerrin Collection at the Houston Museum of Natural Science. Research for this piece was made possible by a National Library of Medicine and National Institutes of Health

Grant for Scholarly Works in Biomedicine and Health (Award Number G13LM011893). Views in this piece are those of the author, not of any granting agency.

1. The items were technically papirosy cases but are termed "cigarette cases" in Western scholarship. I use the more generic "cases" except in quotations from Western scholars.
2. Svetlana Belova, "Vrednye privychki imperatora: Nikolai II kuril 25 papiros v den'," *Moskovskii komsomolets*, November, 9, 2017. Accessed April 22, 2019, https://www.mk.ru/social/2017/11/09/vrednye-privychki-imperatora-nikolay-ii-kuril-25-papiros-v-den.html.
3. Ibid. Christel Ludewig McCanless and Riana Benko, "Fabergé Brick Table Match Holders/Strikers," *Fabergé Newsletter*, Spring and Summer 2019. Accessed April 24, 2019, https://fabergeresearch.com/newsletter-2019-spring-and-summer/.
4. Peter H. Lindert and Steven Nafziger, "Russian Inequality on the Eve of Revolution," *Journal of Economic History* 74:3 (2014), 782; Alexander von Solodkoff, *The Art of Carl Fabergé* (New York: Crown, 1988), 114.
5. Tatiana F. Fabergé, Eric-Alain Koehler, and Valentin V. Skurlov, *Fabergé: A Comprehensive Reference Book* (Genève: Éditions Slatkine, 2012), 424; Matthew Hilton, *Smoking in British Popular Culture, 1800–2000* (Manchester: Manchester University Press, 2000), 403.
6. Belova, "Vrednye privychki imperatora."
7. Dorothy McFerrin, "Cigarette and Vesta Cases," in *From a Snowflake to an Iceberg: The McFerrin Collection* ed. Julie Osterman (Houston: McFerrin Foundation, 2013), 76–7.
8. Ibid.
9. Dorothy McFerrin and Jennifer McFerrin-Bohner, *Fabergé: The McFerrin Collection: The Opulence Continues* (Humble, TX: Artie and Dorothy McFerrin Foundation, 2016), item number 563, p. 19.
10. McFerrin, "Cigarette and Vesta Cases," 103.
11. Michael Brake, *The Sociology of Youth Culture and Youth Subcultures* (New York: Routledge, 2013), 13–19.
12. Henry Charles Bainbridge, *Peter Carl Fabergé: Goldsmith and Jeweler to the Russian Imperial Court, His Life and Work* (repr. 1949; Bungay: Spring Books, 1966), 125.
13. Cynthia Coleman Sparke, *Russian Decorative Arts* (Woodbridge: Antique Collectors Club, 2014), 32–3.
14. Robert N. Proctor, *Golden Holocaust: Origins of the Cigarette Catastrophe and the Case for Abolition* (Berkeley: University of California Press, 2011), 28–30; Jordan Goodman, *Tobacco in History: The Cultures of Dependence* (London: Routledge, 1993), 101–4; Robin Walker, *Under Fire: A History of Tobacco Smoking in Australia* (Carlton: Melbourne University Press, 1984), 1–8; Carol Benedict, *Golden-Silk Smoke: A History of Tobacco in China, 1550–2010* (Berkeley: University of California press, 2011), 131–48; Howard Cox, *The Global Cigarette: Origins and Evolution of British American Tobacco, 1880–1945* (New York: Oxford University Press, 2000), 19–45; John C. Burnham, *Bad Habits: Drinking, Smoking, Taking Drugs, Gambling, Sexual Misbehavior, and Swearing in American History* (New York: New York University Press, 1993), 86–111; Roberta G. Ferrence, *Deadly Fashion: The Rise and Fall of Cigarette Smoking in North America* (New York: Garland, 1989); Gerard S. Petrone, *Tobacco Advertising: The Great Seduction* (Atglen, PA: Schiffer, 1996), 65–9; Nannie M. Tilley, *The R. J. Reynolds Tobacco Company* (Chapel Hill: University of North Carolina Press, 1985), 29–94; Nan Enstad, *Cigarettes, Inc.: An Intimate History of Corporate Capitalism* (Chicago: University of Chicago Press, 2018).

15. Tricia Starks, *Smoking under the Tsars: A History of Tobacco in Imperial Russia* (Ithaca, NY: Cornell University Press, 2018), 1–5.
16. F. V. Greene, *Sketches of Army Life in Russia* (New York: Charles Scribner's Sons, 1880), 14; "Russian Paper Trade: The Manufacture of Paper Cigarette Tubes," in *The World's Paper Trade Review*, March 29, 1907, 8; Ivan Ivanovich Priklonskii, *Upotrebelenie tabaka i ego vrednoe na organism cheloveka vliianie* (Moscow: K. Tikhomivor, 1909), 5; I. Tregubov, *Normal'nyi sposob brosit' kurit'* (Batum: D. L. Kapelia, 1912), 3.
17. M. V. Dzhervis, *Russkaia tabachnaia fabrika v XVIII i XIV vekakh* (Leningrad: Akademii nauk SSSR, 1933), 16.
18. Anon., "Tabachnaia promyshlennost' za 40 let sovetskoi vlasti," *Tabak* 3 (1957), 11; Lev Borisovich Kafengauz, *Evoliutsiia promyshlennogo proizvodstva Rossii (posledniaia tret' XIX v.–30-e gody XX v.)* (Moscow: Epifaniia, 1994), 166, 198, 265.
19. Kathleen Sebelius, *How Tobacco Smoke Causes Disease: The Biology and Behavioral Basis for Smoking-Attributable Disease: A Report of the Surgeon General*, hereafter *SGR* (Rockville, MD: US Department of Health and Human Services, 2010), 110–11; Goodman, *Tobacco*, 5–6; Neal L. Benowitz, "Nicotine Addiction," *New England Journal of Medicine* 362 (2010), 2295–303; David T. Courtwright, *Forces of Habit: Drugs and the Making of the Modern World* (Cambridge, MA: Harvard University Press, 2002), 56.
20. G. G. Smorodinova and B. L. Ulyanova, "The Russian Master Goldsmiths," in *Fabergé and the Russian Master Goldsmiths* ed. Gerard Hill (New York: Macmillan, 1989), 50; Bainbridge, *Peter Carl Fabergé*, 125.
21. Bainbridge, *Peter Carl Fabergé*, 125.
22. Ibid., 109
23. Solodkoff, *The Art of Carl Fabergé*, 21.
24. Sparke, *Russian Decorative Arts*, 137.
25. Sebelius, *SGR*, 120, 181; J. E. Rose, "Multiple Brain Pathways and Receptors Underlying Tobacco Addiction," *Biochemical Pharmacology* 74 (2007), 1263–70; K. Faberstrom, "Determinants of Tobacco Use and Renaming the FTND to the Faberstrom Test for Cigarette Dependence," *Nicotine Tobacco Research* 14 (2012), 75–8.
26. Tatiana F. Fabergé and Valenin V. Skurlov, *The History of the House of Fabergé: According to the Recollections of the Senior Master Craftsman of the Firm, Franz P. Birbaum* (St. Petersburg: Fabergé and Skurlov, 1992), 30.
27. Solodkoff, *The Art of Carl Fabergé*, 17.
28. Daniel Miller, *Stuff* (Cambridge: Polity, 2010), 23–31.
29. Sparke, *Russian Decorative Arts*, 32–3.
30. David Howes, "HYPERESTHESIA, or, the Sensual Logic of Late Capitalism," in *Empire of the Senses: The Sensual Culture Reader* (London: Bloomsbury Academic, 2005), 284–92.
31. Sebelius, *SGR*, 31, 32; Neal L. Benowitz, "Nicotine Addiction," *New England Journal of Medicine* 362 (2010): 2295–303.
32. Howes, "HYPERESTHESIA," 284–92.
33. Sebelius, *SGR,* 181; Rose, "Multiple Brain Pathways," 1263–70; Fagerstrom, "Determinants of Tobacco Use," 75–8.
34. Nicholas J. Saunders, "Bodies of Metal, Shells of Memory: 'Trench Art', and the Great War Re-cycled," *Journal of Material Culture* 5:1 (2000), 43–67.

35. Urban markets found more ready-made papirosy in either loose or pack forms. The countryside relied on self-rolled, makhorka smokes. This resembled the market system of China where urban and rural smokers lived very different experiences. Benedict, *Golden-Silk Smoke*, 11; Prices and brand information from Starks, *Smoking under the Tsars*, 38, 110, 131.
36. Proctor, *Golden Holocaust*, 59
37. John Burnham coined the concept of the "vice industrial complex," *Bad Habits*, 230. Other historians have done a much more thorough exploration of the ways in which the tobacco industry crafted an entire sensory appeal from the snapping open of the pack's cellophane to the first inhalation. See Proctor regarding the multifaceted marketing campaigns of tobacco producers as well as his arguments for plain packaging, *Golden Holocaust*, 56-78, 550.
38. See, for example, David Hammond and Carla Parkinson, "The Impact of Cigarette Package Design on Perceptions of Risk," *Journal of Public Health* 31 (2009), 345-53.
39. McFerrin, "Cigarette and Vesta Cases," 45.
40. *Easter Eggs and other Precious Objects by Carl Fabergé: A Private Collection of Masterworks Made for the Imperial Russian Court* (Washington, DC: Corcoran Gallery of Art, 1961), 10. For a theorist's dissection of the term see Pierre Bourdieu, *Distinction: A Social Critique of the Judgement of Taste* (Cambridge: Harvard University Press, 1984).
41. Tatiana F. Fabergé, Eric-Alain Koehler, and Valentin V. Skurlov, *Fabergé: A Comprehensive Reference Book* (Genève: Éditions Slatkine, 2012), 424; Hilton, *Smoking*, 33-5.
42. Fabergé, Koehler, and Skurlov, *Fabergé*, 424.
43. Fabergé and Skurlov, *History of the House of Fabergé*, 28-30.
44. Starks, *Smoking under the Tsars*, 102-61.
45. Lynda Need, "Mapping the Self: Gender, Space and Modernity in Mid-Victorian London," in *Rewriting the Self: Histories from the Renaissance to the Present*, ed. Roy Porter (London: Routledge, 1997), 184-5; Louise McReynolds, *Russia at Play: Leisure Activities at the End of the Tsarist Era* (Ithaca, NY: Cornell University Press, 2003), 3-6; Anna Fishzon, *Fandom, Authenticity, and Opera: Mad Acts and Letter Scenes in Fin-de-Siècle Russia* (New York: Palgrave Macmillan, 2013), 15; Sally West, *I Shop in Moscow: Advertising and the Creation of Consumer Culture in Late Tsarist Russia* (DeKalb: Northern Illinois University Press, 2011), 5.
46. Alison K. Smith, *For the Common Good and Their Own Well-Being: Social Estates in Imperial Russia* (Oxford: Oxford University Press, 2014), 123-48; Joseph Bradley, *Muzhik and Muscovite: Urbanization in Late Imperial Russia* (Berkeley: University of California Press, 1985), 4; Harley D. Balzer, ed., *Russia's Missing Middle Class: The Professions in Russian History* (Armonk, NY: M. E. Sharpe, 1996), 89-116; Mark D. Steinberg, *Proletarian Imagination: Self, Modernity, and the Sacred in Russia, 1910-1925* (Ithaca, NY: Cornell University Press, 2002), 2-9.
47. See further examples in Sparke, *Russian Decorative Arts*, 32-3.
48. McFerrin, "Cigarette and Vesta Cases," 61.
49. Sparke, *Russian Decorative Arts*, 118; McFerrin and McFerrin-Bohner, *Fabergé*, 20; Solodkoff gives the year as 1884, *Masterpieces*, 33.
50. Porcelain snuffboxes had a long history as gifts. S. Troinitskii, *Farforovyia tabakerki imperatorskago ermitazha* (Petrograd: Starye gody, 1915), 5-7.
51. Fabergé and Skurlov, *History of the House of Fabergé*, 24.

52. Mark Moehrke, "Introduction," in *Fabergé: The McFerrin Collection, the Art of Presentation*, ed. Julie Osterman (Houston, TX: McFerrin Foundation, 2019), 8–9; Tillander-Godenhielm, *Jewels from Imperial St. Petersburg*, 175.
53. Ulla Tillander-Godenhielm, "Foreword," in *Fabergé: The McFerrin Collection*, 3.
54. Bainbridge, *Fabergé*, 49
55. Victoria E. Bonnell, ed. *The Russian Worker: Life and Labor under the Tsarist Regime* (Berkeley: University of California Press, 1983), 106.
56. Belova, "Vrednye privychki imperatora."
57. Ibid.
58. Fabergé, Koehler, and Skurlov, *Fabergé*, 403
59. McFerrin and McFerrin-Bohner, *Fabergé*, item number 538, p. 41.
60. Greene, *Sketches of Army Life*, 5–6.
61. McFerrin and McFerrin-Bohner, *Fabergé*, item number 372, p. 103.
62. Smorodinova and Ulyanova, "The Russian Master Goldsmiths," 48.
63. McFerrin and McFerrin-Bohner, *Fabergé*, item number 372, p. 103.
64. Starks, *Smoking under the Tsars*, 22–4; S. V. Lebedev, N. O. Osipov, N. I. Oprkhorov, and V. G. Shaposhnikov, "Tabak," in *Entsiklopedicheskii slovar' XXXII*, ed. F. A. Brokgauz and I. A. Efron (St. Petersburg: I. A. Efron, 1901), 421; W. A. Brennan, *Tobacco Leaves: Being a Book of Facts for Smokers* (Menasha, WI: Index Office, 1915), 63, 136; Jeff Sahadeo, *Russian Colonial Society in Tashkent, 1865–1923* (Bloomington: Indiana University Press, 2007), 21, 145, 152.
65. Belova, "Vrednye privychki imperatora."
66. Fabergé, Koehler, and Skurlov, *Fabergé*, 197.
67. Scheverell Sitwell, "Foreword," in *Peter Carl Fabergé*, by Henry Charles Bainbridge, viii.
68. Ulla Tillander-Godenhielm, *Jewels from Imperial St. Petersburg* (St. Petersburg: Liki Rossii, 2012), 197, 231; Fabergé, Koehler, and Skurlov, *Fabergé*, 63–5.
69. Tillander-Godenhielm, *Jewels from Imperial St. Petersburg*, 231; Smorodinova and Ulyanova, "Russian Master Goldsmiths," 45.
70. Smorodinova and Ulyanova, "Russian Master Goldsmiths," 47.
71. Fabergé, Koehler, and Skurlov, *Fabergé*, 331; on diamonds, 387.
72. Fabergé, Koehler, and Skurlov, *Fabergé*, 72.
73. Tillander-Godenhielm, *Jewels from Imperial St. Petersburg*, 168.
74. Fabergé, Koehler, and Skurlov, *Fabergé*, 226; Smorodinova and Ulyanova, "Russian Master Goldsmiths," 33.
75. Solodkoff, *Art of Carl Fabergé*, 16; Sparke, *Russian Decorative Arts*, 57–8, 64–7.
76. Starks, *Smoking under the Tsars*, 38–42; Stephen M. Norris, *A War of Images: Russian Popular Prints, Wartime Culture, and National Identity, 1812–1945* (DeKalb: Northern Illinois University Press, 2006), 121, 149.
77. Fabergé, Koehler, and Skurlov, *Fabergé*, 142.
78. McFerrin, "Cigarette and Vesta Cases," 51.
79. McFerrin and McFerrin-Bohner, *Fabergé*, 144.
80. Fabergé, Koehler, and Skurlov, *Fabergé*, 530–2.
81. Ibid., 543.
82. Aleksandr Ivanovich Rupasov, *Agafon Faberzhe v Krasnom Petrograde* (St. Petersburg: Liki Rossii, 2012).

9

# Socialism in One Tank: The T-34 as a Microcosm

Brandon Schechter

*My Tatiana is a rather dirty lady, dangerous and lewd, unlike my old love Argentina. But I don't let her get away with anything and pay little heed to her caprices.*

So wrote Dmitrii Kabanov in a letter to an intimate in March of 1943.[1] He was not bragging about romantic conquests. Kabanov was part of the massive buildup of Soviet forces near the Kursk salient, and he was writing his mother about the difference between the two T-34 tanks he drove and serviced. His letters home contained accounts of the machines he had come to know intimately and personally, as individuals, and to which he bestowed affectionate nicknames. Like tens of thousands of other Soviet citizens, Kabanov's fate was closely tied to the T-34 tank. He drove them, visited the factory that produced the majority of them, and eventually became an expert repair technician salvaging them from the battlefield.

The T-34 tank was the most widely produced tank of the Second World War and by many accounts, the best.[2] It was also a physical embodiment of Stalinism: one of the major fruits of Stalin's crash industrialization, designed by beneficiaries of Soviet social mobility, built mostly by workers learning on the job, and crewed by carefully vetted true believers, this iconic tank was created and animated by the society that formed under Stalin's reign. The T-34 was literally a moving fortress, often isolated and surrounded by enemies, just as the Soviet Union imagined itself in a constant state of siege. It proved to be a remarkably effective weapon in winning a war that many observers thought that the Soviet Union would lose. After victory, this tank became one of the most common monuments to the Red Army's triumph, mounting pedestals from Nizhnii Tagil to Berlin and Prague (Figure 9.1).

The T-34 was both an actual object and a metaphorical microcosm of the state and society that produced it. It was an inanimate thing and an intimate friend and protector to soldiers like Kabanov. The soldier's emotional bond accompanied a unique bodily and physical experience. The tank was a necessity of war and cultural symbol. This chapter begins with a brief discussion of the tank as a tool and its capacities, then examines the tank's development and production. The final sections explore how

**Figure 9.1** Drawing of a T-34, from the cover of *Tank T-34 v boiu* (Moscow: Voenizdat, 1942).

people interacted with the T-34 and the tank's impact on culture both during and after the war.

This is a story of how people touched tanks and tanks touched people. This essay attempts to provide the social life of this tank, along the lines of Igor Kopytoff's seminal essay, focusing on the changing meaning of the object over time and attempts to singularize a mass-produced object as well as drawing inspiration from his conscious blurring of the line between people and things. My overall understanding of material culture and its place has been most influenced by Leora Auslander's call to look "beyond words" to understand history, Bruno Latour's use of objects to anchor actors and their actions, and Elaine Scarry's concept of material objects as embodied knowledge.[3]

## The Thing Itself

Tanks were originally devised as a solution to the problem of the machine gun during the First World War.[4] They could destroy strong enemy positions, serve as mobile protection for their crew, and provide a screen against small arms fire for infantry that followed behind. By the Second World War, tanks had developed into fast-moving, heavily armored machines that fundamentally changed the battlefield, expanding the space of the front and allowing for rapid movement that would have been physically impossible in previous wars. As the Germans had shown in 1939 and 1940, massing tanks in coordination with airpower and artillery could end wars almost as quickly as they began.

Stalin defined the Second World War as a "war of motors" in which machinery would play a decisive role.[5] An arms race that began in the interwar period intensified with the initiation of hostilities, as the battlefield provided a proving ground in which both the speed and urgency of development were greatly accelerated. The T-34 had a number of innovations and initially shocked the Germans.[6] Kabanov wrote in July of 1941: "So far the machine has vindicated itself completely and German shells can't touch its armor ... they do no more harm than a fly to an elephant." Unfortunately, this behemoth required constant maintenance and could be capricious: Kabanov missed his first battle as his tank broke down on the way to the front.[7] Hundreds of these excellent machines would be abandoned in the first days of the war due to breakdowns or lack of fuel. But when they worked, they could be decisive.

Initially virtually impervious to German artillery, in 1941 there was no better medium tank (the workhorse of any army) than the T-34. Although by 1943 the Germans had developed much more powerful tanks, they could never produce them on the scale that the Soviets could manufacture the T-34. This mirrored the overall Allied strategy of creating simple machines that could be produced in overwhelming numbers as opposed to the Axis obsession with innovation and creating wonder weapons, often framed as Ford versus Porsche. By 1943 an individual German tank crew was likely to survive longer in battle, but the army that could field fleets of cheaper T-34s was going to win the war, particularly as the Soviets constantly refined their workhorse.[8]

The T-34 was an impressive, terrifying machine designed to allow a small group of soldiers immense killing potential and the ability to function autonomously. The first version of the T-34 weighed 28.5 tons, could travel up to 50 kilometers per hour, and carried over 700 liters of diesel fuel, a crowbar, a saw, an ax, two spades, and four crew members. The tank also carried a fire extinguisher (which had to be used while wearing a gasmask, as it produced phosgene gas), a medical kit, and (in theory although not always in practice) a radio. Armed with a 76mm cannon, 71 shells, 3 DP machineguns with 1,890 rounds of ammunition, 20 F-1 grenades, and the soldiers' own personal weapons, the tank was virtually a mobile fortress.[9] It featured thick (45mm) armor that was sloped to maximize protection from the front and rear, made of an amalgam of different metals that could absorb the shock of a standard 45mm anti-tank shell with no damage to the crew.[10] Built with function, rather than comfort, in mind, there was effectively no room for soldiers' personal effects, which were often stowed outside the tank itself. One tanker declared "in general real tankers don't have anything—it gets lost in battle."[11] It was furthermore too cramped and cold to sleep in, necessitating tank crews to find shelter or dig themselves a dugout under their tanks.[12] By the end of the war, the revamped T-34–85 weighed 32.7 tons, had traded the 76mm cannon for a much more powerful 85mm cannon, with 55 shells and 860 liters of fuel, and the interior had also been remodeled.[13]

## Production Relationships

The T-34 was a weapon that would shape the battlefields of the Second World War, yet the tank's development and production came at immense cost. The T-34's production was made possible by Stalin's crash industrialization begun a decade before the war, which he justified with appeals to national security. Stalin argued that the Bolsheviks had ten years at most to catch up to the industrialized, capitalist countries that encircled the Soviet Union or they would be defeated.[14] Industrialization would come at an unimaginable cost, paid first and foremost by the Soviet peasantry, and millions of peasants died of starvation as the state prioritized industrialization over the lives of its citizens.[15] The resulting system was not always efficient and often produced substandard items, but Soviet planners expected to do things at a speed and scale that many thought impossible. They consistently valued quantity over quality, pushing their workers to the limit.[16] This would serve them well when the war came.

Hagiographical accounts of the tank's design and production, while eschewing the cost of creating the country's industrial base, point to the Revolution as freeing people to realize their creative and productive potential. As General A. A. Morozov, who oversaw production of the tanks and would become one of the keepers of its memory, declared,

> Despite the lofty virtues of the T-34, it is necessary to underline that the machine was made not by some super-humans or geniuses who came out of nowhere. The T-34 is the fruit of the immense enthusiasm, industriousness and patriotism of Soviet people. The workers of our construction bureau did not have the opportunity to study in famous universities, and they did not have the legacy of prior generations and traditions of developed machine engineering. They were all children of the country of workers and peasants, which had just stood on its feet, newly creating many sectors of industry.[17]

This "fruit of great enthusiasm" was designed and built largely by yesterday's peasants, the type of people unlikely to be serving on construction bureaus in other countries, and the tank would be specially designed to be produced in a country new to wide-scale machine industry.

Soviet leadership promised social mobility and demanded a fanatical work ethic, and perhaps no one personified these two tendencies more than Mikhail Il'ich Koshkin, the main engineer who designed the T-34. A Russian peasant who had served in the tsarist army and then the Red Army, he became the beneficiary of the Communist Party's obsession with education. He graduated from Sverdlov Communist University in 1924, becoming the director of a candy factory, then a full-time party worker. In 1929, he was allowed to pursue an engineering degree in Leningrad, which he finished in 1934. From there his rise was meteoric—an Order of the Red Star in 1936, head of the tank bureau at Kharkov, and finally their head engineer. The main designer of the legendary tank never lived to see it tested in battle: instead he worked himself to death. Returning from a successful demonstration of the T-34 prototypes in Moscow in the fall of 1940, his vehicle flipped near Tula and he was seriously injured. He refused treatment, traveling back to Kharkov. Shortly thereafter, he was hospitalized with pneumonia and died. Koshkin was posthumously awarded the Stalin Prize in 1942 and the Hero of Socialist Labor in 1990, crowning an ideal Bolshevik career. (Unfortunately, and ironically, the Germans destroyed his grave when they occupied Kharkov.)[18]

The T-34 was designed not "to catch up with, but to surpass" other weapons systems, in particular those of the German firm Krupp.[19] It was specifically engineered to be produced by a relatively poor country with limited technological capabilities and largely by unskilled labor.[20] It featured a diesel engine, which was significantly less flammable and more efficient than tanks that ran on gasoline.[21] Wide tracks allowed the T-34 to maneuver in a variety of terrain, including the infamous lack of roads and harsh winters of Russia. The tank had a low profile, making it easier to camouflage and less of a target.[22] It also had a high-caliber cannon that made it particularly deadly.

More important to its success than its innovative characteristics was the fact that it could be produced economically and quickly. The Soviets manufactured the T-34 in shocking numbers, building 58,681 between 1940 and 1945, over ten thousand more than the next most produced tank, the US M-4 "Sherman." It made up between 40 and 80 percent of Soviet tank production every year of the war.[23] By contrast the Third Reich produced a total of just over thirty-five thousand tanks during the war.[24] Soviet workers accomplished this feat in part due to a restriction on new designs during the war, as Stalin forbade the development of new tanks, saying, "You don't design a pump during a fire."[25] The Soviet Union only produced three basic tank chassis during the war, as opposed to the Germans who fundamentally redesigned their tanks several times.[26] The Soviets identified a number of issues with components of the tank before the war and made plans to fix them by 1942, yet the war made fundamental changes impossible.[27] In true Soviet fashion, emphasis was placed on maximum numbers rather than an optimal product.

Soviet workers made tens of thousands of tanks quickly despite being forced to evacuate from western regions and move deep into the hinterland. The only factory that produced the tank before the war, Koshkin's Factory No. 183, dislocated from Kharkov to Nizhnii Tagil in the fall of 1941, taking over and expanding the Uralvagonzavod, which itself had only recently been built during the first Five Year Plan. Factory No. 183 produced over half of the T-34s made during the war (1,675 in Kharkov, 28,952 in Nizhnii Tagil).[28] This factory built the bulk of T-34s, although T-34s were also produced in Stalingrad, Gorky (Nizhnii Novgorod), Omsk, Sverdlovsk (Ekaterinburg), and Cheliabinsk.

While the tank had been designed to be built largely by people with minimal skills (much of the labor force consisted of adolescents learning on the job), by 1942 serious problems had become apparent both with the design of the tank and the quality of tanks being produced. After a series of complaints by tankers, Factory No. 183 held an emergency conference on September 11–13, 1942. The quality of tanks had declined precipitously, with up to 89 percent exhibiting significant cracks in their armor at the time of production.[29] The report filed after the conference could be read as a caricature of Soviet industry that was obsessed with quantity over quality or a beleaguered regime's desperate attempt to expand production under impossible conditions. Rubber, ball bearings, tracks, and a variety of other vital details were in short supply and of poor quality when available. Rubber deficits left large seams in the tank, allowing water to drip into the cabin and potentially damaging electrical parts and rusting components, including ammunition storage, which ultimately led to breakdowns.[30] Workers failed to lubricate fundamental parts of the tank or properly attach bolts to such vital components as the gearshift. According to Stalin, Soviet tanks were also capable of going only a quarter of the distance of German tanks before requiring maintenance.[31]

Constructor bureau chief Morozov's report revealed a haphazard, improvised system and its results. Eighty percent of the workers at the factory were new to the job and lacked proper training, including inspectors responsible for the quality of production. Parts that had been rejected were used anyway and there was no mechanism in place to hold individual workers responsible for faulty work—it was only possible to punish quality inspectors who passed faulty goods. Additionally, highly skilled workers were being called from their stations to do menial tasks such as gathering firewood or unloading cargo and there was no functioning research bureau. The combination of valuing quantity over quality, shifting production thousands of kilometers east, and rapid expansion of the base of workers had all come home to roost. The report called for the return of research bureaus, stricter testing of finished tanks, for each worker to have their own stamp, and the simplification and improvement of parts.[32]

By and large, the situation improved. Workers learned their trade, ersatz materials were found, and the tank was dramatically simplified. By the end of 1942, the inventory of T-34 parts was reduced by 6,237 pieces, with several hundred more eliminated over the next few years. Parts were increasingly stamped or poured, rather than machined, requiring less skilled labor.[33] This had a dramatic impact on both the sturdiness of the machine and the ability to return damaged tanks to service. The simplification of parts evolved alongside an ever more sophisticated system of field repair shops that later in the war could fix complex components such as engines and cannons. One repair master noted that by the end of the war, tanks were routinely returned to service two or three times in the course of a month-long operation, often after their original crews had been killed or wounded.[34]

## Physical and Emotional Relationships

Affective relationships with tanks began before they reached the front. It was not uncommon for a collective farm, factory, region, or even notable individual to donate money to pay for a tank or column of tanks during the war, often honored by the name of the tank or unit. These included "Battle Girlfriend"—a tank paid for by a war widow who later became its driver-mechanic.[35] Kabanov's own Tatiana was officially named *Komsomolets Zabaikalia* and was paid for by miners from Chita's Chernovskii district. It was common for tank crews to write a *Nakaz*—a letter of gratitude in which the crew introduced itself and accomplishments and vowed to destroy the enemy and end the war more quickly.[36] These rituals positioned an individual tank as an embodiment of the connection between front and rear, a major theme in wartime propaganda.[37] Soldiers developed intimate, personal relationships with their tanks, often naming them after historical figures such as Chapaev and Suvorov or affectionately after women such as Kabanov's Tatiana and Argentina.

Alongside love, by design tanks engendered fear. The T-34 caused shock on both sides when it entered combat in June of 1941. The Germans were shaken by the fact that those they saw as Slavic subhumans had developed a tank that was virtually invulnerable to German artillery.[38] The Red Army was stunned by how many tanks it was forced to abandon and how ineffective it was at using them. Many crews lacked time to master the complicated machine. Some received their T-34s a few weeks before the invasion, and the inability to bring fuel and ammunition to encircled forces meant that many abandoned their tanks, often tearfully destroying them before retreating.[39] No weapon better demonstrated the Red Army adage "machinery without people is dead" (i.e., useless).[40] Just as it took time for the workers building T-34s to learn their trades, so too did it take time for tankers and tank commanders to learn how to use these complicated machines and for the Red Army to organize the sophisticated logistics necessary to support tanks. This learning curve would cost many lives. Ultimately, it led the state to value tankers in a way that went well beyond other troops.

A tank crew usually consisted of four soldiers—a commander, a turret gunner-loader, mechanic-driver, and radio operator-machine gunner. The commander was responsible for controlling the tank and keeping it provisioned and functional, with specific tasks assigned to each member of the crew. The turret gunner kept track of all weapons and ammunition, loaded, and (when the tank commander did not take the task on himself) aimed and fired the cannon. The radio operator kept the radio in order, communicated with other tanks, and operated a machine gun. Finally, the mechanic-driver drove the tank and maintained the engine, transmission, air filter, and tracks.[41]

Keeping these machines running was a full-time job, and the mechanic-driver had the worst of it. T-34s leaked, both inside and out, sometimes causing fires.[42] The tanks' air filters underperformed horrendously, the first model having to be cleaned as often as once per hour and later versions every three to five hours. A weak transmission in early models led to frequent breakdowns and massive wear and tear.[43] Manuals and training reminded tank crews that the tank had to be turned on and off and gears shifted in an intricate series of tasks.[44] The fuel tank was to be constantly topped off to keep the tank running and make it less flammable.[45] A variety of lubricants had to be used on different parts and weapons, requiring constant maintenance and occasional repair. The crew had never-ending labor.[46] Kabanov frequently complained of being filthy and even left his fingerprint in motor oil on a letter home.[47] Deep emotions were inspired by these steel monsters, which were said to have their own personalities and on whom their crews depended for survival. As one tanker remarked, "A machine is similar to a living thing: if you take care of her she will never betray you or let you down and will serve you faithfully."[48]

To operate and animate this behemoth, the crew had to function like an organism, each soldier answering for one part of the system. Closed hatches in combat meant that visibility was extremely limited. Gunners often had to aim while moving rapidly over uneven terrain, solving trigonometric equations under fire. They were encouraged to use machine-gun fire or several shots to zero in on their targets, with the mechanic-driver observing where the shot or shell landed.[49] For the first few years of the war, the tank commander also often served as the gunner, with disastrous results—he could either aim the gun or command the crew, but doing both at once was unmanageable. This also meant that T-34s seldom fired while moving, a massive disadvantage. The tank had a tendency to gyrate so severely over uneven terrain that aiming was virtually impossible, due to a weak suspension system. Eventually Stalin gave a special order to encourage tanks to fire "not fearing, if the fire is not always aimed" and a variant of the T-34 had a five-person crew in which the commander just commanded.[50] The mechanic-driver had to constantly keep in mind the type of ground they drove on, because swamps could swallow tanks and mud or turns on weak soil could immobilize them, although the T-34 dealt with rough terrain better than other tanks.[51] Driving the tank required incredible skill and strength. The driver used two levers that controlled each track separately and shifting gears often required two soldiers' efforts.[52] Many considered drivers to be the most important crew member, as their ability to maneuver the tank, and to avoid exposing its vulnerable flanks, is what kept crews alive.[53]

Tanks required a lot of prior planning and information about the enemy to work effectively, and tankers drew maps that contained information about the landscape, enemy, and points for the tanks to regroup.[54] Tankers frequently had to leave the confines of their tank in order to reconnoiter—climbing trees, crawling forward, and gathering as much information as possible before returning. Within the tank, vision was so limited that every crew member was responsible for constant observation of a certain portion of the 360 degrees around the tank through a periscope or slit.[55] When used together, a platoon of tanks functioned like a squad of steel giants, maintaining distance to ensure maneuverability, covering each other, and deploying from columns into battle formations. The turret even moved back and forth while on the march like a giant head.[56] Tanks also provided transportation for soldiers, being exactly the right size to carry a squad—they even had special handles for riders.[57] As soon as the tank stopped anywhere, the crew took stock, replenished supplies, made repairs, and then began a series of new tasks, including the gathering of information, digging their own shelter underneath the tank, and setting up a forward position to guard the tank. A tanker's work was never done.

Everyone was learning on the job in 1941 and 1942. Early in the war, most tankers lacked proper training, having only had a few hours of practice with the tank before seeing combat. Many officers had been promoted rapidly to command newly created formations and found themselves without maps and got lost.[58] Tanks used without proper reconnaissance or coordination were quickly destroyed.[59] As late as the autumn of 1942, it was found that many crews had yet to master these skills and armored unit commanders often just controlled their own tanks rather than commanding their formations.[60] Measures were soon taken to improve cadres and reorganize the armored forces.[61] Initially, this meant reducing the size of armored formations, as neither commanders nor crews could sufficiently control and coordinate large numbers of tanks. As the officers and tankers gained experience, larger and larger formations of concentrated tanks were formed, with a dramatic impact on the battlefield.[62] This process mirrored the process of professionalization within the army as a whole.[63]

The fact that tanks were so expensive and difficult to operate and required reliable, talented crews led to increasingly careful vetting of armor cadres. Kabanov began his service before the war and represented an ideal candidate—a college student from a family of Leningrad workers.[64] As the war progressed, these ideal recruits became a rarity but were prioritized for tank service. A series of orders led to a much more stable social milieu for tankers who were only to be used as specialists and whose service would be attached to one unit. Further orders set out educational and battlefield distinctions that one had to attain to be considered for tanker training and explicitly excluded most people from the formerly occupied territories and everyone from the newly annexed regions of Ukraine, Byelorussia, and Moldova from the honor of operating a tank. These stringent requirements corresponded to a higher status: everyone serving in a tank crew was at least a sergeant (who would command eight soldiers in the infantry), and a tank commander held the same rank as an officer who would command dozens of soldiers in the infantry.[65] The growing esteem of tankers reflected army-wide trends of valuing soldiers and expertise as it became apparent that human resources were dwindling and soldiers needed more than enthusiasm to win.

Some soldiers came to feel themselves as organic parts of the machinery they operated, a realization of a long-standing Soviet trope of the merging of man and machine.[66] Constant maintenance led to soldiers coming to know their machines intimately and tankers being filthy, stained with a variety of liquids that kept the tank running and often covered with soot. Nowhere was this fusion more acute than in operation. Kabanov's letters home boasted how he could eat and drive at the same time, sometimes using the tank to toast bread or that "Now I feel an unusual rush of strength, despite the fact that I haven't let go of the steering levers for two days, I am ready to go all the way to Berlin itself." [67]

He also noted his thoughts in battle, where he both became part of the machine and suffered from its operation:

> We go into the attack with thunder and a crash, then you don't think at all. Forward—I press the starter, full throttle, and the machine rushes out of the woods where it had been camouflaged and waiting for the signal, like a beast. Then the most unpleasant thing is your own cannon: "Boom-mm!"—a wave of air explodes, flames smack your eyes and ears, and in your ears the ringing sound remains "Boom-mm!"—another shot and again the same impressions. It goes on like that endlessly, because my commander fiercely fires the cannon. "Fritzes" are afraid of the tanks, we just have to show ourselves and they start leaving their positions and skedaddling, chasing them is very pleasant and good sport. It's a little worse if they have artillery, then, gritting my teeth, leaning my forehead into the perescope and clutching the steering levers, I start to change course, in order to get out of "Hans'" sights, drive the machine trying to hit the flank of the cannon and crush it with her tracks. I have already crushed three cannons this way. True, the fourth that I was attacking palmed a shell off on us, but I managed to get our damaged machine off the battlefield and our wounded commander managed to put out a fire on the move.[68]

The sense of empowerment and accomplishment could be exhilarating but came with extreme danger. This was made possible by the symbiosis of man and machine in ways that were unique to the tanker's experience.

Steven Jug has posited that all Red Army soldiers underwent a "process of embodied identity formation" during their service. For tankers this experience was defined by their machines, which had distinct smells (diesel, gunpowder, and a variety of chemicals), sounds (the roar of the engine, booming of shells, and thud of bullets hitting armor), sights (mediated by the narrow periscopes and tight confines of the tank), and feelings (the vibration of the tank, being pitched to and fro as it navigated uneven ground, and the more or less constant residue of lubricants and other chemicals on one's hands, face, and overalls).[69] In a functioning tank, soldiers merged with their machines gaining tremendous agency over the outcome of battle, but this could be cut short at any moment as the tank could turn from a weapon of war to a burning hazard.

Losses among both tanks and tankers were tremendous. The Germans noted that tank crews were zealously dedicated, often fighting on after their vehicles were disabled, viewing the tank crews as paragons of Soviet fanaticism.[70] This was in part the result of filtration that accepted only the most loyal elements, and in part due to the potentially suicidal consequences of leaving a tank. There was no way to evacuate wounded soldiers from a tank, and the 1944 *Combat Regulations for Armored and Mechanized Troops* stated, "Every soldier in the crew, if wounded, should exert all of their strength and continue fighting."[71] As in the case Kabanov cites above, the tank crew could only seek medical attention once the vehicle itself was nonfunctional. This meant that if a soldier was killed or wounded, they would often remain in the tank until the end of battle. The dead could merge with the machine—at least one soldier recalled how he used the blood of a fallen comrade to put out a fire in his tank, which led to an unbearable smell.[72] Deprived of their tanks, crewmembers were particularly pitiable, as one veteran described, "Without their tanks, without boots, barefoot, in torn clothing they have a tortured look—filthy, bloody, and burnt."[73]

But burning was part of being a tanker. Tanks and soldiers lived through parallel cycles of use, in which they were damaged/wounded, repaired/healed in the rear and that would only end if they were destroyed/killed, damaged beyond repair/crippled, or if the war ended. One veteran casually wrote his mother that two of his tanks had burned, while another told of a comrade who had escaped from twelve tanks before being killed outside his thirteenth.[74] Early in the war, it was determined that tanks should be sent to existing units rather than be used to form new units, as a unit would lose 70–80 percent of its tanks in two weeks of combat.[75] Germans investigating destroyed tanks that they captured found that the vast majority were hit within six months of manufacture.[76] Possession of the battlefield was particularly important for tanks: even if their crews had been killed, the tanks themselves could be salvaged in whole or in part.[77] By the end of the war, the percentage losses of tanks was greater than among crews, and soldiers who escaped a burning tank outnumbered those who died in them by a ratio of two to one.[78]

The dual cycles of use and recovery led some tankers, including Kabanov, to describe their recovery from wounds in terms used to describe tank repair—"routine maintenance (*tekuiushchii remont*)." Kabanov himself was wounded several times in Tatiana and Argentina. He suffered severe burns, a broken jaw, and the loss of teeth. He glibly wrote home that he would have to grow out his hair to cover his scars but also complained that after his long recovery in the hospital, the worst part of his wounds was when comrades would grimace and "make sympathetic speeches."[79] Each time he was wounded, Tatiana or Argentina also required repairs. Man and machine would meet again for further use. Kabanov continued in this cycle until he was killed while salvaging a tank in January of 1945.[80]

## Tanks as Symbols

The dual cycles of burning and repair ran counter to an official image of tanks as virtually indestructible. The hit "Tanker's March" from the 1939 film *Traktoristy* (*Tractor Drivers*) boasted:

> Our armor is strong and our tanks fast
> And our people filled with bravery
> Roaring with fire, shining with the sparkle of steel
> The machines go into a furious campaign.

The song continued to promise any enemy waiting in ambush that Soviet tankers would fire first and destroy them.[81] Much of the folklore produced by tankers themselves focused on their feelings of vulnerability and spoke to a sense of fatalism that belied official culture, reflecting what they witnessed inside their tanks. Some felt that the regime valued their machines more than their lives:

> Somehow they called me to the Special Section [secret police—B.S.]:
> —Bastard, why didn't you burn with the tank?
> And I tell them:
> —Of course next time I will burn
> It is my duty to burn next time.[82]

Many tankers had a long list of comrades whose deaths they witnessed in the tight confines of their tanks and the T-34 was often referred to as "a coffin for four brothers."[83] A popular frontline song with many variations spoke of a proud fatalism:

> Motors flare with flame
> licking the turret with fiery tongues
> I accept the call of fate
> with a handshake.[84]

During the war tanks became graves for some of their crews and tankers would sometimes use tracks as fencing for their comrades' graves.[85] With victory, scores of T-34s were displayed on pedestals as monuments to Red Army victory in locations as diverse as the factories that produced them, tank schools that trained cadres, and in villages and cities liberated by the Red Army. Within Russia and the former Soviet Union, these monuments were unambiguous symbols of both the sacrifices and technical capabilities that made victory possible. The meaning of these monuments beyond the Soviet Union was unstable, as Soviet tanks could be seen as a symbol of occupation and oppression, particularly after 1956 and 1968. As Rachel Applebaum has shown, tanks turned into monuments could become important sites of contestation of the meaning of the Soviet presence in Europe, as when a young man in Prague painted a T-34 pink in 1991.[86] For most Russians, and many people around the world, the tank remains a symbol of Soviet ingenuity and sacrifice during the war.

In film the T-34 played supporting and starring roles since the 1940s. Tank crews featured in a number of films, while perhaps the most striking post-Soviet casting of the tank is *Belyi tigr* (*White Tiger*) (dir. Karen Shakhnazanov, Mosfil'm, 2012). This film features a Lazarus-like driver-mechanic who remarkably recovers from a fatal wound, loses all sense of his former identity—he is renamed *Naidennov* (Foundson)—and gains the ability to talk to tanks. The film follows Naidennov's quest to destroy the White Tiger—a German tank with metaphysical properties and no human crew, embodying the West's desire to destroy Russia. He is aided by the God of Tanks, whose chariot is a golden T-34. Interestingly enough, the embodiment of the Russian spirit is a human who animates a tank, while the embodiment of Western aggression is a soulless machine animated by pure evil. The top-grossing film of 2019 was simply *T-34* with a plot that centers on German jealousy of both Soviet skills and the tank itself. The writers of *White Tiger* and *T-34* are not the only people seeking to relive the heyday of the legendary tank.

*World of Tanks*, a massive online video game, allows anyone with access to a computer to control a tank, manipulating with a few keystrokes the steel behemoths that required highly skilled and coordinated crews in real life. With over sixty million registered users in 2013, the game set a world record with over a million simultaneous players and had made the Belorussian-based company Wargaming $372 million by 2014.[87] The game itself is free, but players can unlock a variety of features (including customizing their tanks) in the virtual world by paying actual money. The company also offers a variety of merchandise, from shirts and stemware to pins and models, and even publishes scholarly works on tanks.

The T-34's revival in celluloid and pixels is paralleled by their deployment in martial displays on Red Square and Nevskii Prospect in Victory Day Parades. Both the state and private individuals are profiting off the victory of which this tank is a vital and lasting symbol. The fact that the tanks can still run after seven decades is a testament to their legendary fortitude. Just as Victory in the Great Patriotic War has outlived the Soviet Union as a source of pride and identity, so has the T-34, one of its preeminent symbols, outlived the regime that built it.

## Conclusion

If the T-34 has become a prop or even something like a toy today, it played an important role in the defeat of fascism from 1941 to 1945. Tens of thousands of workers turned steel into behemoths and hundreds of thousands of soldiers learned to animate them. The visceral experience of living with and loving these giants—maintaining them, driving them, and burning with them—has been lost or romanticized as they are reborn as pixels and models or remobilized as antiques to serve as synecdoche of the Soviet experience of the war itself. These narratives eschew the human suffering that made both their production and animation possible—transforming the meaning of the tank from a concrete object embedded in a series of relationships into an abstraction that can serve the ends of politics or entertainment.

## Notes

I would like to thank the members of the Columbia Russian History Kruzhok, especially Catherine Evtuhov, Richard Wortman, Boris Gasparov, Mark Lipovetsky, Azat Bilalutdinov, Sam Cogeshall, and Susan Heuman, as well as Mirjam Voerkoelius, Milyausha Zakirova, Alison K. Smith, Matthew Romaniello, and Trish Starks for feedback on this text.

All English translations of lyrics/verse throughout the chapter are the my own, unless otherwise stated.

1. Dmitrii Kabanov, *Pamiat' pisem ili chelovek iz "tridtsatchetverki": Unikal'nye frontovye pis'ma 1941–1945 godov* (Moscow: Atlantida-XXI vek, 2006), 47.
2. The latter is of course a contested claim about which much ink has been spilled.
3. For a thorough discussion of how I approach material culture and its stakes for the Soviet project, see the introduction to my monograph: Brandon Schechter, *The Stuff of Soldiers: A History of the Red Army in World War II through Objects* (Ithaca, NY: Cornell University Press, 2019); Igor Kopytoff, "The Cultural Biography of Things: Commoditization as Process," in *The Social Life of Things: Commodities in Cultural Perspective*, ed. Arjun Appadurai (Cambridge: Cambridge University Press, 1986), 64–91; Leora Auslander, "Beyond Words," *American Historical Review* 110 (2005), 1015–45; Bruno Latour, *Reassembling the Social: An Introduction to Actor-Network Theory* (New York: Oxford University Press, 2005); Elaine Scarry, *The Body in Pain: The Making and Unmaking of the World* (New York: Oxford University Press, 1985).
4. *Posobie dlia boitsa-tankista* (Moscow: Voenizdat, 1941), 1; Rossiiskii gosudarstvennyi voennyi arkhiv (RGVA) f. 4, op. 12, d. 106, ll. 112–122, in A. I. Barsukov et al., *Prikazy narodnogo komissara oborony SSSR 22 iiunia 1941 g.—1942 g.: Dokumenty i materialy. T. 13 (2—2). Russkii arkhiv: Velikaia Otechestvennaia* (Moscow: TERRA, 1997), 334–7.
5. Joseph Stalin, *The Great Patriotic War of the Soviet Union* (Moscow: Progress, 1945), 32.
6. E. Middel'dorf, *Russkaia kampaniia: taktika i vooruzhenie* (St. Petersburg: Poligon, 2000), 288.
7. Kabanov, *Pamiat' pisem*, 16.
8. Sergei Ust'iantsev and Dmitrii Kolmakov, *Boevye mashiny Uralvagonzavoda. Tank T-34* (Nizhnyi Tagil: Media-Print, 2005), 75–105.
9. *Tank T-34 v boiu* (Moscow: Voenizdat, 1942), 1–6; *Rukhovodstvo po ekspluatatsii i obsluzhivaniiu Tanka t-34* (Moscow: Voenizdat, 1943), 52.
10. Galina Chikova et al., *Aleksandr Morozov: Unikal'nye dokumenty, fotografii, fakty, vospominaniia* (Moscow: Izdat, 2009), 78; Ust'iantsev and Kolmakov, *Boevye mashiny Uralvagonzavoda. Tank T-34*, 35–43.
11. Kabanov, *Pamiat' pisem*, 142.
12. Artem Drabkin, ed., *Ia dralsia na T-34* (Moscow: Eksmo, 2005), 170–1; *Posobie dlia boitsa-tankista*, 173–4.
13. Chikova et al., *Aleksandr Morozov*, 78–9.
14. Joseph Stalin, "Tasks of Business Executives," in *Works*, vol. 13 (Moscow: Foreign Languages Publishing House, 1954), via Marxists.org.

15. Lynne Viola, "Collectivization in the Soviet Union: Specificities and Modalities," in *The Collectivization of Agriculture in Communist Eastern Europe: Comparison and Entanglements*, ed. Constantin Iordachi and Arnd Bauerkämper (Budapest: Central European University Press, 2014), 49–77.
16. Stephen Kotkin, *Magnetic Mountain: Stalinism as Civilization* (Berkeley: University of California Press, 1995), 40–2, 46–70; Sheila Fitzpatrick, *Everyday Stalinism Ordinary Life in Extraordinary Times: Soviet Russia in the 1930s* (New York: Oxford University Press, 1999), 101–6; Ust'iantsev and Kolmakov, *Boevye mashiny Uralvagonzavoda*, 35.
17. *T-34. Put' k pobede*, 22–3.
18. *Museum-Memorial Complex "History of the T-34"*. With the passing of Koshkin, A. A. Morozov lead the development and oversaw mass production of the tank. He would become not only a major player in the armor production but also one of the key singers of the T-34's praises. For more background on the development of the tank see Boris Kavalerchik, "Once Again about the T-34," *Journal of Slavic Military Studies* 28:1 (2015), 186–214. Koshkin himself became the subject of a film *Glavnyi konstruktor* (Sverdlovskaia kinostudiia, dir. Vladimir Semakov, 1980), https://www.youtube.com/watch?v=MmQyurj65wc.
19. *T-34 Put' k pobede*, 118.
20. Ust'iantsev and Kolmakov, *Boevye mashiny Uralvagonzavoda*, 11; Chikova et al., *Aleksandr Morozov*, 26, 28; *Muzeinyi kompleks "Istoriia tanka T-34" Dokumental'no-istoricheskii sbornik*, no. 9 (Moscow: Uchrezhdenie kul'tury "Muzeinyi kompleks "Istoriia tanka T-34", 2018), 10.
21. Ust'iantsev and Kolmakov, *Boevye mashiny Uralvagonzavoda*, 48; *T-34 put' k pobede*, 7, 56–7; Chikova et al., *Aleksandr Morozov*, 23–5.
22. Ust'iantsev and Kolmakov, *Boevye mashiny Uralvagonzavoda*, 48, 67.
23. Ibid., 4, 5.
24. Mark Harrison, ed., *The Economics of World War II: Six Great Powers in International Comparison* (Cambridge: Cambridge University Press, 1998), table 1.7.
25. Chikova et al., *Aleksandr Morozov*, 29.
26. Ust'iantsev and Kolmakov, *Boevye mashiny Uralvagonzavoda*, 170.
27. Kavalerchik, "Once Again about the T-34," 207.
28. Biography as presented in the exhibit of the Museum-Memorial Complex "History of the T-34," Sholokhovo, Moscow oblast'.
29. Ust'iantsev and Kolmakov, *Boevye mashiny Uralvagonzavoda*, 66–7.
30. Chikova et al., *Aleksandr Morozov*, 67–76; Kavalerchik, "Once Again about the T-34," 189, 194–5; *T-34. Put' k pobede*, 10, 176.
31. Ust'iantsev and Kolmakov, *Boevye mashiny Uralvagonzavoda*, 52; Morozov, *Unikal'nye dokumenty*, 71–4.
32. Chikova et al., *Aleksandr Morozov*, 67–76.
33. Ust'iantsev and Kolmakov, *Boevye mashiny Uralvagonzavoda*, 184.
34. *T-34 Put' k pobedy*, 217–21.
35. "Voennaia istoriia zhenshchiny i eë tanka 'Boevaia podruga,'" *RIA Novosti*, April 14, 2010, http://ria.ru/ocherki/20100414/222121628.html. Liberty ships in the United States could also be named by those who paid for them, but only after famous people who had passed away.
36. Kabanov, *Pamiat' pisem*, 53–4. On the Nakaz as a genre, see Schechter, "'The People's Instructions': Indigenizing the Great Patriotic War among 'Non-Russians,'" *Ab Imperio* 3 (2012), 109–33.

37. Karel C. Berkhoff, *Motherland in Danger: Soviet Propaganda during World War II* (Cambridge, MA: Harvard University Press, 2012), chapter 3.
38. G. Guderian, *Vospominaniia soldata* (Smolensk: Rusich, 1999), 221–3, 315, 317–18, 322, 337; Andrei Ulanov and Dmitrii Shein, *Pervye T-34: Boevoe primenenie. World of Tanks* (Moscow: Taktikal Press, 2013), 160–4.
39. P. A. Rotmistrov, *Stal'naia gvardiia* (Moscow: Voenizdat, 1984), 54; *Muzeinyi kompleks "Istoriia tanka T-34" Dokumental'no-istoricheskii sbornik*, no.1 (2012), 48; Ulanov and Shein, *Pervye T-34*, 64–91.
40. M. Vistin, "Uchit'sia voevat' tak, kak etogo trebuet delo pobedy," *Bloknot agitatora Krasnoi Armii* 15 (1943), 12–13.
41. *Boevoi ustav bronetankovikh i mekhanizirovannykh voisk Krasnoi Armii, Chast' 1 (Tank, tankovyi vzvod, tankovaia rota)* (Moscow: Voenizdat, 1944). (*BUBiMV-44*), 14–25.
42. Drabkin, *Ia dralsia na T-34*, 167–8.
43. Ust'iantsev and Kolmakov, *Boevye mashiny Uralvagonzavoda*, 47–52, 101–2.
44. *Rukovodstvo po ekspluatatsii i obsluzhivaniiu Tanka t-34*, 17–23.
45. Ibid., 34; Ust'iantsev and Kolmakov, *Boevye mashiny Uralvagonzavoda*, 33.
46. For an exhaustive and exhausting list of procedures, see *Rukovodstvo po ekspluatatsii i obsluzhivaniiu Tanka t-34*, the mid-War manual for T-34 crews.
47. Kabanov, *Pamiat' pisem*, 48.
48. *T-34. Put' k Pobede*, 212.
49. *BUBiMV-44*, 68; *Posobie dlia boitsa-tankista*, 72–83.
50. Ust'iantsev and Kolmakov, *Boevye mashiny Uralvagonzavoda*, 60–2.
51. *Posobie dlia boitsa-tankista*, 118; *Rukovodstvo po ekspluatatsii i obsluzhivaniiu Tanka t-34*, 22–3.
52. Drabkin, *Ia dralsia na T-34*, 26.
53. Rotmistrov, *Stal'naia Gvardiia*, 112.
54. *Posobie dlia boitsa-tankista*, 145–75; *BUBiMV-44*, 185–9.
55. *Tank v boiu* (Moscow: Voenizdat, 1946), 42–7; *Tank T-34 v boiu*, 31–2; *BUBiMV-44*, 70–2.
56. *BUBiMV-44*, 34–8, 59–61; *Posobie dlia boitsa-tankista*, 18.
57. *Boevye priëmy tankistov* (Moscow: Voenizdat, 1942), 36–41.
58. See, for example, Ulanov and Shein, *Pervye T-34*, 156.
59. *BUBiMV-44*, 94–5.
60. RGVA f. 4, op. 12, d. 106, ll. 112–22, in *Prikazy narodnogo komissara oborony SSSR 22 iiunia 1941 g.–1942 g.*, 334–6.
61. RGVA f. 4, op. 11, d. 73, ll. 341–42, in *Prikazy narodnogo komissara oborony SSSR 22 iiunia 1941 g.–1942 g.*, 379–80.
62. Rotmistrov, *Stal'naia gvardiia*, 111, 163–6.
63. Schechter, *Stuff of Soldiers*, 177–80.
64. Kabanov, *Pamiat' pisem*, 4.
65. RGVA, f. 4, op. 11, d. 66, l. 232–234 and RGVA, f. 4, op. 11, d. 66, l. 167, in *Prikazy Narodnogo komissara oborony SSSR 22 iiunia 1941 g.–1942 g.*, 122–3, 114.
66. Peter Fritzsche and Jochen Hellbeck, "The New Man in Stalinist Russia and Nazi Germany," in Michael Geyer and Sheila Fitzpatrick, *Beyond Totalitarianism: Stalinism and Nazism Compared* (Cambridge: Cambridge University Press. 2009), 321.
67. Kabanov, *Pamiat' pisem*, 38, 15.
68. Ibid., 39.

69. Steven G. Jug, "Sensing Danger: The Red Army during the Second World War," in *Russian History through the Senses: From 1700 to the Present*, ed. Matthew P. Romaniello and Tricia Starks (New York: Bloomsbury Academic, 2016), 219–40, quote: 224.
70. Ulanov and Shein, *Pervye T-34*, 154.
71. *BUBiMV-44*, 92.
72. Nauchnyi arkhiv Instituta rossiiskoi istorii Akademii nauk Rossiiskoi Federatsii (NA IRI RAN), f. 2, r. I, op. 120, d. 3, l. 2ob.
73. NA IRI RAN, f. 2, r. X, op. 7, d. 13-b, l. 141.
74. Rossiiskii gosudarstvennyi arkhiv sotsial'no-politicheskoi istorii (RGASPI), f. M-7, op. 2, d. 650, ll. 87; NA IRI RAN f. 2, r. I, op. 120, d. 3, l. 4.
75. *Arkhiv Prezidenta Rossiiskoi Federatsii* (AP RF), f. 3, op. 50, d. 264, l. 166, in Sergei Kudriashov, ed., *Voina: 1941–1945. Vestnik Arkhiva Prezidenta Rossiiskoi Federatsii* (Moscow: Arkhiv Prezidenta Rossiiskoi Federatsii, 2010), 84.
76. Walter S. Dunn Jr., *Hitler's Nemesis: The Red Army, 1930–1945* (Mechanicsburg, PA: Stackpole, 2009), 150.
77. Rotmistrov, *Stal'naia Gvardia*, 171.
78. Ust'iantsev and Kolmakov, *Boevye mashiny Uralvagonzavoda*, 90.
79. Kabanov, *Pamiat' pisem*, 39–40 (quote), 68–72, 81, 113.
80. Ibid., 142.
81. Ivan Pyr'ev, dir., *Traktoristy* (Mosfilm, 1939).
82. N. N. Nikulin, *Vospominaniia o voine* (St. Petersburg: Izdatel'stvo Gos. Ermitazha, 2008), 78.
83. Viktor Kurochkin, "Na voine kak na voine," in *Povesti i rasskazy* (Leningrad: Khudozhestvennaia literatura, 1978), 19.
84. Kurochkin, "Na voine kak na voine," 71–72.
85. Tat'iana Repina (Atabek), *K biografii voennogo pokoleniia* (Moscow: Moskovskie uchebniki i Kartolitografiia, 2004), 113.
86. Rachel Applebaum, *Empire of Friends: Soviet Power and Socialist Internationalism in Cold War Czechoslovakia* (Ithaca, NY: Cornell University Press, 2019), 1, 17, 195–8.
87. https://worldoftanks.com/en/news/announcements/world-tanks-hits-mark-60-million-registered-users/; https://sputniknews.com/business/20140120186729656-Belarusian-Game-Out-Guns-World-of-Warcraft-on-Revenue/.

Part 4

# Preserving Things

# 10

# Binding Siberia: Semen Remezov's *Khorograficheskaia Kniga* in Time and through Time

Erika Monahan

The past happened in color. The archives of early-modern Siberia put this materiality constantly before us, even when we are not looking for it. Thinned pages in the archive harken to the things that filled Siberian towns: the chalices, wine, prayer books, and shining accoutrements for the liturgy shipped to Siberian churches;[1] the fragrant bricks of tea wrapped in leather rolls strapped to the backs of camels; the heavy pistols a merchant carried with him and the red pants listed in his inventory when he died;[2] the smooth leather saddles that adorned fine steeds; the musky moose hides stored in a church;[3] the thick books the military-governor Prince Mikhail Yaklovlevich Cherkasskii imported to Siberia in 1701;[4] the axes, the pans, the nails, needles, mirrors, windows; the innumerable lengths of linens, wools, silks that passed through Siberian towns along with countless fur pelts on their way to the workshops of seamstresses and haberdashers.[5] The paper, ink, wax seals, candles—the stuff with which Siberia's first bureaucrats did the business of empire—that government servitors made trips through bog and taiga to procure.[6] These are the materials—soft, hard, smooth, rough, heavy, light, colorful, faded, new, broken—that made up the material world of early-modern Siberia.

The world these Siberians inhabited was as solid and vibrant to them as it is ephemeral and faded to us. Ice melts. Wood rots. Colors fade. Fabrics turn threadbare. What is left behind for us often is not as it was for those who held, moved, and relied upon these objects. In museums and archives, however, objects and documents lie quietly, accessible to those who travel there with the training to search, touch, and make sense of the scribbling on aging paper. So much of the irrefutable but underconsidered materiality of the world "they" knew is there, offering a real if only partial portal to the past.

Among the telling relics of the early-modern Siberian world, one of the richest sources is a book of maps, the first atlas of Siberia. The atlas, which has long since left Siberia, contains a staggering amount of information, but since its creation the value of this knowledge has changed. The landscape it depicts has been transformed and the atlas's intellectual apparatuses reflect a different era. As an atlas, it is obsolete.

Even with the atlas's digitization in the twenty-first century, the information embedded in the pages of this monument to cartography, now just keyboard strokes away in disembodied form, remains largely inaccessible. Concentrating on the thing itself, then, becomes an object lesson in how historical understanding can never be divorced from context nor the expertise through which we establish understanding. At its conception, the atlas captured a pride in the domains of the Russian Empire. To later authors, it represented Russian backwardness. And to others, it reflected the realities of Russian scientific knowledge, much as did the apothecary ware that it has long outlived.

## The Map

The *Khorograficheskaia kniga*—or *Chorography*—is an object teeming with information.[7] This manuscript atlas was drawn primarily by Semen Remezov (ca. 1642–post-1720). Composed around the turn of the eighteenth century, Remezov's *Chorography* is the earliest atlas of Siberia, produced even before a comparable atlas of Russia itself existed.[8] This rectangular atlas is bound in pasteboard; the cover, once perhaps a rich and solid olive green color, is now flecked and scratched, bearing traces of liquid stains.[9] Along the binding runs a strip of brown buckram, which is a stiff, loosely woven cotton that has been soaked in a sizing agent to add durability. The atlas weighs 2 lbs., 3 oz.[10] Opening the book presents the reader with a portal into early-modern Russia—a heady mix of imperial aspiration, quotidian utility, and bewildering details. It comprises 176 sheets of paper: 172 of those sheets are numbered; one sheet (f.4) is missing; the five unnumbered pages, sometimes with titles for maps that were never drawn, are interspersed, mostly coming at the end of the atlas.

The series of maps is preceded by elaborate front matter. Done in black ink with some red embellishment, these nine sheets of paper contain drawings and prose. This introduction describes the state instructions and rationale that guided the project.[11] In an incomplete and rudimentary way, Remezov describes his method and provides a listing of the contents and a key to symbols. Interspersed in these pages of prose are elaborate drawings.

The front matter is followed by over one hundred maps (and one panorama) on now yellowed paper. Twenty-four maps have fold-out sections. The central organizing principle of the atlas is hydrographic; that is, the maps are organized around river systems. Siberian travel, after all, was oriented around river systems. The maps are drawn in blue, red, and black. Yellow swaths indicate higher ground.[12] Trees are marked throughout in what may once have been a brighter green but has faded to a brownish olive color. With the exception of a single, smaller loose sheet (f. 47), the sheets of paper are 30 cm × 20.5 cm (11.8″ × 8″, 94.4 in$^2$).[13] The pages Semen Remezov drew on are slightly more oblong than that of modern, standard printer paper, with a slightly greater surface area (8.5″ × 11″ paper has an area of 93.5 in$^2$).[14] The sheets have margins on all four sides, into which Remezov's work occasionally spills over, but which slightly reduce the usable area on each page. Considering the modest size, the amount of detail incorporated into these maps is astounding.

This atlas, as we will see below, is based on a massive complex of information and infrastructure. That is, even a "thin" description, confining itself to its functionality, is a complex affair. As it has traveled through time and space, however, the meaning of this thing has changed. Rather than convey information about early modern Eurasian territory, we look to it to convey information about early modern Russian culture and governance. Centuries removed from its creation, it became a symbol of a "national-imperial" past, and, as it resurfaced far from the polity in which it was created, an object of contention. *The Chorography* became coveted not primarily for the geographical and cartographic information it contained, which in the halls of power in its day, was its *raison d'être*, nor for the quotidian information it contained, which marked travel routes for humbler types and may have helped state bureaucrats mitigate property disputes. The *Chorography* no longer fulfills those purposes. Through the centuries, as the ideational complex that made this map comprehensible and functional morphed, the functionality and legibility of the atlas receded. Yet it is nonetheless recognized as an historical treasure.

As the introduction to this volume highlights, matching words to meaning presents challenges when trying to understand things across time; this object is no exception. Shall we call it an atlas or a chorography? The word atlas first appears in European cartography in Mercator's posthumously published 1594 *Atlas sive cosmographicae de fabrica mundi et fabricate figura*.[15] Yet Remezov himself called it a chorography—a description of an area. While his maps display the symbolic representation we associate with maps, Remezov was steeped in a tradition where itineraries and territories were typically reported in prose; the conventions he knew make it easy to understand his word choice. The *Chorography* also displayed many of the attributes of atlases such as Blaeu's *Grand Atlas*. Since chorography is a genre itself that has gone out of style, and much of the information therein is as obsolete as the genre, in the twenty-first century it makes more sense to call Remezov's book an atlas: a collection of maps, which are cartographic products that communicate information through symbols more than words.

Perhaps another reason to drop the chorography label is because so much of the descriptive information therein is difficult to access. While in the most general sense it is obvious that one is looking at maps when perusing the *Chorography*, this atlas is fully legible only to those with the expertise to crack the "codes" through which the atlas's creator communicated his understanding. These codes were layers of meaning required to depict physical space through a series of abstractions—iconic, linguistic, and presentational—as historian Mary Elizabeth Berry framed cartographic knowledge.[16] The knowledge a material object carries can be lost if the requisite knowledge to decipher it is not sufficiently embedded in the thing or does not travel with it. Anthropologist and philosopher Bruno Latour argued that "when the artifact is completed the activity that fit them together disappears entirely. Mastery, prediction, clarity, and functionality are very local and tentative achievements that are not themselves obtained inside."[17] Latour is talking about more technologically advanced things, but his insight resonates at some level with Remezov's atlas. Attempting to read this source forces a reckoning with the immaterial structures, resources, and mentalities that went its creation but have not traveled *a priori* with this thing. In the absence of that full knowledge, much of the descriptive information we associate with a chorography recedes and the geographic information symbolically rendered—as one finds in maps and atlases—remains.

Finally, one of the joys and benefits of a material history approach is to find clues in the object itself that are revelatory of its life story. Yet, the biography of the *Chorography* reveals how much of an object's itinerary might not be captured in the object itself. In other words, the history of Remezov's atlas suggests one limit on studies of material culture, or, at least, reminds the historian how very consequential are the questions we ask about our objects of study.

## The Map Maker

Semen Ul'ianov syn Remezov was the son of a low-ranking "noble" man (*syn boiarskii*) from the Siberian capital of Tobol'sk. His grandfather Mosei had been exiled from Moscow to Siberia for some offense under the first Romanov tsar, Mikhail Romanov, but the family stayed and even prospered in Tobol'sk. Coming of age as an ascendant dynasty was remaking government at the center and stretching its imperial grasp across the Eurasian continent, Semen Remezov served the Tobol'sk administration in various capacities, including but not limited to land surveyor, town planner, architect, and mapmaker.[18] Remezov's drafting skills caught the attention of the tsar. In 1696 the Siberian Office ordered him to prepare a map of all Siberia.

Remarkably, given his modest provincial education, Semen Remezov was up to the task. He built on a slim tradition of mapping Siberia to produce the most comprehensive mapping work the Russian Empire had known to date. He was born into a family already involved in mapping the tsar's domains. In 1667 Tobol'sk governor Petr Godunov had commissioned the first map of Siberia. That map is not extant but a few early copies survive, including one drawn by, it is thought, Ul'ian Remezov, Semen Remezov's father. Both Remezovs also had experience traveling extensively in the Siberian territories around Tobol'sk. Like his father, his duties as an imperial servitor included serving as emissary to various Kalmyk tribes and other groups living in southern Siberia and Central Asia. In 1640, for example, Ul'ian Remezov, Semen's father, was part of a mission that brought gifts from the tsar to the Kalmyk group camped at Lake Yamysh.[19] No doubt it was on trips like these that his son, Semen, accompanying him, took note of the surroundings—the rivers and lakes, the trees, human paths and settlements, and animals living in the vicinity—the features that so charmingly populate his atlas. The experience served Semen well when the state called upon him to inscribe it all.

Unsurprisingly, Remezov did not rely solely on his own travels. He depended heavily on accumulated knowledge produced by previous government-sponsored missions whose mandate—among other aims—was to learn about and map Russia's Eurasian territory.[20] Some expeditions were dedicated to charting territory; more often, Cossacks and servitors conducted trips similar to the 1640 one described above; reporting their itineraries was standard, adding to the data that Remezov entered into his *Chorography*. Fittingly, the very first page of the *Chorography* reproduces a state order directing government servitors in western Siberia to chart their localities and pass their work on to Semen Remezov.[21] Remezov also had drafting help. In addition to having his three sons as apprentices, Remezov may have had a staff of around twenty men working for him, historian L. A. Gol′denberg supposes.[22]

Nor did Remezov's body of sources stop with the archives of information produced by government servitors. As Remezov explains in the introduction to the *Chorography*, he also interviewed—as was the norm—merchants and members of caravans, such as the Muslim Bukharans, thousands of whom resided in western Siberia by the late seventeenth century and had visited the places the Russian state sought to inscribe in the atlas. Gerhard Friedrich Müller, a member of the Russian Academy of Sciences, later reported that Remezov made dedicated trips beyond Tobol′sk to interview experienced merchants about Siberia's geographies. And yet, as the London-based Sir Robert Southwell observed, lauding the Dutchman Nicolaas Witsen (1641–1717), whose map of Eurasia, a cartographic achievement much indebted to Remezov's work, even the benefits of on-the-ground experience had their limits:

> When I consider that the Caravans passing between Muscovy and China are not frequent; that they are confin'd [sic] to certain Paths and Lines and Trade; That the Merchants and common Travellers mind nothing but the Security and Certainty of the Journey, and the Profit that ensues: And that those who should inform them of Extents and Boundaries, are a Rambling and uncultivated Generation, and of various Languages. If after all these impediments, you shall yet be able to shew the Credibility of your Survey, you need think no more of Fame, but only pray for Humility.[23]

In her field-defining *Cartographies of Tsardom*, Valerie Kivelson put to rest Isaac Massa's characterization of Russians as incurious and unobservant people.[24] Rather than indifference, Remezov's atlas is a manifestation not only of prodigious observation born from a desire to know a territory. Such knowing required a massive, empire-spanning investment in acquiring and documenting knowledge. The realization of Remezov's atlas was a product of an imperial infrastructure that organized the charting of such an expanse of territory. The state had begun ordering maps and geographical information about Siberia be sent to Moscow. Thus, when Remezov set to work, by state order, to map all of Siberia, he found that the most up-to-date information had been sent directly to Moscow, rather than to Tobol′sk, the Siberian capital.[25] Therefore, consulting the most current geographical knowledge about Siberia required travel to Moscow. Remezov (taking some of his maps with him) spent six months working at the Siberian Chancellery in Moscow in 1698, where he had access to materials from beyond Muscovy's borders. The state's knowledge-gathering infrastructure, after all, extended to gaining access to cartographical works whose foci extended beyond the bounds of the Russian empire. In Moscow, Remezov studied the cartographic products of busy European printing presses, including the atlases of Abraham Ortelius (1527–1598), Gerhard Mercator (1512–1594), and Willem (1571–1638) and Joan (1596–1673) Blaeu.[26] Remezov also studied Greek, Ukrainian, German, and other Latin works.[27] He encountered and brought to bear information about Russia's neighbors to the south and east in a remarkable map of Central Asia.[28] In sum, acquiring and preserving knowledge of this vast region required much movement of people and paper. More than a testament to one man's ingenuity and persistence, the *Chorography* is the product of a broad state commitment to fixing knowledge about its imperial territory of Siberia and surrounding territories. Capturing Siberia on the page—the epistemological binding of Siberia, that is—involved countless itineraries.

## Binding Siberia

Remezov was the first to map Siberia, but how do his maps fit into the history of cartography? Historian Alexey Postnikov called Remezov's work "the 'swan song' of an uncontaminated indigenous Russian cartography." To be sure, Remezov followed conventions soon to be eclipsed by more modern technologies, but if there was a swan song of uncontaminated indigenous Russian cartography, Remezov was not it.[29] Rather, Remezov's work displays a hybridity of purpose and genre that precludes characterizing it as an isolated, indigenous Russian artifact. The *Chorography* is a material testament to that hybridity. Remezov's replication of the look of printed materials—margins, borders, woodcuts—all on full display in the front matter, is perhaps the most striking example of the appropriation in manuscript form technologies of the printed book. As other historians have noted, comparing the quality of Remezov's mapping to that of Herberstein's amateur 1546 map belies that Western standards were very much on Remezov's mind in doing his own work.[30]

The front matter of the *Chorography* reinforces this story. Remezov included a double-hemispheric stereographic map of the globe, styled on those featured in the Mercator and Blaeu atlases that were available to Remezov in Moscow. The bi-hemispheric globe bears an ecliptic (the curved line tracing the sun's path across the equator), making it suggestive of the most scientifically advanced cartography. It is simultaneously adorned, however, with mythical sea creatures, invoking the imaginative Western European mapping traditions that preceded empirically based representations. Notably, however, no such mythical creatures fill the *horror vacui* in the Siberian maps of the atlas; Remezov's significations there were more quotidian.[31] With diagrams of a sextant-like tool, a compass rose, and a drawing of a compass accompanying the atlas's key to symbols, Remezov associated himself with the tools of the modern surveyor and cartographer (even as compass lines play little role in the atlas). Remezov's use of Latin letters interspersed alongside Cyrillic in the drawings makes plain the varied traditions on which he draws. Though a manuscript, Remezov's *Chorography* mimics atlases produced on a printing press. This following of contemporary trends in cartographical publishing was typical; historian of European maps Benjamin Schmidt observed that, as certain attributes became desirable, they were replicated. Quite soon, "page engravings; their fold-out maps, tables, and explanatory charts; their various textual synopses delivered in tables of contents, chapter overviews, marginalia, and indices" became *de rigueur* in Amsterdam printing.[32]

Another of Remezov's atlases illustrates clear and direct appropriation of a European motif. Valerie Kivelson has persuasively argued that it was seeing the demons in Blaeu's map of Asia that inspired Remezov to add demons to his map of Asia in his *Working Sketchbook*.[33] The visual evidence for such Western influence is convincing: in his *Working Sketchbook* Remezov copied—demons and all—Blaeu's grand atlas map of Asia.[34] Of note, however, is that Russia had its own lore about demons in the desert. The merchant Gavril Romanov's 1674 trade expedition that traveled directly across the Gobi Desert was significant in part because it dismantled lore that circulated among merchants that the Gobi Desert was impassable because of demons.[35] Those closer to this region talked of demons even if there does not seem to be any evidence that they drew them first. In another related example—again, not taken from the *Chorography*—Remezov imitates western European predecessors who located Baba Zlata, the "Golden Woman," in northern Eurasia. The "Golden Woman" appears in several sixteenth-century maps (Sigismund von Herberstein, 1549; Antonius Wied, 1555; Anthony Jenkinson, 1562; Gerhard Mercator, 1595).[36] She also makes an appearance in Remezov, although she loses the Classical statuesque look in his rendering.[37]

Remezov's engagement with Western European cartographic practices was not limited to what he encountered in books in Moscow. He also surely knew Andrei Vinius, a high-ranking Russified Dutchman and distant cousin to Nicolaas Witsen, whose map is mentioned above. Vinius was a long-time correspondent with Witsen, who was a conduit for the latest cartographical trends in Western Europe. Perhaps doing his cousin's bidding, Vinius was deeply interested in the mapping of Siberia: he attempted to sketch a map of Siberia himself prior to 1675; in 1709 he appealed to the Russian government for the privilege of printing Russian maps abroad.[38] Vinius may have been responsible for some of the orders from Moscow instructing Remezov to produce maps, which he then forwarded to Witsen. One wonders if Witsen was referring to Vinius when he wrote, "I have gathered ... a vast number of Drafts made by my own Order, which describe the Territories that I have mentioned."[39] There is more to understand in Vinius's role in the mapping of Siberia, and I have wondered elsewhere if Vinius may have played some role in the single panorama that appears in Remezov's *Chorography*.[40] While the depiction of panoramic city landscapes emerged in Renaissance Europe, to my knowledge Remezov's seventeenth-century panorama of Tobol'sk is unprecedented in Russian graphic traditions to that point.[41] In any case, that one map in Remezov's "Official Map Book" (*Sluzhebnaia chertezhnaia kniga*) is labeled "The Draft of Andrey Andreyevitch Vinius" testifies to this Dutchman's association with the project to map Siberia.[42] Vinius was not Remezov's only European contact interested in cartography. Gol'denberg reported that Remezov met Philip Johan von Strahlenberg and Daniel Messerschmidt, both of whom would produce maps of Siberia, in Tobol'sk.[43]

Whatever Western influences might be manifest in the *Chorography*, the atlas is hardly an exercise in imitation of Western forms. Remezov's encounter with cartographic practices beyond Russia did not result in wholesale appropriation, but rather selective incorporation.[44] Importantly, Remezov's interest in empirically based, information-rich cartographical representations portrayed according to Muscovite conventions jumps from page after page after page. The absence in Remezov's maps of features that became standard in modern maps should not be reason to dismiss their contents.

Pausing on just one discrete page of the *Chorography* allows the viewer to appreciate the tremendous amount of information the knowledge-making infrastructure succeeded in harnessing in one material object. This one map—Map 10.1—depicts a remote region Remezov dubbed the "waterless and barely passable stone steppe" in central Eurasia, an area that roughly corresponds to the regions to which the Remezovs personally traveled in service to the state. This map depicts the source of the Tobol River, hundreds of miles to the south (because Siberian rivers flow northward) of Tobol'sk, Russia's imperial capital in Siberia built at the confluence of the Tobol and Irtysh Rivers. In contemporary parlance the region shown is of the Turgai Plateau in northwest Kazakhstan. Remezov may be indicating a plateau with the yellow line in the upper right-hand corner of the map. Yellow lines indicate raised terrain throughout the atlas. The Urals are indicated on the right of the page. North is at the bottom on this map so that corner indicates an area southeast of the Urals.

The map—even as it is far from the busiest of Remezov's pages—presents us with an array of hydrographic, topographic, demographic, ethnographic, cultural, travel, and imperial information. The map shows us trees, settlements, and other geographical features such as mountains (this yellow line is the Urals; north is at the bottom), mounds (perhaps human-made), and white cliffs along the river are depicted. The yellow line that begins at the center top of the page, then bends to proceed vertically downward along the right edge of the mound is the Ural Mountains. North is at the bottom on this map; the right edge is the western edge of the territory depicted in the frame.

That objective measurements appear very little on the map has largely been seen as a deficit, another indication—along with a lack of lines of latitude and longitude—of Russian backwardness. In Remezov's context, the decision to forego such measures is reasonable. For one, surveying equipment and manpower was in short supply. But there was enough flux in systems of knowledge at the turn of the seventeenth to eighteenth century that objective measures could confuse even as they could clarify.[45] That said, Remezov regularly gives distances in versts (1 verst = 1,067 meters) in his description of the Tobol River. The thirteen maps charting the course of the Tobol River are interspersed with four pages of prose[46] in which he variously references distances with versts. For example, in one section he writes that a certain distance is going by foot or by other means.[47] On routes Remezov may not have traveled himself, he provides a distance given "on good information."[48] Remezov is ever attentive to the practicalities of travel. He reports frequently throughout the atlas how many weeks and days travel a particular itinerary required. He indicates places with white water, important features to be aware of in any river travel. Mode of travel is frequently indicated. Travel times varied by dog sleigh, by boat, by foot, or by season, for example. Typically, Remezov does not indicate variations for the same route; rather, he gives one metric, perhaps signaling how that route was most typically traveled.

This map depicts the headwaters of the Tobol River, nestled in the Ural Mountains. Depicting the headwaters of several significant rivers, any viewer would have understood the area to be higher ground. It is the last in a series of thirteen maps that follow the Tobol River—the first river basin mapped in the atlas—from the city of Tobol'sk where the Tobol River runs into the Irtysh on its way to the confluence with

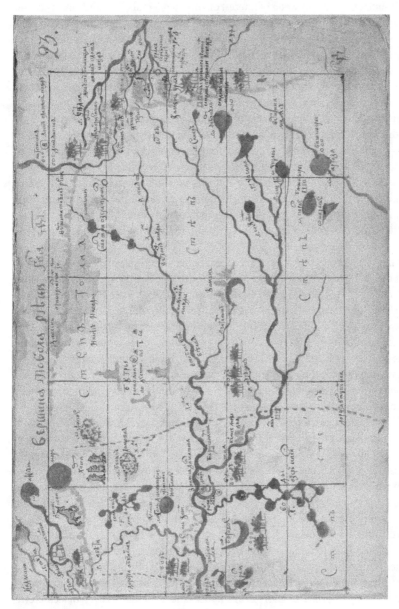

**Map 10.1** Map of the source of the Tobol River in the Ural Mountains, by Semen Ul'ianovich Remezov, *Khorograficheskaya kniga*, f. 23. MS Russ 72 (6). Credit: Houghton Library, Harvard University, Cambridge, Massachusetts.

the Ob River, meandering north toward the Arctic Ocean. On the dozen pages from Tobol'sk to the source of the Tobol, Remezov's maps show a river fed by numerous tributaries, surrounded by many lakes, forest groves, and swamps.

The Tobol is not the only water of interest on this map. We also see fresh and saltwater lakes—salt was a key resource in preservation of meat and fish and the Russian state consequently took a high interest in salt harvesting.[49] We see marshes, that mosquito-nurturing ecosystem in abundance in the hinterlands around Tobol'sk; no doubt they are well known to Remezov. Remezov is conscientious to mark the source of rivers; this map shows a cluster of rivers originating in the Urals. It is the source of the Tobol River that gives this map its title, written in red across the top of the map.

In the top row, second column from the right, according to the map's grid lines—which did not signify latitude or longitude but made copying easier—we see a blue line that ends in the map's yellow arc depicting the southern Urals (again, north is at the bottom on this map). Where this blue line terminates we find the words "source of the Tobol River."[50] (The Russian term for source is *vershina*—literally, summit.) Nearby clusters of trees that appear taller than the mountains reveal the range's unimposing stature. Among the several headwaters this map depicts, the humble Tobol loomed largest in Remezov's hydrographical imagination, for he titled the map after the river upon whose banks he grew up.

The map also shows us roads and resources of commercial potential. On the right edge of the map (somewhere in the southern Urals) we see the notation "Ural silver mines." North of the silver veins (but lower down on the page) and at the very source of the Ufa River, Remezov marked a different mineral resource. Red squares usually designated Russian households/small settlements, but they could also indicate seasonal camps for fur hunters and trappers.[51] In this case the two red squares may similarly indicate a processing camp, perhaps seasonal, but these are not for processing fur. Remezov's tiny notation next to these structures states, "House for mica processing. Mica veins are in the mountains."[52] Slightly north of that is another notation, revealing of the dynamism in Russians' exploitation of Siberia, "New mica places."[53] This is just one of many places in which the atlas seems to convey a dynamic, immediate utility, rather than a static, unchanging reality.

A single horse in the upper left corner indicates "wild horses"—perhaps higher up on the Turgai Plateau—roam there and three ferrets (polecats), hunted for their pelts, perched on hind legs. These animals seem to gaze toward the barren steppe—the feature that dominates this map. Beyond, there are two lakes, depicted with blue spots rather than solid color, seemingly indicating something more boggish than the lakes depicted to the north and west. The words in the top row of the grid across the top center of the map, which is the south in this projection, read, "Naked steppe. No forest. No water." Let the intrepid traveler be warned.

The map is teeming with evidence of human life, past and present. Kurgans—mounds, perhaps burials of past civilizations—and a handful (five) of cemeteries indicate that human presence was not brand new here.[54] Even more prevalent are indicators of contemporary life. A road marked by red dashes cuts its way through the steppe. Over sixty bridges span the Tobol River and its tributaries, connecting the twenty-seven neighborhood outposts (*slobody*) Remezov mapped along the Tobol

River.⁵⁵ In contemporary Russian language, *sloboda* is translated as neighborhood. In seventeenth-century Siberia, a *sloboda* referred to a population point with a church; it may have also had a bazaar where itinerant customs collectors collected taxes, according to administrative documents.

The spectrum of what Remezov captured in his *Chorography*, from the global to the particulars of family settlements, is astounding. In addition to these twenty-seven *sloboda* detailed along the Tobol River, we see several other population points, ranging perhaps from single family settlements to larger villages. Spread throughout the *Chorography* are red circles and red squares. Squares indicate Russian settlements. There are about 2,076 Russian population points (indicated with one, two, or three red squares) throughout the atlas. Circles indicate non-Russian population points, or yurts. The atlas contains about 1,942 yurt population points.⁵⁶ While this data may seem tedious to all but historians of Siberia and multiethnic empire, such information was of vital important to Russian servitors attempting to extract tribute, plan logistics, and assess security in early modern Siberia.

The thirteen maps of the Tobol River system show 213 Russian settlements and 59 yurts, denoting settlements of non-Russians. These Russian settlements are often named. On the northern outskirts of the city Tobol'sk we see one red square marked Remezov, perhaps indicating the family property of our mapmaker.⁵⁷ Along the Tobol River the vast majority of Russian settlements (squares) are accompanied by proper names (Reshetnikov, Kiselev (f. 11); Bulasheva, Repina, Shumiloma [sic], Shestakova,⁵⁸ Mazurova, Volokhova, Lusovaia, Kobylina (f. 12)). This isn't the case for non-Russian (circle) settlements. Of the fifty-nine *iurts*, some are labeled with proper names (Cheburtkinskie, Babasanskie, Akhmanasovy (f. 12), but probably less than half. Some *iurt* settlements are labeled more generically—*Bukhartsy* (f. 11), *Tobol-Turinskie* (f. 11). *Iurt*, we should note, in this context refers not to "yurt"—a round-framed tent, typically associated with Mongol homes, but rather is the word used in seventeenth-century Russian chancellery documents to indicate non-Russian settlements.

With this level of granular detail, it is almost as if the atlas could have doubled as a metaphorical "phone book." This is remarkable when we consider what an imprecise affair the seventeenth-century post was. To be sure, the Russians had adopted many of the features and vocabulary of the Mongol relay (*iam*) system, a sophisticated and efficacious postal network by any premodern standards. "Deliver to so-and-so, wherever you may find him" stood in for specific address on letters to one merchant's agents doing his bidding across Siberia.⁵⁹ While any sort of robust and comprehensive population tracking evaded the early-modern Russian state, Gol'denberg suggests that recording such specifics could help in the event of property disputes.⁶⁰

These basic shapes in red ink scattered across map after map are regular indicators of the multiethnicity and mixed sovereignty of the early-modern Russian empire. This is brought most poignantly home in the occasional diagrams where we see circles and squares crowded together.⁶¹ It brings to mind the complaint of a church official passing through Tobol'sk in 1654: "Christians and Muslims are living in close proximity." The complaint was repeated by another high church visitor from Moscow again decades later.⁶² It seems that the proximity was a reality the strict purveyors of Orthodoxy could not countenance, but that aspiration for an Orthodox fold apart and unsullied from nonbelievers was not entirely conducive to life in the taiga. Speaking of mixing, the map we are considering contains a puzzling deviation from Remezov's typical symbolic system. In the northwest corner of the map (bottom right), we see two settlements along two neighboring lakes: one is drawn with three red squares; the other, with three red circles. Both are labeled "Bashkirs."[63] The reason for this elision is unclear. The map also marks imperial obligations: "Bashkirs live here. They pay tribute in Ufa." "Nogais live here. They pay tribute in Ufa."[64]

## Movement

One of the richest sources of the early-modern Siberian past has not been in Siberia for centuries. Aside from the many itineraries, the travel, and the channeling of information through a knowledge-making infrastructure that went into the making of the *Chorography*, the atlas itself has covered much ground.[65] On the last page of the *Chorography*, there is some (as yet to me) indecipherable script across the center of the page. Below it, there is a shorter notation in a different hand. In the top left-hand corner of the page someone made notations of what the book contained and perhaps included an indecipherable name, although the first initial suggests a name of Yuri, before the date April 11, 1912, written in the same neat hand. Below that notation in the left-hand bottom corner of the page is the official-looking stamp: "Main office of the Countess E. A. Vorontsova-Dashkova." In the right-hand bottom corner of the page is affixed a sticker numbering the manuscript in Harvard's Houghton Library archive. These notations indicate the hands through which this object has passed, providing us just a tease of its itineraries throughout time. Otherwise, the *Chorography*'s movements through the dramatic twentieth century have left no material mark on this object.

The atlas's whereabouts in its first two centuries remain similarly murky. Historians generally think that Remezov intended to present the atlas to Tsar Peter I in 1701 but, probably because he felt it was not sufficiently ready, demurred and instead of presenting it to the tsar in Moscow, took it back to Tobol'sk with him. The *Chorography*, after all, has some blank pages labeled for maps that were intended but never drawn. The atlas likely remained in Tobol'sk with the Remezov family for the duration of Semen's life. Gol'denberg suggests that the *Chorography*, arguably the most detail-rich of all his atlases, served as a resource for producing subsequent cartographical works.

The atlas's whereabouts later in the eighteenth century are less clear. The German academician Gerhard Friedrich Müller, who resided in Siberia from 1733 to 1743 as part of the Second Kamchatka expedition, made notes about the contents of the atlas, which survived in his portfolios. Historian Leo Bagrow asserts that Müller saw the *Chorography* in Tobol'sk, but Gol'denberg is unclear on whether Müller himself held the atlas in Siberia or if he might have used it in European Russia.[66] Gol'denberg seems open to the possibility that the atlas came into the collection of the Vorontsov family during the lifetime of Müller, who died in 1783, noting that Müller was acquainted with the family. Eventually the atlas made its way into the collection of Russian noblewoman E. A. Vorontsova-Dashkova (1845–1924) and bears her stamp. The atlas passed through the hands of other owners, at least one of whom left a notation on the atlas, before being in the possession of the Antiquities Commission in St. Petersburg at the outbreak of the First World War.[67]

On March 12, 1956, the *Chorography* entered Harvard University's Houghton Library collection as part of the "Leo Bagrow Collection of Maps of Siberia."[68] The movement of the atlas from Russia before the First World War to Harvard was much entwined with Leo Bagrow (1881–1957). Born Lev Semenovich Bagrov in Siberia in 1881 to a mother who died soon after and a civil engineer, Bagrow became a cadet in the Russian Imperial Navy, "a career path traditionally reserved for Russian nobility," indicating the social dynamism that characterized late nineteenth-century Russian society.[69] He straddled academia and naval service in a hybrid position that would characterize his entire career. His tours of naval duty were interspersed with study that led to lecturing on cartography and publication of a few articles on the Caspian Sea (1912), Black Sea (1913), and an extensive literature review (1916) on the history of cartography (1916).

The Russian Revolution disrupted but did not derail his career in map history. He and his wife fled Russia for Berlin, Germany, in November 1918. When they fled they brought with them many maps from his personal collection. Bagrow never returned to his homeland but he continued to build his map collection. In the 1920s he cultivated his passion for historical cartography and made ends meet by working for various businesses. This employment allowed him to travel in search of historical maps, which he bought on behalf of others, and for his own collection.

By the 1920s the *Chorography* was part of Bagrow's personal map collection. How he acquired it has been a point of much contention. Gol'denberg alleged that Bagrow stole the atlas. He wrote that in 1914 the atlas was loaned from the archive of the Antiquities (*Arkheograficheskii*) Commission in order to prepare an "Atlas of Asiatic Russia." That Bagrow authored the introduction of this atlas strengthens Gol'denberg's conviction that Bagrow stole the atlas and smuggled "this unique monument to Russian science and culture of the 17th century, properly belonging to the Soviet people" out of the country.[70]

Bagrow, who considered Remezov's *Chorography* the "flower of his collection," told a different story.[71] From his previous work in Russia he was familiar with this cartographical treasure. According to Bagrow, he persuaded the wealthy German industrialist and conservative Reichstag member Hugo Stinnes to purchase, via a proxy, the *Chorography* from a Moscow bookseller in 1923.[72] Heffernan and Delano-Smith, investigating the matter in the archives of the academic journal, *Imago Mundi*, wrote that shortly after Stinnes died in 1924, Bagrow somehow came into possession of the atlas.[73] The details of whether this treasure was smuggled out of Russia by Bagrow or ushered through by an indifferent customs administration remain murky. Bagrow's 1947 comment in *Imago Mundi* about a small manuscript atlas in Stockholm that "was considered lost" does not clarify.[74] Both versions, while mutually exclusive, are theoretically tenable. Indeed, a combination of financial desperation and ideological rejection of bourgeois culture led the officially atheist Bolshevik regime to sell many treasures of the Orthodox Church and Imperial possessions.[75] In his monograph about Remezov's mapping, Gol'denberg maintained that Bagrow's friends made up the story about him buying the atlas to cover up his crime of stealing it.[76] Heffernan and Delano-Smith disagreed, arguing that the *Imago Mundi* archive supports Bagrow's version of events; admittedly, the *Imago Mundi* was founded and managed by Bagrow.

If the Siberian atlas's exodus was not furtive it would mark a departure from a long tradition of smuggling Siberian maps out of Russia. Two and half centuries earlier two Swedes, Prytz and Cronman, had smuggled out furtive sketches that they themselves had drawn in "stolen" private moments of the Godunov map of 1667. At the end of the century Andrei Andreevich Vinius, who served the Russian state for a time as the head of the Siberian Office, channeled information to his cousin and avid amateur cartographer Nicolaas Witsen. Vinius, who may have been responsible for Semen Remezov getting tapped to do more mapping, is also suspected of having smuggled maps out of Russia.[77]

In Berlin, Bagrow continued to pursue his passion for the history of cartography, straddling the academic-antiquities market divide. Book dealers and wealthy businessmen like Stinnes hired Bagrow to seek out historical antiquities. In addition, Bagrow formed the "Circle of Lovers of Russian Antiquities" in 1927. In 1935, just over a decade after Remezov's *Chorography* came into Bagrow's possession, he partnered with Berlin bookseller Hans Wertheim to found *Imago Mundi*, a biennial journal dedicated to the history of cartography. While founding *Imago Mundi* was a solid academic endeavor and did help him, along with his important contributions to scholarship, attain scholarly credibility, his lack of academic pedigree, suspicions about how he spent his war years, and, even according to charitable associates, a prickly personality dogged Bagrow throughout his career.

In 1943, Bagrow traveled to the National Library in Nazi-occupied Paris, France. The National Library in 1942 had acquired from the Paris Geographical Society a collection of more than ten thousand items. While it is typical that Bagrow would have been interested in that acquisition, some suspected that Bagrow's trip, in the wake of Berlin usurping control from the Vichy regime, may have been part of a collaboration with the Nazi program to "repatriate" historical maps.[78] Bagrow and his wife left Berlin on April 23, 1945, just one week before a defeated Adolf Hitler committed suicide. They left on one of the last flights possible with a few cases of books and maps—including Remezov's *Chorography*—and "a small cage containing their pet sparrow." Bagrow took great delight in sparrows, according to the Obituary *Imago Mundi* published about him.[79] There is something poetic in this recollection about a man who devoted so much of his energy to Remezov's maps, counting Remezov's atlas and a pet sparrow as his most treasured items, for the name Remezov derives from the Russian word, *rémez*—a type of small bird in a branch of the sparrow family.[80] The *Chorography* resided in Stockholm, Sweden, until, struggling to make ends meet in Sweden, Bagrow resorted to selling the "flower of his collection."

None of this death and suffering left its material mark on Remezov's *Chorography*. In a volume dedicate to materiality, this excursus into the turbulence that churned around the *Chorography* in the first half of the twentieth century is perhaps a reminder of the limits of a material approach. For all the thousands of facts that are preserved in the materiality of this artifact, and the incidental, unintended clues this "thick thing" carries, the atlas' peregrinations in the Second World War bear no obvious mark that I have discerned.

If its itineraries shaped by historical forces are entirely absent from the object itself, they are not without consequence. First, the suspicion that the atlas was stolen may have contributed to its arrival at Harvard's Houghton Library. When its sale was proposed to the British Museum, the curator who inspected the atlas in 1954 declined to purchase it, referring to it as "allegedly stolen."[81] The atlas was acquired from Orion Booksellers, Ltd., by American philanthropist Curt H. Reisinger, graduate of Harvard Class of 1912, who gifted it to the Houghton Library in 1956.[82] Bagrow and the Houghton library, according to Heffernan and Delano-Smith, were both involved in the negotiations.[83]

A second consequence of the *Chorography*'s travels is that, while they left no mark on the material thing, the movement of this object has informed (and impeded) the development of scholarship. Particularly because there is so much overlap in the works Remezov produced, a comprehensive source study of Remezov's oeuvre is a complicated endeavor. The physical facts of separation may have hindered scholarly progress. Geopolitics and ideological divides have of course done their part, exacerbating logistical difficulties in scholarly cooperation. Scholars to the west of the Iron Curtain had access to the *Chorography* while scholars in the Soviet Union had access to the rest of Remezov's extant works. A. I. Andreev and Gol'denberg studied Remezov and early cartography without access to the *Chorography* while Bagrow studied the *Chorography* without access to Remezov's other two "atlases." If this physical separation complicated the study and historical contextualization of the source, the obstacle should not be overstated: the publisher Mouton & Co. published a facsimile edition of the *Chorography* in The Hague in 1958. An edition of this was first received in a Soviet library in 1959, just one year later. Movement and connections are embedded in the thing's entire history—some preserved, some of them with consequences, but consequences not evident in the document itself.

Today, the *Chorography* lies quietly on a shelf protected from sunlight, elements, and the wear and tear of page turning by patrons in the collection of the Houghton Library at Harvard University in Cambridge, Massachusetts. Its physical location recedes, however, because the digitization of the atlas in 2010 has meant it is effectively, or at least potentially, everywhere all the time in cyberspace.[84] The digitization of this source engenders new contexts. The liberating disembodiment that makes accessing the content so easy may make accessing the context that much more difficult, not least because the accessibility may impart a facile intellectual satisfaction. If this is a tendency, this is not an insurmountable problem, but rather an opportunity for historians. Scholars and platforms can counter this downside of decontextualization and support informed curiosity by more consciously featuring and explicating the materiality of digitized sources.

## Conclusion

Remezov's *Chorography* is a thick and quiet thing. On the one hand, this quiet thing shouts out the tremendous transmission of information, infrastructure, and ambition that went into the making of this thing. It depended on interaction with cartographical production from the west. It built on accumulated knowledge, much of it recorded on paper, even if early historians of Russian mapping may have exaggerated the state of Russian cartography in the sixteenth and early seventeenth centuries. It also relied upon the input and reporting of contemporaries of Remezov who traveled to corners of Eurasia and shared with him what they learned. From the ecliptic circling the bi-hemispheric globe in the front pages to the named individual settlements throughout, the global to local range of this atlas is remarkable: it is both continent-spanning and locally particular cartography. On the other hand, for all the rich and staggering information contained in this material treasure, its utility has receded with time—not only because the landscape and demography it depicted are so altered but also because the intellectual apparatuses and context that made this material "legible" have also receded.

The past happened in color. It played on all five senses. This is a banal but a worthy reminder to those of us who engage with the past primarily through flat, quiet pages. For most of its history, the pages considered here have laid quiet, flat, and out-of-sight. But there is much movement in this thing's past. Before it came to rest in a quiet climate-controlled archive and in cyberspace, highly pixelated and zoomable, it had made peregrinations of its own, just as its author had made extensive peregrinations, by Semen Remezov and by countless others whose intelligence and information went into the binding of Siberia in the pages of the *Chorography*.

## Notes

I would like to thank the editors for their vision, encouragement, insightful comments, and patience in realizing this project. I also express my gratitude to the History Department of Dartmouth College for supporting me with a printed, color copy of Remezov's *Khorograficheskaia kniga*.

1. Gosudarstvennoe biudzhetnoe ucherezhdenie Tiumenkoi oblasti, Gosudarstvennii arkhiv Tiumenskoi oblasti (GBUTO GATO), f. 47, op. 1, d. 261, l. 1 (1684).
2. Erika Monahan, "Gavril Romanovich Nikitin," in *Russia's People of Empire: Life Stories from Eurasia, 1500–Present*, ed. Stephen Norris and Willard Sutherlands (Bloomington: Indiana University Press, 2012), 54.
3. Gosudarstvennoe ucherezhdenie Tiumenkoi oblasti, Gosudarstvennii arkhiv v gorode Tobol'ske (GUTO GAT), f. 156 (Tobol'skaia Dukhovnaia Konsistoriia), f. 156, op. 1, d. 1367, l.32 (1753).
4. N. N. Ogloblin, "Bytovye cherty nachala XVIII veka," *Chteniia OIDR* (1904) kn. 1, Part. 3: Smes', 1 (p. 219 in volume).
5. GBUTO GATO, f. 47, d. 1744, l. 3 (1728).
6. GBUTO GATO, f. 47, op. 1, d. 248, l. 1 (1650); Sankt-Peterburgskii institut istorii Rossiiskoi akademii nauk (SPbII RAN), f. 28, op. 1, d. 778, l. 1, d. 863, 8 ll.; GUTO GAT), f. 156 (Tobol'skaia Dukhovnaia Konsistoriia), op. 1, d. 118, 8 ll.
7. Semen Ul'ianovich Remezov (1642–ca. 1720), *Khorograficheskaya kniga* (cartographical sketch-book of Siberia). MS Russ 72 (6). Houghton Library, Harvard University, Cambridge, MA. https://nrs.harvard.edu/urn-3:FHCL.HOUGH:4435676. Hereafter referred to as Remezov, *Chorography*. The Harvard website translates it differently than I do here.

8. It is typically dated as having been composed between 1697 and 1711. Leo Bagrow wrote that it was begun in 1696, although some images in the atlas were certainly produced earlier. Erika Monahan, "Moving Pictures: Tobol'sk 'Traveling' in Early Modern Texts," *Canadian-American Slavic Studies* 52:3–4 (2018), 261–89.
9. Harvard archivist Christine Jacobson describes pasteboard as "cardboard's seventeenth-century cousin." Email correspondence with Christine Jacobson, Assistant curator of Modern Books and Manuscripts, Houghton Library, July 22, 2020.
10. Email correspondence with Kelly O'Neill, Director of *The Imperiia Project*, Davis Center, Harvard University, July 22, 2020.
11. Conventions were in flux. Placing the index at the back came later, just as putting the title page in the front was a later innovation. Incunabula such as Strabo's *Geography*, for example, placed the title page in the back.
12. L. A. Gol'denberg, *Semen Ul'ianovich Remezov, sibirskii kartograf i geograf, 1642–posle 1720* (Moscow: Nauka, 1965), 183.
13. Email correspondence with Kelly O'Neill, Director, *The Imperiia Project*; Christine Jacobson, Assistant curator of Modern Books and Manuscripts, Houghton Library; David Weimer, Librarian for Cartographic Collections and Learns, Harvard Map Collection, July 22, 2020. I thank these scholars for sharing these material facts about the atlas.
14. Polevoi wrote that this reduced-size map (*chertezh*) was typical of Muscovite models. Boris P. Polevoi, "Concerning the Origin of the Maps of Russia of 1613–1614 of Hessel Gerritsz," in *New Perspectives on Muscovite History*, ed. Lindsey A. Hughes (New York: St. Martin's Press, 1993), 16, 18.
15. Jerry Brotton, *A History of the World in 12 Maps* (New York: Penguin, 2014), 256.
16. Mary Elizabeth Berry, *Japan in Print: Information and Nation in the Early Modern Period* (Berkeley: University of California Press, 2006), 67–8.
17. Bruno Latour, "Can We Get Our Materialism Back, Please?" *Isis* 98 (2007), 141.
18. Gol'denberg, *Semen Ul'ianovich Remezov*; Leo Bagrow, "Semyon Remezov. A Siberian Cartographer," *Imago Mundi* 11 (1954), 111–25; Valerie Kivelson, *Cartographies of Tsardom: The Land and Its Meanings in Seventeenth-Century Russia* (Ithaca, NY: Cornell University Press, 2007), 133–45.
19. Bagrow, "Semyon Remezov," 112.
20. L. A. Gol'denberg, "Russian Cartography to ca. 1700," in *History of Cartography*, Vol. 3, pt. 2, ed. David Woodward (Chicago: University of Chicago Press, 2007), 1887–9; Polevoi, "Hessel Gerritsz's Maps of Russia, 1613–1614," 17. See also Marina Tolmacheva, "The Early Russian Exploration and Mapping of the Chinese Frontier," *Cahiers de Monde Russe* 41:1 (2000), 41–56; Valerie Kivelson, "Early Mapping: The Tsardom in Manuscript," in *Information and Empire: Mechanisms of Communication in Russia, 1600–1850*, ed. Simon Franklin and Katherine Bowers (Cambridge: Open Book, 2017), 23–57.
21. Remezov, *Chorography*, f. 1.
22. Gol'denberg, "Russian Cartography to ca. 1700," 1889.
23. Sir Robert Southwell to Nicolaas Witsen, letter repr. in *Philosophical Transactions* Vol. 16 (1686–92), 493.
24. Kivelson, *Cartographies of Tsardom*, 123.
25. Leo Bagrow, "The First Russian Maps of Siberia and Their Influence on the West-European Cartography of N. E. Asia," *Imago Mundi* 9 (1952), 84.
26. Kivelson, *Cartographies of Tsardom*, 134.
27. Gol'denberg, "Russian Cartography to ca. 1700," 1885.

28. Remezov, *Chorography*, f. 113.
29. Kivelson, "Early Mapping," 54.
30. Kivelson, *Cartographies of Tsardom*, 232n52.
31. Maike Sach, "Symbols, Conventions, and Practices: Visual Representation of Ethnographic Knowledge on Siberia in Early Modern Maps and Reports," in *An Empire of Others: Creating Ethnographic Knowledge in Imperial Russia and the USSR*, ed. Roland Svetkovski and Alexis Hofmeister (New York: Central European University Press, 2014), 178.
32. Benjamin Schmidt, *Inventing Exoticism: Geography, Globalism, and Europe's Early Modern World* (Philadelphia: University of Pennsylvania Press, 2015), 35.
33. Kivelson, *Cartographies of Tsardom*, 133. I have not worked with or seen the *Working Sketchbook* (*Sluzhebnaia chertezhnaia kniga*) in person. Kivelson calls it "the most spectacular of all" Remezov's atlases.
34. Kivelson, *Cartographies of Tsardom*, 134; Kivelson, "Early Mapping," 55. Of note, the map of Asia Remezov copied from Blaeu does not depict the Kamchatka peninsula. The map of the bi-hemispheric globe in the *Chorography*, however, does depict the Kamchatka peninsula.
35. Monahan, "Gavril Romanov Nikitin," 47–56.
36. Sach, "Symbols, Conventions, and Practices," 180.
37. See Daniel Waugh, "The View from the North: Muscovite Cartography of Inner Asia," *Journal of Asian History* 49:1–2 (2015), 81.
38. Bagrow, "The First Russian Maps of Siberia," 85.
39. Nicolaas Witsen to Sir Robert Southwell, undated, letter repr. in *Philosophical Transactions*, Vol. 16 (1686–92), 493.
40. Monahan, "Moving Pictures," 261–89.
41. Jessica Maier, "A 'True Likeness': The Renaissance City Portrait," *Renaissance Quarterly* 65:3 (Fall 2012), 711–52.
42. Bagrow, "The First Russian Maps of Siberia," 86.
43. Gol'denberg, *Semen Ul'ianovich Remezov*, 149, 154; Gol'denberg, "Russian Cartography to ca. 1700," 1901.
44. Valerie Kivelson, "The Cartographic Emergence of Europe?" in *Oxford Handbook of Early Modern European History, 1350–1750*, vol. 1: *Peoples and Places*, ed. Hamish Scott (New York: Oxford University Press, 2015), 27–8.
45. See Gol'denberg, "Russian Cartography to ca. 1700," 1863, Table 62.1.
46. These pages are labeled "caption text of the *Chorography* (*podpis' kherografii*)."
47. Remezov, *Chorography*, ff. 11v., 12v.
48. "*po vestu dobre*" Remezov, *Chorography*, f. 12v.
49. Remezov devoted an entire page to one of the most important salt lakes from which the Russian state harvested, Lake Yamysh, along the Irtysh River. Remezov, *Chorography*, f. 97. For a discussion of this lake, see Monahan, *The Merchants of Siberia*, chapter 5.
50. The source of the Tobol River is also shown in Remezov, *Chorography*, f. 113 (bottom right corner).
51. Trapper is an imperfect translation of the Russian term *promyshlennik*. Since *promyshlenniki* could also be involved in the acquisition of furs through indirect means, such as trade or extortionary acquisition from indigenous Siberians, and involved in the processing and sale of fur pelts, another term sometimes used is the awkward "fur entrepreneurs."
52. *избы у слюдного промысла. Слюдны признаки в горах.*

53. *слюдны новые места*.
54. Remezov, *Chorography*, ff. 11, 12, 21, 23.
55. Ibid., ff. 11–23.
56. My thanks to Jonathan Wright for his research assistance in tallying the population points of the *Khorograficheskaia kniga* in the summer of 2020.
57. Remezov, *Chorography*, f. 11. (B5 in grid)
58. The more we know about Siberian history, the more revealing and interesting these names become. To take one example, one of the villages named is Shestakova. A Cossack ataman by the name of Afanasii Shestakov made a map of northeast Asia, which came to St. Petersburg in 1726. L. Breitfuss, "Early Maps of North-Eastern Asia and of the Lands around the North Pacific: Controversy between G. F. Müller and N. Delisle," *Imago Mundi* 3 (1939), 87.
59. Ogloblin, Obozrenie stolbtsov i knig Sibirskogo prikaza, 2: 206.
60. Gol'denberg, *Semen Ul'ianovich Remezov*, 141.
61. For examples along the Tobol River, see Remezov, *Chorography*, ff. 16, 18, 27.
62. Monahan, *The Merchants of Siberia*, 276.
63. Remezov, *Chorography*, f. 23.
64. Ibid.
65. For a detailed treatment of the chronological and locational composition of the atlas, see Leo Bagrow, "Introduction," in *The Atlas of Siberia by Semyon U. Remezov* (The Hague: Mouton & Co., 1958), 1–17.
66. Bagrow, "Introduction," 16. For compelling evidence that Müller saw the *Chorography* see Bagrow, "Semyon Remezov. A Siberian Cartographer," 115n2.
67. Gol'denberg, *Semen Ul'ianovich Remezov*, 84.
68. Harvard Library, Hollis for Archival Discovery page, https://hollisarchives.lib.harvard.edu/repositories/24/resources/1274, accessed May 27, 2019.
69. Michael Heffernan and Catherine Delano-Smith, "A Life in Maps: Leo Bagrow, *Imago Mundi*, and the History of Cartography in the Early Twentieth Century," *Imago Mundi* 66, supp. 1 (October 2014), 45.
70. Gol'denberg, *Semen Ul'ianovich Remezov*, 83–5. The introduction is listed in the Bibliography of Bagrow's works published in his *Imago Mundi* obituary. "Leo Bagrow," *Imago Mundi* 14 (1959), 10.
71. R. A. Skelton, "Leo Bagrow: Historian of Cartography and Founder of *Imago Mundi*, 1881–1957," *Imago Mundi* 14 (1959), 8.
72. Bagrow, "Introduction," 17; Skelton, "Leo Bagrow," 8.
73. Heffernan and Delano-Smith, "A Life in Maps," 47.
74. Leo Bagrow, "Review of A. I. Andreev," *Ocherki po istochnikovedeniiu Sibiri. XVII vek. Imago Mundi* 4 (1947), 83. In his 1954 article on Semen Remezov, Bagrow declares that the General Map of Siberia is in his possession but is silent on the *Chorography*. See Leo Bagrow, "Semyon Remezov: A Siberian Cartographer," *Imago Mundi* 11 (1954), 116.
75. Among other articles in the collection, see Irina Tarsis, "Book Dealers, Collectors, and Librarians: Major Acquisitions of Russian Imperial Books at Harvard, 1920s–1950s," in *Treasures into Tractors: The Selling of Russia's Cultural Heritage, 1918–1938*, ed. Anne Odom and Wendy Salmond (Seattle, DC: University of Washington Press, 2009), 369–87. This article contains no mention of the Leo Bagrow collection.
76. Gol'denberg, *Semen Ul'ianovich Remezov*, 85, 181.
77. Bagrow, "Introduction," 15–16; Alexey Postnikov and Marvin Falk, *Exploring and Mapping Alaska* (Fairbanks: University of Alaska Press, 2015), 18.

78. Heffernan and Delano-Smith, "A Life in Maps," 53.
79. R. A. Skelton, "Leo Bagrow: Historian of Cartography and Founder of *Imago Mundi*, 1881–1957," *Imago Mundi* 14 (1959), 9.
80. I thank Dr. Barry Scherr for sharing this linguistic information. See *Dictionary of Russian Personal Names*, by Morton Benson, compiler (New York: Cambridge University Press, 1992), 106.
81. Heffernan and Delano-Smith, "A Life in Maps," 59.
82. "Leo Bagrow Collection of Maps," Harvard Library acquisition details, https://hollisarchives.lib.harvard.edu/repositories/24/resources/1274, accessed August 29, 2020.
83. Heffernan and Delano-Smith, "A Life in Maps," 59–60.
84. Emilie Hardman, "Early Maps of Siberia Digitized," *Houghton Library Blog*, April 10, 2010, https://blogs.harvard.edu/houghton/early-maps-of-siberia-digitized/, accessed January 20, 2021.

# 11

# "Rather Poor and Threadbare": Bogoras, Scratching-Woman, and the Intimacy of Material

## Marisa Karyl Franz

In New York City, a coat that once belonged to a Siberian shaman named Scratching-Woman rests in storage.[1] In 1902, Waldemar Bogoras, as part of the Jesup North Pacific Expedition, acquired this coat and passed it on to the anthropology department of the American Museum of Natural History (AMNH).[2] Unlike many ethnographic objects in museum collections that have unknown provenances and erased, forgotten, or hidden histories, this coat is embedded in the intimacies of life and the relationship between two people who found themselves together in a coastal village on the Gulf of Anadyr in the waning days of the Russian Empire.[3]

The Jesup Expedition, which facilitated the AMNH's acquisition of this coat, was an expansive ethnographic undertaking lasting from 1897 to 1902 that had "for its object the investigation of the tribes, present and past, of the coasts of the North Pacific Ocean beginning at the Amoor [sic] River in Asia, and extending northeastward to Bering Sea, thence southeastward along the American coast as far as Columbia River."[4] The detailed ethnographic works that were written by members of the expedition attempted to document all aspects of life ranging from religion to dog and reindeer breeding to the history and geography of the region.[5] The scale of the expedition was vast, and while Boas himself never produced a summative work that drew together the findings from the different expedition members, the subsequent academic engagement on the expedition has stepped in to analyze, critique, challenge, and celebrate the far-reaching material.[6] The coat is at the AMNH now as part of the collection from the Jesup Expedition. Prior to its time at the AMNH, however, the coat belonged to, and was rooted in, the shamanic life of Scratching-Woman. Through the recording of its history and the movement of it across continents, the coat is also entangled with the life of Bogoras.

Bogoras described the coat itself as "rather poor and threadbare" and wrote dismissively about the Chukchi material culture of shamanic dress in comparison with other nations' material shamanic practices in Siberia.[7] However, it is the only Chukchi shaman's coat Bogoras collected at the AMNH, and he centers this poor and threadbare coat and its owner in his account of the shamanic material culture of the Chukchi in his ethnographic monograph *The Chukchee*, including an illustration of it for readers (Figure 11.1). Bogoras's work suggests an ambivalence about the value

**Figure 11.1** Illustration of Scratching-Woman's coat by Rudolf Weber originally published in Bogoras's *The Chukchee*. Credit: American Museum of Natural History, Anthropology.

of the coat as simultaneously visually falling short of the detailed and intricate image of Siberian shamans' coats that are often seen in museums and visual media, while also centering it and its owner in his study. This ambiguity and the relationship between these two people are documented within—but always mediated through—Bogoras's ethnographic records and collections. Bogoras, as a mediator, filters out many of our potential insights into Scratching-Woman's own motivations and desires. Conspicuously absent from the records is an account of how Bogoras acquired Scratching-Woman's coat. Throughout Bogoras's account of Scratching-Woman there are moments of partnership, resistance, distrust, and friendship. While this central question of acquisition remains unanswered, through Bogoras's work, we can see how this coat became something embedded within the intimacies of people's lives, and we can trace its history of movement and transition as a thing in-between different understandings of value, of personhood, of worlds, and of use.

I read this "in-betweenness" as part of the complexity of the coat and as an opening both to consider how Siberian shamanism has been represented within museums and to propose a foregrounding of the troubling and troubled relationships that sat (and sit) at the foundations of ethnographic documentation and collection. Anthropologist Paul Basu writes of the in-betweenness of things, a view that places things in a middle ground, a relational space that challenges the idea of an epistemic object that can serve as a specimen, an example of a category or idea.[8] The in-betweenness of this coat is embedded in the relational space between Bogoras and Scratching-Woman. In this space, the coat is a specimen neither of Chukchi shamanism nor of Siberian ethnographic collecting but is rather an intimate and personal thing that moved between people and places as it traveled from Chukotka to New York City.

Bogoras's dismissive assessment of the visual impact of this coat derives not only from its threadbare appearance but also from its simplicity of design in comparison to the visual repertoire of shamanic coats that are held in collections, photographed, and printed. More commonly in museums and visual media, the shamans' coats presented are highly decorated and elaborate garments covered in fringe, metal ornaments, dyed fabric strips, and large metal plates.[9] At the AMNH, the Siberian displays in the Gardner D. Stout Hall of Asian Peoples include a Nanai shaman's coat with black and red fringe and painted images and a Sakha shaman's coat with intricate metal ornaments hanging off the leather coat and covering the back.[10] Both these pieces are, like Scratching-Woman's coat, associated with the Jesup Expedition, and were collected by Berthold Laufer (the Nanai coat) and Waldemar Jochelson (the Sakha coat) in 1900 and 1902, respectively. The AMNH's decision to show these highly decorated coats in their gallery is in keeping with the practices of most museums with Siberian shamanic displays; the coats selected are usually visually engaging, with complex and intricate ornamentation that does not have to rely on text to suggest to the viewer that these would have been worn outside of everyday mundane dress. Since the eighteenth century, Russian expeditions had been participating in ethnographic research and material collecting for museums, which included shamanic materials. These accounts and images circulated within the Russian Empire and internationally and helped popularize the idea and image of shamanism in Western academic and museum spaces.[11] Images of the intricate coats of shamans have been circulating outside of Siberia since the early 1800s in illustrations from books such as Johann Gottlieb Georgi's *A Description of All the Peoples Living in the Russian State* (1799) and William Alexander's *The Costumes of the Russian Empire* (1803), both of which depict elaborate Siberian shamans' coats in colored plates.[12] The long legacy of circulating coats and illustrations of ornate shamanic coats has established a repertoire of visual references for Siberian shamanic materials that are absent in Scratching-Woman's coat. Scratching-Woman's coat has not been displayed at the AMNH, nor was it one of the pieces included in a 2014–16 project that selected some of the Jesup Collection materials for more intensive study, community consultation and collaboration, and preservation work.[13]

Our repertoire of what Siberian shamans look like continues to be informed by the images of ornately decorated shamanic coats, and implicitly we carry forward Bogoras's assessment of the coat as lacking due to its simplicity. However, if we locate ourselves in the fissures of Bogoras's work, a different perspective on this coat emerges. By recentering on the relational space, the thing itself—the coat—becomes bound to people, places, emotions, spirits, and ancestors. Things are intimate and personal; they are, as Basu reminds us, "entanglements of ongoing social, spatial, temporal, and material trajectories and relationships, dislocations and relocations."[14] Similarly, museum practices are shifting toward a relational methodology grounded in the incorporation of traditional knowledge and care practices, and away from material culture as manifested in an ethnographic object as a static specimen.[15] The materiality of the coat itself is always bound up with the immaterial life of its movements and intimacies. While this was not the stated methodology of Bogoras while he was living at Mariinsky Post with Scratching-Woman, nor of Boas at the AMNH, who oversaw the Jesup Expedition, the prioritization of personalization, relation building, and intimacy within Bogoras's records can draw us into this coat. Rather than reading this coat as a representation of Chukchi shamanism, I move into a space of the joined and severed relationships that make this coat embedded in the lives and movements of two people. In its current position as a museum piece, this coat is still bound up in the in-betweenness of its entanglements with different lives, places, beings, and uses. When framed in the intimacies of life, "all objects are, in a sense, travelling objects" with layered and relational identities that shift and alter the space around them; here, this is the movement of a coat through Chukchi land, the travel between worlds, the taking on and off during shamanic rituals, the patching and mending of leather, and the dislocation and movement away from Scratching-Woman, to Bogoras, and, finally, to the AMNH.

## Mariinsky Post as a Meeting Place

Bogoras and Scratching-Woman encountered each other in Mariinsky Post, a village established by Russian settlers on the Gulf of Anadyr near the Chukchi village Ve$^ɛ$ñ,[16] which had previously been closer to the water (Map 11.1).[17] The settlement was located just below the Arctic Circle, on an estuary of the Anadyr that would freeze over by October 17.[18] By the time Bogoras was there in 1902, small seasonal fairs had started occurring in the town twice a year, one in the spring, and one in the summer around the time when the mail-steamer would arrive, and people across the region would come on dog and reindeer sledges, as well as skin boats from the maritime villages.[19]

For Bogoras, Mariinsky Post was not a home but a place for ethnographic study. He was brought into the Jesup expedition to document the "Eastern Chukchee" for the AMNH, for which, in a draft of the initial invitation to join the expedition, Bogoras was to be paid one hundred dollars a month for his studies that "would be devoted primarily to the ethnology of the people [the Chukchi], including a study of their language and mythology, and anthropometric measurements."[20] Bogoras joined the Jesup Expedition on the recommendation of the Russian Academy of Science and had previously been working as an ethnographer on expeditions with the Imperial Geographical Society in Eastern Siberia.[21] Bogoras has become a foundational scholar in Russian ethnography, but he began his work as an amateur ethnographer during his exile. Born into a Jewish family in Ovruch in the Volyn Governate, he became involved with the populist *Narodnik* movement while at university in St. Petersburg, which led to his exile to the Kolyma region in Northeastern Siberia.[22] Bogoras, like other exiled *Narodniks* including Lev Sternberg and Vladimir Jochelson (both of whom were also involved in the Jesup Expedition), began to engage in ethnographic studies of the local communities; initially, for Bogoras, these were of the Russian settlers in Kolyma, and later, once he learned the language, of the Chukchi.[23] Bogoras was particularly interested in the study of material culture, language, and religion, and, despite Boas's wide-ranging objectives for the Jesup Expeditions that are reflected in the three-volume monograph on the Chukchi, Bogoras's particular areas of interest are apparent

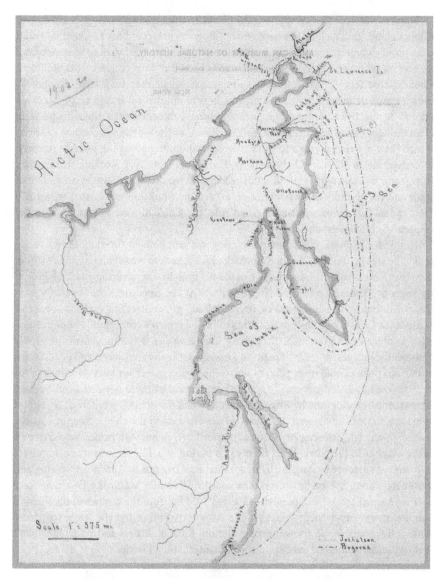

**Map 11.1** A hand-drawn map of the routes taken by Bogoras and Jochelson during the Jesup Expedition, which includes the location of Mariinsky Post on the Gulf of Anadyr. Credit: American Museum of Natural History, Anthropology.

in his writing, and they continued to be important throughout his future career as an ethnographer, as a political figure in the early Soviet Union, and as the director and founder of the State Museum of the History of Religion. These particular interests help contextualize why Scratching-Woman and Chukchi shamanism and its materiality occupy such a central place in Bogoras's work and his proposed cultural exegesis.

Bogoras was dedicated to studying the Chukchi language and culture while living on Chukchi land, and, as Igor Krupnik writes, "Bogoras preserved his Chukchi devotion through his whole academic career and through the Jesup fieldwork as well. Actually, he looked at other Siberian native nations from the perspective of his Reindeer Chukchi experience."[24] Not only is this comparative inclination suggestive of Bogoras's broader interest in evolutionary interpretations of culture but it also emphasizes his unique perspective as an ethnographer that sought to center the Chukchi who were often thought of and framed as the least "civilized" of the Siberian Indigenous nations due to their active resistance to Russian colonization, to paying the *iasak* (a fur tax), to converting to Russian Orthodoxy, and to settlement. Yuri Slezkine summarizes this strong resistance by reminding his readers, "It would take a century and a half of trade and two decades of collectivization to turn the Chukchi into Russian subjects."[25] Despite this history of rejecting Russian rule, the Chukchi were not immune to the impacts of colonial expansion.

In a letter to Boas about his travels, Bogoras emphasized the remoteness of the region he was in, writing, "From Kamchatka I went back to Anadyr along the seacoast, the latter part of which way was not made till now by any civilized man, or indeed by anybody besides a few Chukchee camps."[26] At the same time, however, Bogoras did not document an imagined or romanticized "pre-contact" or primeval space of Indigenous Chukotka. While parts of this subarctic region were certainly unpopulated, what is more often presented throughout *The Chukchee* is the movement of people through the villages, ports, and nations. Russians settle the area, naval and postal ships come into port, people from villages across the region gather for fairs; Mariinsky Post is connected in a vast network. The lived experience of these networks can be seen in moments documented by Bogoras, such as when Scratching-Woman, at one point "during a shamanistic séance," is asked by the assistant of the chief officer of Anadyr, a Russian official, "whether his Second Interior Loan Bond, with prizes, would draw a lucky number in the yearly lottery."[27] By this period, too, English was more dominant as a second language among the Chukchi than Russian, due to American whaling and commerce along the eastern Chukotka coastline.[28] While Mariinsky Post may have seemed a small coastal village where Bogoras lived far from the capitals of the Russian Empire, it was experiencing the vast and complex world of the late Imperial period with political exiles and fermenting revolution, Russian settlers and settlements, and military and commercial expansion through international trade.

## Lives In-between: Scratching-Woman and Bogoras

Scratching-Woman, the first recorded owner of the shaman's coat at the AMNH, was a male Chukchi shaman who lived in Mariinsky Post in the early years of the twentieth century. Scratching-Woman is referred to in Bogoras's writings with male pronouns. Bogoras was aware of gender nonconforming and transgender Chukchi, and he explains that while some shamans were gender-fluid, there were individual Chukchi who would completely abandon "all pursuits and manners of his sex and takes up those of a woman."[29] Here, these women, with the help of spirits, would change their speech, manner, work, and would "after a time take a husband"; about this, Bogoras adds, "I must say that it forms a quite solid union, which often lasts until the death of one of the parties. The couple lives much in the same way as do other people. The man tends his herd and goes hunting and fishing, while the [wife] takes care of the house, performing all domestic pursuits and work."[30] Scratching-Woman, in addition to being identified with male pronouns, also has a wife and tends his reindeer herd suggesting that he lives as a male, and, because of this, I continue Bogaras's use of the pronouns *he* and *him* in referring to Scratching-Woman.

According to Bogoras's account, Scratching-Woman had a hard childhood farther inland in Chukotka near the Russian village of Markovo; his father died while he was a boy after losing a herd of reindeer, and he and his mother nearly starved, which left him "sick and weak."[31] In this state of ill health, having lost his father, and hauling fuel for the wealthier residents of Markovo, Scratching-Woman

> began to beat the drum and to call for the "spirits," and one by one he saw all the supernatural beings (va'ɪgɪt), and he made himself a shaman. The va'ɪgɪt of the Motionless Star came to him in a dream and said to him, "Cease to be such a weakling! Be a shaman and strong shaman, and you will have plenty of food."[32]

Scratching-Woman became a shaman, gained a "good-sized" herd of reindeer, married into a family, and "was no longer an orphan."[33]

As a shaman, Scratching-Woman was able call upon spirits (ke'ʟet) to help him. Bogoras describes some of these in his monograph, including a spirit of a wild reindeer fawn that Scratching-Woman had found trying to suckle on the body of its mother, who had been killed by a wolf whose spirit also came to him.[34] He could also call upon the ke'let of a small mouse "who could travel very fast underground, and was employed for errands requiring haste."[35] Scratching-Woman's work as a shaman is recorded in *The Chukchee* in detail, including his work curing patients, performing cuttings, and releasing curses. Bogoras also directly quotes Scratching-Woman's explanations of different practices, such as the details of an "Incantation of Magic Medicine" that Scratching-Woman explained, stating,

> "If I want to cure some one from a disease, I transform him into earth, and transform myself into a huge bear. I am strong; I am clawing the earth and scattering it around. Then I put the disease into the hole, and cover it with the earth again. Thus I make everything tight." Told by Scratching-Woman (man) at Mariinsky Post, 1900.[36]

Scratching-Woman stands in Bogoras's work as an individual person and shaman; his biography, his life as a shaman, and his ke'let provide details, add depth to him, and present him as a unique person within the context of Bogoras's ethnographic overview of Chukchi shamanism and life in Mariinsky Post.

Bogoras's accounts provide a personal and individualized identity of Scratching-Woman that comes from the intimate in-betweenness of their relationship; however, as an ethnographic subject, Scratching-Woman became "an anthropological classic, the archetype of the arctic shaman."[37] The mobilization of Scratching-Woman as an archetype relies upon Bogoras's characterization and exposition of him as a shaman, rather than the more intimate presentation of him as a man who faced starvation, who called on the spirit of a sulking fawn, and who lived in a Russian village by the sea. Bogoras saw Scratching-Woman as an unstable man, temperamental and violent, and wrote, "The shaman Scratching-Woman manifested symptoms of a nature even more excitable. He could not sit for long in one place, but every little while he would jump up with violent gestures."[38] Bogoras's assessment of Scratching-Woman drew upon and reinforced the idea of the Siberian shaman as "on the verge of insanity," a trope that became part of this "archetype of the arctic shaman."[39] However, between Bogoras's pathologizing and sideways lines, there are also spaces to read against Bogoras. In the same section in which Bogoras characterized Scratching-Woman's nature, Scratching-Woman is quoted explaining, "I will be frank with you. Drink really makes my temper too bad for anything. Usually my wife watches over me, and puts all knives out of my reach. But when we are apart, I am afraid."[40] This personal explanation is framed, however, by Bogoras's more general assertions of the "passion Chukchee have for alcohol" and a glossing over of the affective and intimate expression of fear that Scratching-Woman shares.[41]

Bogoras presents Scratching-Woman as his principal informant about Chukchi shamanism, but he is often dismissive of Scratching-Woman's trustworthiness. Bogoras frequently introduces Scratching-Woman's actions with qualifications that undermine the veracity of his claims and actions; for example, Bogoras writes, "Scratching-Woman pretended to have cut open and put to right internal organs ... and several other parts of the bodies of many patients, although, according to his neighbors, he was too young to claim so many successful cases of treatment."[42] Despite these doubts, Bogoras relied on Scratching-Woman as an informant and a corroborator of accounts given by others. When Bogoras includes a "Chukchee Sketch representing a Shaman praying to the Moon," which was "made by a native of Mariinsky Post, represent[ing] a shaman who crawls on all-fours to invoke the moon ... [and] is supposed to be naked, his head only being covered with a large shamanistic cap," he turns to Scratching-Woman in his text and informs the readers that "Scratching-Woman affirmed that he performed his incantations of this kind without any clothing, but with a shaman's cap on his head."[43] Scratching-Woman nevertheless remains cast as a trickster in Bogoras's work and is presented as misleading people in "shamanic séances" through slights of hand and skilled showmanship. At times, he appears eager to share information and to be proud of his skills, while at others, he is angry and hostile toward Bogoras, and seemingly resents him for his skepticism.[44] In one reading, this is Bogoras's exposition of Scratching-Woman as an "excitable" man, which carries with it echoes of the growing idea of the shaman as a hysteric.[45] Another reading, however, allows us to see these changing attitudes as the emotional shifts over long-term collaboration with, and resistance to, Bogoras.

Through Bogoras's writings and the objects he collected and sent back to the AMNH, an image of Scratching-Woman emerges that is animated and individualized within the wide view of Chukchi life that Bogoras tried to document. What also enters in, however, is the complex relationship that existed between these two men. Bogoras is mediating our meeting and bringing in his own voice to narrate Scratching-Woman. Our decision to accept or call into question Bogoras's records of life in Mariinsky Post must account both for his biases and lacunae and for the position of ethnography and the ethnographer at the turn of century. Igor Krupnik addresses concerns over the accuracy of Bogoras's ethnographic work by examining Bogoras's claim that even the largest villages "of the Maritime Chukchi and Asiatic Eskimos on the Chukchi Peninsula ... have no inner organization and are governed by no one, beyond the custom and the public opinion."[46] Krupnik, however, documents that further ethnographic research revealed complex social structures within the villages, and he uses this to raise questions as to why Bogoras overlooked or failed to see this social organization.

Despite Krupnik's attention to this oversight and misrepresentation of the maritime Chukchi, he also stresses Bogoras's rigor and dedication to ethnographic fieldwork. Krupnik writes that while he was in the village of Ungazik, where Bogoras conducted research between April and June of 1901, he was able to use the list of names Bogoras had compiled as a census to interview elders who could identify the names and map out the social networks between them.[47] While Bogoras may not have been able to see the social organization in these villages, he was able to compile accurate and useful data. Throughout these records, we see the detailed accounts Bogoras provides about the lives lived in Mariinsky Post, but we also see through the filters of both the troubled relationship between Bogoras and Scratching-Woman and the troubling racial, gender, and evolutionary prejudices and biases that have been woven into the archival records. Nevertheless, while our views are filtered, we are still able to look out and see two people who met, talked together, and watched each other.

## A Traveling Object: Scratching-Woman's Coat

Scratching-Woman became an "archetype" of the Arctic shaman through Bogoras's ethnographic writing; however, the materials that belong to him that were sent to the AMNH and described in detail in Bogoras's work have not received the same attention. Bogoras described the coat as "a characteristic specimen" of the garments of a Chukchi shaman.[48] He continued in his writing,

> It is a reindeer-skin coat of the usual Chukchee pattern, with the hair turned inward. It looks rather poor and threadbare. This, however, in the eyes of its owner, only increased its value. The neck and sleeves are adorned with white fringe, and there are, moreover, slits cut along the sleeves and in the front of the skirt below. These slits are ornamented with fringe made of curried leather. The cuts and fringe are considered the characteristic features of the coat, and all shamanistic coats of which I heard were described as garments ripped up all around and adorned with fringe. ... These slits and fringes are usually said to represent the curves and zigzags of the Milky Way. It is quite possible, however, that both the slits and the fringes are simply the best imitation possible to them of the Tungus specimens.[49]

Bogoras's characterization of the coat as "poor and threadbare" and its framing as "the best imitation possible" of coats from the Tungus nation introduces this piece as deficient—despite Scratching-Woman's insistence that this evidence of wear augments the value of the coat. In *The Chukchee*, Bogoras does not explain how the coat moved into his possession after being "acquired from the shaman Scratching-Woman," nor why this seemingly deficient coat was worth collecting and documenting.[50] Without any more information of the circumstances of the acquisition, we are left in a space of absences, and we can only bring with us to this emptied moment of movement between two men the complexly layered relationship that connected them.

In examining the coat now at the AMNH, one sees that the leather is stiff. The coat, which is ninety-six centimeters long by seventy-six across, is well worn and the leather patina is developed over most of the piece. The coat was most likely made up originally of several different pieced parts that were seamed together and have slight variations in their natural tan color. Over time the coat appears to have been repeatedly patched and mended creating a more complex and asymmetric pattern. The patching is clearly defined by the topstitching (most likely done with sinew) along the edges of the patches and elsewhere for mending tears. While most of these patched pieces are also of leather (most likely reindeer), there is one piece of sturdy fabric on the front (visible on the left side of the coat in the illustration in Figure 11.1 as the large rectangular piece with more uniform cross-hatching). There is a line of soft cream fur around the neck, and bands of fur on the arms, wrists, waist, and bottom. The front of the coat and the lower half of the sleeves have slits that are then laced up, and, as Bogoras described, there is leather fringe that is attached at the skirt and the back around the waist of the coat. The only other decorative elements are small metal rings punched through the leather on the sleeve below the shoulder, and at the front, attached at the fur waistline, are a cut-out leather figure and a leather ball-shaped piece filled with reindeer fur, which hangs on a strap connected to the coat at the waistline and has a tail that extends down from the bottom.

Bogoras explains that the ball and the leather figure are important shamanic materials for Scratching-Woman. The leather ball is "an image of tetke'yuñ (vital force), residing in the heart, and therefore having its form," and the figure "represents a re'kkeñ, who was an 'assisting' spirit of the shaman."[51] Bogoras is generally rather dismissive of the shamanic coats of the Chukchi; he writes, "The shamanism of the Chukchee has not reached a stage of development high enough to have drums or clothing of particular form, or, indeed, any special belongings characteristics of itself."[52] Later, he suggests that the absence of particular shamanic clothing is connected to the fact that shamans perform most of their work in the close inner rooms of houses in "total darkness, where the outer appearance of the shaman is of no consequence" and where the "atmosphere, too, is so close, that the shamans, instead of putting on a special garment, are accustomed, on the contrary, to take off their coats."[53] This disrobing for rituals appears as a frequent motif in Bogoras's account, and the movement of the coat on and off appears as a response to the close atmosphere, for "more freedom of movement," and for particular rituals that are done naked, such as the invocation of the moon.[54] Bogoras interprets this as an indication that there is an absence of clothing that is uniquely shamanic among the Chukchi, accounting, perhaps, for the absence of shamanic coats similar to the ornate and highly decorated ones of the Tungus and Sakha nations.[55]

Scratching-Woman's coat has, however, several elements that distinguish it from the more general style of Chukchi reindeer hide parkas. In addition to the tetke'yuñ and re'kkeñ that appear as elements connected to Scratching-Woman's particular shamanic practice, the white fur around the neck and the fringe at the sleeves are a demarcation of the wearer being a shaman.[56] While ritualized disrobing appears in Bogoras's work as a common element of shamanic practice, there are still aspects of the materiality of the coat itself that reflect the particular nature of it as shamanic and personal to the shaman who owns it, here Scratching-Woman. The comparatively simple design does not diminish its identity as an intimate piece of a shamanic material culture. Throughout his work, Bogoras continually frames the Chukchi shamans through comparisons with shamans and shamanic traditions from other Indigenous Siberian nations. Bogoras notes that the Chukchi acknowledge the power of "alien" shamans, particularly the Tungus, and he suggests that this has led to the probable "imitation of the Tungus in regard to the shamanistic coat."[57] The effect of this is that to Bogoras, Chukchi shamanism appears as a diminished religious tradition in comparison, in particular, with that of the Sakha and Tungus nations.

While Scratching-Woman became an "archetype" of the Arctic shaman through Bogoras's work, the image of the ornate shaman's coat—rather than Scratching-Woman's own coat—became the visual and material archetype.[58] This is not to suggest that the archetypal representations of Siberian shamans that have established the repertoire of visual and material images are necessarily inaccurate, and indeed, the ornate and intricate coats seen in museum displays are shamanic coats embedded within different Siberian shamanic material cultural traditions. However, Scratching-Woman's coat, as Bogoras emphasized, does not match this highly decorated and intricately ornamented vision. Scratching-Woman's "poor and threadbare" coat asks viewers to reconsider what the image of a shaman is, and how we have inherited and continue to inhabit a specific and limited space of authenticity in our decisions to circulate and display specific shamanic materials.[59]

Bogoras argued that the Chukchi coat was an imitation of the Tungus coats and positioned it as lesser than them. Within Bogoras's work there are contrasting perspectives on Scratching-Woman's coat—in one view, Scratching-Woman's coat, and the material culture of shamanic dress among the Chukchi, is dismissively presented; in the other view, Bogoras focuses on this coat as the principal example of the "shamanistic garments" and draws our attention to its materiality by his descriptions and the inclusion of an illustration.[60] The coat was important to the presentation of Chukchi shamanic material culture and was embedded within Bogoras's own intimacy with Scratching-Woman that allowed him to see it as important to a particular shaman, a particular man, and a particular space. Unlike many Siberian shamanic coats in collections that date back to the late Imperial through early Soviet eras of ethnographic collecting, we have information about the shaman who owned this coat and the man who collected it. Through these records, we can see the coat as immersed not in an abstract or anonymous space but in a relational and troubled one inhabited by individual people who remain connected through its movement and intimate life as a thing in-between.

In addition to the coat, the AMNH has a cap, two ritual knives, and sound recordings of Scratching-Woman gathered by Bogoras during his time at Mariinsky Post. The cap, also illustrated in *The Chukchee*, is made of hide and fur, and would have sat close to the head.[61] Bogoras writes, "The shamanistic cap which belonged to the garment (Fig. 288 [illustration of Scratching-Woman's coat]) is also supplied with fringes, with a tassel on the top and a long double tassel on the left side. The tassels are of the type adopted for magic purposes; that is, they are formed of alternating pieces of white and black fur."[62] These two long tassels extend from the cap and reach down well past where the shoulders would be; they are of brown leather with white fur rings every few inches, and on one side there is a short string of red, white, and pale blue beads attached closer to the head.

The two knives are quite different from one another but were used together so that Scratching-Woman could cut and open a body.[63] They are both included as sketches in Bogoras's work and were displayed as part of the 1988 *Crossroads of Continents: Cultures of Siberia and Alaska* exhibition at the Smithsonian's National Museum of Natural History.[64] One is an iron blade set into a wooden handle with two leather cut strips threaded through the end of the wood and a large black bead strung between them, which "Scratching-Woman asserted ... was received by his grandfather directly from the ke′let." The other piece, which Bogoras calls a knife, but is named as a "shaman's director" in the AMNH's catalog, is a rectangular piece of ivory that tapers at the ends.[65] There are three pairs of holes through the ivory; through several of these holes are threaded leather straps attaching three leather images. These images are of "a ke′lE from the 'direction' of the darkness" that has arms that extend past its legs; the "ke′lE Iu′metun" (defined elsewhere in Bogoras's work as a disease that manifests as "a kind of violent nervous affection, which comes on at night like nightmares" and is attributed to spirits that the Chukchi "do not like even to mention their names");[66] and an "image represent[ing] a crawling 'spell,' which one of the enemies of the shaman sent to attack him; but he intercepted it on the way and thoroughly subdued it, so that it began to do his bidding."[67] Like the coat, these two knives are entangled with Scratching-Woman's particular relationships with the ke′let, and with his grandfather who also had a connection to these spirits, who gave him the bead attached to the iron knife's handle.

## Intimacy in Museum Records

In the AMNH's catalog, these different pieces from Scratching-Woman are not connected with, nor embedded in, the lives and intimacies bound up in their creation, use, or acquisition. The coat, cap, and knives each appear in the museum's records as separate pieces (though each has references to Bogoras's *The Chukchee*) and the provenancial information is centered on Bogoras as the donor and the Jesup Expedition as the context for acquisition, but no mention is made of Scratching-Woman in the catalog as the owner of all three. It is rare for museums to have specific Indigenous people named as the owners of pieces, particularly when the collections date back almost 120 years, and it is even rarer that there is also documentation of their individuated personal lives, beliefs, and practices. The ability of a catalog to metaphorically and literally place museum objects in one space or another separates this collection, recreating the coat, cap, and knives as separate pieces. With the exception of the cap, which is identified as Chukchi but has its locale listed as "Siberia," all these pieces are specifically located as from Mariinsky Post and the Anadyr region.[68] While this locates these pieces in a particular place, the records still transform these highly specific and personal things into generic objects—in these records, these things are no longer seen as Scratching-Woman's coat with his tetke'yuñ and re'kkeñ, or as his knife with a bead from his grandfather that was given by the ke'let. We lose the intimacy of Scratching-Woman and the layering in-betweenness of Bogoras as collector, ethnographer, confidant, and skeptic, and instead we are presented a record of a Chukchi "coat, shaman's" and a "shaman's knife."[69]

In their work on cataloging and Indigenous museology, Cara Krmpotich and Alexander Somerville call for the inclusion of affective language and knowledge in museum catalogs to engage visitors with the emotional, experiential, and sensorial "relationship between material culture and human bodies."[70] Their work suggests a shifting of museum engagement with material culture toward an understanding of collections as a gathering of intimate and relational things. Scratching-Woman's coat was intimately worn, made, and embedded within life at Mariinsky Post, within Chukchi material culture, and within the shamanic traditions that Scratching-Woman followed. Scratching-Woman tells us in Bogoras's work that the worn nature of the coat "only increased its value."[71] Bogoras's seeming dismissal of the assessment and framing of the coat as "poor and threadbare" offers an opening for us to engage with the divergent understandings of value that the coat, as a material object, is moving between. By approaching these divergent understandings of the coat's value as affective responses rooted in the layered histories behind these two men, we can engage this intimate material as an embedded microhistory of a relationship that expands outward to place these men and these materials not as archetypes of a shaman, an ethnographer, or a Siberian village; rather, we expand into the complexities of ethnographic records and histories of power that configure some places as particular and others as generic, giving some people names and others types.

The intimacy of the archival record of Scratching-Woman extends to sound recordings that Bogoras made of Scratching-Woman in Mariinsky Post. He writes,

> I tried to make a phonographic record of the "separate voices" of the "spirits." For this purpose I induced the shaman Scratching-Woman to give a séance in my own house, overcoming his reluctance with a few extra presents. The performance, of course, had to be carried out in utter darkness: and I arranged my machine so as to be able to work it without any light. Scratching-Woman sat in the farthest corner of the spacious room, at a distance of twenty feet from me. When the light was put out, and "spirits," after some "bashful" hesitation, entered, in compliance with the demand of the shaman, and even began to talk into the funnel of the gramophone. The records show a very marked difference between the voice of

the shaman himself, which sound from afar, and the voices of the "spirits," who seemed to be talking directly into the funnel.[72]

Here, we encounter Scratching-Woman in Bogoras's home; we hear his reluctance, and his voice. The AMNH and the Archives of Traditional Music at Indiana University have preserved these sound files. Through these Scratching-Woman and the spirits can be heard speaking in their own voices. At the exhibition "Drawing Shadows to Stone: Photographing North Pacific Peoples, 1897–1902," which ran from November 1997 to March 1998, these sound recordings made by the members of the Jesup Expedition were played for visitors together with explanations of the wax cylinder recording technology. These sounds became museum things within the exhibition through the preservation of voices etched in wax.[73]

## Conclusion

Scratching-Woman's coat challenges the archetype of shamanic dress and the values of museum display and cataloging. The coat is entangled in the "ongoing social, spatial, temporal, and material trajectories and relationships, dislocations and relocations" of Scratching-Woman, Bogoras, and the AMNH.[74] The in-betweenness and movement of this coat allows us to approach the affective and relational nature of both Scratching-Woman and Bogoras to each other and to the materiality of the thing itself. These layered relations should not be stacked on top of one another, allowing only the topmost to appear, but rather expanded outward connecting to other associated objects in the AMNH's collection, to the history of ethnography and museum collections, to the histories of imperial Russia and the Chukotka coastline, and to the lives of a formerly exiled ethnographer and a former orphaned shaman sharing a room in the dark with the voices of spirits.

## Notes

I would like to thank the participants at two workshops, "Museums, Religion, and the Work of Reconciliation and Remembrance" and "Materials and Materiality in Russia and the Soviet Union," where I was able to present portions of this work. Additionally, I would like to thank Jane Anderson, Antonia Behan, Nika Collison, Cara Krmpotich, Maureen Matthews, Irina Mihalache, Matthew Romaniello, Alison Smith, and Tricia Starks for their questions and comments that helped me to look at aspects of my research from other angles and in more depth. Finally, I am grateful for the support of the American Museum of Natural History, especially Laurel Kendall for her support and encouragement of this research.

1. "Coat, Shaman's." 70/6708. American Museum of Natural History.
2. I have chosen to maintain the spelling of Waldemar Bogoras in accordance with the spelling used on his English-language publications, rather than following more common transliteration practices, which would render the name Vladimir Bogoraz. Other Russian names will be transliterated according to the Library of Congress

ALA-LC Romanization system, unless, like Bogoras, there is a widely used English alternative, for example, Nicholas II rather than Nikolai II, or Yakutsk instead of Iakutsk.
3. Waldemar Bogoras, *Memoirs of the American Museum of Natural History Volume XI Part II—the Chukchee—Religion*, reprint ed. (New York: AMS Press 1975).
4. Franz Boas, *The Jesup North Pacific Expedition: I—Facial Paintings of the Indians of Northern British Columbia* (New York: G. E. Stechert, 1900), 4.
5. While I maintain the use of Bogoras's spelling of *Chukchee* when referring to his publication, I switch to the more contemporary transliteration (Chukchi) in all other cases.
6. For a small sampling of this prodigious field see Laurel Kendall and Igor Krupnik, eds., *Constructing Cultures Then and Now: Celebrating Franz Boas and the Jesup North Pacific Expedition* (Washington, DC: Arctic Studies Center, Museum of Natural History, Smithsonian Institution, 2003); Igor Krupnik and William W. Fitzhugh, eds., *Gateways: Exploring the Legacy of the Jesup North Pacific Expedition, 1897–1902* (Washington, DC: Arctic Studies Center, Smithsonian Institution, 2001); Laurel Kendall et al., eds., *Drawing Shadows to Stone: The Photography of the Jesup North Pacific Expedition 1897–1902* (New York: American Museum of Natural History in association with the University of Washington Press, Seattle, 1997); Susan Roy, *These Mysterious People: Shaping History and Archaeology in a Northwest Coast Community* (Montreal: McGill-Queen's University Press, 2010); Douglas Cole, *Franz Boas: The Early Years, 1858–1906* (Seattle, DC: University of Washington Press, 1999); Igor Krupnik, "'Jesup Genealogy': Intellectual Partnerships and Russian-American Cooperation in Arctic/North Pacific Anthropology," *Arctic Anthropology* 35:2 (1998), 199–226.
7. Bogoras, *The Chukchee*, 458.
8. Paul Basu, *The Inbetweenness of Things: Materializing Mediation and Movement between Worlds* (London: Bloomsbury, 2017), 2–3.
9. Some museums with contemporary displays of these intricately decorated and ornate Siberian shamanic coats include the AMNH in New York City, the Quai Branly in Paris, the Russian Museum of Ethnography in St. Petersburg, the Oslo Museum of Cultural History in Norway, and the Krasnoyarsk Regional Museum of Local History in Krasnoyarsk.
10. "Coat, Shaman's." 70/695. American Museum of Natural History; "Coat, Shaman's." 70/8861. American Museum of Natural History.
11. Andrei A. Znamenski, *The Beauty of the Primitive: Shamanism and Western Imagination* (Oxford: Oxford University Press, 2007); Han F. Vermeulen, *Before Boas: The Genesis of Ethnography and Ethnology in the German Enlightenment*, Critical Studies in the History of Anthropology (Lincoln: University of Nebraska Press, 2015); Nathaniel Knight, "Nikolai Kharuzin and the Quest for a Universal Human Science: Anthropological Evolutionism and the Russian Ethnographic Tradition, 1885–1900," *Kritika: Explorations in Russian and Eurasian History* 9:1 (March 10, 2008), 83–111; Catherine B. Clay, "Russian Ethnographers in the Service of Empire, 1856–1862," *Slavic Review* 54:1 (1995), 45–61; Roland Cvetkovski and Alexis Hofmeister, eds., *An Empire of Others: Creating Ethnographic Knowledge in Imperial Russia and the USSR* (Budapest: Central European University Press, 2014).
12. See, as examples, William Alexander, *The Costume of the Russian Empire, Illustrated by a Series of Seventy-Three Engravings* (London: Printed for William Miller by Howlett and Brimmer, 1803); Johann Gottlieb Georgi, *Opisanie vsekh obitaiushchikh*

v Rossiiskom gosudarstve narodov (St. Petersburg: Imperatorskaia Akademiia Nauk, 1799).
13. Note: Due to Covid-19 and the closure of the AMNH, the museum was unable to verify unequivocally that the coat had not been displayed in the old Siberia hall; however, the archival records I worked with at the AMNH did not indicate any exhibition history for this piece.
14. Basu, *The Inbetweenness of Things*, 2.
15. For works that address this shifting museum practice both in general and through specific relationships see Ruth B. Phillips, "Re-Placing Objects: Historical Practices for the Second Museum Age," *Canadian Historical Review* 86:1 (March 17, 2005), 83–110; Joshua A. Bell, "A Bundle of Relations: Collections, Collecting, and Communities," *Annual Review of Anthropology* 46:1 (2017), 241–59; R. Eric Hollinger et al., "Tlingit-Smithsonian Collaborations with 3D Digitization of Cultural Objects," *Museum Anthropology Review* 7:1–2 (2013), 201–53; Cara Ann Krmpotich and Laura L. Peers, *This Is Our Life: Haida Material Heritage and Changing Museum Practice* (Vancouver : UBC Press, 2013); Michael M. Ames, *Cannibal Tours and Glass Boxes: The Anthropology of Museums* (Vancouver: UBC Press, 1992); Marilena Alivizatou, *Intangible Heritage and the Museum: New Perspectives on Cultural Preservation* (Walnut Creek, CA: Left Coast Press, 2012).
16. In Bogoras's transcription system for Chukchi $^\varepsilon$ indicates a "very deep laryngeal intonation" and ñ, a "nasal *n* sound" (Bogoras, *The Chukchee*, 10).
17. Ibid., 28.
18. Ibid., 25.
19. Ibid., 59.
20. Letter to Waldemar Bogoras from the Anthropology Dept. of the AMNH, December 6, 1898, New York.
21. Franz Boas, "Waldemar Bogoras," *American Anthropologist* 39:2 (1937), 314.
22. Sergei Kan, "'My Old Friend in a Dead-End of Empiricism and Skepticism': Bogoras, Boas, and the Politics of Soviet Anthropology of the Late 1920s–Early 1930s," *Histories of Anthropology Annual* 2 (2006), 34; Igor Krupnik, "Waldemar Bogoras and the Chukchee: A Maestro and a Classical Ethnography," in *The Chukchee*, ed. Waldemar Bogoras, Michael Duerr, and Erich Kasten, Erich (Fürstenberg: Kulturstiftung Sibirien, 2017), 9–10.
23. Dmitry Arzyutov and Sergei A. Kan, "The Concept of the 'Field' in Early Soviet Ethnography: A Northern Perspective," *Sibirica* 16:1 (2017), 39.
24. Igor Krupnik, "The 'Bogoras Enigma': Bounds of Cultures and Formats of Anthropology," in *Grasping the Changing World*, ed. Václav Hubinger (New York: Routledge, 1996), 43.
25. Yuri Slezkine, *Arctic Mirrors: Russia and the Small Peoples of the North* (Ithaca, NY: Cornell University Press, 1994), 17.
26. Letter, Bogoras to Boas, April 16, 1901, Jesup North Pacific Expedition Archive (1897–1902), AMNH Archives.
27. Bogoras, *The Chukchee*, 430.
28. Slezkine, *Arctic Mirrors*, 107.
29. Bogoras, *The Chukchee*, 450.
30. Ibid., 451.
31. Ibid., 423–4.
32. Ibid., 424.
33. Ibid.

34. Ibid., 436.
35. Ibid., 437.
36. Ibid., 503.
37. Andrei A. Znamenski, *The Beauty of the Primitive: Shamanism and Western Imagination* (Oxford: Oxford University Press, 2007), 80.
38. Bogoras, *The Chukchee*, 427.
39. Znamenski, *The Beauty of the Primitive*, 80.
40. Bogoras, *The Chukchee*, 428.
41. Ibid..
42. Ibid., 466.
43. Ibid., 449.
44. Ibid., 229.
45. Znamenski, *The Beauty of the Primitive*, 79–101.
46. Waldemir Bogoras, "Chukotskii obshchestvennyi stroi po dannym fol'klora," *Sovetskii Sever* 6 (1930), 70, quoted in Krupnik, "The 'Bogoras Enigma,'" 35.
47. Krupnik, "The 'Bogoras Enigma,'" 37.
48. Bogoras, *The Chukchee*, 458.
49. Ibid., 458–9.
50. Ibid., 458.
51. Ibid., 459.
52. Ibid., 457.
53. Ibid., 458.
54. Ibid., 432, 449.
55. Ibid., 458.
56. Ibid.
57. Ibid., 459.
58. For more information on the history of representing Siberian shamans, see Znamenski, *The Beauty of the Primitive*; and Silvia Tomášková, *Wayward Shamans: The Prehistory of an Idea* (Berkeley: University of California Press, 2013).
59. For discussions of shamanism and the politics of authenticity and cultural revival in the more contemporary context, see Morten Axel Pedersen, *Not Quite Shamans: Spirit Worlds and Political Lives in Northern Mongolia*, Culture and Society after Socialism (Ithaca, NY: Cornell University Press, 2011); Laurel Kendall, *Shamans, Nostalgias, and the IMF: South Korean Popular Religion in Motion* (Honolulu: University of Hawaii Press, 2009); Marjorie Mandelstam Balzer, *Shamans, Spirituality, and Cultural Revitalization: Explorations in Siberia and Beyond*, Contemporary Anthropology of Religion (New York: Palgrave Macmillan, 2011).
60. Bogoras, *The Chukchee*, 457–60.
61. "Shaman's Hat." 70/7495. American Museum of Natural History; Bogoras, *The Chukchee*, 459.
62. Ibid., 459.
63. Ibid., 466
64. William W. Fitzhugh, Aron Crowell, and National Museum of Natural History (U.S.), eds., *Crossroads of Continents: Cultures of Siberia and Alaska* (Washington, DC: Smithsonian Institution Press, 1988), 248.
65. "Shaman's Director." 70/6793. American Museum of Natural History.
66. Bogoras, *The Chukchee*, 42.
67. Ibid., 466.
68. "Shaman's Hat." 70/7495. American Museum of Natural History.

69. "Coat, Shaman's." 70/6708. American Museum of Natural History; "Shaman's Knife." 70/6792. American Museum of Natural History.
70. Cara Krmpotich and Alexander Somerville, "Affective Presence: The Metonymical Catalogue," *Museum Anthropology* 39:2 (September 1, 2016), 178.
71. Bogoras, *The Chukchee*, 458.
72. Ibid., 436.
73. Molly Lee, Review of *Review of Drawing Shadows to Stone: Photographing North Pacific Peoples (1897–1902); Drawing Shadows to Stone: The Photography of the Jesup North Pacific Expedition, 1897–1902*, by Laurel Kendall et al., *American Anthropologist* 100:4 (1998), 1006.
74. Basu, *The Inbetweenness of Things*, 2.

# 12

# "Kunststchutz" in the War of Annihilation or the Power of Images against Ideology

Ulrike Schmiegelt-Rietig

The State Novgorod Museum-Reserve has in its collections one of the finest and most ancient icons of Russia, an extraordinary, huge image of Saints Peter and Paul, which once was part of the main iconostas of Novgorod's St. Sophia Cathedral. According to the legends about the history of Novgorod Velikii, Saint Vladimir himself brought it back to Kiev from his initial baptism in Kherson.[1] Created in the mid-eleventh century, it is a Byzantine work in style, but likely created by a Greek or even a Russian artist on site in Novgorod.[2]

The painting, one of the oldest representations of the apostles in conversation, shows the two apostles in full figure. Peter carries three keys, the wood of the cross, and a parchment scroll in his hand, identifying him as the first representative of Christ on earth; Paul appears with the Holy Scriptures. They turn to each other in concentrated conversation. Between them, the image of Christ appears like a vision. Despite the poor state of preservation of the almost one thousand-year-old icon, the extremely fine technique is still visible. The original parts of the robes show delicate shades of blue, white, light rose, and golden yellow. The painting is executed with greatest precision down to the smallest detail of the ornaments on the hems of the robes. The apostles have expressive physiognomies of unusual individuality.[3] Through eye contact with one another, they are at the same time removed into a sphere to which the viewer does not have access (Figure 12.1).

Over almost a thousand years, the icon left Novgorod only twice, in both cases because of warfare. Ivan IV (the Terrible) abducted it after he subdued Novgorod in the sixteenth century, and German occupiers took it away in 1942. It seems almost a miracle that the icon survived and returned to its home after the Second World War was over. It would have been much more likely to perish, just like so many other cultural assets in the Soviet Union did.

Military conflicts greatly affect material culture. In particular, since the turn of the nineteenth/twentieth centuries cultural assets more and more fell victim to warfare, most notably in Germany's war against the Soviet Union, when National Socialist strategy aimed for the enemy's complete annihilation. This was due to an ideology that declared the superiority of the "Aryan" (or "Nordic") race, considered Jews but also Slavic peoples as "subhuman," and planned their extermination. This led to a

**Figure 12.1** Icon of Saints Peter and Paul with *oklad*, around 1050. Photo Eugen Fink, Pskov 1942. © Bildarchiv Foto Marburg/Eugen Fink.

fundamental difference between Nazi warfare on the Western and the Eastern front. Although since the Napoleonic wars, France was considered the "Erbfeind," the Germans nevertheless admired French (as well as Netherlandish) culture. Therefore, although the occupied countries in Western Europe faced large-scale looting of Jewish collections, the occupying forces mostly spared the public collections and did not (or at least rarely) commit willful destructions of cultural assets. In the East, however, cultural assets would either be appropriated as "Germanic" or "European" by the occupying forces or dismissed as primitive, worthless, and therefore released for destruction. In other words, Nazi ideology extended its obsession with race to material objects, leading it to value and therefore seek to preserve some objects, while discarding most of the others.

How this piece survived is one of this chapter's narratives. Tracing the Icon of Saints Peter and Paul becomes the Leitmotif that binds together the chapter's two main stories: the account of the military art protection unit that came into being at the Headquarters of the Army Group North in Pskov and the story of one of the institution's members, Werner Körte (1905-1945), told by his private record that lays bare his shifting attitudes about his job and his emotional reaction to the objects.

## Kunstschutz

Appropriating cultural assets was a general pattern of Nazi warfare in Western, Central, and Eastern Europe. Several authorities as the Foreign Office, the SS (Schutzstaffel), and first and foremost the "Reichsminister für die besetzten Ostgebiete" (RMO) (minister for the occupied Eastern territories) Alfred Rosenberg (1892/93-1946) installed special task forces. Rosenberg created the "Einsatzstab Reichsleiter Rosenberg" (ERR) ("Reichsleiter Rosenberg Taskforce"), which was commissioned to confiscate cultural goods of all social groups hostile to National Socialism, and any valuable cultural assets in the occupied territories.[4] Within the "Wehrmacht" several departments were involved with the appropriation of cultural assets among which military art protection units played a central role. Such a department was first established at the German military command for France and modeled on the military art protection units created during the First World War. In those units, professionals, mostly art historians, monument conservators, and architects, were commissioned to organize the protection of cultural assets in the occupied countries according to the 1907 Hague Regulations for Warfare.[5] Contemporary German reports described the measures as a full success.[6] But later accounts suggest that the German art protection units did not achieve very much. They were weak and their commitment came late.[7]

Despite the model and its failure, the High Command of the Armed Forces did not make any plans for art protection units as the Second World War began. Instead, suggestions from outside the Army High Command forced the creation of basic military art protection.[8] In May 1940 the art historian and curator of the Rhine Province, Franz Graf Wolff-Metternich zur Gracht (1893-1978) was appointed military art conservator for France.[9] Among other things, he organized a photographic campaign to document the cultural assets in occupied France, and stubbornly defended French state collections from other Nazi authorities. Apart from France, Belgium, and the Netherlands, military art protection units deployed in Greece and Serbia as of 1941 and in Italy as of 1943.[10]

In the occupied territories of the Soviet Union the situation at first glance seems completely different because there are hardly any indications of the existence of military art protection units in the sources. In fact, in a letter from July 3, 1941, the "Oberkommando des Heeres" (OKH) (Army High Command) wrote to Minister of Education Bernhard Rust that "a permanent military administration will not be set up in the occupied Soviet territories." As soon as the military operations progressed far enough, regional civil administrations, so-called "Reichskommissariate" under the direction of RMO Rosenberg, were to be set up. Before then, military conditions would presumably "not allow in-depth measures to secure the museums and monuments,"[11] and after the establishment of civilian administrations, a military art protection unit would be obsolete. However, in 1944 Wolff-Metternich wrote in his final report summarizing the work of the unit under his command that "in the first months of occupation of Russian territories to the establishment of the Eastern Ministry" a representative had been sent to Russia, who was commissioned to prepare the installation of an art protection organization.[12] Wolff-Metternich's report was true: as soon as the military situation permitted, a young archeologist and civil employee of the OKH, Reinhold Strenger (1903–1966), was sent as an observer. Furthermore, unexpectedly and contrary to the official plans, a small military art protection unit emerged in northwest Russia. Under the direct authority of the high commander of the army group, it tried to secure the cultural goods of the region.

## Military Art Protection in Northwest Russia

The founder of military art protection in Northwest Russia was Captain Ernstotto Graf zu Solms-Laubach (1890–1977), whose most infamous act would be the organization of the dismantling and deportation of the Amber Chamber from the Catherine Palace in Pushkin in October 1941.[13] Born in 1890, he first studied medicine, but after fighting in the First World War, he changed to art history and got his doctoral degree in Marburg in 1925.[14] In October of that year, he was employed as a research assistant in the Städel Art Institute in Frankfurt (Main),[15] where he later became curator of the Sculpture Collection and in 1938 was appointed director of the Frankfurt city History Museum. On March 1, 1941, Solms was drafted despite his age because he had been an officer of the First World War. He was soon promoted to captain.[16] In May, he was transferred to a Feldkommandantur newly established in his Hessian military district under the command of the 285th Security Division and the Army Group Rear Area Command North. Since securing conquered territory was one of the tasks of the Army Group Rear Area Command, these units were also responsible for constructing military administration structures. The staff mainly consisted of older reserve officers and soldiers not suitable for the front.[17] Presumably, Solms was posted at the Feldkommandantur for use in military administration. Solms's unit was stationed in Pskov, at the headquarters of the High Command of the Army Group North. From here he developed his initiatives in service of art protection.

Solms expressed astonishment at the Wehrmacht's lack of interest in art protection, as he wrote to the liaison officer of the 18th Army in the Foreign Office in April 1942. He pointed out that he had been entrusted as conservator on his own initiative and was formally put in this position only in December.[18] Solms would describe this quite differently later: testifying in the Nuremberg OKW process in 1948, he stated that he had been appointed due to the initiative of the commander of the 18th Army Georg von Küchler, who "wished to protect Russian cultural heritage from being destroyed by the effects of war, but also against the desires of other authorities."[19] The statement undoubtedly aimed at clearing Küchler of one of the charges laid against him: the destruction of cultural assets. Which version of the story is true remains unclear. Most likely Solms himself worked to establish art protection and Küchler supported his commission.[20] Officially, Solms was ordered to secure treasures in the area of Army Group North by the end of September in 1941.

First of all, in September 1941, he reopened the Pskov City Museum. According to an article in the *Frankfurter Generalanzeiger* of September 15, 1941, which reported on Solms's activities in Pskov, he must have been entrusted to take care for the treasures and cultural assets in the sphere of his military unit even earlier. The article states that Solms had arranged an exhibition in Pogankiny Palaty (the City Museum), within a few weeks of his arrival in Pskov, using art he recovered there. The article lauded the exhibition as "on the one hand, a place of quiet observation and spiritual recovery for the German soldiers and, on the other hand, a worthy and expert storage of old European art." The author of the article seemed especially impressed by the quantity and quality of objects, probably mostly works by German or Western European artists as well as works of Russian origin, especially icons and ecclesiastical crafts, chasubles, gospel books, and missals.[21]

In March 1942, Solms began to build up a working group for art protection systematically by requesting professionals stationed in units in the area.[22] These were officers and soldiers from divisions of Army Group North, who in their civilian lives worked as art historians—custodians, assistants, volunteers—or as restorers and photographers in museums or archives. The practical handling of museum objects, the exemplary collecting, preserving, and researching of traditional and contemporary material culture had made up their everyday professional life before they were called up. For most of them, military art protection was a welcome opportunity to escape the front for a while.

The working group also included Russian experts. The most important was the Novgorod archaeologist Vasilii Ponomarev (1907–1978), who worked for the German art protection throughout the occupation, first in Novgorod and as of summer 1942 in Pskov. In 1944, he left the country together with the German troops and lived in Marburg until the 1970s. The artists Natal'ia (1880–1963) and Tat'iana Gippius (1877–1957), sisters of Russian poetess Zinaida Gippius (1869–1945), also from Novgorod, cooperated with the restoration of icons. They also evacuated during the retreat to Germany. Unlike Ponomarev, they returned to Novgorod after the war.

Overall, it is clear that the establishment of a military art protection unit in the Russian Northwest did not follow a preplanned concept but rather came into being as a spontaneous reaction to conditions on site. Solms, who was able to enforce his ideas because of his social position, his age, his technical competence, and his good relationships, played the decisive role.

## The Power of Images

The art historian Werner Körte, who joined the working group for a short time in July and August 1942, is the most interesting member of the art protection group in Pskov when it comes to the question of material culture. He had studied art history, archeology, history, and philosophy and got his doctoral degree at the University of Leipzig in 1929.[23] In Freiburg he had qualified as a professor and received a professorship in art history in Innsbruck in 1939. Körte had become involved in the SA early on and was a staunch supporter of National Socialism. After being drafted in 1939, Körte served in an artillery regiment, first in France, then in the Soviet Union. From November 1941 he was lieutenant and commander of a unit of the Coast Guard in Peterhof. Here he occupied himself with the history of the Imperial palaces, made guided tours through the palace complex for senior officers, and wrote about the increasing destruction. Starting in July 1942, he worked for Solms for five weeks.[24] In 1944, the now father of four boys was transferred to the reserve. In spring of 1945 he again volunteered in a mountain infantry unit and was shot by Serbian partisans in Carinthia in April 1945.[25]

Körte left behind extensive writings. First there is his diary, which he kept in the form of short notes in small annual calendars. Mostly he recorded key details of his everyday life on the front and thoughts about the course of the war, noted family events about which his wife but also other relatives informed him, or with whom he corresponded. He wrote about his professional and scientific plans, wrote art-historical considerations, and repeatedly described his impressions of Russia and the cultural landscape of Northwest Russia. Körte also maintained extensive correspondences. His most important and most regular contact person was his wife Elisabeth. She reported on her life in Innsbruck, their sons, housing worries, and other things; he wrote about his everyday life in Russia. Elisabeth, like her husband, had studied art history. Also like him, she was convinced of National Socialist ideology and shared his belief that the war against the Soviet Union was a necessary step for Germany's further development.[26] They communicated as equals their thoughts on war as well as art and art history. The war correspondence of the Körte couple differs fundamentally from the average field mail between couples, which normally hardly ever gives a deeper insight into their personal thought.[27]

Körte also corresponded extensively with his colleagues in art history. He had a most intense exchange with his colleague and close friend Harald Keller (1903–1989), who like Körte was posted in Peterhof, although in a different military unit. With his former supervisor and mentor from his time at the university of Freiburg's Institute for Art History, Professor Kurt Bauch (1897–1975), Körte shared his views on their common scholarly interests. The two men were colleagues who shared professional interests and political views, especially a positive attitude toward National Socialism. This relationship gave rise to a series of newsletters initiated by Körte among Bauch's and Körte's students and colleagues from the Freiburg school to keep in touch during wartime. The series started in 1939 and ended with a last letter to the few survivors in summer of 1946.[28] In the newsletters, Körte's commitment to military art protection was discussed at the beginning, without judgment. This was something Körte frequently did by himself, to varied effect. The letters and notes, in which Körte reflects on his views, scientific attitudes, plans, and goals, offer a deep insight into his work for military art protection. Additionally, Körte began to record ideas for his postwar academic work. He also compiled lectures and guided tours about the cultural assets of the area where he was stationed. All these documents have been carefully preserved by his family since his death.[29]

Apart from the richness of data, there is another aspect that raises interest in his written legacy: Körte was the only member in the work group set up by Solms who had no contact with museum work as a civilian. His self-perception as an art historian was characterized by a predominance of art theory, to which Körte intended to make an explicit contribution in his further academic life. One concept that appears repeatedly in his letters is what he called "The Power of the Image." His writings suggest that he planned a larger work on this question and that he used his time at the front to conceptualize the project. At the end of his work in Pskov, he wrote to his wife,

> My work here was a very interesting tension ... Especially the "power of the image" is well preserved; the single thoughts begin to join together, and here in Russia, especially the chapter on the night side of the issue, the magic of the image is very advanced. If I have time to let the writing mature, then it will be a big thing that Heidegger should enjoy.[30]

Körte did not have this time. The work was never written, although hints are scattered throughout his notes. In March 1943, for example, he wrote that the war effort reduced art historians to viewing individual works without access to comparative material. This, he hoped, would "rediscover the absolute, unparalleled dignity of the work of art" and ultimately true art could be precisely defined.[31] What he formulated here is a critique of the comparative methodology in art history, which had been established by the previous generation of scholars. Probably not by coincidence Körte mentioned the name of Erwin Panofsky in this context, the German-Jewish emigrant, renowned for his work in art theory and most eminent representative of iconology, the method created by Aby Warburg in Hamburg. It would have been more obvious to blame Richard Hamann, who was the first to systematically establish the principle of constant image comparison. It seems as if Körte considered the methodology of the Jewish scholar more mistaken than that of the communist, but at least "Aryan," professor.

Körte had extensive knowledge of European art from ancient Greece through the Middle Ages to the present and a profound appreciation for the history of style. For his research interests these were more means to an end than value in themselves and so he looked a little contemptuously at the art historians who devoted themselves exclusively to applied art history in the museum business. Furthermore, his way of thinking was shaped by belief in the different creative powers of races. As a result, he presumed Russian culture to be inferior and at its best derivative. He did not expect any noteworthy works of art or cultural assets to be found in Russia. Körte's work in Pskov was therefore a new experience in practical museum work and applied science and at the same time a confrontation with the material heritage of the occupied area, which produced, as we will see later, unexpected results.

Körte's stationing in military art protection did not come unexpectedly or spontaneously. Before being stationed in Pskov in July 1942, Count Solms apparently had inquired about suitable specialists in the area. He had already tried to have Körte's friend Harald Keller moved to his unit. In April 1942, Körte himself noted the possibility of an assignment to do catalog work for the 18th Army.[32] At that moment, it did not seem to have been inconvenient to him. However, this does not indicate an interest in or an accepting of military art protection. Rather, it had to do with Körte having personal difficulties with his superior, as he also noted several times, albeit very cautiously. Among other things he complained about a lack of appreciation, a contested vacancy in his unit, as well as dealing with errors and other disputes so that on February 26, Körte asked himself, "Should I apply for a transfer?"[33]

Körte already knew from his friend the art historian Harald Keller about the problems military art protection faced. In November 1941, the commander of the 212th Infantry Division stationed in Peterhof, Theodor Endres, had commissioned Keller to secure the works of art still to be found in the palace and surrounding smaller palaces and to confiscate objects from the staff's offices and from the officers' mess.[34] Keller had been ambivalent about his mission. After the destruction caused by fighting and willful damage and theft by German soldiers, there was hardly anything left worth saving.[35] At the same time, Keller found his mission, lasting from November 1941 to January 1942, a chance "to get out of the trenches." Thus he tried to establish contact with Count Solms, hoping that the acquaintance from before might have a job for him.[36] He was successful, and in April 1942 Solms requested him for his unit. But after he had completed his mission in Peterhof, Keller was so disillusioned that he refused to accept further activities in military art protection, when Count Solms finally asked for him.[37] Instead, he drew Solms's attention to his friend Körte.[38] To Körte he wrote about the requirement that he had "passionately resisted," that art protection was a "terrible post, since one was expected to take icons and furniture from the officers" who had taken it first. Finally, he warned Körte that he probably now would be "the next victim"—without revealing that this was due to his own recommendation.[39] Thus being aware of some negative aspects military art protection might have for himself, Körte was not pleased when he got his new assignment. On July 1, 1942, his diary reads "command to protect art in Pleskau—unfortunately."[40]

A few days after his arrival in Pskov, Körte wrote to his wife,

> While the best things by Bernt Notke, Benedikt Dreyer, etc. which were not properly recovered in Lübeck and were therefore destroyed by the fires, we save, with enormous effort, the sometimes quite moderate Russian icons from Novgorod ... Yes, an irony of fate wanted us to recover Russian valuables, while the Russians

have taken with them the famous German bronze doors of the twelfth century in Novgorod when they left.[41]

In one of his notebooks, he confirmed,

> It feels so mad to salvage old Russian icons here, while at home the highest sanctuaries of our people, the Cologne churches of St. Martin, St. Gereon and Maria im Capitol are destroyed to the ground.[42] The best art protection would be to help to win the war quickly.[43]

It becomes clear that Körte's rejection of his mission at the art protection unit was based on two interlinked reasons. On the one hand, because of his low opinion of Russian art, he did not consider the objects worth the effort, especially as truly valuable art was lost elsewhere. On the other hand, he thought it necessary to achieve victory as quickly as possible in order to save the cultural goods back in Germany.

## Novgorod

Körte's worldview was soon to be shaken by his interaction with cultural artifacts from one of the oldest Russian cities: Novgorod. German troops took the city on August 19, 1941. In this area, the occupiers could not move further eastward, so the city remained virtually on the front line at the Volkhov for the rest of the occupation.

German experts inspected the cultural assets of Novgorod as soon as possible. One of the first to come was the abovementioned archeologist Reinhold Strenger, who arrived in early September.[44] At that time, the eastern part of the city was still embattled, so he had to restrict his visit to the Kremlin or Sophia side west of the river Volkhov. He found the building of the Picture Gallery intact. The exhibition of the "Propaganda Museum," however, was destroyed by the soldiers. The archiepiscopal library was locked, as it was supervised and guarded by the local army commander. Saint Sophia Cathedral was intact except for the main dome. According to Strenger, the Russians had evacuated the "most significant" artworks and other cultural goods before the Soviet troops had left the city. Nevertheless, he demanded to have the cathedral locked, "because of the danger that visitors would remove parts of the valuable art objects still inside the cathedral."[45] Almost simultaneously, but no later than early October 1941, the photographer Ernst Baumann (1906–1985) captured images of St. Sophia Cathedral from the northwest, with no signs of damage,[46] as well as from the interior of the cathedral, where he documented the iconostasis.[47]

The archeologist Vasilii Ponomarev also took eyewitness notes of Novgorod during and immediately after the capture by Germans. Like Strenger, he reported that the architectural monuments were essentially still intact at the start of German occupation. According to Ponomarev's descriptions, the long trench warfare that followed proved fatal. The front came to a virtual standstill here in the winter of 1941–2, and for the next two years German and Soviet units faced each other across the river Volkhov. The Soviet Artillery shelled Novgorod frequently, which led to the destruction or severe damage of numerous monuments.[48] The first victim was St. John's Church; its dome was hit in early September. In the resulting fire a large part of the collections stored in the church were destroyed. Ponomarev wrote of tens of thousands of objects, including about three thousand icons and the entire collection of his grandfather Vasilii Peredolskii (1833–1907), which had been confiscated in the 1930s.[49] The Cathedral of the Epiphany, too, was hit and set ablaze. The fire destroyed the eighteenth-century iconostasis, but the murals survived almost undamaged except for those in the ruined dome and apses. Many churches in the city center suffered similarly at the beginning of the occupation. As far as he could observe it, Ponomarev described all the damage. However, the churches east of the river, which suffered most, were out of reach for him due to the ongoing fights.[50] Subsequently, churches in villages east of the river were damaged. The Church of the Savior of Neredica and the Assumption Church in Volotovo were left as rubble—one by October 1941 and the other after the two and a half years of fighting.

In October 1941, Ponomarev was charged with securing the remaining collections. He had most of the artworks and other goods left in the museums and repositories taken to St. Sophia Cathedral, which became a central repository. Ponomarev was tasked to rate the objects according to their museum value. In addition, he created a list of the art treasures gathered in St. Sophia Cathedral, since corresponding lists were requested by the "Wirtschaftsstab Ost" (Economic Staff "East") or by the working group "Ostland" of the ERR in January 1942.[51]

In the spring of 1942, one member of the ERR, art historian Dietrich Roskamp (1907–1967), wrote a report on the actual state of Novgorod, which gives an impression of how the cultural assets and architectural monuments had survived the winter. Not a single building had remained undamaged. Crumbling masonry, damaged roofs, and broken windows represented a great threat to the monuments. Snow lay in all churches so that the objects within were endangered by moisture. Roskamp stated that the Spanish soldiers of the "Blue Division" who were stationed in Novgorod alongside the Germans caused the greatest damage. They broke open and looted locked churches, stole icons and crucifixes, cut the embroidery from Altar cloth and liturgical vestments, broke porcelain, and defiled and looted graves. In some cases they even burned icons for heat.[52]

On June 5, 1942, Soviet artillery units started to shoot at the Novgorod Kremlin. Twenty artillery shells hit the Sophia Cathedral. The northern part was the worst affected. The Christ-Pantocrator fresco was destroyed and several vaults collapsed. The local army commander reported the damage and demanded removal of all cultural assets, since he assumed there was no hope that the "Bolsheviks" would spare them.[53] The occupiers made minimal repairs. In makeshift fashion, they closed accessible holes in the roof and walls. The iconostases were dismantled and icons temporarily placed in the lower sacristy. All other items were hidden under the tower stairs. The frescoes of St. Constantine and St. Helena, as well as the fourteenth-century stone Alekseevski Cross, were given a protective coating of brick.[54] It was only after this attack that concrete steps were taken to remove the cultural assets.

In the first days of July, Solms removed the icons from the collections of the Museum of Ancient Russian Art as well as from the churches of Novgorod and its surroundings. He gathered the icons from the main iconostasis of the St. Sophia Cathedral, from the iconostasis of the Nativity of Mary Chapel, from the St. Peter-and-Paul Church, the Assumption Cathedral of the Monastery of St. Anthony, and the Apostle Philippus Church and transferred them to Pskov. From the iconostasis of St. Nicholas Cathedral in the Yaroslav's Court and from the Church of the Transfiguration of Christ on Ilyinka Street only a few icons were recovered. Before dismantling, the iconostases were photographed.[55] In addition to icons from the St. Sophia Cathedral, Solms removed the bishop's and tsar's throne, two mosaic plates, and some archaeological objects, carved crosses including a famous miraculous Cross from 1548 and the Lyudogoshchin Cross from 1359. He also had some wooden statues evacuated, for example, a carved figure of the holy martyr Paraskjeva Pjatnica, a Christ in the dungeon, and some small figures of gods who had been deposited there as part of the security measures. Some icons were left back in the lower sacristy as was the sarcophagus with the remains of the holy bishop Nikita. Hardware and other metal objects remained hidden under the stairs.

The most detailed description of the operation came from Ponomarev, who had de facto responsibility for Novgorod's art treasures after the withdrawal of the Soviet troops in 1941 and who was the only one who knew the inventory exactly. No object lists from that transfer survived. It is likely that when the evacuation was prepared in July, there was simply no time to compile them. What remained in Novgorod is undocumented. Since Soviet bombardment continued and was triggered by visible movement, removal took place at night. For several days, wagons drove near the city at dusk. Solms, who supervised the dismantling himself, had the artworks taken to the train station by trucks and loaded by prisoners of war. He refrained from having the archives removed because of the poor conditions.[56] He took with him the Russian helpers, Vasilii Ponomarev and the sisters Tat'iana and Natal'ia Gippius.

On July 5, 1942, Werner Körte received the icons and all archaeological objects from Novgorod in Pskov. Under his supervision, they were taken to the repository of the museum in the Dormition (Uspenskaya-Paramenskaya) church.[57] Körte got support from a small group of Russian workers: two prisoners of war had to lift and carry the icons; Ponomarev and the sisters Gippius helped with the scientific work.[58] Körte inventoried the icons, a work he finished by July 24.[59] Unfortunately, his inventory can no longer be found. Some pieces seem to have fascinated Körte so much that he documented them for his own use. He did this carefully for the elaborate carvings of the Lyudogoshchin Cross, for example, even making a sketch.

Working with these cultural goods brought Körte's art-historical world outlook almost to collapse. Having been very critical about the art protection measures before, shortly after his arrival in Pskov he wrote,

> I am completely enchanted by the world of icons that we have to recover here. It is not as if I were looking for the Russian as such in them, but I do feel very vividly that the Byzantine-Romanesque foundations of Russian art are very similar to those of German and Italian; and since we brought here over 300 icons from Novgorod, partly from the thirteenth century, I live among these heavy wooden boards in the middle of the great world from which Giotto once rose.[60]

Körte's delight in the icons, which he had despised so much at the beginning, demonstrates how these objects inspired his vague thoughts on the "power of the image." He literally experienced them. This is the dark side of this power, the magic of the images, he reflected on in his letter to his wife.[61] In that case, though, he did not indicate that he described an immediate personal experience.

The magic manifested itself particularly when dealing with the revered icons from Novgorod's St. Sophia Cathedral, works of art anchored in Russian Orthodox spirituality. There can be no doubt that it was the encounter with the original, the direct experience of the materiality of the icons, their physical presence, size and weight of the huge wooden panels, as well as the high quality painting, that particularly affected him. The finely nuanced details of the representations became an almost cathartic moment for Körte's perception of Russian culture. The thoughts about the "dark side" of the "power of the image," its "magic," recorded at the end of Körte's mission, related to this physical experience. Even the jaded expert and connoisseur could not escape this "image act."[62] The intensity of his experience on the one hand is due to the fact that in Körte's conception the image was given a fundamental and nonspiritual power. Thus, his theoretical considerations turned into a self-fulfilling prophecy. Dealing with the works of art by hand was an unusual or even new experience for him, which certainly intensified the "image act."

Körte found his balance again toward the end of his mission:

> My art-historical view of the world was thoroughly disturbed here; according to the old scheme, I had always meant that in the eleventh, twelfth, and thirteenth centuries east of the river Elbe there was wilderness, and much deeper wilderness on east of the river Vistula. Instead, here in the north, at the Ilmensee, all of the sudden we find advanced crossed-dome churches, as they might stand in Palermo, with huge fresco cycles dating of 1060, 1108, 1156, etc., in which the entire Christian iconography, with Navicella, Lamentation, etc. is fully developed.[63]

He acknowledged that Russian art had a three-century lead over the German East, but now he flipped this story to one that once again gave superiority to German art. It deserved even greater praise precisely because it had been backward in comparison to this Russian art—now he could claim that German art outperformed Russia "in an unprecedented steady development" until the beginning of the eighteenth century.[64]

## The Museum in Pskov and Later Exhibitions

Until the recovery of the Novgorod cultural assets Solms's activities, apart from the reopening of the Pogankiny Palaty, had mainly consisted of recovering what the Germans considered the most significant cultural assets from the residences around Leningrad and preparing them for evacuation. By summer 1942 Solms, who took a lot of creative freedom for his task, had established regular museum work in the Pogankiny Palaty. All objects were inventoried, described, photographically documented, restored if necessary, and exhibited if possible. Ponomarev, the expert on ancient Russian art, set up a card catalog of the Novgorod and Pskov icons in which he noted which church each icon came from and correspondingly tagged them. Altogether, this was very careful, up-to-date, and professional work that met the standards of larger museums at any place in peacetime.

Photographs document some of the exhibition spaces and thus give an impression of the architecture of the medieval building as well as the exhibition structure and contents. A hall on the ground floor with magnificent ceiling paintings was dedicated to ancient weapons and contained a knight's armor, a miniature cannon, as well as various other weapons and parts of armor. In another room, arts and crafts ranging from a tiled stove and single stove tiles to ceramic vessels and bronze church bells were arranged. Furniture and paintings lined the halls of the ground floor. The rooms on the upper floor displayed ancient Russian art, icons, and religious crafts. The most important icons were on display in the main hall of the upper floor, the former dining room. Here hung many of the Novgorod icons, such as the celebrated Byzantine Peter and Paul icon mentioned at the beginning, along with its traditional silver *oklad*, as well as a fourteenth-century icon of Saints Boris and Gleb (Figure 12.2).

After the defeat of the Germans at Stalingrad, which made even the most convinced National Socialists doubt the "Endsieg,"[65] the Soviet Army began to push back German troops. In March 1943 the Headquarters of the Army Group North in Pskov started a careful review of which departments needed to remain within the city; expendable services should be scaled down, disbanded, or transferred back

**Figure 12.2** View of the exhibition in the *Pogankiny Palaty*. In the background on the right the icon of Saints Peter and Paul. Photo: Eugen Fink, Pskov 1942. © Bildarchiv Foto Marburg/Eugen Fink.

home. No further troops should enter the city.[66] From late autumn 1943 on, Solms had the art treasures evacuated west. The first station was Riga. There Solms handed over most icons to the staff of the ERR, who took the icons and other cultural objects to Colmberg castle near Ansbach in Franconia. Why the Army Group North gave up most of the before jealously guarded artworks is unknown. Even an indication of the exact date is missing; the only secure information is that in April 1944 most icons were in the ERR's hands.[67]

The most valuable icons and objects from the Imperial palaces remained with the armed forces. They were exhibited in the Latvian National Gallery, renamed "Deutsches Landesmuseum" in early summer 1944, exclusively for Wehrmacht members.[68] Solms even had a catalog created, but this seems to be lost.[69] Apparently, the Riga exhibition contained the best objects of the Pskov exhibition, including about sixty icons, among them the Novgorod "Boris and Gleb" and the Byzantine "Peter and Paul" icon, as well as the Lyudogoshchin cross. Despite the risk of destruction of the objects by air raids, the authorities refused to close the exhibition and bring the objects to a safe haven as quickly as possible, because "the objects, salvaged by the German soldiers at risk of their lives, should be of continued benefit for them, therefore the exhibition will remain in place for the unforeseeable future."[70] In other respects it was "very likely that the new Army Museum in the fortress Boyen close to Lötzen planned by the Führer would have a section on Russian art, in which the Riga pieces were to be displayed."[71]

Another exhibition with icons from the collection point in Pskov, namely the show "Pflug und Schwert in Russlands Norden" (Plow and Sword in Russia's North), was shown in the city of Breslau (Wrocław) from April to May 1944. Christian Gündel (1903–?), who had been employee of Breslau Castle Museum before the war, organized the exhibition for Solms. Conceived as a temporary exhibition, other than those in Riga and Pskov, it aimed primarily at the German civilian population. It was designed to convey an impression of the "life, struggle and performance of the soldiers" in northwestern Russia.[72] The show was a complete success: after just one month, more than fifty thousand visitors had seen it. Afterward it was to be sent to Prague for about four weeks.[73] However, this did not happen anymore.

## Epilogue: The Balance of the Military Art Protection in Russia

Solms left Riga for the exhibition in Breslau. From April 1944 to early spring of 1945, he had German cultural goods evacuated from the Baltic region, from repositories in East Prussia and in Silesia, partly on behalf of the department "Chef der Heeresmuseen,"[74] partly for German noble families who had taken their treasures to their palaces and country houses to save them from air raids. The remaining files of the working group were brought to Werro in southeastern Estonia, where the headquarters of the Army Group North had moved. Werner Körte was stationed here since the summer of 1943. Apparently, he had been, again and very much against his wishes, transferred to the rear.[75] It is almost an irony of fate that Körte, who had been so critical of the deployment of Pskov military art protection, became the one who had to sort the files.[76] He also wrote a final report.

The files were lost. Maybe Werner Körte had destroyed them, or perhaps they were left behind and fell to Soviet hands. Körte's report, however, was preserved in one copy, which he himself had sent to Alfred Stange, professor for art history at the University of Bonn.[77] It was a sober survey of the activities of Solms's staff in Pskov, which was intended to present the efforts of Army Group North for Russian art in a positive light and justify the failures of military art protection. The text is a sharp contrast to everything Körte had written for himself, for his wife, and for his friends, with no traces of his skepticism at the beginning, nor his ideologically justified contempt for the Russian culture, or the shock of discovering its quality and the theory-based mastering of his unexpected enthusiasm. Today it reads as if the writer finally closed a door behind himself.

The military art protection of the Army Group North was a failure indeed, at least if one assumes that the protection and preservation of cultural assets in their original state and place was the goal. Nothing of that could be realized. None of the architectural monuments could be saved from damage by the acts of war or, in the worst, from complete destruction, and the movable cultural assets were largely deported to the west—with no idea of returning them at any future point. Other art protection officers—the American and British Monuments Men, the Soviet Trophy Brigades, and other Soviet military units—finally brought exactly these cultural goods back to the Soviet Union, a result that German plans never considered.

The objects in the Riga exhibition were actually transported westward in June or July 1944. They reached the small town of Mühlberg on the Elbe. There Russian troops on their advance found forty crates of property from the Novgorod State Museums and sent them back to Moscow, where they were stored in the Central Restoration Department.[78] Only a few labels taken from the objects, showing that they had been part of the Riga exhibition, are still kept there.[79] Maybe the famous Peter and Paul icon from Novgorod was in one of these crates. Unfortunately, the main documentation of the find turned out to be untraceable, so we cannot be sure whether every single item took this path as part of its return. Whatever the route, the icon of St. Peter and Paul returned to Novgorod, where the icon fascinates and enchants visitors to this day.

## Notes

This paper is based on materials compiled as part of the research project "Russian Museums in the Second World War." Together we investigated the German art theft in northwestern Russia. The research project was carried out from 2012 to 2014 by the Prussian Cultural Heritage Foundation (Stiftung Preußischer Kulturbesitz) in Berlin. The Volkswagen Foundation generously supported it. Scientific director was the former founding director of the Research Center for Eastern Europe in Bremen, Wolfgang Eichwede. In the German-Russian cooperation, my colleagues and I worked intensively with many employees from the State Museums of Novgorod and Pskov, as well as the Palace Museums Tsarskoe Selo, Peterhof, Gatchina, and Pavlovsk. I am deeply indebted to all of them for the wonderful cooperation.

1. Mikhail V. Tolstoi, *Sviatyni i drevnosti velikago Novgoroda* (Moscow: Universitetskaia Tipografiia, 1862), 70, 99.
2. Viktor N. Lazarev, *Russkaia ikonopis' ot istokov do nachala XVI veka* (Moscow: Iskusstvo, 1983), 33.
3. Nikodim P. Kondakov, *Die russische Ikone*, 4. Bde (Prague: Seminarium Kondakovianum, 1928–33); Lazarev, *Russkaia ikonopis' ot istokov do nachala XVI veka*, 163.
4. For more details, see Patricia Kennedy Grimsted, "Reconstructing the Record of Nazi Cultural Plunder. A Survey of the Dispersed Archives of the Einsatzstab Reichsleiter Rosenberg (ERR)," http://www.errproject.org/survey.php.
5. Christian Fuhrmeister, Johannes Griebel, Stephan Klingen, Ralf Peters, eds., *Kunsthistoriker im Krieg: Deutscher Militärischer Kunstschutz in Italien 1943–1945* (Cologne: Böhlau, 2012); Christina Kott, "Der deutsche 'Kunstschutz' im Ersten und Zweiten Weltkrieg. Ein Vergleich," in *Deutsch-französische Kultur- und Wissenschaftsbeziehungen im 20. Jahrhundert. Ein institutionsgeschichtlicher Ansatz*, ed. Ulrich Pfeil (Munich: R. Oldenbourg, 2007), 137–53; Christina Kott, *Préserver l'art de l'ennemi? Le patrimoine artistique en Belgique et en France occupées, 1914–1918* (Brussels: PIE-Peter Lang, 2006); Lutz Klinkhammer, "Kunstschutz im Propagandakrieg: Der Kampf um die Sicherstellung der italienischen Kunstschätze 1943–1945," in *Kunsthistoriker im Krieg: Deutscher Militärischer Kunstschutz in Italien, 1943–1945*, ed. Christian Fuhrmeister, Johannes Griebel, Stephan Klingen, Ralf Peters (Cologne: Böhlau, 2012), 49–73, 49.
6. Paul Clemen, *Kunstschutz im Kriege. Berichte über den Zustand der Kunstdenkmäler auf den verschiedenen Kriegsschauplätzen und über die deutschen und österreichischen Maßnahmen zu ihrer Erhaltung, Rettung, Erforschung* (Leipzig: E. A. Seemann, 1919). See also Kott, "Der deutsche "Kunstschutz" im Ersten und Zweiten Weltkrieg," 142.
7. Hermann Burg, *Kunstschutz an der Westfront. Kritische Betrachtungen und Erinnerungen* (Charlottenburg: Deutsche verlagsgesellschaft für politik und geschichte, 1920).
8. Dagobert Frey, Bericht über meine Tätigkeit in Polen, NARA, OMGUS—Cultural Affairs Branch, Records Relating to Monuments, Museums, Libraries, Archives, and Fine Arts, Dagobert Frey, s.p. [BL. 44–65]; Sabine Arend, *Studien zur deutschen kunsthistorischen "Ostforschung" im Nationalsozialismus: Die Kunsthistorischen Institute an den (Reichs-) Universitäten Breslau und Posen und ihre Protagonisten im Spannungsfeld von Wissenschaft und Politik* (PhD dissertation, Berlin, 2009), http://edoc.hu-berlin.de/dissertationen/arend-sabine-2009-07-15/PDF/arend.pdf, 571.
9. "Über meine Tätigkeit als Beauftragter des Oberkommandos des Heeres für den Schutz der Werke der Bildenden Kunst von 1940–42." Grundsätze und Arbeitsmethoden von Franz Graf Wolff Metternich, Bundesarchiv–Militärarchiv, MSG 2/3244; published in French by Jean Cassou, ed., *Le Pillage par les Allemands des œuvres d'art et des bibliothèques appartenant à des juifs en France: Recueil des documents* (Paris: Editions du Centre, 1947), 149–77.
10. Bundesarchiv—Militärarchiv, RH 3/154, Bl. 5–39, Franz Wolff-Metternich, Abschließender Bericht über die Arbeit des Kunstschutzbeauftragten in der Zeit von Mai 1940–September 1944, Bl. 22. Thanks to Christian Fuhrmeister for pointing this out.
11. Archiv des LVR, Nachlass Franz Graf Wolff-Metternich, 68.
12. Bundesarchiv–Militärarchiv, RH 3/154, Metternich, Abschließender Bericht, Bl. 17/18.

13. Archiv des LVR, Legacy of Franz Graf Wolff-Metternich, 68; Legacy of Georg Stein, Private archive. BA–MA, RH 20-18/1203, Bl. 205 verso; BA–MA, RH 24–50/163, Bl. 8.
14. Ernst Otto Graf zu Solms-Laubach, *Die Wormser Bauschule in Hessen und ihre Grundlagen in Deutschland und Oberitalien* (PhD dissertation, Marburg 1927). See Institut für Stadtgeschichte Frankfurt am Main, Personal files, Dr. Graf zu Solms-Laubach, Bl. 1.
15. Institut für Stadtgeschichte Frankfurt am Main, Personal files, Dr. Graf zu Solms-Laubach, Bl. 2.
16. Institut für Stadtgeschichte Frankfurt am Main, Personal files, Dr. Graf zu Solms-Laubach, Bl. 122.
17. Jörn Hasenclever, *Wehrmacht und Besatzungspolitik in der Sowjetunion: Die Befehlshaber der rückwärtigen Heeresgebiete 1941–1943* (Paderborn: Schöningh, 2010), 149f.
18. PA–AA, R 60769.
19. Solms affidavit for v. Küchler in the judgement of Nuremberg against the Army High Command. Staatsarchiv Nürnberg, Rep. 501, IV, KV-Prozesse, Fall 12, F 3, Dok. Nr. 62.
20. Werner Körte mentioned the good relations between Solms and Küchler as well as the fact, that Küchler personally supported Solms' ideas. Werner Körte am 8.7.1942, private archive.
21. Frankfurter Generalanzeiger, 15.09.1941.
22. Ulrike Schmiegelt-Rietig, Graf Ernstotto zu Solms-Laubach, "Biograficheskii ocherk," in *Gorod Pushkin: dvortsy i liudi*, ed. I. K. Bott (St. Petersburg: GMZ "Tsarskoe Selo," 2015), 146–163; Ulrike Schmiegelt-Rietig, "Ernst Otto Graf zu Solms-Laubach. Museumsdirektor in Frieden und Krieg," in *Archiv für Frankfurts Geschichte und Kunst* 78 (2019), 154–67.
23. Werner Körte, *Die Wiederaufnahme romanischer Bauformen in der niederländischen und deutschen Malerei des 15. und 16. Jahrhunderts, Wolfenbüttel 1930* (PhD dissertation, Leipzig 1930).
24. Werner Körte, diary of 1942, private archive.
25. Staffing plan; letters and notes by Werner Körtes, private archive; personal files at Deutsche Dienststelle—WAST.
26. Statement of Körte's eldest son in several conversations with the author.
27. Klaus Latzel, *Deutsche Soldaten - nationalsozialistischer Krieg? Kriegserlebnis - Kriegserfahrung. 1939–1945* (Paderborn: Schöningh, 1998). The author of the random reading of letters in the collection of field mail letters in the Berlin Museum of Communication was able to get an impression of the quality of the usual field mail. About the collections. https://sammlungen.museumsstiftung.de/feldpostbriefe/ (last on May 31, 2020).
28. Albert Ludwig University of Freiburg. University archive.
29. I am especially grateful to Werner Körte's eldest son, who generously provided the material.
30. Werner Körte to his wife on July 31, 1942. Private archive.
31. Werner Körte, diary March 10, 1943. It is a single sheet from the estate. Private archive.
32. Werner Körte in his diary, April 21, 1942. Private archive.
33. Diary Werner Körte on February 26, 1942. Private archive.
34. Harald Keller, November 22 and 25, 1941. Private archive.
35. Harald Keller, letter to his wife, November 25, 1941. Private archive.

36. Harald Keller, letter to Graf zu Solms-Laubach, winter of 1941. Private archive.
37. Harald Keller, letter to his wife, April 25, 1942. Private archive.
38. Harald Keller, letter to his wife, June 5, 1942. Private archive.
39. Harald Keller, letter to Werner Körte, June 14, 1942. Private archive.
40. Werner Körte in his diary, July 1, 1942. Private archive.
41. Werner Körte, letter to his wife, July 6, 1942. Private archive. Werner Körte alludes to the destruction of the historical town of Lübeck on March 29, 1942, by an air raid by the Royal Air Force.
42. Körte is writing about the Royal Air Force's attack on Cologne on May 30–31, 1942.
43. Werner Körte, *Geschichte meiner Arbeit. 1928–1942. Gedanken und Pläne*. The large-scale notebook contains only a few pages from Körte's time in Pskov. Private archive.
44. CDAVO, f. 3676, op. 1, d. 138, l. 550.
45. Ibid.
46. BArch—Bildarchiv, Bild 101 III, Baumann—052.
47. Ibid., Bild 4–7.
48. V. S. Ponomarev, "Sud'by monumental'nykh pamiatnikov Velikogo Novgoroda," Vstupitel'naia stat'ia by N. N. Grinev, *Ezhegodnik Novgorodskogo gosudarstvennogo Muzeia-Zapovednika 2005* (Velikii Novgorod: Novogorodskii gosudarstvennyi ob'edinennyi muzei-zapovednik, 2006), 228–53, here, 240.
49. Ibid.
50. Ibid., 241.
51. CDAVO, f. 3676, op. 1, d. 149, l. 16.
52. CDAVO, f. 3676, op. 1, d. 149, l. 570 ff.; vgl. auch CDAVO, f. 3676, op. 1, d. 149, l. 580.
53. CDAVO, f. 3676, op. 1, d. 149, l. 555.
54. V. S. Ponomarev, "Sud'by monumental'nykh pamiatnikov," 243.
55. Unfortunately the photographs seem to be lost; despite intense research they have not been retrieved.
56. State Archives Counsellor Mommsen memorandum about his excursion to Pskov and Dorpat from August 18 to 22, 1942. BArch Koblenz, R 90/173, o. Fol.
57. Werner Körte, entries in his diary on July 5 and 6, 1942. Private archive; see also: Ponomarev, Gibel' Novgoroda; Grinev and V. S. Ponomarev, 244.
58. Werner Körte, letter to his wife Elisabeth on July 19, 1942, private archive.
59. Werner Körte, entry in his diary on July 24, 1942, private archive.
60. Werner Körte, letter to Kurt Bauch, July 12, 1942, private archive.
61. Werner Körte, letter to his wife, July 31, 1942, private archive.
62. About the theory of "image act" see Horst Bredekamp, *Theorie des Bildakts* (Berlin: Suhrkamp, 2010).
63. Werner Körte, Die grauen Hefte, private archive.
64. Ibid.
65. Even a staunch supporter of National Socialism like Werner Körte became insecure for a short time in the face of the defeat. Werner Körte, Tagebucheinträge vom 31. Januar bis 12. Februar 1943, private archive. See also Bernd Wegner, "Von Stalingrad nach Kursk," *Ostfront 1943/44: Der Krieg im Osten und an den Nebenfronten*, ed. Karl-Heinz Frieser and Klaus Schmider (Munich: Verl.-Anst., 2007), 3–79, here 3–8.
66. BArch RH 19 III / 253, Bl. 26f.
67. Files of the Ic (that is the intelligence officer/third general staff officer) of the Army Group North. BArch RH 19 III / 385, Bl. 7.
68. BArch RH 19 III / 385, Bl. 3.
69. Ibid., Bl. 7f.

70. Ibid., Bl. 7.
71. Ibid., Bl. 7.
72. BArch RH 19 III / 486, Bl. 81.
73. BArch RH 19 III / 385, Bl. 9.
74. Institut für Stadtgeschichte Frankfurt am Main, S 2/ 7.089, o. Fol.
75. For example, Werner Körte, letter to his wife Elisabeth, December 3, 1943; diary of 1944, private archive.
76. Werner Körte, diary, April 14, 1944, private archive.
77. Estate of Alfred Stange, Archive of the Institute of Art History at the University of Bonn.
78. GARF, f. A-534, op. 2, d. 10, ll. 59.
79. Corinna Kuhr-Korolev, Ulrike Schmiegelt-Rietig, and Elena Zubkova, *Raub und Rettung: Russische Museen im Zweiten Weltkrieg* (Vienna: Weimar, 2019), 299.

# Select Bibliography

Adler, Ken. "Making Things the Same: Representation, Tolerance and the End of the Ancien Regime in France." *Social Studies of Science* 28:4 (1998): 499–545.
Adler, Ken. "Thick Things: Introduction." *Isis* 98:1 (2007): 80–3.
Akinsha, Konstantin. "Between Lent and Carnival: Moscow Conceptualism and Sots Art: Differences, Similarities, Interconnections." In *Moscow Conceptualism in Context*. Ed. Alla Rosenfeld. New Brunswick, NJ: Jane Voorhees Zimmerli Art Museum, 2011. 24–47.
Alivizatou, Marilena. *Intangible Heritage and the Museum: New Perspectives on Cultural Preservation*. Walnut Creek, CA: Left Coast Press, 2012.
Ames, Michael M. *Cannibal Tours and Glass Boxes: The Anthropology of Museums*. Vancouver: UBC Press, 1992.
Antonova, Katherine Pickering. *An Ordinary Marriage: The World of a Gentry Family in Imperial Russia*. Oxford: Oxford University Press, 2013.
Antonova, Katherine Pickering. "'Prayed to God, Knitted a Stocking': Needlework on a Nineteenth-Century Russian Estate." *Experiment: A Journal of Russian Culture* 22 (2016): 1–12.
Appadurai, Arjun, ed. *The Social Life of Things: Commodities in Cultural Perspective*. New York: Cambridge University Press, 1986.
Applebaum, Rachel. *Empire of Friends: Soviet Power and Socialist Internationalism in Cold War Czechoslovakia*. Ithaca, NY: Cornell University Press, 2019.
Appleby, John H. "Humphrey Jackson, F.R.S., 1717–1801: A Pioneering Chemist." *Notes and Records of the Royal Society of London* 40:2 (1986): 147–68.
Arel, Maria Salomon. *English Trade and Adventure to Russia in the Early Modern Era: The Muscovy Company, 1603–1649*. Lanham, MD: Lexington Books, 2019.
Arzyutov, Dmitry, and Sergei A. Kan. "The Concept of the 'Field' in Early Soviet Ethnography: A Northern Perspective." *Sibirica* 16:1 (2017): 31–74.
Auslander, Leora. "Beyond Words." *American Historical Review* 110 (2005): 1015–45.
Bagrow, Leo. "The First Russian Maps of Siberia and Their Influence on the West-European Cartography of N. E. Asia." *Imago Mundi* 9 (1952): 83–93.
Bagrow, Leo. "Semyon Remezov: A Siberian Cartographer." *Imago Mundi* 11 (1954): 111–25.
Bainbridge, Henry Charles. *Peter Carl Fabergé: Goldsmith and Jeweler to the Russian Imperial Court, His Life and Work*. Reprint ed. Suffolk: Spring Books, 1966.
Balzer, Harley D., ed., *Russia's Missing Middle Class: The Professions in Russian History*. Armonk, NY: M. E. Sharpe, 1996.
Balzer, Marjorie Mandelstam. *Shamans, Spirituality, and Cultural Revitalization: Explorations in Siberia and Beyond*. New York: Palgrave Macmillan, 2011.
Basu, Paul. *The Inbetweenness of Things: Materializing Mediation and Movement between Worlds*. London: Bloomsbury, 2017.
Beckert, Sven. *Empire of Cotton: A Global History*. New York: Knopf, 2014.

Beckwith, Christopher. "Tibetan Treacle: A Note on Theriac in Tibet." *Tibet Society Bulletin* 15 (1980): 49–51.
Bell, Joshua A. "A Bundle of Relations: Collections, Collecting, and Communities." *Annual Review of Anthropology* 46:1 (2017): 241–59.
Benedict, Carol. *Golden-Silk Smoke: A History of Tobacco in China, 1550–2010*. Berkeley: University of California Press, 2011.
Berg, Maxine. "In Pursuit of Luxury: Global History and British Consumer Goods in the Eighteenth Century." *Past and Present* 182 (2004): 85–142.
Berg, Maxine. *Luxury and Pleasure in Eighteenth-Century Britain*. Oxford: Oxford University Press, 2005.
Berg, Maxine, Felicia Gottman, Hanna Hodacs, and Chris Nerstrasz, eds. *Goods from the East, 1600–1800: Trading Eurasia*. London: Palgrave Macmillan, 2015.
Berg, Mikhail. *Literaturokratiia*. Moscow: Novoe literaturnoe obozrenie, 2000.
Berkhoff, Karel C. *Motherland in Danger: Soviet Propaganda during World War II*. Cambridge, MA: Harvard University Press, 2012.
Biedermann, Zoltán, Anne Gerritsen, and Giorgio Riello, eds. *Global Gifts: The Material Culture of Diplomacy in Early Modern Eurasia*. Cambridge: Cambridge University Press, 2018.
Billington, James H. *Russia in Search of Itself*. Washington, DC: Woodrow Wilson Center Press, 2004.
Blackwell, William L. *The Beginnings of Russian Industrialization, 1800–1860*. Princeton, NJ: Princeton University Press, 1968.
Bogatyrev, Sergei. "The Patronage of Early Printing in Moscow." *Canadian-American Slavic Studies* 51:2–3 (2017): 249–88.
Boivin, Nicole. *Material Cultures, Material Minds: The Impact of Things on Human Thought, Society, and Evolution*. Cambridge: Cambridge University Press, 2008.
Bradley, Joseph. *Muzhik and Muscovite: Urbanization in Late Imperial Russia*. Berkeley: University of California Press, 1985.
Braudel, Fernand. *Civilization and Capitalism, 15th-18th Century*, Volume 2, *The Wheels of Commerce*. Trans. Siân Reynolds. New York: Harper & Row, 1979.
Breen, T. H. "An Empire of Goods: The Anglicization of Colonial America, 1690–1776." *Journal of British Studies* 25:4 (1986): 467–99.
Bren, Paulina, and Mary Neuberger, eds. *Communism Unwrapped: Consumption in Cold War Eastern Europe*. New York: Oxford University Press, 2012.
Brewer, John, and Roy Porter, eds. *Consumption and the World of Goods*. New York: Routledge, 1993.
Britenkova, Liudmila. *Samovary Rossii: populiarnaia entsiklopediia*. Moscow: Khobbi Press, 2010.
Broman, Thomas H. *The Transformation of German Academic Medicine, 1750–1820*. Cambridge: Cambridge University Press, 1996.
Brooks, Crispin. "On One Ancestor: Vasilisk Gnedov in the Work of Sergej Sigej and Ry Nikonova." *Russian Literature* 59:2–4 (2006): 177–223.
Bruegel, Martin. "A Bourgeois Good? Sugar, Norms of Consumption and the Labouring Classes in Nineteenth-Century France." In *Food, Drink and Identity: Cooking, Eating and Drinking in Europe since the Middle Ages*. Ed. Peter Scholliers. Oxford: Berg, 2001. 99–118.
Brumfield, William Craft. *Landmarks of Russian Architecture: A Photographic Survey*. Abingdon: Routledge, 1997.

Bulakh, A. G. "Ornamental Stone in the History of St Petersburg Architecture." *Global Heritage Stone: Towards International Recognition of Building and Ornamental Stones*. Geological Society, London, Special Publications 407:1 (2015): 243–52.

Bundel, Richard, and Angela Tregear. "From Artisans to 'Factories': The Interpenetration of Craft and Industry in English Cheese-Making, 1650–1950." *Enterprise & Society* 7:4 (2006): 705–39.

Burgess, Rebecca, and Courtney White. *Fibershed: Growing a Movement of Farmers, Fashion Activists, and Makers for a New Textile Economy*. White River Junction, VT: Chelsea Green, 2019.

Burnham, John C. *Bad Habits: Drinking, Smoking, Taking Drugs, Gambling, Sexual Misbehavior, and Swearing in American History*. New York: New York University Press, 1993.

Castree, Noel. "Commodity Fetishism, Geographical Imaginations and Imaginative Geographies." *Environment and Planning A* 33 (2001): 1519–25.

Chartier, Roger. *The Order of Books: Readers, Authors, and Libraries in Europe between the Fourteenth and Eighteenth Centuries*. Trans. Lydia G. Cochrane. Stanford, CA: Stanford University Press, 1994.

Chikova, Galina, et al. *Aleksandr Morozov: Unikal'nye dokumenty, fotografii, fakty, vospominaniia*. Moscow: IzdAT, 2009.

Christian, David. "Silk Roads or Steppe Roads? The Silk Roads in World History." *Journal of World History* 11:1 (2006): 1–26.

Classen, Constance. *The Deepest Sense: A Cultural History of Touch*. Urbana: University of Illinois Press, 2012.

Clay, Catherine B. "Russian Ethnographers in the Service of Empire, 1856–1862." *Slavic Review* 54:1 (1995): 45–61.

Cole, Douglas. *Franz Boas: The Early Years, 1858–1906*. Seattle, WA: University of Washington Press, 1999.

Cookson, Gillian. *The Age of Machinery: Engineering the Industrial Revolution, 1170–1850*. Woodbridge: Boydell Press, 2018.

Courtwright, David T. *Forces of Habit: Drugs and the Making of the Modern World*. Cambridge, MA: Harvard University Press, 2002.

Cox, Howard. *The Global Cigarette: Origins and Evolution of British American Tobacco, 1880–1945*. New York: Oxford University Press, 2000.

Cracraft, James. "James Brogden in Russia, 1787–1788." *Slavonic and East European Review* 47:108 (1969): 219–44.

Crespo, Horacio. "Trade Regimes and the International Sugar Market, 1850–1980: Protectionism, Subsidies, and Regulation." In *From Silver to Cocaine: Latin American Commodity Chains and the Building of the World Economy, 1500–2000*. Ed. Steven Topik, Carlos Marichal, and Zephyr Frank. Durham, NC: Duke University Press, 2006. 147–73.

Crosby, Alfred W., Jr. *America, Russia, Hemp, and Napoleon: American Trade with Russia and the Baltic, 1783–1812*. Columbus: Ohio State University Press, 1965.

Cross, Anthony. *"By the Banks of the Thames": Russians in Eighteenth Century Britain*. Newtonville, MA: Oriental Research Partners, 1980.

Cross, Anthony. *By the Banks of the Neva: Chapters from the Lives and Careers of the British in Eighteenth-Century Russia*. Cambridge: Cambridge University Press, 1997.

Cruickshank, Pippa. "Flax in Croatia: Traditional Production Methods, the Use and Care of Linen in Folk Costumes and Implications for Museum Conservation." *Textile History* 42:2 (2011): 239–60.

Crummey, Robert O. "The Silence of Muscovy." *The Russian Review* 46:2 (1987): 157–64.
Curry-Machado, Jonathan, ed. *Global Histories, Imperial Commodities, Local Interactions*. Houndmills: Palgrave Macmillan, 2013.
Cvetkovski, Roland, and Alexis Hofmeister, eds. *An Empire of Others: Creating Ethnographic Knowledge in Imperial Russia and the USSR*. Budapest: Central European University Press, 2014.
Darnton, Robert. *The Kiss of Lamourette: Reflections in Cultural History*. New York: W. W. Norton, 1990.
Davydova, Sof'ia. "Russian Lace and Laceworkers: A Historical, Technical, and Statistical Investigation." *Experiment: A Journal of Russian Culture* 22 (2016): 161–72.
De Laet, Marianne, and Annemarie Mol. "The Zimbabwe Bush Pump: Mechanics of a Fluid Technology." *Social Studies of Science* 30:2 (2000): 225–63.
De Munck, Bert. "Artisans, Products and Gifts: Rethinking the History of Material Culture in Early Modern Europe." *Past and Present* 224:1 (August 2014): 39–74.
De Vos, Paula. "The Science of Spices: Empiricism and Economic Botany in the Early Spanish Empire." *Journal of World History* 17:4 (2006): 399–427.
Dennison, Tracy, and Sheilagh Ogilvie. "Does the European Marriage Pattern Explain Economic Growth?" *Journal of Economic History* 74:3 (2014): 651–93.
DeSoucey, Michael. "Gastronationalism: Food Traditions and Authenticity Politics in the European Union." *American Sociological Review* 75:3 (2010): 432–55.
Dicken, Philip, Philip K. Kelly, Kris Olds, and Henry Wai-Chung Yeung. "Chains and Networks. Territories and Scales: Toward a Relational Framework for Analysing the Global Economy." *Global Networks* 1:2 (2001): 89–112.
Douglas, Mary, and Baron Isherwood, eds. *The World of Goods: Towards an Anthropology of Consumption*. New York: Basic Books, 1979.
Downes, Stephanie, Sally Holloway, and Sarah Randles, eds. *Feeling Things: Objects and Emotions through History*. Oxford: Oxford University Press, 2018.
Drabkin, Artem, ed. *Ia dralsia na T-34*. Moscow: Eksmo, 2005.
Dumschat, Sabine. *Ausländischer Mediziner im Moskauer Russland*. Stuttgart: Franz Steiner Verlag, 2006.
Dunn, Walter S., Jr. *Hitler's Nemesis: The Red Army, 1930–1945*. Mechanicsburg, PA: Stackpole, 2009.
Eichenbaum, Boris. "How Gogol's 'Overcoat' Is Made." In *Gogol from the Twentieth Century*. Ed. Robert A. Maguire. Princeton, NJ: Princeton University Press, 1974. 269–91.
Engel, Barbara Alpern. "Not by Bread Alone: Subsistence Riots in Russia during World War I." *Journal of Modern History* 69:4 (1997): 696–721.
Enstad, Nan. *Cigarettes, Inc.: An Intimate History of Corporate Capitalism*. Chicago: University of Chicago Press, 2018.
Fabergé, Tatiana F., Eric-Alain Koehler, and Valentin V. Skurlov. *Fabergé: A Comprehensive Reference Book*. Geneva: Éditions Slatkine, 2012.
Ferrence, Roberta G. *Deadly Fashion: The Rise and Fall of Cigarette Smoking in North America*. New York: Garland, 1989.
Findlen, Paula, ed. *Early Modern Things: Objects and Their Histories, 1500–1800*. New York: Routledge, 2013.
Fisher, Tom. "Fashioning Plastic." In *The Social Life of Materials: Studies in Material and Society*. Ed. Adam Drazin and Susanne Küchler. London: Bloomsbury Academic, 2015. 119–36.

Fishzon, Anna. *Fandom, Authenticity, and Opera: Mad Acts and Letter Scenes in Fin-de-Siècle Russia*. New York: Palgrave Macmillan, 2013.
Fitzpatrick, Sheila. *Everyday Stalinism Ordinary Life in Extraordinary Times: Soviet Russia in the 1930s*. New York: Oxford University Press, 1999.
Frank, Andre Gunder. *ReORIENT: Global Economy in the Asian Age*. Berkeley: University of California Press, 1998.
Franklin, Simon. "Printing and Social Control in Russia 1: Passports." *Russian History* 37:3 (2010): 208–37.
Franklin, Simon. "Printing and Social Control in Russia 2: Decrees." *Russian History* 38:4 (2011): 467–92.
Franklin, Simon. "Printing and Social Control in Russia 3: Blank Forms." *Russian History* 42:1 (2015): 114–35.
Franquemont, Abby. *Respect the Spindle*. Loveland, CO: Interweave Press, 2009.
Franquemont, Edward, and Christine Franquemont. "Learning to Weave in Chinchero." *Textile Museum Journal* 26 (1987): 55–79.
Frey, James W. "Prickly Pears and Pagodas: The East India Company's Failure to Establish a Cochineal Industry in Early Colonial India." *The Historian* 74:2 (2012): 241–66.
Fritzsche, Peter, and Jochen Hellbeck. "The New Man in Stalinist Russia and Nazi Germany." In *Beyond Totalitarianism: Stalinism and Nazism Compared*. Ed. Michael Geyer and Sheila Fitzpatrick. Cambridge: Cambridge University Press, 2009.
Gänger, Stefanie. "World Trade in Medicinal Plants from Spanish America, 1717–1815." *Medical History* 59:1 (2015): 44–82.
Gaustad, Stephanie. *The Practical Spinner's Guide: Cotton, Flax, Hemp*. Loveland, CO: Interweave Press, 2014.
Gerritsen, Anne, and Giorgio Riello, eds. *The Global Lives of Things: The Material Culture of Connections in the Early Modern World*. London: Routledge, 2016.
Gestwa, Klaus. *Proto-Industrialisierung in Russland: Wirtschaft, Herrschaft und Kultur in Ivanovo und Pavlovo, 1741–1932*. Göttingen: Vandenhoeck & Ruprecht, 1999.
Girouard, Mark. *Life in the English Country House: A Social and Architectural History*. New Haven, CT: Yale University Press, 1978.
Gol'denberg, L. A. *Izograf zemli sibirskoi: zhizn' i trudy Semena Remezova*. Magadan: Magadanskoe knizhnoe izdatel'stvo, 1990.
Goodman, Jordan. *Tobacco in History: The Cultures of Dependence*. London: Routledge, 1993.
Greve, Charlotte. "Zaumland. Serge Segay and Rea Nikonova in the International Mail Art Network." *Russian Literature* 59:2–4 (2006): 445–67.
Grewe, Bernd-Stefan, and Karin Hofmeester. "Introduction: Luxury and Global History." In *Luxury in Global Perspective: Objects and Practices, 1600–2000*. Ed. Karin Hofmeester. New York: Cambridge University Press, 2016. 1–26.
Griffin, Clare. "Disentangling Commodity Histories: *Pauame* and Sassafras in the Early Modern Global World." *Journal of Global History* 15:1 (2020): 1–18.
Griffin, Clare. "Russia and the Medical Drug Trade in the Seventeenth Century." *Social History of Medicine* 31:1 (2018): 2–23.
Guerrini, Anita. "The Material Turn in the History of Life Science." *Literature Compass* 13:7 (2016): 469–80.
Hammond, David, and Carla Parkinson. "The Impact of Cigarette Package Design on Perceptions of Risk." *Journal of Public Health* 31 (2009): 345–53.
Hans, Nicholas. "Russian Students at Leyden in the 18th Century." *Slavonic and East European Review* 35 (1957): 551–62.

Harrison, Mark, ed. *The Economics of World War II: Six Great Powers in International Comparison*. Cambridge: Cambridge University Press, 1998.

Hart, Peggy. *Wool: Unraveling an American Story of Artisans and Innovation*. Atglen, PA: Schiffer, 2017.

Hartwick, Elaine. "Geographies of Consumption: A Commodity-Chain Approach." *Environment and Planning D: Society and Space* 16 (1998): 423–37.

Hawkins, Gay. "Plastic and Presentism: The Time of Disposability." *Journal of Contemporary Archaeology* 5:1 (2018): 91–102.

Heffernan, Michael, and Catherine Delano-Smith. "A Life in Maps: Leo Bagrow, *Imago Mundi*, and the History of Cartography in the Early Twentieth Century." *Imago Mundi* 66, supp. 1 (Oct 2014): 44–69.

Heinrich, Linda. *Linen: From Flax Seed to Woven Cloth*. Atglen, PA: Schiffer, 2010.

Hellie, Richard. *The Economy and Material Culture of Russia, 1600–1725*. Chicago: University of Chicago Press, 1999.

Hilton, Matthew. *Smoking in British Popular Culture, 1800–2000*. Manchester: Manchester University Press, 2000.

Hoffmann, Viktoria von. *From Gluttony to Enlightenment: The World of Taste in Early Modern Europe*. Urbana: University of Illinois Press, 2017.

Hollinger, R. Eric, et al. "Tlingit-Smithsonian Collaborations with 3D Digitization of Cultural Objects." *Museum Anthropology Review* 7:1–2 (2013): 201–53.

Hopkins, Terence K., and Immanuel Wallerstein. "Commodity Chains in the World-Economy Prior to 1800." *Review* 10:1 (1986): 157–70.

Hoskins, Janet. "Agency, Biography and Objects." In *Handbook of Material Culture*. Ed. Chris Tilley, Webb Keane, Susanne Küchler, Mike Rowlands, and Patricia Spyer. London: Sage, 2006. 74–84.

Howes, David, ed. *Cross-Cultural Consumption: Global Markets, Local Realities*. London: Routledge, 1996.

Howes, David. "HYPERESTHESIA, or, the Sensual Logic of Late Capitalism." In *Empire of the Senses: The Sensual Culture Reader*. Ed. David Howes. London: Bloomsbury Academic, 2005. 281–303.

Howes, David. *Sensual Relations: Engaging the Senses in Culture and Social Theory*. Ann Arbor: University of Michigan Press, 2003.

Hughes, Lindsey. "Russian Culture in the Eighteenth Century." In *The Cambridge History of Russia: Volume 2: Imperial Russia, 1689–1917*. Ed. Dominic Lieven. Cambridge: Cambridge University Press, 2006. 65–91.

Hunter, Janet, and Helen Macnaughton. "Gender and the Global Textile Industry." In *The Ashgate Companion to the History of Textile Workers, 1650–2000*. Ed. Lex Heerma van Voss, Els Hiemstra-Kuperus, and Elise van Nederveen Meerkerk. Farnham: Ashgate, 2010. 703–24.

Ippolitova, A. B. *Russkie rukopisnye travniki XVII–XVIII vekov: issledovanie fol'klora i etnobotaniki*. Moscow: Indrik, 2008.

Jackson, Peter. "Commodity Cultures: The Traffic in Things." *Transactions of the Institute of British Geographers*, New Series 24:1 (1999): 95–108.

Janecek, Gerald. "A. N. Cicerin, Constructivist Poet." *Russian Literature* 25 (1989): 469–524.

Janecek, Gerald. *Everything Has Already Been Written: Moscow Conceptualist Poetry and Performance*. Evanston, IL: Northwestern University Press, 2018.

Janecek, Gerald. *The Look of Russian Literature: Avant-Garde Visual Experiments, 1900–1930*. Princeton, NJ: Princeton University Press, 1984.
Janecek, Gerald. "Tysiacha Form Ry Nikonovoi." *Novoe literaturnoe obozrenie* 35 (1999): 283–319.
Jug, Steven G. "Sensing Danger: The Red Army during the Second World War." In *Russian History through the Senses: From 1700 to the Present*. Ed. Matthew P. Romaniello and Tricia Starks. London: Bloomsbury Academic, 2016. 219–40.
Kahan, Arcadius. "The Costs of 'Westernization' in Russia: The Gentry and the Economy in Eighteenth-Century Russia." *Slavic Review* 25:1 (1966): 40–66.
Kahan, Arcadius. *The Plow, the Hammer, and the Knout: An Economic History of Eighteenth-Century Russia*. Chicago: University of Chicago Press, 1985.
Kan, Sergei. " 'My Old Friend in a Dead-End of Empiricism and Skepticism': Bogoras, Boas, and the Politics of Soviet Anthropology of the Late 1920s–Early 1930s." *Histories of Anthropology Annual* 2 (2006): 33–68.
Kaplan, Herbert H. *Russian Overseas Commerce with Great Britain during the Reign of Catherine II*. Philadelphia, PA: American Philosophical Society, 1995.
Kavalerchik, Boris. "Once Again about the T-34." *Journal of Slavic Military Studies* 28:1 (2015): 186–214.
Keenan, Edward L. "Muscovite Political Folkways." *Russian Review* 45:2 (1986): 115–81.
Kendall, Laurel. *Shamans, Nostalgias, and the IMF: South Korean Popular Religion in Motion*. Honolulu: University of Hawai'i Press, 2009.
Kendall, Laurel, and Igor Krupnik, eds. *Constructing Cultures Then and Now: Celebrating Franz Boas and the Jesup North Pacific Expedition*. Washington, DC: Arctic Studies Center, Smithsonian Institute, 2003.
Kendall, Laurel, et al., eds. *Drawing Shadows to Stone: The Photography of the Jesup North Pacific Expedition 1897–1902*. New York: American Museum of Natural History in association with the University of Washington Press, Seattle, 1997.
Khmeleva, Galina, and Carol R. Noble. *Gossamer Webs: The History and Techniques of Orenburg Lace Shawls*. Loveland, CO: Interweave Press, 1998.
Khudin, K. S. "Stanovleniie mozhzhevelovoi povinnosti v Rossii v XVII v. (po materialam fonda Aptekarskogo prikaza RGADA)." *Vestnik RGGU* 21 (2012): 118–26.
Kivelson, Valerie. "Angels in Tobolsk: Celestial Topography and Visionary Administration in Late Muscovite Siberia." *Harvard Ukrainian Studies* 28:1/4 (2006): 543–56.
Kivelson, Valerie. *Cartographies of Tsardom: The Land and Its Meanings in Seventeenth-Century Russia*. Ithaca, NY: Cornell University Press, 2007.
Kivelson, Valerie. "Early Mapping: The Tsardom in Manuscript." In *Information and Empire: Mechanisms of Communication in Russia, 1600–1854*. Ed. Simon Franklin and Katherine Bowers. Cambridge: Open Book, 2017. 23–58.
Kleimola, Ann. "Regulating Icon Painters in the Era of the Ulozhenie: Evidence from the Russian North." *Russian History* 34:1/4 (2007): 341–63.
Klein, Lawrence E. "Politeness and the Interpretation of the British Eighteenth Century." *Historical Journal* 45:4 (2002): 869–98.
Klein, Ursula, and Wolfgang Lefèvre. *Materials in Eighteenth-Century Science: A Historical Ontology*. Boston, MA: MIT Press, 2007.
Knight, Nathaniel. "Nikolai Kharuzin and the Quest for a Universal Human Science: Anthropological Evolutionism and the Russian Ethnographic Tradition, 1885–1900." *Kritika* 9:1 (2008): 83–111.
Komaromi, Ann. "The Material Existence of Soviet Samizdat." *Slavic Review* 63:3 (2004): 597–618.

Komaromi, Ann. "Samizdat and Tamizdat." In *Vladimir Nabokov in Context*. Ed. David Bethea and Siggy Frank. Cambridge: Cambridge University Press, 2018. 166–73.

Komaromi, Ann. *Uncensored: The Quest for Autonomy in Soviet Samizdat*. Evanston, IL: Northwestern University Press, 2015.

Kopytoff, Igor. "The Cultural Biography of Things: Commoditization as Process." In *The Social Life of Things: Commodities in Cultural Perspective*. Ed. Arjun Appadurai. New York: Cambridge University Press, 1986. 64–94.

Koroloff, Rachel. "Travniki, Travniki and Travniki: Herbals, Herbalists and Herbaria in Seventeenth-Century and Eighteenth-Century Russia." *ВИВЛIОѲИКА: E-Journal of Eighteenth-Century Russian Studies* 6 (2018): 58–76.

Kotkin, Stephen. *Magnetic Mountain: Stalinism as Civilization*. Berkeley: University of California Press, 1995.

Kotsonis, Yanni. *States of Obligation: Taxes and Citizenship in the Russian Empire and Early Soviet Republic*. Toronto: University of Toronto Press.

Kozintseva, R. I. "Uchastie kazny vo vneshnei torgovle Rossii v pervoi chetverti XVIII v." *Istoricheskie zapiski* 91 (1973): 267–337.

Krmpotich, Cara, and Alexander Somerville. "Affective Presence: The Metonymical Catalogue." *Museum Anthropology* 39:2 (2016): 178–91.

Krmpotich, Cara, and Laura Peers. *This Is Our Life: Haida Material Heritage and Changing Museum Practice*. Vancouver: UBC Press, 2013.

Krupnik, Igor. "The 'Bogoras Enigma': Bounds of Cultures and Formats of Anthropology." In *Grasping the Changing World*. Ed. Václav Hubinger. New York: Routledge, 1996.

Krupnik, Igor. "'Jesup Genealogy': Intellectual Partnerships and Russian-American Cooperation in Arctic/North Pacific Anthropology." *Arctic Anthropology* 35:2 (1998): 199–226.

Krupnik, Igor, and William W. Fitzhugh, eds. *Gateways: Exploring the Legacy of the Jesup North Pacific Expedition, 1897–1902*. Washington, DC: Arctic Studies Center, Smithsonian Institute, 2001.

Kuhr-Korolev, Corinna, Ulrike Schmiegelt-Rietig, and Elena Zubkova. *Raub und Rettung: Russische Museen im Zweiten Weltkrieg*. Vienna: Weimar, 2019.

Kukui, Il'ia. "Laboratoriia avangarda: zhurnal *Transponans*." *Russian Literature* 59:2–4 (2006): 225–59.

Lakhtikova, Anastasia. "Professional Women Cooking: Manuscript Cookbooks, Social Networks and Identity Building in the Late Soviet Period." In *Seasoned Socialism: Gender and Food in Late Soviet Everyday Life*. Ed. Anastasia Lakhtikova, Angela Brintlinger, and Irina Glushchenko. Bloomington: Indiana University Press, 2019.

Latour, Bruno. *Reassembling the Social: An Introduction to Actor-Network Theory*. New York: Oxford University Press, 2005.

Levin, Eve. "Healers and Witches in Early Modern Russia." In *Saluting Aron Gurevich: Essays in History, Literature and Other Related Subjects*. Ed. Yelena Mazour-Matusevich and Alexandra Korros. Leiden: Brill, 2010. 105–33.

Lincoln, W. Bruce. *The Great Reforms: Autocracy, Bureaucracy, and the Politics of Change in Imperial Russia*. DeKalb: Northern Illinois University Press, 1990.

Lindert, Peter H., and Steven Nafziger. "Russian Inequality on the Eve of Revolution." *Journal of Economic History* 74:3 (2014): 767–98.

Lounsbury, Carl R. "Architecture and Cultural History." In *The Oxford Handbook of Material Culture Studies*. Ed. Dan Hicks and Mary C. Beaudry. Oxford: Oxford University Press, 2010. 484–501.

MacFadyen, Joshua. *Flax Americana: A History of the Fibre and Oil That Covered a Continent*. Montreal: McGill-Queen's University Press, 2018.

McCants, Anne E. C. "Exotic Goods, Popular Consumption, and the Standard of Living: Thinking about Globalization in the Early Modern World." *Journal of World History* 18:4 (2007): 433–62.

McDonald, Peter D. "Implicit Structures and Explicit Interactions: Pierre Bourdieu and the History of the Book." *The Library*, ser. 6, 19:2 (1997): 105–21.

McFerrin, Dorothy, and Jennifer McFerrin-Bohner, *Fabergé: The Mcferrin Collection: The Opulence Continues*. Humble, TX: Artie and Dorothy McFerrin Foundation, 2016.

McKendrick, Neil, John Brewer, and J. H. Plumb. *The Birth of a Consumer Society: The Commercialization of Eighteenth-Century England*. Bloomington: Indiana University Press, 1982.

McReynolds, Louise. *Russia at Play: Leisure Activities at the End of the Tsarist Era*. Ithaca, NY: Cornell University Press, 2003.

Melillo, Edward D. "Global Entomologies: Insects, Empires, and the 'Synthetic Age' in World History." *Past and Present* 233 (2014): 233–70.

Mendels, Franklin F. "Proto-Industrialization: The First Phase of the Industrialization Process." *Journal of Economic History* 31 (1972): 241–61.

Meshalin, I. V. *Tekstil'naia promyshlennost' krestian Moskovskoi gubernii v XVIII i pervoi polovine XIX veka*. Moscow: Institut istorii, 1950.

Miller, Daniel, ed., *Materiality*. Durham, NC: Duke University Press, 2005.

Miller, Daniel. *Stuff*. Cambridge: Polity, 2010.

Miller, David. "Monumental Building as an Indicator of Economic Trends in Northern Rus' in the Late Kievan and Mongol Periods, 1138–1462." *American Historical Review* 94:2 (1989): 360–90.

Mintz, Sidney W. *Sweetness and Power: The Place of Sugar in Modern History*. New York: Penguin, 1985.

Mohanty, Gail Fowler. *Labor and Laborers of the Loom: Mechanization and Handloom Weavers, 1780–1840*. New York: Routledge, 2006.

Monahan, Erika. "Gavril Romanov Nikitin: A Merchant Portrait." In *Russia's People of Empire: Life Stories from Eurasia, 1500–Present*. Ed. Willard Sunderland and Stephen Norris. Bloomington: University of Indiana Press, 2012. 47–56.

Monahan, Erika. *The Merchants of Siberia: Trade in Early Modern Eurasia*. Ithaca, NY: Cornell University Press, 2016.

Monahan, Erika. "Moving Pictures: Tobol'sk 'Traveling' in Early Modern Texts." *Canadian-American Slavic Studies* 52:3–4 (2018): 261–89.

Mt. Pleasant, Alyssa, Caroline Wigginton, and Kelly Wisecup. "Materials and Methods in Native American and Indigenous Studies." *Early American Literature* 53:2 (2018): 407–44.

Munting, Roger. "The Russian Beet Sugar Industry in the XIXth Century." *Journal of European Economic History* 13:2 (1984): 291–309.

Nappi, Carla. "Surface Tension: Objectifying Ginseng in Chinese Early Modernity." In *Early Modern Things: Objects and Their Histories, 1500–1800*. Ed. Paula Findlen. New York: Routledge, 2013. 31–52.

Need, Lynda. "Mapping the Self: Gender, Space and Modernity in Mid-Victorian London." In *Rewriting the Self: Histories from the Renaissance to the Present*. Ed. Roy Porter. New York: Routledge, 1997. 167–85.

Norris, Stephen M. *A War of Images: Russian Popular Prints, Wartime Culture, and National Identity, 1812–1945*. DeKalb: Northern Illinois University Press, 2006.

Odom, Anne, and Wendy R. Salmond. *Treasures into Tractors: The Selling of Russia's Cultural Heritage, 1918–1938*. Seattle, WA: University of Washington Press, 2009.

Ogilvie, Sheilagh, and Markus Cerman. *European Proto-Industrialization: An Introductory Handbook*. Cambridge: Cambridge University Press, 1996.

Osterman, Julie, ed. *Fabergé: The McFerrin Collection, The Art of Presentation*. Houston, TX: McFerrin Foundation, 2019.

Osterman, Julie, ed. *From a Snowflake to an Iceberg: The McFerrin Collection*. Houston, TX: McFerrin Foundation, 2013.

Parthasarathi, Prasannan. *Why Europe Grew Rich while Asia Did Not: Global Economic Divergence, 1600–1850*. Cambridge: Cambridge University Press, 2011.

Pedersen, Morten Axel. *Not Quite Shamans: Spirit Worlds and Political Lives in Northern Mongolia*. Ithaca, NY: Cornell University Press, 2011.

Pennell, Sara. *The Birth of the English Kitchen, 1600–1850*. New York: Bloomsbury Academic, 2016.

Perkins, John. "Sugar Production, Consumption and Propaganda in Germany, 1850–1914." *German History* 15:1 (1997): 22–33.

Perloff, Marjorie. *The Futurist Moment: Avant-Garde, Avant Guerre, and the Language of Rupture*. Chicago: University of Chicago Press, 1986.

Perloff, Nancy. *Explodity: Sound, Image, and Word in Russian Futurist Book Art*. Los Angeles: Getty Research Institute, 2006.

Phillips, Ruth B. "Re-Placing Objects: Historical Practices for the Second Museum Age." *Canadian Historical Review* 86:1 (2005): 83–110.

Phipps, Elena. *Looking at Textiles: A Guide to Technical Terms*. Los Angeles: J. Paul Getty Museum, 2011.

Pokhlebkin, V. I. *Natsional'nye kukhni nashikh narodov*. Moscow: Pishchevaia promyshlennost', 1978.

Pomeranz, Kenneth. *The Great Divergence: China, Europe, and the Making of the Modern World Economy*. Princeton, NJ: Princeton University Press, 2000.

Postnikov, Alexey, and Marvin Falk. *Exploring and Mapping Alaska*. Fairbanks: University of Alaska Press, 2015.

Pretty, Dave. "The Cotton Textile Industry in Russia and the Soviet Union." In *The Ashgate Companion to the History of Textile Workers, 1650–2000*. Farnham: Ashgate, 2010. 421–48.

Principe, Lawrence M., and William R. Newman. "Some Problems with the Historiography of Alchemy." In *Secrets of Nature: Astrology and Alchemy in Early Modern Europe*. Ed. William R. Newman and Anthony Grafton. Boston, MA: MIT Press, 2001. 385–431.

Proctor, Robert N. *Golden Holocaust: Origins of the Cigarette Catastrophe and the Case for Abolition*. Berkeley: University of California Press, 2011.

Pronin, Alexander, and Barbara Pronin. *Russian Folk Arts*. South Brunswick, NJ: A. S. Barnes, 1975.

Rappaport, Erika. *A Thirst for Empire: How Tea Shaped the Modern World*. Princeton, NJ: Princeton University Press, 2019.

Rappe, Tamara. "Catherine II and European Decorative Arts." In *Catherine the Great: Art for Empire*. Ed. Nathalie Bondil. Montreal: Montreal Museum of Fine Arts, 2005.
Rec, Agnieszka Anna. "Transmutation in a Golden Age: Reading Alchemy in Late Medieval and Early Modem Cracow." Unpublished PhD diss., Yale University, 2016.
Rieber, Alfred J. *Merchants and Entrepreneurs in Imperial Russia*. Chapel Hill: University of North Carolina Press, 1982.
Riello, Giorgio. *Cotton: The Fabric That Made the Modern World*. Cambridge: Cambridge University Press, 2013.
Riello, Giorgio, and Prasannan Parthasarathi, eds. *The Spinning World: A Global History of Cotton Textiles, 1200–1850*. Oxford: Oxford University Press, 2009.
Robbins, Bruce. "Commodity Histories." *PMLA* 120:2 (2005): 454–63.
Roberts, Graham H., ed. *Material Culture in Russia and the USSR: Things, Values, Identities*. London: Bloomsbury Academic, 2017.
Romaniello, Matthew P. *Enterprising Empires: Russia and Britain in Eighteenth-Century Eurasia*. Cambridge: Cambridge University Press, 2019.
Rotmistrov, P. A. *Stal'naia gvardiia*. Moscow: Voenizdat, 1984.
Roy, Susan. *These Mysterious People: Shaping History and Archaeology in a Northwest Coast Community*. Montreal: McGill-Queen's University Press, 2010.
Rublack, Ulinka, and Giorgio Riello, eds. *The Right to Dress: Sumptuary Laws in a Global Perspective, c. 1200–1800*. Cambridge: Cambridge University Press, 2019.
Rupasov, Aleksandr Ivanovich. *Agafon Faberzhe v Krasnom Petrograde*. St. Petersburg: Liki Rossii, 2012.
Ryckbosch, Wouter. "From Spice to Tea: On Consumer Choice and the Justification of Value in the Early Modern Low Countries." *Past and Present* 242 (2019): 37–78.
Sahlins, Marshall. "Cosmologies of Capitalism: The Trans-Pacific Sector of the 'The World System.'" *Proceedings of the British Academy* 74 (1988): 1–51.
Scarry, Elaine. *The Body in Pain: The Making and Unmaking of the World*. New York: Oxford University Press, 1985.
Schechter, Brandon. "'The People's Instructions': Indigenizing the Great Patriotic War among 'Non-Russians.'" *Ab Imperio* 3 (2012): 109–33.
Schechter, Brandon. *The Stuff of Soldiers: A History of the Red Army in World War II through Objects*. Ithaca, NY: Cornell University Press, 2019.
Schiebinger, Londa. *Plants and Empire: Colonial Bioprospecting in the Atlantic World*. Cambridge: Harvard University Press, 2004.
Schmidt, Benjamin. *Inventing Exoticism: Geography, Globalism, and Europe's Early Modern World*. Philadelphia: University of Pennsylvania Press, 2015.
Schönle, Andreas. *The Ruler in the Garden: Politics and Landscape Design in Imperial Russia*. Oxford: Peter Lang, 2007.
Schotsmans, Eline M. J., et al. "Interpreting Lime Burials. A Discussion in Light of Lime Burials at St. Rombout's Cemetery in Mechelen, Belgium (10th–18th Centuries)." *Journal of Archaeological Science: Reports* 3 (2015): 464–79.
Sedov, P. V. *Zakat Moskovskogo tsarstva. Tsarskii dvor kontsa XVII veka*. St. Petersburg: Dmitrii Bulanin, 2008.
Shapin, Steven. "The Invisible Technician." *American Scientist* 77:6 (1989): 554–63.
Skelton, R. A. "Leo Bagrow: Historian of Cartography and Founder of *Imago Mundi*, 1881–1957." *Imago Mundi* 14 (1959): 4–5, 7–12.
Slezkine, Yuri. *Arctic Mirrors: Russia and the Small Peoples of the North*. Ithaca, NY: Cornell University Press, 1994.

Smith, Alison K. *For the Common Good and Their Own Well Being: Social Estates in Imperial Russia*. New York: Oxford University Press, 2014.

Smith, Alison K. "A Microhistory of the Global Empire of Cotton: Ivanovo, the 'Russian Manchester.'" *Past & Present* 244:1 (2019): 163–93.

Smith, Alison K. "New Town, New Townspeople: Transforming Gatchina in the 1790s." *Вивлиоѳика: E-Journal of Eighteenth-Century Russian Studies* 7 (2019): 86–101.

Smith, Pamela H. *The Body of the Artisan: Art and Experience in the Scientific Revolution*. Chicago: University of Chicago Press, 2004.

Smith, Pamela H. "Making and Knowing in a Sixteenth-Century Goldsmith's Workshop." In *The Mindful Hand: Inquiry and Invention between the Late Renaissance and Early Industrialization*. Ed. Lissa Roberts, Simon Schaffer, and Peter Dear. Amsterdam: Koninklijke Nederlandse Akademie van Wetenschappen, 2007. 3–57.

Smith, Pamela H. "Science on the Move: Recent Trends in the History of Early Modern Science." *Renaissance Quarterly* 62:2 (2009): 345–75.

Smith, Pamela H., Amy R. W. Meyers, and Harold J. Cook, eds. *Ways of Making and Knowing: The Material Culture of Empirical Knowledge*. Ann Arbor: University of Michigan Press, 2014.

Smith, Robert. "Runners and Rituals in Early Russia." *Costume: Journal of the Costume Society* 38 (2004): 41–9.

Smith, Robert E. F. "Whence the Samovar?" *Petits Propos Culinaires* 4 (1980): 57–72.

Smith, Robert E. F., and David Christian. *Bread and Salt: A Social and Economic History of Food and Drink in Russia*. Cambridge: Cambridge University Press, 1984.

Smith, Woodruff D. *Consumption and the Making of Respectability, 1600–1800*. New York: Routledge, 2002.

Smith, Woodruff D. "From Coffeehouse to Parlour: The Consumption of Coffee, Tea and Sugar in North-Western Europe in the Seventeenth and Eighteenth Centuries." In *Consuming Habits: Global and Historical Perspectives on How Cultures Define Drugs*. Ed. Jordan Goodman, Andrew Sherratt, and Paul E. Lovejoy. 2nd ed. New York: Routledge, 2007. 142–57.

Smith-Peter, Susan. "Sweet Development: The Sugar Beet Industry, Agricultural Societies and Agrarian Transformations in the Russian Empire, 1818–1913." *Cahiers du monde Russe* 57:1 (2016): 101–24.

Smith-Peter, Susan. *Imagining Russian Regions: Subnational Identity and Civil Society in Nineteenth-Century Russia*. Leiden: Brill, 2018.

Stahl, Ann Brower. "Material Histories." In *The Oxford Handbook of Material Culture Studies*. Ed. Dan Hicks and Mary C. Beaudry. Oxford: Oxford University Press, 2010. 150–72.

Starks, Tricia. *Smoking under the Tsars: A History of Tobacco in Imperial Russia*. Ithaca, NY: Cornell University Press, 2018.

Stasov, Vladimir. "Russian Folk Ornamentation: Embroidery, Weaving and Lace." *Experiment: A Journal of Russian Culture* 22 (2016): 178–98.

Steinberg, Mark D. *Proletarian Imagination: Self, Modernity, and the Sacred in Russia, 1910–1925*. Ithaca, NY: Cornell University Press, 2002.

Steiner, Peter. "On Samizdat, Tamizdat, Magnitizdat and Other Words That Are Difficult to Pronounce." *Poetics Today* 29:4 (2008): 613–28.

Stevens, Scott Manning. "Tomahawk: Materiality and Depictions of the Haudenosaunee." *Early American Literature* 53:2 (2018): 475–511.

Tagliacozzo, Eric, and Wen-chin Chang, eds. *Chinese Circulations: Capital, Commodities, and Networks in Southeast Asia*. Durham, NC: Duke University Press, 2011.
Tempest, Snejana. "Stovelore in Russian Folklife." In *Food in Russian History and Culture*. Ed. Musya Glants and Joyce Toomre. Bloomington: Indiana University Press, 1997.
Tilley, Christopher. *Metaphor and Material Culture*. Oxford: Blackwell, 1999.
Tomášková, Silvia. *Wayward Shamans: The Prehistory of an Idea*. Berkeley: University of California Press, 2013.
Topik, Steven C., and Allen Wells. "Commodity Chains in a Global Economy." In *A World Connecting, 1870–1914*. Ed. Emily S. Rosenberg. Cambridge: Belknap, 2012. 593–814.
Trentmann, Frank. *Empire of Things: How We Became a World of Consumers, from the Fifteenth Century to the Twenty First*. New York: Harper Perennial, 2016.
Turnau, Irena. "Aspects of the Russian Artisan: The Knitter of the Seventeenth to the Eighteenth Century." *Textile History* 4:1 (1973): 7–25.
Uglow, Jenny. "Vase Mania." In *Luxury in the Eighteenth Century: Debates, Desires, and Delectable Goods*. Ed. Maxine Berg and Elizabeth Eger. New York: Palgrave, 2003. 151–62.
Ulanov, Andrei, and Dmitrii Shein. *Pervye T-34: Boevoe primenenie. World of Tanks*. Moscow: Taktikal Press, 2013.
Unkovskaya, Maria. *Brief Lives: A Handbook of Medical Practitioners in Muscovy, 1620–1701*. London: Wellcome Trust, 1999.
Unkovskaya, Maria. "Learning Foreign Mysteries: Russian Pupils of the Aptekarskii Prikaz, 1650–1700." *Oxford Slavonic Papers* 30 (1997): 1–20.
Ust'iantsev, Sergei, and Dmitrii Kolmakov. *Boevye mashiny Uralvagonzavoda. Tank T-34*. Nizhnyi Tagil: Media-Print, 2005.
Veblen, Thorstein. *The Theory of the Leisure Class*. Oxford: Oxford University Press, 2007.
Vermeulen, Han F. *Before Boas: The Genesis of Ethnography and Ethnology in the German Enlightenment*. Lincoln: University of Nebraska Press, 2015.
Viola, Lynne. "Collectivization in the Soviet Union: Specificities and Modalities." In *The Collectivization of Agriculture in Communist Eastern Europe: Comparison and Entanglements*. Ed. Constantin Iordachi and Arnd Bauerkämper. Budapest: Central European University Press, 2014. 49–77.
Von Solodkoff, Alexander. *The Art of Carl Fabergé*. New York: Crown, 1988.
Wallerstein, Immanuel. *The Modern World System: Capitalist Agriculture and the Origins of the European World-Economy in the Sixteenth Century*. New York: Academic Press, 1974.
Warde, Paul. "Trees, Trade and Textiles: Potash Imports and Ecological Dependency in British Industry, c. 1550–1770." *Past and Present* 240:1 (2018): 47–82.
Waugh, Daniel C. "The View from the North: Muscovite Cartography of Inner Asia." *Journal of Asian History* 49:1–2 (2015): 69–95.
Weinberg, Bennett Alan, and Bonnie K. Bealer. *The World of Caffeine: The Science and Culture of the World's Most Popular Drug*. New York: Routledge, 2002.
West, Sally. *I Shop in Moscow: Advertising and the Creation of Consumer Culture in Late Tsarist Russia*. DeKalb: Northern Illinois University Press, 2011.
White, Lynn, Jr. "Technology Assessment from the Stance of a Medieval Historian." *American Historical Review* 79:1 (1974): 1–13.
Whited, Tamara L. "Terroir Transformed: Cheese and Pastoralism in the Western French Pyrenees." *Environmental History* 23:4 (2018): 824–46.
Wong, R. Bin. *China Transformed: Historical Change and the Limits of European Experience*. Ithaca, NY: Cornell University Press, 1999.

Wye, Deborah. "Art Issues/Book Issues: An Overview." In *The Russian Avant-Garde Book: 1910–1934*. Ed. Margit Rowell and Deborah Wye. New York: Museum of Modern Art, 2002. 10–23.

Yoder, Audra. "Tea Time in Romanov Russia: A Cultural History, 1616–1917." Unpublished PhD diss., University of North Carolina at Chapel Hill, 2016.

Zinzendorf, Christian, and Johannes Zinzendorf. *The Big Book of Flax*. Atglen, PA: Schiffer, 2011.

Znamenski, Andrei A. *The Beauty of the Primitive: Shamanism and Western Imagination*. Oxford: Oxford University Press, 2007.

Zupanov, Inez G., and Angela Barreto Xavier. "Quest for Permanence in the Tropics: Portuguese Bioprospecting in Asia (16th–18th Centuries)." *Journal of the Economic and Social History of the Orient* 57:4 (2014): 511–48.

# Index

Abramtsevo 1
Adler, Ken 6
agriculture 36–7, 104, 108
Aksakov, Sergei 1
alcohol 18–19, 106, 198
   *see also* vodka
Aleksander Nevskii Monastery 1
Alexander III, Emperor 135, 137, 142, 145
American Museum of Natural History (AMNH) 8, 191, 193–5, 196–202, 204
   *see also* Jesup North Pacific Expedition; Waldmar Borogaz
Ancient Russian Art, Museum of 218
anthropology 5–6, 121, 191–2, 195, 197
   *see also* Arjun Appadurai; Bruno Latour; Clifford Gertz; Daniel Miller; David Howes; Edward Franquemont Mary Douglas; Igor Kopytoff; Igor Krupnik; Jesup North Pacific Expedition; Waldemar Bogoras
Apothecary Chancery 22–7
apothecary ware
   Gzhel clay 22–7
   immateriality 7–8, 10, 17, 24–5, 172
   Russian medicine 17–27
Appadurai, Arjun 3
architecture 45, 220–1
   *see also* built environment; construction; limestone
Army Museum 222
art *see* avant-garde; conceptualism; constructivism; folk arts; icons; neoclassicism; samizdat; socialist realism
art protection *see* Kunstschutz; military art protection
artists 1–2, 10, 51–6, 59–63, 209, 213
   *see also* samizdat

atlas *see* chorography
avant-garde 51, 53–6, 58–60
   *see also* samizdat
Astrakhan 73, 79–80

Bagrow, Leo 182–5
Bainbridge, Henry Charles 137–9
Bartelik, Marek 59–60
bioprospecting 9, 71–2, 82
Black Sea 135, 145–6, 183,
Bogoras, Waldemar 191–204
Bourdieu, Pierre 52
Braudel, Fernand 4
Breen, T. H. 6
Breslau Castle Museum 222
British Museum 185
built environment 7, 10, 33–5, 37–41, 43–6, 90, 109
   *see also* architecture; construction; limestone
Bunge, Nikolai Kh. 105–6

cartography
   *see also* geography; Leo Bagrow; Semen Remezov
   European 173
   Russian 176, 186
   Siberian 176–81
Catherine II, Empress 1, 36–7, 40, 121, 124–5, 129–30, 146
Chartier, Robert 52
Chikhachev plaid 87–90, 93
   *see also* textiles
China 25, 120–1, 137, 175
chorography 8, 171–86
   *see also* cartography; geography
Chukchi 10, 191–203
   *see also* Scratching-Woman; shamanism; Siberia
Collins, Samuel 73–4, 76

commodity 3–5, 9, 80
   see also apothecary ware;
      bioprospecting; Chikhachev plaid;
      cotton; flax; limestone; linen;
      medicine; sugar; textiles; tobacco
construction
   see also architecture; built
      environment
   Chancellery 39
   materials 34–5 37, 39, 43–5
   military administration 212
   railroad 106
   Tallinn 37
   village of Gatchina 41–3, 46
constructivism 56, 58
   see also art
consumers
   December Conference 110
   middle-class 4
   organizations 110
   preindustrial 94
   Russian 7, 72, 104
   semi-industrial 94
   subconscious 140
   sugar 7–9, 106–8
   Western European 7, 71–2
consumption
   connoisseurship 142
   conspicuous 5
   global 4
   legal restrictions on 4
   localization 5
   per-capita 104
   sugar 103–4, 103–9
   tea 122
Construction Chancellery 39
   see also construction
Cossacks 24–6, 174
cotton 5, 88, 91, 94. 95–7, 172
   see also textiles
Crimea 145–6

Daniel, Wallace 95–6
Darnton, Robert 52
Deutsches Landesmuseum 222
Dorozhaevo 90
Douglas, Mary 5
Duma, Third 106–13

East Asia 21
   see also China
Eastern Front 8, 211
   see also Second World War
economy
   see also commodities; consumers;
      consumption; *normirovka*
Elizaveta, Empress 1
Emancipation 94
   see also peasantry
embodiment 153, 158, 164, 185
   see also sensory
emotions 6
   see also production relationships
Europe see Western Europe

Fabergé
   Agathon 148
   Peter Carl, 135–48
factory 1, 43, 80, 82, 89, 91, 93–5, 105, 107,
      109–13, 124–5, 140, 153–8
   see also industrialization
femininity 137, 145–8
   see also gender
fetish see commodity
Finland 136, 141
First World War 113, 136, 138, 148, 154,
      183, 211–12
   flax 7, 75–6, 81–2, 87–8,
      91, 94, 97
   see also linen; textiles
folk art and motifs 1, 125, 146, 163
foreign merchants 73–5
   see also merchants
Fonvizin, Denis 119
Forest Greenhouse 33–4
   see also architecture
Franquemont, Edward 92

Gatchina 33–4, 40–43, 45–6
Gatchina Palace Estate Museum 33–4
gender 121, 138, 145–8, 196, 199
   see also femininity; masculinity; men;
      Scratching-Woman; women
geography
   see also cartography
   North Pacific Ocean 191
   Russian Empire 3, 36, 171–5, 181–6

# Index

Gerritsen, Anne 19
Gertz, Clifford 6
glue 7, 9, 71–2
   identifying 72–6
   making 76–81
Gmelin, Samuel Gottlieb 79–80
Gol'din, Efim S. 111
Golitsyn family 122–4
Gzhel clay 22–7

Hamburg 23–4, 75, 215
Hartwick, Elaine 5
hemp 75–6, 79, 81–2
   *see also* textiles
Howes, David 140

icons 9–10, 26–7, 209–11, 213–23
Indigenous Studies 21
industrialization 1, 87–9, 94–7, 106, 114, 153–6
   *see also* factory
Ippolitova, A. B. 26
Iroquois *see* Native American
Isherwood, Baron 5
isinglass 7, 9–10, 34
   identifying 72–6
   making 76–81
Ivan IV (the Terrible) 1–2, 11, 79
Ivanovo 87, 91–7

Jackson, Humphrey 77–80, 82
Jesup North Pacific Expedition 191–6, 202, 204
   *see also* American Museum of Natural History; Scratching-Woman; shamanism; Walter Bogoras

Kahan, Arcadius 5
Kaluga Cossack *see* Cossacks
Kapustin, Mikhail Ia. 106–7
Karelian birch 135–6, 138, 142–3, 145–6
Kazan' 37, 72–3, 79
Keenan, Edward L. 21
Khudin, K. S. 26
Kiev Market Committee 105–6
Kitai-gorod merchants 26, 44
   *see also* merchants

Kivelson, Valerie 175–7
Klein, Ursula 20
Kokovtsov, Vladimir N. 104, 106, 112–13, 116 n.57
Kopytoff, Igor 2–3, 154
Koroloff, Rachel 26
Körte, Werner 9, 211, 214–23
Koshkin, Mikhail Il'ich 9, 156–7
Kozintseva, R. I. 74–5
Krasheninnikov, Stepan 75
   *see also* Second Kamchatka Expedition
Krmpotich, Cara 203
Krupnik, Igor 196, 199
Kunstschutz 211–14, 222–3
   *see also* artists; military art protection, museum; Werner Körte

Laet, Marianne De 20, 22
language *see* semantics and terminology
Latour, Bruno 154, 173
Lefévre, Wolfgang 20
*lekarstvo* 23 *see* medicine
Lem, Vladimir 35–7, 40
Leningrad 53–9, 156, 160, 220
   *see also* St. Petersburg
Lepekhin, Ivan Ivanovich 79
lime burning 39–42
lime cycle 35–9
limestone 35, 39–43
linen 75–6, 79, 87–94, 96–7, 171
   *see also* flax; textiles
locality 33–5, 39–43, 96–8
   *see also* Gzhel clay
Lounsbury, Carl R. 34

Mamontov, Savva Ivanovich 1, 146
Marx, Karl 4–5, 55
masculinity 138, 148
   *see also* gender
maternal lineages 88–9
McDonald, Peter 52
medicine 7, 17–19, 23, 27, 197
memory 6
   *see also* emotions
men 1–227
   *see also* war

merchants
  British 80, 129
  European 76
  foreign 74
  Kitai–gorod 26
  Russian 71, 74
  wine 74
Meshalin, I. V. 95
Messerschmidt, Daniel Gottlieb 75, 177
military art protection 212–14
  see also Kunstschutz
Miller, Daniel 139
Ministry of Finance 105, 107, 111–12
Mol, Annemarie 20
Moscow 1, 6, 17, 22, 24–7, 36, 37, 44–5, 51, 53, 56, 59–62, 72–3, 91, 96–8, 112, 125, 147–8, 156, 174–5, 182–3, 223
Moscow Conceptual Circle 59–62
  see also samizdat
Müller, Gerhard Friedrich 77, 79, 175, 182–3
  see also Second Kamchatka Expedition
Murdoch, William 80–2
museum
  American Museum of Natural History 8, 191
  Army Museum 222
  Breslau Castle Museum 222
  British Museum 185
  Deutsches Landesmuseum 222
  Gatchina Palace Estate Museum 33–4
  Metropolitan Museum 88
  Museum of Ancient Russian Art 218
  National Fine Arts Museum of the Republic of Sakha (Yakutia) 128
  Novgorod State Museums 223
  Propaganda Museum 217
  in Pskov 220–2
  Pskov City Museum 213
  records 202–4
  of Russian Matryoshkas 1
  Smithsonian's National Museum of Natural History 202
  State Historical Museum 145
  State Museum of the History of Religion 195
  Victoria and Albert Museum 122

Nappi, Carla 25
National Fine Arts Museum of the Republic of Sakha (Yakutia) 128
Native Americans 19, 21
Nazi 10, 184
  see also Eastern Front; Kunstschutz; Second World War
neoclassicism 45, 122, 126
  see also art
neofuturist 53–9
  see also artists; samizdat
Nicholas II, Emperor 1, 135–7, 145
Nitsch, Hermann 58
nobility 94, 122, 124, 183
*normirovka* 104–14
  see also economy; sugar market
Novgorod 34, 217–220
Novgorod State Museums 223
Novitskii, Iosif I. 107–12

oil 4–5, 159
Orlov, Grigory 40

papirosy 7, 135, 137–8, 140, 145
  see also tobacco
Pallas, Peter Simon 79–80
Paris Exhibition 1
Paul, Emperor 33
Paul of Aleppo 43
*pech'* see stove
peasantry 1, 9, 22, 24, 41–3, 89–96, 104, 107, 112, 136, 142, 156
Peter I, Emperor 1, 7, 17, 36, 38–9, 43–5, 74, 75, 122–3, 125, 128, 182
Peterhof 34
Pleasant, Alyssa Mt 21
Pomet, Pierre 74, 76, 78
*prianik* (gingerbread) 58–9, 103
Prigov, Dmitrii 60
production relationships 155–8
  physical and emotional 158–62
Propaganda Museum 217
Pskov City Museum 213
Pudost' stone 33, 34, 39
Pudovskaia 40

quicklime 35–8
  see also lime cycle

# Index

Red Army soldiers 161–2
Remezov, Semen 9, 26–7, 174–82
revolution
   industrial 92
   of 1905 87, 145
   of 1917 8, 148, 156, 183
Ridley, Mark 23
Riello, Giorgio 19
Royal Society (Britain) 77–80
Russian Academy of Sciences 75–7, 79–81, 175, 194
   *see also* Second Kamchatka Expedition
Russian revolution *see* revolution

St. Petersburg 1, 7, 9, 33–46, 71, 76–7, 80–1, 107, 109, 111, 112, 127–9, 135, 183, 194
   *see also* Leningrad
samizdat 7, 8, 10, 51–63
   *see also* Moscow Conceptual Circle; neofuturist; transfurist
samovar 51, 119–26, 129–31
Schiebinger, Londa 71
Scratching-Woman 196–202
Second Kamchatka Expedition 75, 182
   *see also* Gerhard Friedrich Müller; Stepan Krasheninnikov
Second World War 6, 8, 33, 153–5, 184, 209, 211
   *see also* Eastern Front; T-34 tank
semantics and terminology 8–9, 22–24, 54–55, 60, 72, 121, 124, 142, 145, 181, 194–6
sensory 2, 6, 7–8, 11, 38, 58–9, 80–1, 89, 103, 135, 138–41, 154–5, 161–2, 171, 186
   *see also* embodiment
serfs *see* Emancipation; peasantry
Sergiev Posad 1, 58
shamanism 192–3, 198
   *see also* Chukchi; Scratching-Woman
Sheremetev, Dmitrii Nikolaevich 96
Siberia 8, 9, 75, 146, 171–84, 191–99
   *see also* Chukchi; Jesup North Pacific Expedition; Tobol'sk
Sitwell, Sacheverell Reresby 146
slaked lime *see* lime cycle
Slavophiles 1
Smith, Pamela H. 19–20, 25–6

Smithsonian's National Museum of Natural History 202
Somerville, Alexander 203
Soviet Sots Art 59–60
spindle 92
Stalin, Joseph 154, 155, 157, 159
State Historical Museum 145
State Museum of the History of Religion 195
Stevens, Scott Manning 19
stove (*pech'*) 10, 125, 127–30, 221
Strahlenberg, Philip Johan von 75–6
Strangways, Horner Fox 40
sugar 4, 7, 9–10, 103–14
   *see also* normirovka
Sverchkov, Ivan 26
swim bladder 71–81
   *see also* isinglass

T-34 tank 153–64
tank crews 159–62
tariffs 44–5, 105, 115 n.22, 123
tea urns 119–20, 125–30
   *see also* samovar
terminology *see* semantics
textiles 88, 90, 94–6
   *see also* Chikhachev plaid; cotton; flax; hemp; linen
theriac 23
   *see also* medicine
Tillander-Godenhielm, Ulla 144
Tilley, Christopher 121
tobacco
   *see also* papirosy
   cases 138–48
   gender 145–8
   sensory and prompts 138–40
   smoking, distinction 140–5
Tobol'sk 174–5, 177, 180–2
   *see also* Siberia
transfurist 53–9
   *see also* artists; samizdat
transportation 38, 44, 72–3, 93, 160
Tula 124–5, 156

Urals 123, 146, 178, 180
Ushakov, Semyon 26–7

Veblen, Thorstein 5, 104
    see also consumption
Victoria and Albert Museum 122
Visconti, Placido 41
Vladimir province 9, 87–97
vodka 39, 58–9, 87, 106
    see also alcohol

Wallerstein, Immanuel 4
war see First World War, Second World War
Western Europe 7, 10, 20–1, 120–5, 130, 176, 211

Western Pop Art 59
Whitworth, Charles 75–6
Wigginton, Caroline 21
Witte, Sergei Iu. 106, 112–13, 116 n.57
Wisecup, Kelly 21
women 7, 94, 196–9, 202–4
    household serfs 90, 93
    smoking 138, 145
    spinning wheel 92

Zimbabwe Bush Pump 20, 22
Znachko-Iavorskii, Igor 43–4

Printed in the USA
CPSIA information can be obtained
at www.ICGtesting.com
LVHW011647091223
766046LV00004B/111

9 781350 186064